Cuban Revelations

Contemporary Cuba

UNIVERSITY PRESS OF FLORIDA

Florida A&M University, Tallahassee
Florida Atlantic University, Boca Raton
Florida Gulf Coast University, Ft. Myers
Florida International University, Miami
Florida State University, Tallahassee
New College of Florida, Sarasota
University of Central Florida, Orlando
University of Florida, Gainesville
University of North Florida, Jacksonville
University of South Florida, Tampa
University of West Florida, Pensacola

CUBAN REVELATIONS

Behind the Scenes in Havana

Marc Frank

University Press of Florida

Gainesville

Tallahassee

Tampa

Boca Raton

Pensacola

Orlando

Miami

Jacksonville

Ft. Myers

Sarasota

This book may be available in an electronic edition.

18   17   16   15   14   13   6   5   4   3   2   1

Frank, Marc.
Cuban revelations : behind the scenes in Havana / Marc Frank.
p. cm. — (Contemporary Cuba)
Includes bibliographical references and index.
ISBN 978-0-8130-4465-1 (alk. paper)
1. Cuba—Foreign relations—United States. 2. United States—Foreign relations—Cuba.
3. Cuba—Social conditions—1990– 4. Cuba—Politics and government—1990– 5. Cuba—
History. 6. Castro, Fidel, 1926– 7. Castro, Raúl. I. Title. II. Series: Contemporary Cuba.
E183.8.C9F69 2013
327.7291073—dc23   2013015084

The University Press of Florida is the scholarly publishing agency for the State University System
of Florida, comprising Florida A&M University, Florida Atlantic University, Florida Gulf Coast
University, Florida International University, Florida State University, New College of Florida,
University of Central Florida, University of Florida, University of North Florida, University
of South Florida, and University of West Florida.

University Press of Florida
15 Northwest 15th Street
Gainesville, FL 32611-2079
http://www.upf.com

To Dhara and Ivet

Contents

Preface

Secretive Cuba can only be covered by asymmetrical reporting. Journalism 101 may prove helpful in structuring your stories, but it will not get you very far in actually reporting on a land where rumors and disinformation abound and there are very few press conferences and press releases. In Cuba the officials, diplomats, foreign businessmen, and citizenry are wary of foreign media, and the government-controlled local variety reveals little. Triangulating fragments of information, using your imagination to get around obstacles, pushing the envelope, painstaking source development, and legwork are the only methods for cracking the silence. This book builds on my reporting over the years and thus relies on these same methods.

Cuban Revelations is about a critical moment in the Caribbean island's history. Fidel Castro was forced by illness to step aside after nearly half a century in power, and the decision was soon taken to transform a Soviet-style socialist system, put in place soon after the Revolution, into a new model closer to that of Asian Communism, in particular in Vietnam. The introduction provides a brief sketch of the author, his family, Cuba, and its history. Part I takes the reader through the horrific crisis that followed the Soviet Union's demise and Fidel Castro's final years in power: understanding that period is essential to understanding what followed. Part II covers Raúl Castro's first years in office, and the third and fourth sections examine the extraordinary changes he proceeded to introduce. The conclusion tackles the always tricky question of Cuba's future. Throughout, the impact of U.S. policy on Cuba is examined.

Some of the interviews in the book first appeared in my articles and a few were conducted by surrogates. All translations, unless indicated otherwise, are my own. All unpublished documents are translated verbatim. Secondhand accounts of important events within the leadership and Communist Party are just that, secondhand accounts, though I trust my sources and have done everything within my power to ensure their accuracy. Where possible I have named those quoted in the book. Where requested, only a first name appears, and in some cases none at all.

Introduction

Distinguished visitors from the United States and other lands—politicians and their staffs, diplomats, academics, businessmen, and my colleagues—often seek me out for a chat over lunch or dinner at one of the ever-growing number of Havana restaurants, or a mojito, Cuba libre, or daiquiri at the bar, or an espresso and mellow cigar at an outdoor café as dusk sets in with a refreshing breeze and the always colorful Cuban life streams by. My new acquaintances invariably want to know what brought me to Cuba and what it has been like working as a journalist in "enemy territory" for twenty-five years.

I joke that covering Cuba is like covering the White House. "You're nice to them and they're nice to you," I say. "Get nasty or probe too deeply and doors begin to close." Or I use the analogy of covering crime and, at the same time, doing a little investigative reporting on police brutality and corruption. "All of a sudden the cops are sending menacing looks your way and no longer giving you tips or vital information for a story." Doors were usually opened for me when I covered Cuba, and from there Latin America, in the 1980s as a young, leftist reporter. When I returned in the 1990s to report on the country for the mainstream media, those same doors were usually shut tight.

Covering Cuba is actually more difficult than covering the White House or the local crime beat. It is rather like working under a state of emergency or covering a war, which is what the government insists has existed with the United States for more than half a century. Everything you write is read by the authorities after publication. While accredited writers and photographers are free to roam at will, television is more difficult, and official interviews are practically nonexistent. There are no spokespeople here to brief you. If the functionaries at the International Press Center (which is attached to the Foreign Ministry and gives you your credentials to work) do not like what you say about Cuba, they call you in and let you know. Sometimes they even kick you out or refuse to renew your credentials. They do not censor your stories before publication, jail you, torture you, or try to kill you. My Cuban wife's extended family, and the dozens of friends and acquaintances you will meet in the pages to come, have never been questioned or harassed. But I can speak only for myself. And I am a resident foreign journalist, not someone who comes for a week or two, nor a Cuban journalist—official or dissident, print or blog, writing for the domestic audience or abroad. That's a whole other story best left for those reporters to tell.

I point to my grandfather when asked what drew me here. Waldo Frank arrived on the Caribbean island's shores soon after the 1959 revolution, the first well-known U.S. writer, and a man much hailed in Latin America, to visit at the invitation of the recently victorious revolutionaries eager to tell their version of events. He quickly wrote and published, in 1961, *Cuba: Prophetic Island*. Waldo, a man both blessed and cursed with the courage to be different, moved fairly early in his career from literary criticism and fiction to also writing a number of nonfiction books about Spain, Latin America ("América Hispana," he would call it), and the latter's relations with the United States. He proved sympathetic to the region's straining at the bit, pulled tight by a still fairly new U.S. jockey racing neck-and-neck down life's path with the Soviets. The wild, bucking animal had spit out the bit held by Spain for centuries and had thrown off the rider. Waldo wrote *The Re-discovery of America* in the 1920s, *South American Journey* appeared in 1943, and in 1951 he published *Birth of a World: Bolívar in Terms of His Peoples*. My grandfather's books, particularly his biography of Latin America's independence hero, Simón Bolívar, written at the invitation of Venezuelan president Rómulo Gallegos, captured the attention and acclaim of many of the region's intellectuals, including those soon to be plotting and fighting in Cuba. They quickly published a local edition. After his visit to the island, Waldo helped found the Fair Play for Cuba Committee, which at the time was made up of many prominent personalities, among them Norman Mailer, Truman Capote, James Baldwin, Jean-Paul Sartre, Allen Ginsberg, and Carleton Beals.

I tell my new acquaintances that back in 1984, when I first set foot in the country, I was a tender thirty-three and a tireless crusader for social justice. I had come of age during the civil rights movement and the Vietnam War, the assassinations of President John F. Kennedy, Robert Kennedy, and Martin Luther King Jr. I spent my last year in high school and six months after graduation working in Massachusetts juvenile jails under a reform-minded commissioner named Jerome Miller, and then a year organizing street gangs to keep kids from killing themselves and each other and out of that juvenile justice system. I attended Rutgers University. There followed a long stint aiding and organizing the unemployed in the 1970s, then years as a union organizer and officeholder. The inauspicious beginning of my reporting career consisted of writing, laying out, publishing, and then distributing student, community, and union fliers and newsletters, not journalism school. I had kept a mimeograph machine in my living room since my college days. There was no Internet or social networking at the time, and I quickly discovered there were no mimeograph machines in Cuba—at least not in anyone's living room.

Latin America, the Caribbean, and Cuba were not complete strangers to me when an opportunity came along to live in the always intriguing and contentious island nation. The area was merely background noise, a vague image of underdevelopment, dictatorship, revolution, and military conflict as the Cold War raged and I went about my daily business. I had never traveled in the region. I planned to stay a few years to experience firsthand what socialism was really all about, and then return to the United States. I became fascinated by the country and its people and stayed on until 1991, only to return again to Cuba in December 1993 at the depths of the post-Soviet crisis. Next thing I knew, the place had become my second home.

Making one's way to Cuba from the United States proved long and tortuous in 1984, despite the mere ninety miles separating the two countries. There were only a few direct charter flights each week, and piles of paperwork required by Washington. I felt like a criminal sneaking off to the Bahamas for a flight into enemy territory—even though I took pride in never breaking the law and signed every article I wrote once I arrived. There were just a handful of Americans living in Cuba at the time, most either on the lam or in love. I was an exception.

I was not planning to write this book, despite the encouragement of many friends over the years. I would protest that I had written a book after my first stay in the country and it proved a time-consuming task with little financial reward. In 1993, at a time when the world gave Castro and his revolution weeks, or at most months, before they followed European Communism into the dustbin of history, I explained in *Cuba Looks to the Year 2000* why they both would still be very much around at the turn of the century.

I changed my mind about writing another book when Fidel Castro decided he had had enough of my snooping around. In an aside during a major speech on May 1, 2006, Castro railed at me for reporting he had tried, but failed, to turn around a dismal sugar harvest. He did not use my name, but I was the only foreign journalist regularly covering that worst harvest in a century and reporting that Castro had personally, and to no avail, taken over its direction earlier that year.[1] And in case there was any doubt about whom he meant, government minders (officials assigned to look after foreign journalists) were soon knocking on the Reuters News Agency door to let me know. A few lines in an April 13 article on the failed harvest may have caught Castro's attention at that moment.

President Fidel Castro, alarmed by the industry's decline and soaring prices, held an emergency meeting of the industry in mid-February. Castro ordered daily reports from the 42 mills in operation, a crash planting plan and more supplies and said essential spare parts for agricultural equipment should be flown in from Europe, according to a summary of the meeting seen by Reuters.

And just how had Marc Frank managed to see a summary of that meeting? Then, a few weeks later, during a May 24 appearance on television, Castro said:

Speaking of journalists, on May 15, there are 36 news stories on Cuba. . . . These groups exist in the world and they are people paid in dollars by the United States. . . . Some of them are spying on our institutions, some of them are truly insolent. . . . Various things could be done to them; one could tell them, "Look, go to your home." [There are] even some foreigners, spying, searching for news, bribing [people] whenever they can, writing trash, twisting it all. Look at the issue of the sugarcane harvest, the country just accomplished a feat. On February 14, only 13 percent of the sugar was harvested, and we made it to 90 percent by the end of the harvest. I already spoke some about this.[2]

The International Press Center repeatedly let Anthony Boadle, head of the Reuters office at the time, and me know that I was the object of Castro's wrath.

Fidel's message was clear enough. I was sniffing around too much. My coverage of the demise of the once-proud sugar industry was so accurate that a source said that Ulises Rosales Del Toro, a powerful general and Communist Party leader who headed the Sugar Ministry, was sure I was bribing someone in his office. How else could I have seen the Castro meeting transcript, or broken the story a few years earlier that half the country's mills would close? There was another way. A friend of my wife, who worked for the ministry, began lamenting about the plans to close mills without having any idea that this might be news. Then I went to a few sources outside the ministry to confirm. I ended up being the last of a long list of foreign journalists to receive a tongue-lashing from Castro, the man most Cubans referred to as the Comandante, before he was forced from power by intestinal bleeding and a series of surgeries just a few months later.

May through July of 2006 proved the most difficult period of the quarter century I have reported on Cuba. I was sure that expulsion was right around the corner. The minders were all over me everywhere I turned! I have no idea why it didn't happen. One never knows for sure why the government kicks a journalist out, or decides not to. Perhaps Castro learned I was Waldo Frank's grandson. Fidel took ill less than three months later, at the end of July, and the matter could simply have been dropped due to the new circumstances.

I had a lot more time on my hands, because I had to slow down and be more careful. It was like jumping off the tracks with a freight train bearing down on you. I decided that taking a breather was worthwhile if the payoff was to still be in the neighborhood for the huge story of Cuba after Castro, which was surely coming soon. Besides, Cuba and I had both changed over the years, and the itch to write this book, and clarify my thoughts in the process, would not go away. Then historic events began to unfold before my eyes. Writing this book simply kept me content and relatively sane throughout my down period. And after that—well, I simply had to finish it and get it out as the Castro era neared its end, Latin America welcomed the island back into the fold, and Cuba began to dramatically change its old Soviet-style ways and break fifty-year-old social and economic taboos one after the other.

The Family

As a foreign journalist in Cuba I am very fortunate. When you marry a Cuban, you marry the entire family, and I mean the extended one. Your doors are always open to them with no invitation necessary, or time limits, or ifs, ands, or buts. Then again, so are their homes and hearts open to you, a huge advantage for a reporter washed up on the shores of this hermetic Caribbean island.

Marlene León Reyes, when we met in 1995, came with eighteen aunts and uncles and more than fifty cousins, who were scattered from one end of the island to the other and of every political stripe and fancy. Only one uncle lived in the United States. Rosalia, Marlene's mother, hailed from a huge family of poor peasants in eastern Cuba's mountains who supported Castro's rebel troop, resulting in a death warrant being put out for her maternal grandfather and numerous raids on their humble home. Marlene's father, Miguel, was one of eight children born to farmers in central Cuba, where Marlene grew up. Miguel began working in the fields at the age of eight and cutting sugarcane, the first of twenty harvests for him, at the age of fourteen. They have lived Cuba's revolutionary history and each drawn their own conclusions, as has everyone in the clan. Most of the family still make their home on the island, although a few of the aunts and uncles have passed away, and one aunt has joined her daughter in Florida. A dozen or more of the cousins have moved on to the United States and Europe. Their families, in Cuba and elsewhere, are smaller, usually counting just one or two offspring. Marlene, when we were courting in the 1990s during the worst of the post-Soviet depression, managed to take me around the entire island for the once-over by just about every one of her aunts and uncles and many of her cousins, who were more like parents and siblings to her. I could never remember who was who: there were far too many, and their names and lineage were far too complicated. The clan members would joke that I should put their pictures and names on my wall and try harder to memorize the family tree. They all remembered my name—a real live gringo, and a journalist to boot, had appeared in their midst.

Marlene, a registered nurse for more than thirty years, is very Cuban indeed and therefore able to make friends with just about anyone. She comes from the *campo* or countryside, marking her character with a natural generosity and remarkable ability to focus on the positive qualities in others. It seems that she not only knows but is actually on friendly terms with half of Havana, Miami, and Madrid! I have come to know many of her friends over the years, and I am grateful for having had that opportunity.

Dhara, my American daughter from a previous marriage that ended in 1994, and Ivet, my Cuban stepdaughter, attended the local schools right up through university and medical school. There were always plenty of young people hanging around my home, using the forbidden Internet to chat with friends recently gone to Miami or Madrid, and gawking at Miami TV stations ("Wasn't that guy here just last month?") or the sports channels to cheer on Cuban baseball players in the big leagues ("Go Duque!") on my satellite television, also off limits to them. I have held numerous discussions with my daughters and their friends about why so many young people feel they face a dead-end future, catch the Caribbean's "island fever," and leave.

Welcome to Cuba

Irene Aloha Wright, a U.S. historian, journalist, and business consultant, published a wonderful book in 1910 called *Cuba*, with a brilliant introduction to the island that still rings true more than a century later.

> After one has resided in Cuba through ten years, he ceases to hold any dogmas or doctrines concerning this country, which has, very justly, . . . been called the land of topsy-turvey. Here logic and rational sequence are not the rule. Life runs, not like reality, but after the style of librettos of stage plays. From largest to smallest, contradiction exists in all the details of our daily life. Here there are woods which sink and stones which float. Here the executive pardons persons not yet convicted of any crime, and the congress legislates against incorrigible suicides. Business firms send creditors no bills, but signed receipts instead, to dun them. Here black is not necessarily black, but may carry a legal document to prove its color

white; white is not surely white, but may only "pass" for such. Under these, and a thousand other circumstances of which they are typical, one learns to hesitate to call a spade either a qualified shovel or an agricultural implement, but compromises by stating, if one must commit oneself, that at a given time and at a given place it looked to one something like an *azadón*.[3]

I am indebted to Richard Bebbington, a dear friend and the Finnish consul general in Havana through 2011, for discovering Wright's book and thereby giving me the perfect dodge for the puzzled questions of those who look me up to pick my brain when passing through Havana. When diplomats tell me they have done their job by the rules of the game and still have no idea what's going on, or journalists commiserate on the impossibility of getting the place just right, I refer them to Ms. Wright. After all, it took that quite brilliant lady ten years of walking Havana's streets, sailing around the island on steamships with her ailing mother, riding the new rails, and visiting small western-style pioneer U.S. settlements throughout the country on horseback to get the place just right—by figuring out that she never quite would.

Richard, a businessman turned dean of Havana's diplomatic community, had lived in Cuba for as long as I had. He bought and sold old books about the island, among his many hobbies (which, also fittingly, included cars, especially antique racing cars). Over the years, I bought from Richard dozens of books dating all the way back to the 1800s—and just as many from the used-book vendors camped out at Colonial Havana's Plaza de Armas in front of the former Spanish captain general's quarters, which became the U.S. governors' office after Spain ceded Cuba to the United States in 1899.

The books invariably describe the hues of green through yellow and brown of Cuba's semitropical landscape, changing their mixes and shades with the mountains, hills, plains, and valleys. The sun seems always present, dazzling the eye as it rises, blinding and searing by noon, and once more taking one's breath away with its beauty and sense of approaching relief as it sets. Then there is the rich coffee, the splendid rum, and the exquisite cigars. Visitors, down through the centuries, write of the dry "winter" season from November through April and then the summer rains, humidity, and heat. There is no real autumn or spring on this island of extremes. It is stiflingly hot and humid in the summer season, especially June through September.[4] Come November, the weather is absolutely gorgeous into April, except for the occasional cold front blowing in from the north—the waves swamping the seaside drive and sending the capital's inhabitants scampering from their favored perch. The Cubans pull out their *abrigos* or overcoats and bundle up. The tourists flock to the spectacular beaches. Elegant, slender, pinwheel-topped royal palms that bend easily with the winds, and thick-trunked ceiba trees that withstand them, stand guard over the centuries, survivors of the hurricanes for opposite reasons, embraced and bathed, as is the island, by calming and transparent turquoise and emerald waters. Nature, that greatest of artists, brushed the scene with breathtaking explosions of flowers of every imaginable color, shape, and size springing forth from more than 3,000 types of flowering trees and plants. Cuba's flora counts more than 7,000 varieties, nearly half of which are indigenous to the island. Its fauna is more limited: the most dangerous animal is a disease-carrying mosquito, the most exotic animals are the world's tiniest frogs, and the most bothersome, after the mosquitoes, and, at least for me, are the gigantic flying cockroaches. Christopher Columbus was only the best known of many outsiders to catch their breath upon sighting Cuba and exclaim that it was the loveliest land they had ever laid eyes on. The country's beauty has proved both a blessing and a curse to its residents, as outsiders repeatedly try to take it from them.

The old books also invariably describe the warmth and hospitality of the island's residents and their resilience in the face of natural adversity and the tragedy of some four centuries of Spanish colonialism, slavery, and subsequent failure to properly govern their land. No visitor to the island fails to be impressed to this very day by the sip of dark, sweet coffee that even the humblest of Cubans offers the stranger. "If asked to name the most prominent or salient characteristics dominating the Cuban race, we should probably be justified in saying: unfailing hospitality, exceptional courtesy, and unmeasurable love of children," writes Willis Fletcher Johnson in his voluminous *History of Cuba*.[5] In colonial times, land grants included a legal obligation to provide travelers with shelter and nourishment.

This book is about the dramatic events unfolding in Cuba today. The end of Revolutionary Cuba's egalitarian project as it came to be known in the twentieth century and the country's struggle to find a new path into the twenty-first, without losing the revolutionary ideals and social gains it is famed for, as the *historicos*—the men and women who made the Revolution and defended it against all odds—inevitably pass away. Yet it is impossible to understand the Cubans and what is taking place today without at least a cursory knowledge of past events as an introduction to the island and its inhabitants.

Life has always been difficult for the majority of Cubans and remains so. Those with us today are the survivors and come from a survivor stock. They are the fruit of a cruel natural selection. Hundreds of thousands of human beings perished before their time, and many more suffered, in a beautiful Cuba turned into a nightmare by man and nature (hurricanes and disease) well before a young, bearded and rifle-toting Fidel Castro stomped onto the stage.

The Indians were wiped out by the Spanish sword, the Cross, and forced labor soon after their discovery in the 1500s; countless African slaves met a similar fate during the centuries that followed. Spaniards and slaves were tortured by raiding pirates, and then gutted with a cutlass. Their towns were burned and the women gang-raped in an age when there was no penicillin to cure venereal disease. Pirates were hunted down and dealt with just as mercilessly by master, freeman, and slave, united in fear against that peril. Rebelling nationalist Creoles (Cubans of mainly Spanish heritage) and freed slaves were killed at the hands of the hundreds of thousands of Spanish soldiers sent to put them down in the 1800s, with the help of their local collaborators. Tens of thousands of Spanish soldiers were felled by disease and the machetes of Cuban independence fighters, known as the *mambises*. Innumerable women, children, and elderly perished from hunger and disease when the Spaniards herded the population into towns in the 1890s to keep the rural folk from providing support to the rebelling islanders, earning Spain the indignation of an American press and public whose government soon intervened.

The neighbor to the north already loomed large in the minds and hearts of Cubans long before it put an end to Spanish rule in 1898. When the "Yankees" threw out the British, many islanders longed for help to do the same to the Spanish, and some believed Cuba should join the just emerging Union and become another state. A majority of Cuba's elite, who were slaveholders themselves, sided with and helped the South during the War between the States and dreamed of some sort of U.S. status. Cuban patriots, including national apostle José Martí, found refuge in the United States, where they plotted their independence war and sought support from the Cuban American community and the U.S. public and government.

What sort of relationship should Cuba have with the colossus right next door? Geography, history, and the remarkable development of the United States have made the Cubans' dilemma just as inevitable as its neighbor's interest in the largest of the Antilles and concern over what transpires there. The domestic debate between "annexationists" and "nationalists"—and those who try to moderate—has raged for centuries and became a central, politically polarizing theme of domestic politics with the United States' intervention, occupation, Platt Amendment, and transformation of Spain's colony into a U.S. neo-colony.

The Spanish-American War of 1898 was the United States' first significant foray onto the world stage. Cuba, Puerto Rico, and the Philippines quickly changed masters. A fierce independence war raged in Cuba at the time, and the local rebels played an important role in the quick success of the U.S. intervention, though they were blatantly snubbed when the handover from Spain was signed and were subsequently disarmed. Cuba lay in ruins, its cities filthy, its 1.5 million residents on the verge of starvation. All agree, the United States did a remarkable job cleaning up the place during the close to four years of occupation that followed, but it left a political mess.

An electoral law, imposed on the country in 1901, gave suffrage to a few hundred thousand Cuban males over twenty-one who could read and write, or possessed at least $250 of property, or had fought for independence. A Constituent Assembly, dominated by the former independence fighters, was elected. An uncontested presidential election produced the land's first president, Tomás Estrada Palma. Estrada lived in the United States, where he had worked closely with José Martí and enjoyed good relations with Washington. Most Cubans were pleased with the choice. The Cuban flag rose over Havana and other cities on May 20, 1902, Ascension Day; Estrada became president and the U.S. troops and the much respected governor, Leonard Wood, departed amid near delirium on the island. But the new constitution contained the Platt Amendment—imposed on the Constituent Assembly by the United States through the threat of continued occupation. The amendment gave Washington veto power over many issues of state, leasing rights to lands for military and other naval purposes (Guantánamo), and the right to militarily intervene as it deemed fit. The lone-star Cuban flag finally flew, but it was already tattered.

The majority of Cubans were patriotic, illiterate, and destitute. Spanish rule and slavery had corrupted the land and its morals. There had been government motivated solely by graft and enforced by barbarous cruelty for centuries. Neither Washington nor the Cubans were ready for good government, though by all accounts Estrada's came close. What followed his four years in office can only be described as outrageous, with but a few exceptional moments. There was blatant electoral fraud, armed political revolts and assassinations, and massive and often open plundering of the treasury. Successive governments focused on Havana and the big cities and ignored the countryside, which was left to the big landholders—many from the United States—and their hated rural guard. Washington's management of Cuba was dictated by its own political and economic agenda and favored the American over the Cuban, the local corrupt politician over the honest one, the scoundrel over the gentleman, and the collaborator over the patriot. U.S. interventions on various scales, from the reoccupation of 1906–9 to the sending of warships into Havana Bay and marines to guard U.S. property, stoked youthful patriotism, resentment, and radicalism.

General Gerardo Machado, an officer during the independence war who turned failed politician and then businessman with close links to U.S. interests, was elected president in 1925. His rule was a harbinger of what would come thirty years later. Within three months Machado set a death squad upon a prominent political opponent. Then came torture, and many more assassinations and disappearances, as the United States looked the other way. By the time Machado "ran" for office again in 1929, no one dared run against him. Machado's second term in office coincided with the Great Depression and the ruin of the sugar industry. The combination of hard times, torture, selective political murder, and links with U.S. capital—spiced as it was with the Russian Revolution of 1917 and the rise of Communism—proved a recipe for disaster. Resistance, especially by students and workers, grew, and with it the official terror, opposition bombings, and eye-for-an-eye assassinations. A general strike, combined with a last-minute nudge from Washington in 1933, finally forced Machado to flee. The masses quickly took vengeance on his thugs and lackeys. Cuba's youth had been radicalized and, through the Directorio Estudiantil (Student Directorate), exercised real power for months and some influence for years.

Hudson Strode, in his detailed account of Cuba from its discovery through the Machado years, describes the student leaders in an account of a meeting, soon after Machado fled, with U.S. Ambassador Sumner Wells, even as U.S. battleships hovered nearby.

> The thirty radical young men of the *Directorial Estudiantil* sat around a long table in a private home, like students at an economics seminar. They were not easy to address. It was like speaking with youth who had returned from hell. All thirty of them had suffered imprisonment, twenty-seven of the thirty had been tortured, seven had been castrated.[6]

When Machado fled, Carlos Manuel de Céspedes was appointed president. The son of the country's independence hero and first president of the Nation in Arms during the independence wars was a good choice, but he proved no match for the forces that the Machado years and the Russian Revolution had unleashed. Within twenty-four hours of his inauguration, a group of army sergeants led by court stenographer Fulgencio Batista took over the military and forced the president to resign. The radicalized students supported the coup and together with the military appointed a five-member commission to govern the land. The commission appointed Ramón Grau San Martín provisional president. The real local power, Batista, bided his time. The other power, the Student Directorate, those thirty young men, quickly dictated a series of social and economic reforms and declared the Platt Amendment dead.

The United States refused to recognize the Grau San Martín government, unlike Machado's, and in January 1934 Batista had him replaced by Carlos Hevia, the agriculture minister and a graduate of the U.S. Naval Academy.

Various forces pushed Hevia out just a few days later, to be replaced by long-time politician Carlos Mendieta, who had run against Machado in 1925. The United States quickly recognized the new government and offered aid and improved trade conditions. To many people's surprise, the new Cuban president quickly veered to the left, enacting various social reforms and nationalistic laws that guaranteed Cuban employment in foreign firms, and insisting the Platt Amendment must go. On May 29, 1934, a new treaty with the United States abrogated its right to intervene in Cuba. More favorable trade agreements with the United States quickly followed. Roosevelt's New Deal had arrived. Batista lingered, the students pondered and protested, the workers organized, the Communists agitated, and fresh U.S. capital, goods, tourists, and the Mafia arrived. Batista ran for election in 1940 and won. Cuba's future dictator "retired" to the United States, to be followed in office by Grau San Martín in 1944 and Carlos Prío Socarrás in 1948, both of whom, along with some further reform, engaged in electoral fraud, graft, and political gangsterism on a grand scale. Fidel Castro came of age and appeared at the University of Havana. Batista returned to Cuba after winning a seat in the Senate in 1948, seizing power in 1952 when faced with certain defeat in a new bid for the presidency. Cuba's exercise in democracy had proved anything but successful and Washington's good stewardship a sham.

One of the most controversial questions about Cuba is what life was like before the coup and revolution. Was it as bad as Fidel Castro and his followers claim, or moving in the right direction, as those he drove from power and fortune insist? There is no question that economic and social progress was made in the period after Machado, despite terrible governance, but it was uneven at best, and it coincided with out-of-control and heartless greed. I have searched out and read many books about the island written in the 1940s and 1950s, from travelogues and guides to U.S. technical studies commissioned by the Cuban government. And of course I have met countless Cubans who were alive during that period.

Consuelo Hermer and Marjorie May in their 1941 *Havana Mañana: A Guide to Cuba and the Cubans* paint a lovely picture of a gay and colorful island on its way up in the world. Havana appears a paradise lost and the countryside a scene of endless charm. There are brilliant portraits of the Cuban character. It is the most positive and disinterested book I have read about that period but, in their own unconscious identification with the local elite and Jim Crow America, the authors reveal the seeds of that world's demise.

There is a widespread delusion among Americans that Cubans are a mongrel people. This is completely untrue. The real Cuban is either of pure

Spanish descent or a combination of Spanish and French, or German, or Italian ancestry. . . . Like other countries, Cuba has its Mulattoes but it takes a completely thoughtless individual to suppose that this class represents the true Cuban.[7]

Lowry Nelson, a sociology professor from the University of Minnesota, studied the country in 1945 and 1946 for the U.S. Department of State, and then published a fascinating book in 1950 titled *Rural Cuba*. He clearly was witness to what the tour writers missed. Alongside a fabulously rich and very aristocratic elite and a growing middle class, many Cubans were suffering: "Cuba presents a paradox on a grand order. Nature is bountiful. Climate and soil combine to provide extraordinary fruitfulness with even nominal care. . . . Yet the masses of Cuba's rural population are impoverished, ill housed, ill fed, and poorly clothed," he wrote.[8]

That paradox is brilliantly brought to life by Erna Fergusson in her book *Cuba*, published in 1946 after she traveled the island and visited with both the elite and those beating the first drums of the revolution soon to come. Of a drive with a "lovely lady" in Havana, she wrote:

> We were driving at the edge of a deep arroyo within which were rows of sad-looking shacks, built of old boards and palm slabs, windowless, gardenless. The lady was pointing the other way. "Those new apartment houses have every convenience of the best American houses; they are wonderful for young couples or for women living alone. Of course," sweeping a delicate hand toward the arroyo, "we'll have to get all that out. But that will be attended to. We have such a dreadful time with those people. You will see, out by the Yacht Club, how they are encroaching with their hideous shacks."[9]

According to just about every account, the situation deteriorated rapidly in the 1950s under Batista and the U.S. Mafia. Common sense will do here. You have to be extraordinarily greedy, corrupt, and brutal to lose not only power but an entire socioeconomic system to a revolution led by a bunch of kids.

In 2009 I bought a used copy of my grandfather's book on Cuba from my friend Pepe, a visually impaired young man who plied old books on the streets of the Cuban capital. Pepe would call me whenever he came across books on Cuba in English. He had no idea that this volume's author was my grandfather. What luck! At $10, the weathered paperback proved more than I bargained for. I discovered that at least one person living in Cuba in those convulsive revolutionary days did not like Waldo Frank's ponderings. The name scrawled in blue pen on the title page was Sylvia Cannon and, under *Cuba: Prophetic Island*, the same blue ink blared out in block capital letters: A REALLY INNOCENT BOOK. FROM A REALLY INNOCENT MAN. BUT WRONG AND BLIND.

Thus begins a harsh critique by the book's previous owner, so infuriated and bitter that she rails at his words in the margins. Waldo wrote that the birth of a new and independent Cuba was under way, symbolizing the region's thirst for independence and social justice, and that Castro, whatever he might be or become—and Waldo repeatedly warned of the dangers—was no ordinary Latin American capitalist dictator or European Communist tyrant, because he was as one with the vast majority of his people, and especially the youth.[10]

Where my grandfather described how the young lawyer Fidel Castro had taken Fulgencio Batista's coup to court in the early 1950s and failed, Ms. Cannon scribbled in the margin: "he could do that and now?" When Waldo wrote that only then did Castro exercise his "right to insurrection against illegal tyranny and oppression," the book's owner retorted: "a right which he denied us now." The angry woman from the past crossed out "to the Cubans," where my grandfather wrote that Castro, plotting his return to Cuba from exile in Mexico, planned to deliver Cuba to them, replacing the words with "to him." Where Waldo said that it is "the nature of evil men to be stupid," referring to Cuban dictators Batista and Machado, that blue script bristling in the margin, apparently referring to Castro, replies "not always." The book's owner gave Waldo credit just once, saying "this is relatively true," where he wrote that Cuba was forced by the United States into the arms of the Soviet Union through "its now open economic war." Was Waldo right or was Cannon? Perhaps neither was absolutely right nor completely mistaken. It was a long, long time ago.

What puzzled so many people in the 1990s was why Cuba did not follow the Eastern European Communist countries into the dustbin of history. "So what's the difference between Cuba and the Soviets? How come they fell and Cuba hasn't?" Senator Christopher Dodd asked me over breakfast at the U.S. Interests Section in Havana one morning in 1999. Diplomatic relations had ended soon after the Revolution, and the U.S. embassy was closed. Switzerland began handling matters for Washington on the island until President Jimmy Carter brokered the opening of lower-level Interests Sections, still under Swiss sponsorship, in both countries' capitals. "Well, for one thing, we had diplomatic relations and traded with the Soviets and Eastern Europe," I replied to Senator Dodd. "The Soviets were an empire, Cuba is not. Russia was Eastern Europe's historic colonizer and oppressor, while many in Latin America viewed Spain and then the United States in the same light," I continued. "Nobody forced socialism down the majority of Cubans' throats, let alone the dominant power in the region, the United States," I said. "Finally, Eastern Europe looked to Western Europe and in particular Germany as a developed capitalist model to follow, but what do the Cubans have to look forward to? Should they follow the model of the Dominican Republic, Jamaica, Puerto Rico, or Central America? These are relatively poor countries dependent on developed capitalist countries, a reality quite different from ours."

These days I'm asked why Cuba doesn't follow on the heels of Tunisia, Egypt, Yemen, Syria, Libya, and other Middle Eastern and North African kingdoms and autocracies. I reply:

- There is no significant Internet or satellite TV penetration.
- The demographics are completely different.
- It is relatively easy for young people to emigrate.
- There is comparatively good and free health care and education for all.
- The police and military do not systematically brutalize and bloody the population.
- The leaders and their families are not stealing the oil wealth and openly fooling around at European casinos.
- You are allowed to drink, party, and have sex out of wedlock.
- Women are relatively liberated.
- There is no developed business class.
- The United States does not have diplomatic and economic relations with Cuba.
- Soaring wheat prices fueled the fire in lands where the poor rely on bread, while in Cuba the government has made sure that rice and beans are available for all.
- There have been three grass-roots discussions on what ails the country over the last five years.
- The government has launched a significant reform of the economy, is lifting some onerous regulations on daily life, and has promised minor political reform.
- The Cubans cherish their hard-won social peace.

After Fidel Castro's death, and that of his brother Raúl and the few remaining members of their original troop, the Cubans will no doubt spend decades coming to their own conclusions about Castro's revolution and his long, roller-coaster rule, and examining their own choices to emigrate or stay. As the reader will discover, the discussion is already under way in Cuba, as policies imposed in the troubled Cold War years are finally revisited in search of a better future.

More than 70 percent of Cubans alive today, both in Cuba and abroad, were born after the bitter "divorce" that was the Revolution. In Cuba, they believe that the Soviet-style system, put in place in the heat of violent confrontation with the United States and the losers in the battle that unfolded on the island, no longer serves their interests. A growing majority of Cubans living in the United States and other lands believe that the most comprehensive and longest-lasting sanctions ever imposed by one country on another—known as the U.S. trade embargo—are counterproductive and must go. Thanks to U.S. president Barack Obama and Cuban president Raúl Castro, the two parts of the whole that is the Cuban nation began mingling like never before in 2010, fomenting what inevitably will be their country's future. This book is but a curtain-raiser for the drama that is yet to come.

PART I

Revolution on the Ropes (1994–2008)

1

Trauma

We used to make hamburgers out of grapefruit rinds and banana peels; we cleaned with lime and bitter orange juice and used the black powder in batteries for hair dye and makeup.

Havana nurse

I flew into Havana in December 1993, having been away from Cuba for almost three years. It was late in the evening and, looking down, I could see that the sprawling capital city of 2.2 million people, with an average building height of just two stories, was blacked out and there were few, if any, headlights moving along the roads. That was a sharp contrast to the first time I saw Havana from the air in 1984, a well-lit and bustling city. With the demise of the Soviet Union, that world was gone. Now the country stood alone. Cuba was bankrupt and extraordinarily vulnerable before its nemesis the United States and bitter exiles in Miami. The Soviets had purchased Cuban sugar at well above market prices and sold the island oil and military supplies at well below market prices, a subsidy worth some $5 billion per year. Close to 90 percent of all other Cuban exports, from nickel to oranges, went to the Soviet bloc, which in turn was the source of just about all the island's imports and financing, including for a military that would now be reduced from 300,000 troops to 60,000. What would take the old Cuba's place, I wondered, and how much time and suffering would be needed to get there? A longing for Cuban coffee tugged at my soul, and I could swear the sweet smell of espresso wafted through my nostrils. I thought of all the people who had become my friends in the 1980s: some had braved the harsh conditions in the city below to find an apartment for my wife at the time, our child, and me—to fix it up and have a bit to eat, a package of coffee, a bottle of rum, and a bicycle waiting for us. It would be months before we could purchase a car (an old Soviet Lada from the Russian embassy) and years before I would once more enjoy a relatively stable supply of running water and electricity.

I landed in a world that resembled the aftermath of a natural disaster or war. The gross domestic product had fallen 35 percent over just three years, industrial production and supplies for agriculture 80 percent, and foreign trade 75 percent, according to the government. The lights were off more than they were on, and so too was the water, which was pumped from reservoirs to hundreds of thousands of house and apartment-building cisterns in cities and towns. Smaller pumps sent the water up to rooftop tanks from which it flowed down to the faucets. The pumps—and thus the water—stopped when the electricity did, if they had not already been idled for lack of spare parts. Public transportation—which was the only legal transport available, in a land where the purchase of cars dating after the 1959 Revolution was banned without special government permission—had all but ground to a halt. City suburbs and rural towns were left isolated. There were few cars and buses on the road, and the railways quickly deteriorated. Single-gear bicycles (just about the only aid, along with fans, the Chinese provided at the time) and horse-drawn contraptions were prevalent. One of my friends biked miles to work at the port of Havana every morning, saying to himself, "You can do it, you can do it." Food was scarce and other consumer goods almost nonexistent. Workers continued to receive a state wage even as most factories and farms owned by the now-bankrupt government were idled for lack of supplies and markets. The budget deficit soared, and more currency was printed to finance it. There were plenty of pesos but nothing to buy, and so its value plummeted. The U.S. dollar traded for 150 pesos on the black market, compared with 5 to 7 pesos in 1989. The price of rice, the Cuban staple, climbed from next to nothing to 35 pesos a pound, except for a limited amount that was subsidized as part of the government's World War II–style food ration, while state salaries and pensions averaged around 200 pesos per month.[1] The guaranteed, subsidized daily liter of milk for the sick, the elderly, and children up to age sixteen now went to children through age seven at best, and the older kids received perhaps a few liters of soy yogurt a week. Even a couple of malanga (a root vegetable) for grandma's stomach ailments became hard to come by, no matter the price. Average caloric and protein consumption fell below the United Nations' minimum requirement for the first time since the early 1970s. Some Cubans, mainly women, began to go blind or suffered other nervous-system disorders from the shock of losing their meat-based diet so quickly, combined with the stress of trying to keep their homes together and their families fed. Lice roamed the day care centers and elementary schools, and bacteria multiplied in the hospitals. Doctors set broken bones without anesthesia. Oxen, not tractors, plowed the fields, butterflies replaced pesticides to control insects, and worm dung was the only fertilizer. It was a haunting time that still sends shivers down Cubans' spines. A generation grew up craving eggs, and when they were obtained, the shells were ground into powder and mixed with sugar water. I still rush through my shower for fear the water will vanish before I can rinse off the soap.

The government adopted the strategy of building a new economy—which it called the "emerging" economy—based on newly legalized dollars and fueled by tourism, joint ventures with foreign businesses, and family remittances. Carlos Lage Dávila, a young doctor and Castro aide, was put in charge of the plan. At the same time the old, decaying economy still remained, operating in pesos. Cuba's dual monetary system was born. The authorities hoped the dollar-driven economy would prove strong enough to avoid a complete collapse of the peso system, save free health and education services, and, over time, pull the country up by its bootstraps. Ironically, in the 1960s Cuba's youthful leaders had toyed with the idea of eliminating money altogether. Now they found themselves with two currencies instead of one, the Cuban peso and the U.S. greenback, and the latter quickly became the currency of choice for state businesses and the population.

Castro made concessions to the "enemy": he eased restrictions on Cuban Americans visiting their homeland and on most Cubans traveling to the United States and other capitalist countries, though they were heavily taxed; he allowed remittances from abroad for the first time and opened the country to some Western investment. A crash plan to develop international tourism, shunned for decades, began, and Castro stomped around the country apologizing for the decision while insisting there was no choice. He delivered the bad news to scientists that in the future the pharmaceuticals they developed would have to be exported, not donated as in the past. This was followed by legalization of some types of self-employment so people could mount home-based businesses. Hundreds of comparatively well stocked, air-conditioned, and clean state-run dollar shops opened for better-off Cubans, side by side with the now all-but-empty, hot and dingy peso shops for the less fortunate. At the same time, the government said it would hold firm on its basic socialist principles of sharing the wealth, imposing a minimum 240 percent markup at the "dollar stores" and maintaining a subsidized, though dwindling, food ration, free social services, and subsidized utilities, culture, and sports.

Tourism development was just getting under way when I arrived, and the combination of the terrible times and the new glitter proved too much for some. One evening in 1994 I was having a drink with Steven Cagen, a visiting photographer friend, in the lobby bar of the Copacabana Hotel, located on First Avenue along the northern coast in the Miramar district of Havana.[2] When the clock struck ten, opening time for the hotel's disco, a parade of provocatively dressed women entered from the rear door that connected the bar with the pool and the disco. The ladies of the night passed by our table, trying to strike up conversation or making suggestive facial expressions in hopes of hooking a date. My well-traveled friend turned to me and said, "I've only seen something this crass in one other place in the world: Saigon during the war."

Fidel Castro had declared a Special Period in Times of Peace, a set of emergency measures planned in case of a military confrontation with the United States and a naval blockade of the island. The official, Soviet brand of Communist ideology was discredited. At the same time, the Cuban variety always had a strong local and Third World twist in the national independence apostle, the brilliant and versatile José Martí, Latin American independence leader Simón Bolívar, Fidel Castro, and Che Guevara. Nationalism, fed by official claims of successfully parrying U.S. efforts to do in the revolutionary government, military victory in southern Africa, support for Latin American insurrections, medical and other technical aid to poor countries, and better health and education than in Eastern European Communist lands, had kept the revolutionary flame flickering even as a creeping, creepy Soviet-style bureaucracy threatened to snuff it out.[3] Castro now referred more frequently to Martí and Guevara than to Karl Marx and V. I. Lenin. He decried the excesses of Stalinism, the corruption of the Russian Communist Party, and the chaos that followed the Soviet Union's collapse, but recalled that the Soviets played a positive role in the defeat of Germany in World War II, the liberation of much of the world from Western colonialism, and Cuba's development. Lenin and his revolution were still hailed as an important milestone in humanity's quest for justice, and the United States was still berated as an "evil empire" now unopposed on the world stage. Mikhail Gorbachev was scorned well before he did his famous television commercial for Pizza Hut.[4]

There was no significant aid, little credit, and no international lending organization to bail the country out. China was hesitant to help a government that had sided against it during its long and bitter dispute with the Soviets. The United States ratcheted up the political and economic pressure in hopes of forcing the increasingly desperate Cubans to rise up and finally topple Castro. The Miami exile establishment was jubilant and expectant. Violent attacks by exiles increased, and a few Cubans hijacked boats and planes to leave the island.

Hijackings, Riots, and Rafters

My future wife, Marlene, lived in Regla, on the opposite side of the bay from the colonial district of Havana. Every morning she would take the ferry across, a fifteen-minute journey, and then hitch or walk to work (see map of Old Havana, page 45). One fine day in the summer of 1994, one of those ferries was hijacked by knife-wielding men and taken out to sea. The U.S. Coast Guard welcomed as future citizens those who wielded the weapons and a few dozen passengers who took the opportunity to migrate to the United States, while other passengers opted to return home. Soon another ferry was taken, and another; a man was killed in one of the incidents. Marlene was scared to death she might find herself on a hijacked harbor boat, clearly unfit for ocean travel, with her child still at home. These boats resembled tin cans and were decades old, not the modern variety; they barely made it across the bay. Marlene was on friendly terms with the local captains, and they all advised her to find another route. For weeks she refused to go to work, or took hours getting there via the back roads around the bay. She began taking diazepam, generic Valium, and would continue to do so for a number of years. Doctors prescribed tons of the stuff at the time, mainly to nerve-wracked women. The men got rum and beer *al granel*, which meant the booze came in tanks served on the street or dispensed at the local bodega, or ration store, more often than not diluted with water by enterprising state distributors.

Summer rioting erupted in Havana in 1994 for the first time since the 1959 revolution, and the massive 1994 exodus that followed saw thousands of Cubans take to the sea toward Florida in everything from fishing boats and inner tubes to makeshift wooden and Styrofoam rafts.

I was taking a midday walk near the harbor in the colonial part of the city on August 4, 1994, when the area's mood turned ugly. Cries of "Lancha, lancha," or "Ferry, ferry," echoed through the narrow streets as hundreds of people poured down to the bay in hopes of escaping the post-Soviet crisis by hijacking an arriving boat. When police blocked their path, a riot broke out. The air became charged with electricity as stones began to fly. I was reminded of the antiwar violence I grew up with while a teenager in Cambridge, Massachusetts. The difference was that nothing was set ablaze here, there was no tear gas, and there were no riot police. Bused-in construction workers, some with metal rods in hand, quickly restored order. And then Castro appeared and waded into the crowds of supporters who poured into the streets from nearby office buildings chanting "Fidel! Fidel!" as the stone throwers melted away. Troops from the Ministry of the Interior hit the streets for the first and only time during my years in the country. A few dozen Special Forces jeeps, with 50-caliber machine guns mounted at the rear, rolled into town after the riot, and for a week the three-man teams, in their spiffy uniforms and red berets, lounged on street corners, chatting with residents.

Castro accused the United States of being behind the ferry hijackings and then encouraging them to continue by granting the hijackers and passengers entry into the country. A man had died and his murderer was free in Miami, Castro charged during a nationally televised appearance a few days after the riot.

Cuba could no longer be held responsible for policing its borders and would-be rafters, he announced. The immigration crisis of 1994 was on and would end only with the signing of new immigration agreements with the United States.[5]

The *balsero* (rafter) crisis was quite spectacular and very big news indeed. One could go to the beach in Cojimar, just east of Havana, and witness dozens of people readying all kinds of makeshift craft to set out to sea, where the U.S. Coast Guard waited just a few miles offshore to pick them up and take them to the Guantánamo Naval Base on the eastern tip of the island, eventually to be processed for entry into the United States. I would often drive along the coastal highway west of the city to Mariel, the scene of an earlier Cuban rush to U.S. borders via the sea. Most of the roadway runs along the top of small hills overlooking the water. One could see old, rickety fishing boats, overloaded with people, heading off from coves along the northern coast. Yet most residents went about their business as if nothing was going on. I found over time that this was "normal" in Cuba. There would be an event that caused massive international attention, and the Cubans would serenely go on with their lives. "Fidel does this every once in a while to let out the bad blood, like doctors in feudal times," a middle-aged woman said with a smile and a shrug when I picked her up hitchhiking in Havana.

Hugo Chávez

Fidel Castro stood on the tarmac at Havana's José Martí International Airport as the commercial flight came to a stop before him. It was Tuesday, December 13, 1994, four months after the riot and ensuing rafter crisis. President William Jefferson Clinton had hosted the first Summit of the Americas in Miami a few days earlier, with the aim of forming a free trade agreement in the hemisphere. Castro was the only area leader not invited. It was not a head of state who stepped off the plane onto a red carpet, watched by a national television audience and saluted by a military band playing each country's anthem, but Hugo Chávez, a retired lieutenant colonel in Venezuela's armed forces.

Chávez, just turning forty and visibly underweight, had only recently been released from prison, where he was serving time for leading a failed 1992 coup.[6] He had formed a leftist organization that claimed the mantle of Simón Bolívar, also a Venezuelan. Chávez, whose popularity skyrocketed with his coup attempt, jail time, and demands to share the country's vast oil wealth with the poor, was a nobody and persona non grata in the Americas. But Castro and his intelligence services thought otherwise. "There's nothing strange about it," the Cuban leader responded to reporters when asked about Chávez's reception, usually reserved for a head of state. "I wish I had as many opportunities to welcome personalities as important as this one."

According to my sources, the two men talked day and night on that first visit by Chávez to Havana, but no information about their conversations has ever been published. Chávez would later say he was interrogated for hours by an "eagle-eyed" Castro as he sized up the young Venezuelan. When the two men appeared in public, it was to heap praise upon one another and scorn on the Americas Summit and the U.S.-proposed free trade agreement. I have never seen Castro so happy and content. The Cuban leader acted like a giddy child in Chávez's company as they inaugurated a statue of Simón Bolívar on Presidente Boulevard in Vedado, and then went on to Havana University. There Chávez delivered a televised speech, endlessly praising Castro and Cuba, trashing U.S. trade plans, and predicting that the two countries would join "as one river flowing toward a better future for the region."

Treasures for Sale

Chávez departed and the crisis continued. Cubans scrambled to unload treasures hoarded during decades of isolation from the capitalist world: antique furniture, U.S. coins and baseball cards, jewelry, gold, silver, stamps, cigar bands, porcelain, art, and whatever else they had from prerevolutionary days. Foreign collectors scooped it all up and took it out of the country for a handsome profit. The government soon opened a business to buy people's treasures. I used to marvel at the silver certificates and U.S. coins that had been stashed for decades and now were in circulation with the legalization of the dollar. They are long since gone, but pre-Revolution U.S. baseball cards, *Life* magazines, Coca-Cola signs, cameras, and other paraphernalia from the 1950s and before can still be had—including, of course, cars. Some "tourists" arrived to take away the ladies too.

"Everything has just disappeared: the food, clothes, soap, makeup, lights, buses, taxis, water, cooking fuel," said Isabel, a university student. "One day we had more than enough to survive, and the next day there was nothing, except in the hotels and other places for the tourists. I started falling, tumbling head over heels down a big dark hole. It is a terrible feeling. If I pass a foreigner, I reach out to grab his hand. I'll do almost anything to break this endless fall. Then he lets go, and I keep falling until I can grab on to the next, and the next. If I am lucky, I wind up spending a whole week at the beach away from Havana. I pray every day one of them will yank me out of here for good. It is not the Revolution's fault, and least of all Fidel's. He has done his very best to improve our lives. Most of all, I blame the United States and the Russians."

Isabel was dressed in a sheer black dress that clung to every curve of her twenty-year-old body. She was sitting in the lobby bar of the Riviera Hotel, waiting to be picked up. Isabel no doubt found plenty of men willing to "hold her hand." She was in perfect health, with smooth olive skin, black hair, a beautiful smile, and dazzling green eyes. Out in the lobby, there were dozens of similarly clad young women lounging around the entrance to the Palacio de Salsa. It was 1995, and the Palacio was Havana's hottest nightclub, where women were said to sometimes take off their shirts and dance on the tables as the island's top salsa bands pounded out rhythms from midnight until dawn. U.S. mobster Meyer Lansky, who built the Riviera in the 1950s, would have been proud. I came to view the amount of prostitution in Havana, and the bribing of police, tourism workers, and cabbies that it required, as a good gauge of the strength of the government and the economy. The massive prostitution of those days showed just how weak the government was, and the ebb and flow of the trade since then seems to have been a good barometer of the social and economic situation.

The vast majority of women, however, simply struggled to survive. "We used to make hamburgers out of grapefruit rinds and banana peels; we cleaned with lime and bitter orange juice and used the black powder in batteries for hair dye and makeup," said one of the nurses gathered around my patio table after the worst of the crisis had passed, while the others laughed nervously. Another recalled that "vanguard" workers were rewarded each month with a ticket they could redeem for a single real—not soy—hamburger. "I remember the 1980s when they used to award us fans, radios, washing machines, trips, and even cars," said another nurse.

I often sat on street corners during those years of crisis and watched people going about their business: *abuelos* (grandparents) waiting in lines for the rationed family basics; parents taking children to school in their cute red-and-white Pioneer uniforms, somehow clean and pressed, and struggling to get to and from work; and men, young and old, on bicycles, delivering a daily government-rationed paltry roll to each citizen. "Why do they bother?" I wondered. "They are working almost for free." Even Irene Aloha Wright, whom we met in the introduction, and who said she could never quite figure Cuba out, would have marveled at the scene. But to work and school, field and office, ration store and wherever, the Cuban majority trudged, often smiling and joking. I decided you would make a fortune if you could patent as an antidepressant whatever brain chemical kept the Cubans' spirits up through the hard times.

Dissent

Some Cubans, though, had had enough. Thousands emigrated legally each year, and just as many illegally, while a few were willing to brave the state's wrath and demand change. The dissidents turned to (or were driven into) the arms of U.S. and European diplomats, who welcomed them with meals, cocktail parties, funds, and advice to promote democracy, human rights, and civil society. Tiny groups, called associations of independent journalists, doctors, farmers, and librarians appeared. More than one U.S. diplomat referred to the dissidents-turned-journalists as "our independent journalists." Some—for example, a leader of the doctors and another of the ad-hoc reporters—would later surface as government agents and finger their peers in a notorious 2003 crackdown on dissent.

The Communist Party had dropped its ban on religious believers in its ranks in 1991 and then replaced the definition of the state as "atheist" in the constitution with the word "secular." Religious congregations grew as the various denominations reached out with promises of emotional security, food, medicine, and other aid pouring in from their fellows abroad. But although many outside the country forecast that Cubans would seize upon His Holiness's presence to erupt in protest over totalitarian rule, Pope John Paul II came and went in 1998 without creating so much as a ripple inside the country. Christmas once more became a holiday. The papal visit did prove important in legitimizing believers: My wife's nephew Rubén—just entering his teens at the time and now a pastor—told me that when he used to walk to church in central Cuba he would have to sometimes brave disapproving stares, scowls, and comments. But no longer; if he encountered them, he would respond, feeling very empowered, "And what about Fidel and the Pope?"

Some Miami-based exile organizations declared war on the new tourism industry. They fired machine guns at hotels and beaches from speedboats. In the late 1990s a bombing spree, hitting more than a dozen hotels, nightclubs, and restaurants, forced us to keep our kids and our partying away from tourism-oriented establishments until the ring of Central American perpetrators was finally brought down. The four captured terrorists confessed that the ring had been organized by Cuban exile and former CIA operative Luis Posada Carriles. That terror campaign killed an Italian tourist and injured numerous other tourists and Cubans.

On July 12, 1997, I was standing outside the Capri Hotel at the corner of 21st and N Streets in the Vedado district of Havana, just a block from the equally famous Hotel Nacional, when bombs went off in the two establishments' lobbies one right after the other.[7] Bombs don't go *bang!* but *kabooooom!* as glass and furniture fly. I had run into an old friend from the 1980s, Martica, and her five-year-old daughter, on their way to a children's activity at the Salón Rojo (once the casino) attached to the hotel.[8] Luckily, when the bomb blew the Capri lobby apart a few minutes later, the activity had already begun and no children were physically hurt, although many no doubt were traumatized.

Almost every Cuban has similar stories to tell about such events from personal experience or passed on by friends and family.[9]

Fog Lifts over Shattered Island

Castro disciple Hugo Chávez became president of oil-rich Venezuela in 1999. For the drowning Cubans, it was as if a man on a passing boat had appeared out of nowhere and thrown them a life preserver. Venezuela would guarantee Cuba oil, the oxygen needed to breathe life into its all-but-asphyxiated economy. Cuba would provide the medical, education, sports, intelligence, and other technical assistance that Chávez needed to jump-start his populist agenda and win elections and referendums. Castro visited Venezuela, and Chávez repeatedly visited Havana. There were baseball games and other stunts aimed at making Venezuelans and Cubans comfortable with one another and their respective Comandantes. Chávez has received far more official Cuban media attention than any other foreign leader in the Revolution's history.

The Cubans and their leaders, with some relief now in sight, had a chance to take a deep breath and look around as a new century dawned. The demise of the Soviet Union, the tightening of the U.S. embargo, and the Cuban policies that followed had not led to the demise of Castro and the Revolution, but had undermined the egalitarianism built up by the original revolutionary project and resulted in the stratification of society. The old structures and policies no longer fit the new social reality. The food ration went to the better-off as well as the poor, as did subsidized utilities, transportation, and just about everything else. Petty theft, the black market, and the corruption it depended on burgeoned, as people sought not just to survive but to obtain the consumer goods that for the first time were available in the foreign-exchange stores, tourism hotels, and related non-hotel establishments. The grossly underpaid economic bureaucracy more and more turned to embezzlement and kickbacks.

Cuba's young leaders had not only toyed with eliminating money, but they all but eliminated financial management, taxes, and accounting in the 1960s. They viewed and vilified accountants as being responsible for helping politicians and the wealthy pillage the treasury for decades. The Soviet-style bureaucracy kept few books, but plenty of everything else. After the Soviet Union's fall, the corruption did seem to increase and appeared more glaring and intolerable. "Of the 300 audits we conducted last year, 46 percent were satisfactory or acceptable. The rest, or 54 percent, were deficient or bad," Lina Pedraza, director of the government's National Auditing Office, told Cuba's official media in 2001. Her office examined the accounts of the island's most important companies, most of them in the emerging dollar-driven economy and tourism sectors. A similar number of audits in 1999 found that only a third of the firms had their books in order, and that was an improvement over 25 percent the previous year.[10]

Up through the early 1990s, moving abroad, let alone to the United States, was considered tantamount to treason. Communist Party members, for example, were not allowed to write letters to, or talk with, their relatives in the United States. Possessing dollars or other foreign currencies was a crime punishable by up to two years in prison. Foreign-exchange stores were supposedly for foreigners only. There was just one foreign-exchange supermarket in Havana, known on the streets as "God's store." There were few consumer goods other than those from the Soviet bloc. No Yankee chewing gum, peanut butter, or hot dogs could be found on the streets. Foreign journalists used to go to the Fourth of July reception at the U.S. diplomatic mission looking for hot dogs. The mindset was such that when a Brazilian subsidiary of the British Tobacco Company formed a joint venture in the early 1990s to produce cigarettes, it at first had problems manufacturing and selling the company's best known brand: Hollywood (an American name if there ever was one). Today, Hollywood cigarettes are everywhere, and so are chewing gum, peanut butter, and hot dogs, the *perros calientes* in fierce competition with the Cuban pork sandwiches called *pan con lechón*, on Havana's streets.

One of the reasons there was so little unrest at the height of the post-Soviet crisis was that residents with family abroad, embezzling bureaucrats, cultural figures, some academics, fledgling entrepreneurs, and people who stole state goods and services to resell on the black market found themselves living better than they ever had, as the dollar circulated legally, foreign-exchange stores opened, communication with family abroad and remittances were encouraged, some small business was allowed, and big-spending tourists and Cuban Americans were welcomed. The overwhelming majority of Cuban emigrants through 2000 were white. Those least likely to revolt took the brunt of the economic collapse: Communist Party members and true believers, as well as Afro-Cubans with less representation within the bureaucracy and fewer relatives abroad. While officials, security personnel, and professionals (such as scientists, doctors, nurses, and teachers) had very low state salaries, those Cubans who received remittances or tips from tourists, or ran small businesses or private farms, or went on paid government missions and exchanges overseas, or earned foreign-currency bonuses working for joint venture and foreign trading companies, or sold their art and intellectual prowess abroad, or embezzled and diverted goods, or hustled tourists and worked the black market—all these had a much higher purchasing power. On the one hand, Cubans with regular access to foreign exchange were now living better than in their wildest dreams, with access to Western consumer goods that were unavailable before 1994. On the other hand, Cubans caught in the peso economy saw their real wages plummet to around 20 percent of what they had been.[11] Maids, nannies, and gardeners made a comeback.

The faithful sometimes sold their homes—which often had been virtually given to them by the government—to the "new rich," an under-the-table transaction because by law a dwelling could only be traded up or down by a single room, a barter transaction known as a *permuta*. Entire middle-class neighborhoods appeared to change hands, with the "new rich" now a majority and government supporters a minority. While homes were registered in peso values dating back to the 1960s, by the turn of the century everyone in Havana and much of the rest of the country knew their dwelling's true market value in dollars. It was a sign of the times. Underground real estate agents, with their connections in the corrupt bureaucracy, did a brisk business arranging chains of trades with money flowing beneath the surface and proper papers guaranteed above. This contrast between the haves and have-nots, based on access to dollars and with no relation to ideology, values, effort, responsibility, or education, was known on Cuba's streets as the inverted pyramid and became a powerful force corroding the old system, its ideals and morals. Hotel bartenders, waitresses, and taxi drivers working the tourism sector often made more in a day through various schemes than government officials, doctors, and university professors did in a month. A few hundred dollars from a relative in Miami made you wealthy compared to those stuck in the old peso economy. A trick or two per week made you rich in your family and barrio.

Stratification

Cuba prides itself on being the most egalitarian society in Latin America, but beginning in the 1990s inequality grew. Various economists, with some access to official information, said that by the year 2000 around 85 percent of the country's private savings were held in 15 percent of the bank accounts, and 15 percent of savings in the hands of the other 85 percent of depositors. Cuba's Gini coefficient, an international standard widely used to measure income inequality, rose from .24 in 1986 to .38 in 2000, according to Havana University professor Mayra Espina in a paper published in Cuba and later in the United States.[12] Perfect equality would earn a 0 on the index and complete inequality a .99. The index does not take into account health care and education, which are universal and free in Cuba. Taking them into account, the Gini coefficient was estimated by sociologists at .30.[13]

Another way to look at stratification is to divide the society into tenths.

Dividing the population into ten groups by income, studies found a 15-to-1 difference in purchasing power between the top tenth and the bottom tenth. Another internal study found that 20 percent of Havana's population could be considered impoverished and an additional 30 percent "vulnerable." Access to foreign exchange and consumption at the corresponding state-run stores was considered the most important differentiating factor.[14]

It is important to note that the Gini index and the decimal approach measure income, not ownership or wealth. So comparing inequality in Cuba with that of the rest of the region at the close of the twentieth century was a bit of a stretch, because in Cuba the state, not individuals, controlled all major means of generating wealth, and the bare-bones basics were subsidized and guaranteed for all.

The 1990s proved a desperate time for the island's people, who were forced to scramble on a daily basis to survive. Cubans will never forget the trauma, and they still exhibit signs of anxiety as they tell stories about how they managed through that period. Years later some remained in shock. Without their strong extended families at home and abroad, the neighborliness of the barrios and churches, the aid of Hugo Chávez, and the leadership of the Castro brothers, socialist Cuba would be no more. But the cost was very high: the egalitarian social and economic system they built was left in shambles by the crisis that followed the demise of European Communism, and by the very measures taken to overcome it. Che Guevara's "new man" was on the decline, along with a society based on collective work and consumption designed to foster him (and her). The struggle for survival and self-interest were gaining ground. Fidel Castro would spend his last years in power trying to overcome the ideological, social, and economic damage wrought on his revolution by forcing the Pandoras of self-interest and inequality back into their box. In sharp contrast, Fidel's brother Raúl, upon taking over in 2006, determined that the social changes under way were irreversible, and that a new economic and social model of harnessing them rather than squashing them was the only way the Revolution could survive.

2

Castro Falters

I joked, saying it was a rehearsal. You could say I was pretending
I was dead, to see what my burial would look like.

Fidel Castro, after fainting during a speech in 2001

I was manning the Reuters office alone on Sunday afternoon, June 23, 2001, watching Fidel Castro deliver one of his marathon speeches before 70,000 supporters just outside Havana. The phone rang and I turned from the television to answer. When I looked back at the screen, the camera was panning away from the podium toward the back of the obviously agitated crowd. "What the hell?" I said to myself. Nelson Acosta, our Cuban reporter on the scene, quickly called. Castro, more than two hours into his speech, under a broiling sun, had fainted. Bedlam ensued as I rushed to flash the news and contact other staff. Castro was quickly surrounded by his entourage and carried to a nearby ambulance, where he revived, and in less than thirty minutes he returned to announce he was fine and depart. Cuba's leader went on television that evening to finish what he had to say and assure Cubans and the world that he was still at the top of his game. Castro pointed out that many people at the rally had fainted from the heat before he did. Indeed, Christian, a fireman friend of mine who was there, said he revived a dozen people before Fidel collapsed. But this was the first time the iconic figure, nearing his seventy-fifth birthday, had shown any physical vulnerability or inability to carry out his political responsibilities.

Castro's speech that day was to launch a campaign for the return of five Cuban agents sent to Florida in the 1990s to keep an eye out for any unusual activity at local military bases that might signal a threat to the island, and to infiltrate Cuban exile organizations, some of which espoused "armed struggle" against Castro and believed attacking tourism, diplomatic, and other soft targets was "freedom fighting." The Cuban leader charged that a few years earlier, as bombs exploded in Havana hotels, he had handed over intelligence information to the Clinton administration on exile activity related to the terror campaign, only to have it used to track down the agents sent to keep an eye on the "terrorists." The five Cubans had recently received extremely long prison terms for conspiracy to commit espionage and, in three cases, life terms for conspiracy to commit murder for regularly providing information that "contributed" to Cuba's 1996 shooting down of two exile-piloted planes, killing all four Cuban Americans aboard. Later, two of the three Cubans' life sentences would be reduced to long terms. The movement for the agents' freedom was to be modeled after the just-concluded successful effort to wrench castaway Elián González from his Miami relatives and secure his return to Cuba and his father. But now all attention was on Castro, instead of on the agents who became known as the Cuban or Miami Five. His invincible image was shattered. And that image was almost indistinguishable from the Cuban state itself. Newspaper headlines and TV news anchors around the world reported—some with sympathy, others straight-faced, and still others with barely concealed glee—that Castro was only human after all. Cubans began to discuss the possibility that the Comandante should retire or play a lesser role. The international news media ordered their television crews and photographers from that day on to keep their lenses on Castro every time he appeared inside Cuba or abroad. Cuban television was told just the opposite, to pan away at the first sign of trouble.

"I joked, saying it was a rehearsal. You could say I was pretending I was dead, to see what my burial would look like," Castro said when, apparently fully recovered and in good humor, he appeared on television that same evening. He gave a full and humorous account of what had happened earlier in the day. Castro said there was still a lot he wanted to do and he would be "a bit more prudent" in the future and put on his cap before going out to speak under the tropical sun. Castro ended his appearance after about two hours. "I feel good . . . my blood pressure is the same as when I was thirty, usually 110 over 70 and a normal pulse, and I hope, please, that they let me work in peace," he said.[1]

Castro Up Close

A year later I staked Fidel Castro out for eight hours at the Havana Convention Center and, as dawn broke, I snagged him. As I stared into Fidel's bloodshot eyes, his right hand rested on my shoulder for support, his face just a few inches from mine. I wondered how long he would survive. It wasn't that the Cuban president was in poor health for his age, quite the contrary. He had just spoken to a meeting of Latin American economists for seven hours (from nine o'clock the previous evening to four in the morning of September 21, 2002)! Then he chatted with the mainly left-leaning participants for another hour—posing for photos, signing autographs, talking earnestly at one moment and joking around at another.

Fidel entered the hallway of the Convention Center still on his feet, though a bit shaky. He was disheveled, visibly exhausted, eyes bloodshot, and with wispy strands of gray hair going every which way. "If he pushes the envelope like this every day," I thought, "how long will a man his age last, even if he is Fidel Castro?"

A few of us had waited for hours in hopes of that rare chance of talking with the legendary figure. "The hurricane, are you going?" an Associated Press colleague shouted, capturing Castro's attention as he very slowly, really shuffling, walked toward the exit. Hurricane Isidore was swirling across the tip of Cuba's westernmost province of Pinar del Río, a hundred miles away. Castro wearily turned back to let us know that he was indeed on his way at that very moment. "And the other hurricane," I shouted. Castro turned toward me and asked, "What other hurricane?" Hundreds of Americans were expected in Havana the following week for an agricultural trade show, the first such event since the 1959 revolution. U.S. food sales to Cuba for cash had just begun, under a 2000 exception to the trade embargo; again, the first such business relations with the island in decades. "The Americans, they are coming next week," I said. Castro hit my softball question out of the park. He sauntered over, placed his lanky right hand on my left shoulder for support, and his twinkling, searching jet-black pupils peered into mine from the pink that had been the whites of his eyes.

"I am very happy they are coming. . . . We have dealt with many of them, and they are really people who leave a good impression," Castro said, still lucid enough to adopt a diplomatic tone. We chatted, nose to nose, for twenty minutes about the event. "They are excellent and educated people. They have been respectful, and I have not seen arrogance in any of them," he said about talks with executives from agribusiness giants such as Archer Daniels Midland and Cargill, the U.S. Chamber of Commerce, and powerful farm groups like the U.S. wheat, rice, and poultry associations.

Castro soon lumbered off to his Mercedes-Benz and Hurricane Isidore. He was surrounded by his men, dressed as he was in olive-green military garb and black boots, pistols holstered to their broad black leather belts. I kept thinking about how old and tired the "invincible" bearded one looked and the damage he had just inflicted upon himself and was certainly inflicting every day. What drove this man to work so hard, day and night: power, ideology, the craving of attention, love of country and humanity, or perhaps a chemical imbalance? Was it all of the above? "He is a proud man who no doubt wants to die with his boots on, fighting for the cause," I thought. "He is going to work himself to death within five years."[2] (He almost did. Castro was forced by illness to cede power four years and eight months later.)

The last time I saw Fidel Castro up close was on July 1, 2004, when he turned up at a reception at the Argentine ambassador's residence to talk with a business delegation from one of the most fertile provinces of the South American country about buying food. Castro always traveled through Havana in a three-car Mercedes motorcade, escorted by motorcycle police. The sleek black sedans, bodyguards at the windows, would speed through the streets—cleared before them by perfectly choreographed police—and swoop up to whatever their destination in a display of force and purpose, always with a few Russian Ladas and an ambulance not far behind. Castro, and his bodyguards and aides, piled out of the cars and went straight to the back patio of the Argentine ambassador's residence, wading through and ignoring reporters and guests. All, except the young foreign minister Felipe Pérez Roque and the bodyguards, were old. Castro emerged after the four-hour meeting and chatted for a while with the press and guests waiting in the wings. His face was spotted with big brown-to-black age marks, and from behind you could see that his shoulders were those of an old man, although from a distance his uniform made them appear broader and sturdier.

Castro's Tumble

Then, on October 20, 2004, Castro tripped while descending from the speaker's platform at a graduation ceremony for art instructors in central Villa Clara Province. The backdrop for his speech was the mausoleum that holds the remains of fellow revolutionary Ernesto "Che" Guevara and his ill-fated Bolivian troop. Castro fractured his left knee and his right upper arm. Local viewers did not see the fall because the cameras quickly panned away, but CNN and other foreign media that do not broadcast inside the country caught the moment for the international audience. Castro was picked up by bodyguards and placed in a chair, where he was attended to by his doctors. Sweating profusely from the pain (and he was never known to sweat), the Cuban president asked for a microphone and told the crowd of about 30,000 people and the national television audience, with local cameras once more focused on him, that there was no cause for alarm. "Dear graduates and other guests, I ask your forgiveness for having fallen. To prevent speculation, I observe that I have a fracture in my knee and maybe in an arm too. I'm not sure yet," he said. "I will recover as soon as possible, but as you can see, I can speak even if they put me in plaster and I can continue my work."[3] Later it would be learned that Castro's kneecap was shattered into eight pieces and his upper arm had sustained a serious fracture that hampers his movement to this day.

Castro's dramatic tumble provoked new questions about how long he could remain at Cuba's helm. It was becoming painful indeed to watch the iconic figure struggling against the vagaries of age as his hours-long speeches became ever more meandering. In his prime, Castro could talk for hours without a text, going off on many tangents but always returning to the main theme, weaving a whole out of many parts, like the ribbon-holding dancers around a maypole. Now, sometimes, he would go off on tangents and prove unable to weave them back into his main subject, leaving his audience confused and those maypole ribbons going every which way.

"He asked that it be made known he is in condition to continue attending to fundamental questions in close cooperation with government and Party leaders," an official statement said, the day after Castro's tumble.[4] Before his fall, Castro was already walking with difficulty, and I was convinced he would never walk again. But he staged a remarkable recovery, continuing to talk as only he can—first from a sitting position and seen only from the waist up, later from a wheelchair. Within a year he was walking again and once more completely dominating Cuba's political space and the day-to-day administration of the country. Castro's Battle of Ideas, built on the struggle around the child castaway Elián González, and in which the art instructors played a part, was in full swing.

Elián and the Battle of Ideas

I was flipping through the *Boston Globe* the day after Thanksgiving in 1999 and saw a small article on an inside page about a Cuban boy found adrift off Miami. He was apparently the only survivor of yet another immigrant tragedy at sea. I thought little of it, and turned my attention to my family, gathered in Massachusetts to share the holiday. I returned to Cuba a few days later to witness young people rallying one evening before the U.S. Interests Section and demanding the repatriation of Elián González. Union of Young Communists leader Otto Rivero and others stood atop a jeep in the center of a vacant lot fronting the U.S. mission, venting through a bullhorn their anger at Miami exiles and U.S. imperialists for "kidnapping" the boy. At the time, there was nothing but a parking lot and an empty two-block grassy wasteland alongside of the building, which stood beside the seaside drive in Vedado, looking out over the Gulf of Mexico. A single billboard nearby boasted a cartoon of an oversized Cuban *mambí,* looming out of Cuba and pointing his finger at a caricature of Uncle Sam across the Florida Straits, with the caption "Mr. Imperialist, we are not the least bit afraid of you." Within months a huge outdoor amphitheater, as well as a paved space for rallies and other activities such as concerts and graduations, would replace the vacant land as the battle for Elián heated up. It was named the Anti-Imperialist Tribuna, and dubbed the Demodrome by Cubans. Later it would be extended when the Interests Section parking lot was dug up and flagpoles erected to its very door as tensions heightened with the Bush administration. A statue of José Martí, holding a child and pointing accusingly at the U.S. diplomatic building, now stands where the bullhorn-toting youth once were atop the jeep. Cubans joke that Martí is pointing the way to the U.S. consular offices where hundreds line up every day in search of visitor and permanent entry visas.

Within weeks of that first protest, the entire country seemed to rise up around Elián's father, Juan Miguel González, as he struggled to recover his son caught in the riptide of the great Cuban ideological divide on either side of the Florida Straits. Fidel Castro's last great international and domestic campaign against his foes in Washington and Miami was on. The boy would return to Cuba in June 2000, an international and domestic superstar and catalyst of newfound energy among the Cubans, especially the youth.[5]

The rally on the vacant Havana lot proved the first of weekly Saturday-morning speak-outs in every nook and cranny of the country, led by youth and combining national and local speakers, musicians, dancers, and poets of all ages with local history, culture, and patriotic rhetoric. The rallies, under the banner of the Battle of Ideas, continued well after Elián's return. Between December 1999 and March 2005 there were 185 of the Saturday speak-outs or Tribunas Abiertas, at least one in each of 169 Cuban municipalities. Every event was televised to the nation and broadcast on various radio stations, the crowds waving little Cuban flags on sticks as they were entertained by local talent and speakers demanding the return of the Cuban Five and denouncing Miami exiles and Washington.[6] Raúl Castro, not Fidel, attended most of the local events, flag in hand, although he rarely spoke. The speak-outs represented a dramatic increase in the younger Castro's public presence even as Fidel faltered, and gave him the perfect opportunity to meet and size up the local leadership. Were the brothers already preparing the transition?

Fidel Castro worked to capitalize on the enthusiasm generated during the battle for Elián, and funds flowing in from Venezuela and now a more forgiving China, through the organization of dozens of youth-directed programs to rebuild social services and infrastructure and recruit disaffected young people to become teachers, health care providers, and social workers. Castro and the leaders of the young people, led by Otto Rivero, spent hours every day planning and carrying out various projects, with budgets in the hundreds of millions of dollars. The movement called the Battle of Ideas was head-quartered alongside Castro's office. Youth leaders gained tremendous power as representatives of Castro's revolutionary will and newfound wealth. They worked parallel to, and sometimes bossed around, government and Communist Party officials.

One of my best friends at the time was a Japanese diplomat named Kenya Uno. The Japanese worked hard to identify and get to know young Cubans they viewed as future leaders, often hosting them in Japan. Otto Rivero certainly appeared to be one of them. Sitting with Kenya in 2003 at the Meliá Havana Hotel, across from the Havana International Trade Center in Miramar, where his embassy was located, I learned over coffee that a meeting with Rivero had finally been set up. "Ask him how often he meets with Castro and for how long," I said. Kenya asked and was told by Rivero: "Over the last 450 days we met maybe 430 times for between two and four hours each time." Indeed, according to my sources, Castro would meet with Rivero and other young people late every evening and into the early morning hours, planning the next day's work, including prime-time television propaganda through a current-events talk show begun during the Elián days, called *Mesa Redonda*, or *Roundtable*.

The rapidly aging Fidel Castro was not happy with the social stratification and the petty and not-so-petty larceny that the post-Soviet crisis had wrought. He understood that there was a growing gap between the leaders and the led, especially the youth, and appeared determined to tackle the bureaucratization and stratification of his revolution by pitting his young followers against these growing domestic ills and, by implication, against an important segment of the Communist Party, which made up the bureaucracy's ranks.

Castro, by 2002, with Chávez now firmly in power in Venezuela and China more willing to open its purse strings, had also begun to roll back the reforms of the 1990s. He recentralized the foreign currency entering the country, froze new licenses for many types of small private businesses, and reduced from 450 to just over 200 the joint ventures and production agreements with mainly Western companies. At the same time he launched the Battle of Ideas and new "internationalist" programs such as Plan Milagro, which provided free eye care and surgery to hundreds of thousands of people in the region, and began training tens of thousands of young people from the area as doctors and other health care providers.

Providing ideological cover for the youth movement was the true purpose of Castro's famous November 2005 speech at Havana University, where he refuted rumors he had Parkinson's disease by speaking for hours without so much as a twitch, and made news by openly admitting his mistakes.

Here is a conclusion I've come to after many years: among all the errors we may have committed, the greatest of them all was that we believed that someone really knew something about socialism, or that someone actually knew how to build socialism. It seemed to be a sure fact. . . . Whenever they said: "That's the formula," we thought they knew. Just as if someone is a physician. . . . Is it that revolutions are doomed to fall apart, or that men cause revolutions to fall apart? . . . The consequences of errors committed by those in authority are terrible, and this has happened more than once during the revolutionary processes. . . . This country can self-destruct; this revolution can destroy itself, but they [the United States] can never destroy us; we can destroy ourselves, and it would be our fault.

Castro then announced that he was mobilizing former dropouts turned social workers, teachers, art instructors, and health workers as the battering rams against creeping corruption, and that he planned to use university students and others in the fight, as needed.

At the moment, while I'm talking to you about this . . . we are working, we are moving toward full changes in our society. We have to change again, because we have gone through some very difficult times, and these inequalities and injustices have arisen, and we are going to change this situation. . . . We have to be resolute. . . . Either we radically defeat these problems or we die.[7]

And so Castro turned to his young followers to launch his final battle against what he saw as an increasingly corrupt and stratified society although, ironically, some of those at the very top of the movement would soon be imprisoned for accepting kickbacks from foreign and domestic firms. The first target of the campaign was the country's fuel distribution system. Even as the Saturday-morning speak-outs, organized by the young people, continued, thousands of student-age youths took over gas stations and started working in refineries and riding in fuel trucks where it turned out up to half of the precious resource was being stolen. The young people also raided bakeries, looking for stashed wheat and lard and checking how many rolls were needed to meet a neighborhood quota, then adjusting wheat and other deliveries accordingly. Soon groups of youths were in the barrios, exchanging high-wattage lightbulbs for more efficient ones and taking a census of each home's living conditions as they began replacing energy-wasting appliances with millions of Chinese-made refrigerators, stoves, and pressure cookers, sold on credit to Cuba. The better-off Cubans fretted they were being classified as the "new rich" currently berated by Castro, even as he staged repeated million-man marches and other activities in front of the U.S. Interests Section. The movement came to an abrupt end when Fidel stepped aside in 2006.

Preparing for the Inevitable

Castro's deteriorating presence and anxiety-provoking behavior signaled that the end of his rule was near. The glacier of public denial of what Castro's enemies called the "biological solution" and Cubans called "the biological fact" began ever so slowly to move, as officials and government media prepared the public.

So did the United States. Secretary of State Condoleezza Rice reconvened Washington's Commission for Assistance to a Free Cuba in December 2005 "to develop a concise but flexible strategic plan that will help the Cuban people move rapidly toward free and fair democratic elections . . . to marshal our resources and expertise and encourage our democratic allies to be ready to support Cuba when the inevitable opportunity for genuine change arises."[8] The cabinet-level commission had already put together a 450-page plan to tighten sanctions and increase support for the Castro brothers' opponents during President George W. Bush's first term, and the previous year a transition co-coordinator was appointed to carry out its recommendations. "U.S. policy must be targeted at undermining this succession strategy," the transition report said of plans for Raúl to take over.

The Cuban National Assembly of People's Power, a single-chamber parliament that includes the country's national and provincial Communist Party and government leaders, held an end-of-the-year session in 2005 that dealt extensively, if delicately, with the inevitable. For the first time since my arrival in Cuba, the entire session was open to diplomats and foreign journalists.[9]

Central Bank president Francisco Soberón and Felipe Pérez Roque, then foreign minister and a Castro protégé who had yet to turn forty, delivered the closing remarks that were televised to the nation as Castro sat quietly at their side. Soberón took the floor first.

> In the USSR the errors made led to popular unrest caused, among other reasons, because of the poor functioning of the economy. . . .
>
> It is true that in our specific situation, we have a colossal safeguard of Socialism that is our faith in our people, in Fidel and Raúl. But if we do not manage to continue to increase the standard of living of the population and guarantee a program of sustainable development we are running the risk that these great personalities will become the only pillar that maintains this system.[10]

Pérez Roque delivered the closing speech at the parliament meeting, a role that traditionally was Fidel's. It was an optimistic review of the international and domestic situation, highlighting the need to prepare for Castro's passing and new U.S. efforts to annex the country. "We have to preserve the victorious revolution in the future when there is a void no one can fill . . . and so one of the profound themes of this assembly's organizers was that the enemy has put its hopes not in defeating us now, but after," said Pérez Roque, who was considered at the time to be a leading voice of an up-and-coming generation of thirty-to-fifty-year-olds who dominated the provincial Communist Party and government organizations and, increasingly, the middle echelons of the military and security apparatus.[11]

The year 2006 kicked off with publication of *Cien horas con Fidel* or *One Hundred Hours with Fidel*, a question-and-answer autobiography with the collaboration of *Le Monde Diplomatique* editor Ignacio Ramonet.[12] Castro talks about his life and work and provides his point of view on any number of controversial questions raised by his myriad biographers. Did Castro's early childhood mark him for life as a narcissist and a rebel against the establishment? Was he a political opportunist and even a gangster in his college days? What was he really up to when, as a student, he joined an expedition to topple a Dominican Republic dictator? Did he just happen to be in Colombia when a popular presidential candidate was assassinated and an urban rebellion broke out? Why did Castro resort to armed rebellion, and when did he become a Communist? What did he know about the Bay of Pigs invasion before it began? How crazy was he during the missile crisis? Why did Castro move Cuba into the Soviet camp and crush all opposition? What was he thinking when he sent tens of thousands of troops to Angola to fight South African forces? What was Castro's relationship with Che Guevara, Raúl Castro, and other personalities, including Pope John Paul II? What were his experiences taking on ten U.S. presidents? The questions and his answers continue through the collapse of the Soviet Union, more recent repression of opponents, and his relationship with Venezuelan president Hugo Chávez. The more-than-750-page book, published in various languages by various publishers under various titles, was a sort of last-will-and-testament in interview format that ensured that Castro's side of the story would get into all serious biographies and histories written long after his death. These days Castro is working on his memoirs, again in oral history format, with official biographer Katiuska Blanco Castiñeira; two volumes have appeared.[13] But when the collaboration with Ramonet was published, was the timing a mere coincidence?

Raúl Castro began openly talking about what would happen when his brother was no longer around, emphasizing the importance of the Communist Party, not the Battle of Ideas, and moving away from the high-energy and very personalized style associated with Fidel. "Only the Communist Party, as the institution that brings together the revolutionary vanguard and will always guarantee the unity of Cubans, can be the worthy heir of the trust deposited by the people in their leader," Raúl said in a speech to military officers six weeks before stepping in for Fidel. Raúl spoke similarly at a meeting of the Party Central Committee in June 2006, a month before his brother took ill. A twelve-member Secretariat was named to take on new executive powers at the same meeting. Fidel, turning eighty, and Raúl, seventy-five, were on the Secretariat, but most of its members were from a younger generation of leaders who came to political maturity in the 1980s and 1990s.[14]

Castro had long suffered from intestinal problems, and his doctors most likely warned that at some point hemorrhaging and surgery were probable if he didn't slow down. He did not.

3

The Big Bang

I was on the bus going to work this morning when this guy started yelling that it was a good thing Fidel was sick. A whole lot of people jumped on the fellow and threw him off, just like that. Then they all went back to whatever they were doing or talking about, as if nothing had happened, nothing was wrong.

Havana doctor

The "Big Bang," as we journalists dubbed Fidel's death or incapacitation, came as we expected in a land known for being able to keep a secret—unexpectedly. Our cell phones were always by our sides for the call that would inevitably come someday, setting off complicated plans to cover one of the most impor tant stories on the planet. We dreaded being out of the country when the news broke, in case we were unable to get back in. Some media kept offices or string- ers on board in Cuba just to be in position for the event and its expected after- math. The common wisdom was that many of us would be out of a job soon after Castro's death, as the island receded from its larger-than-life place in the news and the world's interest.

I happened to be walking through the narrow, weathered streets of Old and Central Havana on that Monday evening, July 31, 2006, when the call finally came. I had crossed the two-block-long Central Park, having first navigated the Paseo de Martí, the once-splendid boulevard universally called the Prado, that runs for about a mile from the old U.S.-style capitol building down to the sea and that serves as the border between Old Havana and Central Havana. The capital's aristocrats, from the late 1800s into the early years of the twentieth century, would parade their womenfolk in horse-drawn carriages up and down the Prado before dinner. The carriages were gradually replaced by the auto- mobile. Young men lounged along the boulevard's lovely laurel-shaded center walkway guarded by statues of roaring lions, hoping to catch a young lady's eye.[1] The boulevard was built over a broader clearing that separated the wall protecting the old town from the forest and the ever-present danger of raiding pirates, buccaneers, and European soldiers. While most streets in Havana are numbered, those in Old and Central Havana have names. El Prado translates as "the meadow."[2]

Today the Prado is a chaos of antique U.S. cars, vintage Soviet Ladas and Polish Fiats, newer European and Asian models, and motorcycles and scooters, all dodging Chinese tour buses, an occasional horse-drawn carriage, careless jaywalkers, and those Cuban inventions the *cocomóvil* and the *bicitaxi*. The former resembles a three-wheeled yellow ladybug with an open front and is powered by a motorbike; the latter is a local version of the rickshaw, pulled by modified bicycles.

I passed Ernest Hemingway's Floridita haunt, advertised as one of the seven best-known bars in the world, ready to plunge down the bustling shopping street of Obispo (named after a bishop who once did the same) toward the harbor, then through the old city's narrow byways, parks, and squares. You can sip a daiquiri if you like, next to a bronze likeness of Papa Hemingway sitting at the Floridita bar, but at an outrageous price. Daiquiri is the name of the town in eastern Cuba where U.S. troops first landed in 1898 to end Spanish rule.

The American author must have taken the same walk as he headed for the Ambos Mundos Hotel on Obispo Street a few blocks from the harbor, where, in room 511, he began his novel *For Whom the Bell Tolls*. The Cubans' home life in the area, within crowded, stifling hot, and once-elegant apartment buildings turned tenements—every window and door open for air—spills onto the streets and alleys, bathed by the din of human chatter and music, boys playing stickball, smells of cooking rice, beans, chicken, pork, coffee, and leaky sewers.

Hemingway's other famous Havana watering hole, the Bodeguita del Medio bar and restaurant, is a five-minute walk from Ambos Mundos Hotel, just off Cathedral Square, though some historians insist he stepped into the place only once. Another spot graced by Hemingway, Sloppy Joe's, just a few minutes' walk from the Floridita and closed for decades, reopened in 2013. Hemingway soon settled down at Finca Vigía (Lookout House), his estate just east of the capital. Hemingway lived in his beloved spread from 1940 to 1960, finished that book there, and also wrote *The Old Man and the Sea*, among other tomes.

I walk for pleasure and work. I soak up Cuba as best I can and try to understand what it is like living day to day and only for the day, as so many here do. I have no doubt I would immediately sense the slightest change in public mood in the barrios of avant-garde Vedado, working-class Marianao, and the Central and Old Havana that I know so well and that are two of the three most densely populated districts in the country.

My mobile phone rang: a Cuban friend alerting me that the nightly government newscast had just announced that Fidel Castro would issue a proclamation at 9:15 that evening. This was strange indeed, even for Cuba, where the government often communicates through stiff communiqués. I hurried home to learn that my stepdaughter's boyfriend had called, asking why mili-

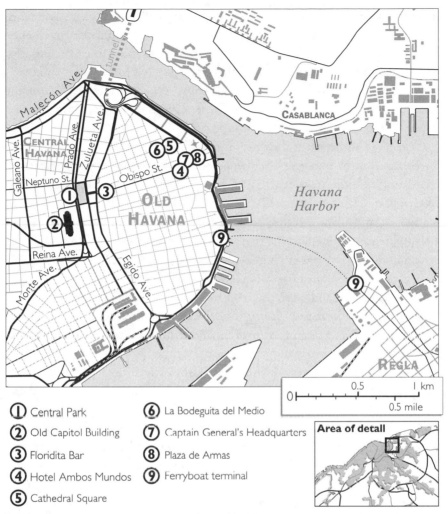

① Central Park
② Old Capitol Building
③ Floridita Bar
④ Hotel Ambos Mundos
⑤ Cathedral Square
⑥ La Bodeguita del Medio
⑦ Captain General's Headquarters
⑧ Plaza de Armas
⑨ Ferryboat terminal

Area of detail

Old Havana, showing the locations made famous by Ernest Hemingway and the route he (and I) often walked down Obispo Street. Map created by Armando Hugo Portela.

tary reserves were being mobilized in his neighborhood. "They are going door to door," Raimy said. I notified my clients at the time, Thomson Reuters, the *Financial Times*, and ABC News, that something important was about to happen.

It was not the graying and sometimes meandering Comandante who appeared on television at exactly 9:15 p.m., but his tense personal aide-de-camp, Carlos Valenciaga. Fidel Castro had temporarily ceded power to undergo emergency surgery for intestinal bleeding. Castro, in a statement read by Valenciaga, said he would not be able to work for a number of weeks and, "due to the fact that our country faces a threat from the Government of the United

States in circumstances such as these," was provisionally appointing his brother Raúl Castro, then seventy-five, to his three positions: commander in chief of the armed forces, president of the Councils of State and Ministers, and first secretary of the Communist Party. "This operation has forced me to take several weeks off," Castro said. The "extreme stress" of recent work had "brought about an acute intestinal crisis with persistent bleeding which made it necessary for me to undergo complicated surgery."

Castro was immersed at the time in "revolutionary offensives" at home and abroad, buoyed by his successful campaign for the return of young castaway Elián González and by the advent of friend and fellow revolutionary Hugo Chávez in oil-rich Venezuela. Castro and Chávez had teamed up to offer oil, health care, and education to other area governments in an attempt to extend their influence and undermine that of Washington. Confrontation with the Bush administration was at its peak, with massive rallies and marches taking place at the U.S. diplomatic mission in Havana.

Castro, as always and despite nearing his eightieth birthday, was at the center of all government initiatives, seeing himself as the "main driving force" behind nearly everything. "I provisionally delegate my functions as the main driving force behind the National and International Public Health Programme to the member of the Politburo and Minister of Public Health, comrade José Ramón Balaguer Cabrera," a doctor and fellow traveler since the earliest days of the Revolution. "I provisionally delegate my functions as the main driving force behind the National and International Education Programme to comrades José Ramón Machado Ventura and Esteban Lazo Hernández, members of the Politburo." Both men would rise in power in the coming years. "I provisionally delegate my functions as the main driving force behind the National Energy Revolution Programme being implemented in Cuba and abroad as part of a scheme of collaboration with other countries to comrade Carlos Lage Dávila," the most important rising young star in the land, who would soon be disgraced. "The funds corresponding to these three programmes, namely Health, Education and Energy, should continue to be administered and given priority, as I myself have been doing, by comrades Carlos Lage Dávila, Secretary of the Executive Committee of the Council of Ministers, Francisco Soberón Valdés, Minister and President of the Central Bank of Cuba, and Felipe Pérez Roque, Minister of Foreign Relations, who have worked with me on this and who should form a commission to this end," Castro said.[3] Eighteen months later, Castro would officially resign as president, and within two years the Battle of Ideas would be over; most of Castro's cabinet, including Lage, Pérez Roque, and aide Valenciaga, would be sacked (Soberón resigned); and memories of the time when life was turned upside down by long speeches and anti-U.S. marches and rallies would be fading, even though Cuba's alliance with Venezuela and other revolutionary governments, and its support for even less well-off countries, continued.

July 31, 2006, marked the start of one of the most remarkable chapters in Cuba's history. The whereabouts of the iconic figure and his exact condition remained secret not for days, weeks, or months, but for nearly three years, as the much-awaited transition from his overwhelming presence in Cubans' lives unfolded and the inevitable questioning of his rule and revamping of his policies began. Not until five years later would all doubts be removed that Raúl was really running the country and that he enjoyed the support of his brother as he relentlessly worked to bring a semblance of order back to the island, lift some restrictions on personal liberties, call for term limits, remake the economy, and, in the process, reverse many of the policies and taboos both men had supported for decades. The secrecy was no small feat, right next door to the United States and its massive intelligence-gathering capabilities, and with an army of foreign diplomats and assorted secret agents, not to mention foreign journalists, working day and night in Havana to discover Castro's whereabouts, condition, and influence. We did not know it at the time, but an ongoing guessing game of how and where Fidel was, and how much influence he still wielded, had begun. For all we knew back then, Cuba's leader was already dead.

Castro's Legacy

The world's media had been preparing for Castro's death ever since he fainted in 2001. U.S. television networks' special-events teams planned for his demise and funeral much as they would for the deaths of former U.S. presidents, the pope, or the queen of England. It was a huge story. The announcement that he was ill was the top news around the world. Castro had presided over a tiny island nation of just 11.2 million inhabitants, a drop in the bucket in a world of 7 billion souls, and it was a poor land with few natural resources aside from real estate, bays for ports, sugar, coffee, tobacco, nickel, and cobalt. Offshore oil exploration had yet to begin. So why was his death seen as an epic event?

Castro was one of the best-known and most controversial personalities alive, both revered and despised, as are most historic political and military figures in their times. The carefully crafted figure of an austere and defiant revolutionary—with his pistol at the hip, his military cap, Roman nose, beard, and uniform with no medals or stars—was etched in the minds of people the world over for half a century. Castro was the last of the key players from the 1962 Cuban missile crisis that brought the world, for the first and only time, to the brink of nuclear annihilation. His revolution was the first in the Western

Hemisphere to definitively break away from the United States; it defeated the U.S.-sponsored Bay of Pigs invasion and, under Castro's leadership, became a flashpoint for the Cold War as Cuba allied with the Soviet Union and defied the most powerful country in history right next door—and, much to the world's surprise, continued to do so even after the Soviet Union's demise. Castro had escaped scores of assassination attempts by the United States government, the mob, and Cuban exiles. The Cuban government claims to have foiled more than 630 plots. He had survived ten U.S. presidents' efforts to kill or oust him.

With the exception of South Africa's Nelson Mandela, Castro was the last of the romantic revolutionary figures that emerged in the twentieth century as colonialism collapsed. The Cuban Revolution unfolded at a time when poor countries were breaking away from the rich countries' parasitical grip. Castro became a voice for many of those countries' aspirations, and Cuba an idealized symbol to follow as poor nations struggled to develop and provide the most basic essentials to their peoples. Cuban troops under Castro's command were decisive in ending South African apartheid, liberating Namibia from South Africa, and defending Angola from a South Africa–promoted civil war, a truly historic and remarkable feat. The Cuban Revolution, with its purist ideology and egalitarianism, its medical and educational support for other poor countries, its development of the best health, education, and other services in the Third World despite U.S. sanctions, its sports prowess, and its propaganda machinery, proved one of the most profound challenges to the international status quo in modern history, perhaps best compared for its zeal and odds-against image with Sparta or the first days of the Paris Commune.

Dictator, megalomaniac, tyrant, narcissist, hero, prophet, historic leader, idealist, utopian, revolutionary, god, or the devil: whatever one believes, there is no doubt that Fidel Castro does not come from an ordinary mold and has managed to leave quite a ripple or two in what is for small and poor countries the otherwise huge, deep, and practically unmovable body of water we call world history, let alone the tsunami he caused in Cuba's and Latin America's. *Time* magazine, in April 2012, would declare Castro one of the one hundred most influential personalities in history.

ABC News, the *Financial Times*, and Reuters had long since worked out detailed personnel and technical plans to cover Castro's death, his funeral, and the possible drama—if not mayhem—that might follow, as Cubans on both sides of the Florida Straits reacted to the end of his long rule. The common wisdom was that if there was any trouble on the island, relatives in Miami might well take to their boats to rescue their loved ones, causing a confrontation with Cuban authorities, an immigration crisis, and perhaps U.S. intervention. My clients were as prepared as they could be when the news broke. I remained wide awake for the next forty-eight hours; my first stop after dictating a story for the *Financial Times* was the Associated Press television office, which had rented time to ABC News from its live-shot balcony, with the backdrop Havana Bay, the Moro Castle, and the sea toward Florida beyond.

August 1, 2006 (ABC News, *Good Morning America*)

Diane Sawyer on camera (OC). But let's start now with that breaking news out of Havana. Fidel Castro's brother Raúl in power right now, while the nearly eighty-year-old leader undergoes surgery. It is the first time he has relinquished any of his duties since he came to power in 1959. And this morning we are there, from Havana to Washington to Miami. We're going to begin in Miami, 228 miles from Havana, home to 650,000 people of Cuban descent.

Diane Sawyer (OC). And ABC's Jeffrey Kofman brings us the latest. Jeffrey, what are they saying there? What are you hearing?

Jeffrey Kofman (OC). Good morning, Diane. You can hear the horns blaring. That's an indication of what they're saying here. This is Southwest 8th Street, Calle Ocho, in the heart of Miami's Little Havana. Overnight, it erupted into a spontaneous street party, so much so that buildings had to close in the street. You know, with more than a million Cuban Americans here in South Florida, they've been waiting almost half a century for word of Castro's death. Simply hearing that he's gravely ill, though, was cause enough for celebration . . .

Cuban male (OC). I am waiting forty year for this moment, for the big, the big moment, for Cuban people is this . . .

Jeffrey Kofman (OC). People here have known the news for about three hours. All they know for sure is that Fidel Castro is gravely ill. But that is all they need to know. For them, that means the end is near. Many here believe it's already happened.

Cuban female (OC). It's the happiest day of our lives. We've waited for this for so long. We can't believe it.

Jeffrey Kofman (OC). But he's not dead. He's just . . .

Cuban female (OC). Oh, my God, he's probably dead since Monday.

Diane Sawyer (OC). That's right, Jeffrey. But the news they have been hoping for down in Miami. Well, as Jeffrey mentioned, there was a special bulletin that went on Cuban TV last night in the words, allegedly, of Fidel Castro. And moments ago, I spoke with ABC's Marc Frank in Havana to find out what he learned from the Cuban people last night, the reaction to this breaking news about their leader . . .

Marc Frank voice-over footage (VO). He's eighty years old. He fell two years ago. He fainted five years ago. And so it's not a total surprise. But certainly people are, are frightened, they're anxious. They've only known Fidel, most people in this country have lived only under Fidel Castro, and they don't know what to expect next.

Diane Sawyer (OC). Is he feared or respected, is he beloved? How beloved?

Marc Frank (OC). Well, I think he's beloved by some and not by others. I know many people who cry at the mere thought of him dying. I know others who laugh. I know others who can't wait. So, I think it's a mixed bag. Certainly, many people here look at him kind of as a living George Washington or Abraham Lincoln, while others look at him as a dictator. So it depends who you talk to.

Diane Sawyer (VO). From your knowledge, and not that there is a precedent for this, but from your knowledge of how announcements come about in Cuba, if in fact he were gravely ill, not coming back—some people speculated that he already died—if that were the case, do you think that they would be making this kind of announcement?

Marc Frank (OC). My own opinion and that of some other people I've talked to is that they made this announcement probably a few days after his operation and after he came through the operation, and that they would not have made it if he wasn't, in their opinion, on the road to some kind of recovery. So my opinion is that he's probably gone through the operation, has come out of the, you know, the first forty-eight hours, and they felt confident enough to put out the statement.

As part of foreign media planning for the Big Bang, we assumed that the Cuban government would not let reporters into the country for a number of days, perhaps until the funeral, nor allow U.S. television networks to go live with the news. We proved wrong about the latter but right about the former. Some news agencies slipped staff into the county as tourists and reinforced their Miami, Washington, and Mexico bureaus. Many U.S. publications, such as the *New York Times*, *USA Today*, and *Newsweek*, also sent reporters in undercover, while hundreds of journalists around the world simply waited for permission to enter—a permission that never came.

The day after the proclamation, at 6:30 p.m. on Tuesday, a second Castro communiqué was broadcast over television and radio, announcing that his health and whereabouts were state secrets. "I cannot make up good news, because that would be unethical; and if there were bad news, these will only be of benefit to the enemy. Given the specific situation facing Cuba and the plans designed by the empire, the information about my health condition becomes a state secret that cannot be continuously disseminated," the statement said.[4]

Calm in Cuba

I kept busy when the story broke doing phone interviews for ABC radio and television and spots for the company's Miami affiliate. It was a bit strange reporting on Miami television that there was complete calm inside Cuba, given local expectations to the contrary. The situation was surreal. There was high drama and even hysteria abroad. The Cubans went about their day-to-day lives as usual, flocked to the beach to escape the heat, hung out along Havana's seaside drive, and lined up for visas at the U.S. Interests Section and the Canadian and Mexican embassies, with an eye to the U.S. border. I took to doing stand-ups on Cuba's streets as the population went about its business, so that viewers in Florida could see the scene for themselves. Talk on Havana's buses centered on an August increase in the number of eggs rationed to the population, but at a higher price.[5] Remember Ms. Wright from the introduction? The U.S. writer who in 1910 said that what you see in Cuba is not always what it appears to be, at least not for long. "I was on the bus going to work this morning when this guy started yelling that it was a good thing Fidel was sick. A whole lot of people jumped on the fellow and threw him off, just like that. Then they all went back to whatever they were doing or talking about, as if nothing had happened, nothing was wrong," Martica, a doctor friend of mine, said a few days after Fidel's proclamation.

The vast majority of Cuban Americans were not partying in Little Havana. They were at home following the news and trying to get through to relatives. Marlén, a friend who worked at the state-run telephone monopoly, said the international circuits were jammed for days. Cubans joked at cafes and on my patio over coffee, beer, and rum about panicked friends and family members calling them from abroad to see if they were all right and advising them to stay inside and stock up on fuel and food.

The Bush administration apparently believed its own rhetoric that the Cuban government was about to implode and that a handful of isolated dissidents openly allied with it would move the masses into action. White House spokesman Tony Snow called Raúl Castro "Fidel's prison-keeper" the day after Fidel Castro stepped aside, adding, "There are no plans to reach out."[6] President Bush and Secretary of State Condoleezza Rice urged Cubans that first week, in broadcasts over U.S.-government-operated Radio and Televisión Martí, to work for a democratic change on the island. They promised support for efforts to build a transition government committed to democracy, and threatened retribution against those who repressed the masses when they rose up.[7] One had to scratch one's head. First, no one could see Televisión Martí due to Cuban government jamming, and few listened to Radio Martí, although it was often on the air.[8] Second, the island was going about its business as usual and dissidents were nowhere to be seen. There was no trouble and thus no increase in repression.

I spent the weekend after Castro's proclamation talking with Cuban friends and acquaintances. They were as surprised as the outside world that they had made it through a week with Fidel Castro out of power and apparently at death's door. Worries proved unfounded that the government might collapse, that boats might leave Miami harbors, that social unrest would break out, or that a mass migration by sea would provoke a U.S. intervention. "I think we gave everyone, including ourselves, a lesson in civility. Everyone was at their post, sad about Fidel, without panic or chaos," said high school teacher Alberto Martínez. But others, tired of the years of hardship and what they saw as excessive government control over their lives, had a different take. "The people are unhappy but scared because they don't know what will come after. We are waiting for something, but don't know what. It's not like Cubans want capitalism, just a change—but to what, we ask," another doctor friend of mine said.

More than 70 percent of Cuba's 11.2 million people were born after Castro's guerrillas swept down from the mountains and know nothing but his rule and socialism. Horror stories of the corruption and brutality that preceded him are as abundant on the island as are the horror stories in Miami of the Castro brothers' brutality. "My generation has never lived through a change of president, so we did not know what to expect," said my wife's twenty-two-year-old nephew Rubén, who, like Marlene, is from Violeta, a sugar town in central Ciego de Ávila Province. He was living with us at the time while studying magic at the National Circus School in Havana and has since gone on to become an evangelical pastor. "That's what the younger generation fears, not just the sadness over Fidel, but the political question, that is what I'm scared of. I didn't know how the people would react," chimed in Malisa, Rubén's brother's girlfriend, who was a computer teacher from the same town. Osmani, Rubén's twenty-five-year-old brother, said it might be a good idea for Castro to semiretire and stay around a while to smooth out future wrinkles—a view expressed by people from every generation. "The best option is for him to slow down because his health is no good anymore to continue as he has," Rubén said, as the other young people, on vacation in Havana, nodded their heads. "The best is for him to stay as a figure, the figure everyone will follow, but not make the most important decisions, because at his age his reasoning is not the same," said Osmani. (And, yes, as I said in the introduction, a Cuban's door is always open to family, and they were all camped out in my far too chaotic home.)

Gradually Cubans began to grapple seriously with the reality that Castro's rule was nearing its end, if not already over. "He is a figure who left a clear mark on Cuba's history, who achieved many benefits for the poor, but Fidel's time has passed," said veterinarian Antonio, a fierce critic of today's Cuba. "Life really improved through 1990, when the Soviets stopped supporting us. Since then it has been all downhill. Obviously many factors have contributed to the current situation besides Fidel, so there is no reason to wish him dead." A friend and mid-level Party member in the city of Camagüey, alluding to prerevolutionary governments, told me she feared a crook would somehow take over again.

Playing Detective

Those first few weeks covering Castro's ceding of power were crazy indeed, but foreign journalists had a second and more difficult task that did drive us all nuts—not for weeks, but for months and years. We were expected to figure out whether Castro was really alive, or dead or near death; what ailed him and, later in the saga, how his recovery was proceeding and, therefore, how much power he still wielded. The world, and we reporters, were kept guessing and confused from the start: Castro appeared and vanished in videos, photos, occasional meetings with foreign guests, writings, and comments from other Cuban leaders and Venezuelan president Hugo Chávez. Secrecy and sowing confusion were state strategy as the transfer of power unfolded smoothly under the very nose of an extraordinarily hostile Bush administration and Miami political establishment. How much of the game of razzle-dazzle was planned, and how much improvised as Castro went through the ups and downs of what turned out to be his long illness and numerous operations, is still not known.

My many years covering Cuba proved invaluable in sorting through reliable and unreliable information and at least taking a good guess at what was going on amid an avalanche of rumors. An analogy would be listening to the world's cell phone traffic in search of the next terrorist attack. It helped to know the language and culture as one sorted through the noise; to have an idea of how the Cuban government acted and an instinctive knowledge of Cuban society.

Fidel Castro and his government insist they never lie to their people. That's very doubtful, but I also doubted that Castro was planning to leave this world with a big lie or that Cuba's new leadership would be so stupid as to start governing with one. That would have destroyed the Comandante's persona and the new government's credibility. I reasoned that the government would let its supporters know the general situation, which they would believe, and bank on its enemies' not believing the information anyway, with Cuban counterintelligence perhaps spreading rumors among diplomats, foreign journalists, and governments abroad to ensure even more confusion in enemy ranks. Wishful thinking is dangerous indeed when it comes to Cuba, where authorities count on its coloring what their enemies perceive.

I was skeptical of the first report that Castro had cancer, leaked to Brazilian officials and through them to one of that country's largest newspapers, the *Folha de São Paulo*.[9] At the time there was no great trust between the governments of Cuba and Brazil, and important Cuban leaders flatly denied that Castro had cancer. I was also suspicious of the detailed descriptions that began floating around Havana's diplomatic community about Castro's operation, their sources saying that cancerous growths had been found and removed (there are no such leaks in Cuba). At meetings with clients preparing for the Big Bang, I insisted that there would be no social unrest upon Castro's death. Quite the contrary, I believed there would be a cathartic show of grief. When Castro fainted, and later shattered his knee and broke his arm, there was no change in public mood as I walked Havana's most impoverished barrios. Most of the people I talked with expressed sympathy for the "old man." So I believed the government did not need to lie to its people and, if that were the case, why would they? I tended to take what officials were stating as more or less the truth.

I pieced together a picture of what had happened to Castro, developing a method I used over and over again in the coming months and years. I more or less believed official generalities, but combined them with exhaustive investigation through friends, acquaintances, and long-proved sources. Claudia Daut, our Reuters photographer, watched Castro closely through her lens on July 26 and said that by the time he delivered his second speech of the day in eastern Holguín, he was pale and perhaps on the verge of fainting.[10] Castro usually delivered just one speech on the Day of Rebellion, but this time he had first spoken in eastern Granma Province, in sweltering heat, then gone to neighboring Holguín to inaugurate a battery of diesel-powered generators as part of his "energy revolution."[11] A friend said that his neighbor, who was a plumber for the Council of State, the policy branch of Cuba's government, was called to fix a leak at a doctor's home. The doctor's wife complained that she had hardly talked with her husband since he was called to the emergency on the twenty-sixth or early on the twenty-seventh of July. An internist friend told me it would take at least forty-eight hours to determine whether a patient Castro's age had made it through major abdominal surgery and had a good chance of survival. I figured the announcement was true, just postponed until after the operation proved initially successful. That was typical of Cuba's leadership, and it made sense. They hedged, left the time of the operation open, and waited to see if Fidel survived before making any announcement—but they had not lied about his being alive. As the ABC crew raced around Havana on Tuesday,

August 1, our Cuban cameraman saw a friend who was a Castro bodyguard. Remember, there were many, and just about everyone claimed to know one of them. I watched from afar as they spoke earnestly with one another. The friend had also heard that Castro was operated on before July 31, and said he came out alive from surgery. Ricardo Alarcón, a Castro confidant and president of the National Assembly, told a mutual friend that Castro was sitting up and demanding the phone.

I e-mailed my clients on August 2: "Fidel on the night of 26th, or on 27th, went into a crisis and had emergency surgery. . . . By 31st they believed he was through the worst and made statement. The future depends on his full recovery which will be weeks."[12] Chuck Lustig, ABC's international news director at the time, was in Cancún, Mexico, with fifteen other people trying to get into Cuba. Chuck e-mailed back: "Do you believe he is stable and not critical at this point?" I replied, "Stable, but given his age he certainly is in serious condition for the coming days. . . . I have paid for a vacation with my kid to Brazil the 17th to 27th. Decided have to cancel because anything might occur in coming weeks." Chuck and his crew gave up trying to get into Cuba and went home, and I gave my daughter the bad news that our adventure of a lifetime was called off.

The kicker, or punch line, of the Big Bang's first week came in a cryptic statement on the front page of the Monday, August 7, edition of the Communist Party's newspaper *Granma*.

AS RESISTANT AS A CAGUAIRÁN

A few hours ago, after spending time with the president and impressed at his recovery, a friend said to us: "He is a Caguairán!"

In the eastern region, Caguairán is the name given to one of the trees that has the most precious, hard and resistant wood. In the western part of the island, the same tree is known as Quiebra Hacha (Ax Breaker) for its resistance.

The Caguairán is incorruptible, compact, of an extraordinary hardness, wrote the Cuban scholar Tomás Roig in his botanical dictionary. Its color is a reddish purple, with a straight, durable and consistent grain. It attains a height of 50 feet and a trunk of 16 inches in diameter. The characteristics of this tree make it ideal for lasting works.

The Caguairán flourishes in the easternmost part of the country and grows in woods on lime soil or in the mountains.

To most outside observers, the note was strange indeed, but Reuters's Cuban employees, used to the Communist Party's ways of speaking, had no doubt that it meant that Fidel Castro was very much alive.

Dead or Alive

I was repeatedly called by clients, fellow reporters, and friends as Fidel Castro aged, asking if it was true that he was dead or dying. Some of my acquaintances would desperately want some kind of assurance besides "Everything seems normal here," but it wasn't as if I could call the Foreign Ministry every few months and say, "Gee, guys, is it true this time that Castro kicked the bucket and you're keeping it a secret?" There was only one thing to do. I would hop in my car and drive by the Palace of the Revolution, the Communist Party and government headquarters facing Revolution Square behind the huge monument to José Martí. I would drive around the complex to its right, swing left behind the buildings and left again up Boyeros Avenue with the Palace of the Revolution now on my left and the Defense Ministry on my right, then left again down the Paseo in front of the Martí statue where May Day marches are held, hang a quick right, then another, passing the Interior Ministry and then the Communications Ministry to my left, and then turn left back up Boyeros and return to the Reuters office. It took about thirty minutes. "No tanks, no unusual troop movements, the guards are still lounging under the palm trees," I would report. Needless to say, with Castro sidelined, the rumors became more persistent, and the drive was an almost monthly, and at times weekly or even daily, routine.

On October 28, 2006, the first and only video of Fidel Castro alone since he had taken ill three months earlier was broadcast by Cuban television. The legendary figure looked far worse than in previous clips. The flow of optimistic statements out of Havana and Caracas slowed. Castro failed to appear at a series of important events in November and December 2006, including the postponed birthday event that he himself had set for December 2, Armed Forces Day, in his proclamation. Bush administration officials said Castro had just weeks, perhaps months, to live and reiterated that he had cancer. The *Financial Times* once again asked me to review his obituary. "Hi Marc, if you've got time could you take a quick look at this obituary, written some time ago and recently updated? If there are any obvious howlers let me know. Best, Richard."[13] And I received this e-mail from ABC News in December 2006: "The FBI has informed the Miami PD that there may be an announcement in a day or two regarding Castro. In other words, they think it is much more likely that he is dead than they did last time."

On December 24, 2006, Dr. José Luis García Sabrido, chief surgeon at Madrid's Gregorio Marañón Hospital, flew to Cuba and became the first and only foreign doctor known to have examined Castro. Headlines such as SPANISH DOCTOR RUSHED TO CASTRO'S BEDSIDE spurred new speculation that he had cancer or some other terminal illness. Dr. García Sabrido returned to Spain

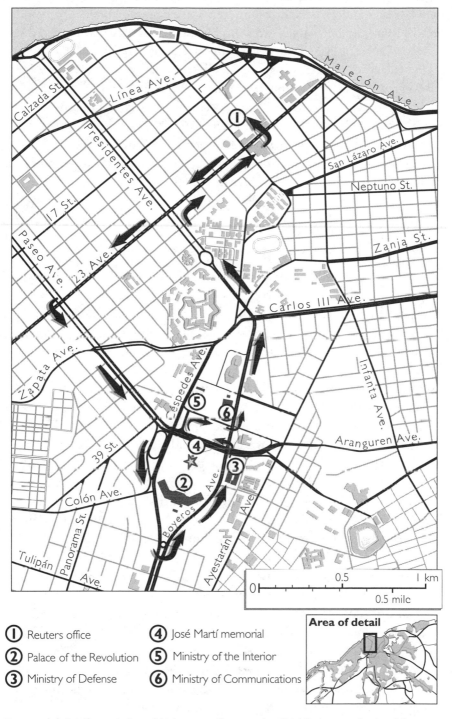

Area of detail

① Reuters office

② Palace of the Revolution

③ Ministry of Defense

④ José Martí memorial

⑤ Ministry of the Interior

⑥ Ministry of Communications

Havana, showing the route I would take to see if rumors that Fidel Castro was dead or dying were true or false. Map created by Armando Hugo Portela.

two days later and gave the first informed outside opinion on Castro's condition. "His physical activity is excellent, his intellectual activity intact, I'd say fantastic: he's recovering from his previous operation," the doctor told reporters in Madrid. "He hasn't got cancer. . . . While respecting confidentiality, I can tell you that President Castro is not suffering from any malignant sickness. It is a benign process in which there have been a series of complications," García Sabrido said.[14] A few weeks later, on January 16, 2007, just as everyone was settling in to the idea that Castro would be around for a while longer (leaving me in relative peace, and my car in the garage), Spain's *El Pais* newspaper dropped a bombshell, reporting in detail on Castro's condition. My cell phone rang well before dawn, and it kept ringing all day long.

CHAIN OF FAILED MEDICAL ACTIONS AGGRAVATED CASTRO'S CONDITION

A serious infection in the large intestine, at least 3 failed operations and various complications are keeping the Cuban dictator, Fidel Castro, with a very serious prognosis, according to medical sources from the Gregorio Marañón hospital in Madrid. José Luis García Sabrido, chief of surgery who went to visit Fidel Castro last December, works in this hospital center. According to the sources consulted, Castro, 80, suffered a severe inflammation of the large intestine named diverticulitis since before the summer (he transferred power in July). It's characterized by inflamed anomalous bags in the intestine that can lead to infection and bleeding, causing hemorrhages, similar to appendicitis. . . . In the summer, the Cuban leader bled heavily in his intestine. This condition brought him to the operating table, according to the same medical sources. His health condition, however, worsened because the infection spread causing peritonitis, an inflammation of the membrane covering the digestive organs. In this first operation, the surgeon proceeded to remove a part of the large intestine, the "sigma," and another part in the rectum, the two areas most affected by diverticulitis. The surgeon had to choose between 2 procedures: the first consisted of an ileostomy, the opening of an artificial anus in the abdomen during the weeks when the affected area of the colon recuperated. During this time, the patient excretes into a bag until the second intervention connects the large intestine with the rectum to reestablish the natural dynamic. The surgeon, on the other hand, opted for the second technique, that directly connects the traversing colon (the central part of the large intestine) with the rectum. Castro's progress was not good. The infection that he suffered stopped the intersection between the colon and the scarred rectum, and his abdomen was flooded with feces, causing another bout of peritonitis. During the second intervention, the doctors cleaned and drained the affected area, removing his whole large intestine and creating an artificial anus. After the second operation, Castro did not heal (scar) well, either. Additionally, his health worsened with a condition in the bile passage. One of the medical sources indicates he suffered a distended gall bladder (an inflammation of the gall bladder and the bile passages that are attributed to the lack of blood circulation, and also surgical manipulation). This situation has a high mortality rate (about 80 percent).[15]

ABC News and the rest of the planet's media went into overdrive trying to confirm the story and figure out the medical implications.

Doctor García Sabrido talked with CNN, Reuters, and others within a few days about the *El Pais* story. "The only truthful parts of the newspaper's reports are the name of the patient, that he has been operated on, and that he has had complications. The rest is rumors," he said.[16]

Venezuelan president Hugo Chávez waxed optimistic about his friend and mentor a week after the *El Pais* scoop, stating on January 24, 2007, in Caracas: "Lage told me Fidel walked for I don't know how many minutes yesterday. And he's walking more than I am, almost jogging."[17] Chávez appeared in Havana a few days later, and a video of him with Castro followed on January 30, this time showing the Cuban leader standing, apparently sipping juice, looking a bit better than in the previous video from October, and stating, "This is not a lost battle."

On February 27, 2007, six months after taking ill, Castro popped up on the phone for thirty-two minutes, talking and joking about current events with Chávez on the Venezuelan president's weekly television show, *Aló Presidente*.

Chávez. Let's see who is calling from Havana. Bring me some coffee, please.
Castro. Hello. Hello. Do you hear me?
Chávez. Who is calling?
Castro. Can you hear me?
Chávez. I hear you.
Castro. Distinguished and dear friend, how are you?
Chávez. [Words inaudible]
Castro. I am listening to you on *Aló Presidente*, all the figures you have cited. I find your argument very good regarding the growth of the GDP, over the drop in unemployment. Many interesting things.
Chávez. [In English] How are you?
Castro. Go ahead, go ahead. Ask me.

Chávez. [In English] How are you?

Castro. [In English] Pretty well. [Laughter]

Chávez. You have no idea how happy it makes us to hear your voice and to know you are well.

Castro. Thank you.

Chávez. We are surprised. We are pleasantly surprised. We were, as almost always, talking about you a while ago. . . .

Castro. I always knew I would end up on *Aló Presidente*. . .[18]

Castro, on March 10, 2007, during a visit to Haiti by the Venezuelan leader, had a long chat by phone with Chávez and Haitian president René Préval, which was later broadcast by the Cuban state media.[19] Gabriel García Márquez finally managed to see his old friend around that same time, and a picture of the two, for the first time showing Castro out of doors, was published in Colombia's *El Tiempo*.[20] García Márquez told *El Pais* that the two men had walked and chatted. "He is the same Fidel as ever," Gabo said.[21] On March 28, 2007, the first of what would become countless Castro columns on various topics was published and broadcast by the state media. Castro continued to gain strength over the next few months, writing and meeting with a number of allies, as Chávez and Cuban officials issued glowing reports of his recovery. More photos and videos appeared of the Comandante meeting with his guests.

Castro revealed a bit about his health for the first time in one of his columns, first called *Reflections of the Commander in Chief* and later, after he retired, *Reflections of Comrade Fidel*, this one dated May 23, 2007, almost a year after stepping aside. "The news dispatches talk of an operation. . . . Well then, it was not just one operation but several. Initially, it was not successful and this implicated a prolonged recovery period. For many months I relied on intravenous procedures and catheters for the greater part of my nutrition."[22]

Castro would later describe his situation in a 2010 interview with the Mexican newspaper *La Jornada*. "I came to the point of being dead. . . . I no longer aspired to live, or far less. . . . I asked myself on various occasions if those people [his doctors] were going to let me live in those conditions or if they were going to let me die. . . . Then I survived, but in very poor physical shape. I reached the point of weighing just over fifty kilos," or something over 110 pounds on his six-foot-three frame, Castro was quoted as saying. "Sixty-six kilograms," or 145 pounds, corrected his wife, Dalia Soto del Valle, who was present at the interview. "Imagine. A guy of my height weighing sixty-six kilos," Castro added.

"He could barely write with some fluidity, because he not only had to learn to walk again, but at his 84 years of age he had to learn again to write," wrote *La Jornada*'s editor in chief, Carmen Lira Saade.[23]

Over the first year of Castro's illness, seven videos of the Cuban leader were broadcast, four with Chávez, one with U.N. Secretary General Kofi Annan (to prove the others were not fakes), one of him alone, and one of Castro being interviewed by a trusted Cuban journalist. Each clip was just a few minutes in length, edited and shot with a backdrop that made it impossible to identify the location.[24] Then in October 2007, as a new wave of Castro death rumors circulated, Chávez was again with Castro in Cuba, and again talked with him on the phone during his regular Sunday television show, this time broadcast live in both countries from the Che Guevara mausoleum in Villa Clara Province. It was the first time Cubans had heard their leader live and in conversation in more than a year—and the last until three years later, when he suddenly emerged from seclusion.

4

Raúl Pinch-Hits

I think Raúl would be a good president because he tells the truth. When he says to you, "This is green," it's because it is green. But he does not have the vision, charisma, and drive of Fidel.

My wife's aunt Paca

If Cuba's weaning from Fidel Castro was blessed by Hugo Chávez and oil-rich Venezuela's peaceful revolution, it was cursed by the government's and state-run economy's inefficiency, bureaucracy, growing inequality, and the malaise left behind by fifteen years of crisis. On the one hand it was the best of times, with Hugo Chávez in power in Venezuela and much of Latin America and the Caribbean shifting to the center-left and embracing Cuba. On the other hand it was the worst of times as the country's charismatic leader faded at a moment when many a Cuban's spirit was ebbing and the leadership's ability to move the bureaucracy and communicate with the masses was weaker than it had ever been.

As the dust settled from the economic collapse and social dislocation of the 1990s, and without Castro around to spin his oratory magic, it was evident that one of the world's last remaining Soviet-style economies had exhausted its potential and needed a very serious makeover. The public's feelings were exemplified by a blog on bureaucracy written in 2007 by Luis Sexto, a columnist for the Union of Young Communists' *Juventud Rebelde* newspaper and winner of Cuba's highest journalism award in 2008, which in part read:

> At this precise moment, the inflexibility, paperwork, and inefficient administration the Royal Academy dictionary ascribes to bureaucracy have mediocritized and decontextualized the prerogatives of the Cuban socialist state.[1] It has been a sort of twisted fairy godmother: everything touched by her magic wand turns into a caricature of socialist aspirations. It spoils and leaves festering everything creative brought by Castro's Revolution to Cuba....
>
> In Cuba, according to popular opinion, bureaucratic attitudes provide a problem for every solution, with a "no" for a "yes." And they dissolve ev-

ery initiative in papers and meetings. And they see reality through their colored glasses or from their balconies, usually high up, above and distant from the streets or workplaces. Or through reports that are usually altered by those who don't wish the truth to be known. . . .

Any project of renewal and improvement of socialism in Cuba will not only have to deal with the U.S. opposition and its permanent war, and with those who push for capitalism within the island, but will also have to face and abolish the bureaucratic resistance. . . .

. . . Bureaucratic actions—tiresome, limiting, and alienating—tend to destroy the cause of socialism in people's hearts.[2]

But how had such a state of affairs come to pass? A walk on the wild side, in this case the *campo*, helps unravel the mystery. If you venture into Cuba's countryside, you soon discover that the extraordinarily hospitable inhabitants can own cattle but cannot kill and eat the beasts—or sell them for slaughter, except with permission from the state and even then only to the state. The "you can't kill your cow law" has no religious basis. During my many years on the island I never met a Cuban Hindu. Nor are Cubans worried about their weight or cholesterol count. They fry everything in lard and oil. Islanders are definitely not vegetarians. They love to gather entire extended families and friends to roast and feast on pork and mutton and, if they only could, beef. In fact, you often hear the hysterical screeching of pigs, even in the cities and towns, as their owners drag them out on roofs, patios, and sidewalks for slaughter. So why can't a hardworking Cuban farmer, let alone a cattle rancher, kill and then eat or sell his own livestock when he damn well pleases?

When Fidel Castro swept into power, the downtrodden—what with rents slashed, utility rates cut, land handed out, and huge cattle estates nationalized—had more money and greater opportunity to buy beef and rustle cattle, and they had a relative feast after the famine. You have to understand that for almost a century cattle ranching was the most important agricultural use of land after sugar, though the regular consumption of beef and milk remained out of reach for many Cubans, who settled for jerked beef when possible, salted fish, eggs, rice, goat, pork, chicken, and beans. The herd came under additional pressure due to poor management, as inexperienced farmers and workers replaced nationalized owners of huge ranches and their top Cuban employees who left for the United States. Then in 1961 there was drought and in 1963 the devastating Hurricane Flora. And so the state, as it often did in those early days, resorted to a "temporary" restriction to protect cattle, which in the end proved not so temporary.[3]

After Hurricane Flora wiped out 20 percent of the country's herd, the government declared it a crime to kill cattle without state authorization, including one's own, assuring the public the measure was temporary and due to its policy of seeing to it that every child had fresh milk at a subsidized price. Over time the state proved incapable of significantly increasing the herd and letting go of its monopoly on killing cattle and purveying beef and milk. A new rationale was needed. Beef became a rich-country luxury item that poor places like Cuba and a starving world with its children in need of milk could ill afford. Fidel Castro has been known to explain in detail that beef protein conversion rates are higher than any other meat's, which means it takes more feed and water to produce a pound of beef than a pound of pork or chicken, let alone an egg, and besides, cows produce milk. As for the bulls, eventually they were slaughtered, but only by the state after serving whatever purpose it deemed advisable. So not killing one's cattle, the narrative went, was a perfect example of placing our neighbors' needs before our own, of putting the less well-off and the vulnerable before the better off, of burying that ego and animal desire for beef in a higher consciousness that requires a minor sacrifice for the common good. Consciousness over animal instinct, Fidel Castro would insist.

But how does a government go about stopping a farmer from throwing a party and barbecuing up big juicy steaks? Well, it first appeals to his better side—think of those kids, those grannies, the infirm! How could you eat that steak! Then it appeals to patriotism and revolutionary spirit—the nation and revolution need your cow and its milk to survive and make us strong in a hostile world. Then the state takes over everything and generously helps you raise cattle by providing state veterinarians, state credits, feed, and other inputs—your livestock now exist in part thanks to the people, so do not kill any cattle without checking with us first! Finally, Fidel sets the example—neither I, nor any other leader, shall eat beef, unless for reasons of state and protocol we have absolutely no choice. Just in case moral persuasion doesn't work, as we have already seen, laws and regulations are drawn up that make it a crime to mess with cattle, even your own.

Now comes the really hard part. How is the government to know if one of the millions of cows and bulls out there winds up in its owner's or someone else's tummy without permission? In 1964 all Cubans were ordered to register their cattle, even if they had only one animal. The position of agriculture inspector, or cattle counter, was soon created, with responsibility, among other matters, for reporting how many head of cattle, of what type, age, and so forth, a farmer or cooperative or state ranch had at any given moment. But what if an inspector agreed not to count a farmer's latest calf, hidden in the barn, for a cut of the meat? After all, everyone knows each other in the countryside.

Well, the position of inspector of the cattle inspectors was created, with responsibility for reporting on whether the inspectors were doing their jobs or gaining weight, and of course municipal, provincial, and national commissions followed to "coordinate" and "supervise" and pass final judgment on controversial cases. Presto! A bureaucracy was born.

So a farmer who has slaughtered a cow reports she was stolen, or it just so happened that poor old Bessie was hit by a train or a vintage Chevy when the brakes failed. It was only logical to eat her, he explains, rather than let the carcass rot in the tropical heat. How could the state prove otherwise? It couldn't. There was only one solution. Assume the farmer is always lying and fine him no matter what happened to that missing animal. The farmer is guilty, period—at times victimized twice, by a thief and the state, by a train or Chevy and the state. Thus it became a risky business even for a true-believing revolutionary farmer to raise a cow in Cuba for milk, and I have talked to a few old-timers who simply concluded it was not worth the bother.[4]

Did all the rules, regulations, restrictions, inspectors, inspectors of the inspectors, committee meetings, lies, and fines at least lead to an exponential increase in the herd and milk? When Fidel Castro, his bearded rebels, and a far broader coalition of patriots triumphed over dictator Batista there were 5,385,000 head of cattle in the country, according to government statistics. In 1980 there were 5,057,000, and in 1989, as the Soviet Union crumbled, there were 4,970,000. In 2005 the government reported just 3,700,000 head of cattle, and as the decade ended, 4,000,000.[5] Milk production, which was 600 million liters per year in 1959, did increase to more than 900 million liters per year in the 1980s. But by 2000, after the Soviet Union's fall, milk output was back to 600 million liters, and in 2005 just 350 million liters, increasing to 629.5 million liters in 2009. The nation's herd had shrunk more than 20 percent since the "you can't kill your cow law" was decreed, and milk production was similar to 1958. Meanwhile, the population had nearly doubled.[6]

Who can go to church and then deny that guaranteeing milk for children, the elderly, and the sick takes precedence over eating steak or roast beef for Sunday dinner? But like so many issues facing Raúl Castro when he took over for his brother, first temporarily in August 2006, then as president on February 24, 2008, the question, with the country importing more than 50 percent of its even bare-bones supply of milk, was whether there was a better way to accomplish that same altruistic goal. To date, the "you can't kill your cow law" still stands, though its days, like those of so many other regulations and the bureaucracies they spawned, are surely numbered, and producing beef for consumption has made a comeback along with the hamburger. "The state can regulate its relations with individuals, but not relations between them," economic reform czar Marino Murillo would soon preach. Let alone between them and their animals, one might add.

Many other Cuban secrets can be unlocked by taking a closer look at the "you can't kill your cow law," because it sometimes seemed, back then when Raúl took over, that there was a "you can't do" law for just about everything. For example, why do those vintage U.S. cars still ply Cuba's streets? There was a "you can't sell or buy a car law" in Cuba too, unless the car was on the road before 1959 or you received special government permission. If you owned a car purchased after the Revolution, you bought it from the government, often at a subsidized price, and signed a paper that you would not sell it except to the state. That's why there are so many vintage U.S. cars on the road, as they were the only ones Cubans could buy and sell freely until October 2011, when all used cars became available.[7]

Raúl Castro

Fidel Castro was determined to tackle the bureaucratization and stratification of his revolution by mobilizing young followers to defend his vision of an egalitarian society through the Battle of Ideas. Raúl Castro would take a different tack. The brothers shared the same goal of preserving the Revolution. Perhaps with Fidel sidelined Raúl could not risk destabilizing the country, but it is more likely he had grave concerns about the youth movement all along and believed the system should adapt to economic and social change and not the other way around. What's certain is that he embarked on a very different approach to the same problems, relying on the very institutional structures Fidel Castro had sidestepped and bashed, in particular the military, the Communist Party, the government, and traditional forms of soliciting ordinary Cubans' views and participation, which were abandoned over the previous decade by his aging and ever more autocratic older brother.

In Eastern Europe the mass of citizens within the system of the Soviet's orbit, who nevertheless wanted change, was known as the Grey Zone. These people were driven by more than economic hardship and social repression. Nationalist sentiment against imperial Russia burned below the surface. At the time of the Soviet collapse, the situation in Cuba was different. Cuban Communist Party surveys, according to my sources, found that most people supported the government, a small percentage actively opposed it, and maybe 30 percent were passive bystanders, the Grey Zone. The Miami-based *Nuevo Herald* in January 1995 reported on an underground survey conducted in conjunction with Gallup that found that, despite the grave crisis, 76 percent of those polled were somewhat or very satisfied with their lives and 58 percent felt the Revolution had had more successes than failures, while 31 percent thought otherwise. It is safe to say that by the time Raúl took over, the majority of Cubans, having suffered through years of crisis, could be counted as within the Grey Zone and were increasingly restless for change. Raúl set about trying to win them back.

Raúl took over for his brother on July 31, 2006, but said nothing in public for almost three weeks and was seen only once in graphics with Chávez and Fidel on the latter's eightieth birthday. The younger of the brothers finally communicated to the nation and the world in his usual straightforward way on August 18, but in the form of an obviously staged "interview" with the editor of the Communist Party daily, *Granma*. Raúl, speaking in his office at the Defense Ministry instead of the Party and government headquarters, reinforced the idea that Fidel's return was possible. Raúl said that in the meantime he had no intention of governing like his brother. "As a matter of fact, I am not used to making frequent appearances in public, except at times when it is required. Moreover, I have always been discreet, that is my way, and in passing let me clarify that I plan to continue that way."[8]

My wife's mother was one of twelve children, eight girls and four boys, born to poor peasants in the Sierra Maestra, the mountains of eastern Cuba where Fidel Castro's revolution began. All but two were still alive in Cuba when Raúl took over, and they remembered cooking and washing clothes for ragtag bands of beardless boys and bearded young men, including some of their cousins, who often passed by their humble home seeking food and refuge from Batista's troops. One of the girls, Francisca "Paca" Reyes Corona, at twenty-two, ran messages and cooked for the revolutionaries. She married one of Raúl's men. Atilano Frómeta deactivated unexploded bombs dropped by the Cuban air force and turned them into mines for the revolutionaries until one blew up in his face, disabling him for life.

"I think Raúl would be a good president because he tells the truth. When he says to you, 'This is green,' it's because it is green. But he does not have the vision, charisma, and drive of Fidel," Francisca said. She was sitting on the back patio of her humble Mangoba home on the outskirts of Havana in early 2006, before Raúl took over, as I prepared a story about the younger Castro to mark his seventy-fifth birthday. Atilano had passed away a year earlier. The home had been given them by Raúl after the Revolution, and they had moved west to Havana from Oriente. "Raúl always takes care of his people. That is why they are so devoted to him," she said, surrounded by mango, orange, and grapefruit trees, a sugarcane patch, chickens, pigs, and dogs.

Hal Klepak of the Royal Military College of Canada, a military historian specializing in Latin America who had developed numerous contacts while researching his book on the Cuban armed forces,[9] had no doubt the younger

Castro brother was up to the job. "He needs to be taken very seriously. He is a leader in his own right, but a loyal one to his boss, his brother. Raúl was the longest serving defense minister in modern history, almost a fifty-year stint, a truly remarkable situation," Klepak said over lunch in Havana. "Raúl has proven himself with the armed forces, and his people scoff at the idea that he has no charisma, leadership skills, or sense of humor."

Frank Mora, an expert on the Cuban military at the National War College in Washington, who under President Obama would move into Latin American affairs at the Pentagon, concurred over the telephone. "Raúl is his brother's keeper in many ways, but in many other ways he is his own man. . . . He is credited with building the revolutionary armed forces, demonstrates management skills and leadership skills. I think he is someone who is taken very seriously in Cuba."

Brian Latell, who watched the Castro brothers for decades at the CIA and wrote a book on the Castros,[10] said in a telephone interview from Miami, "If the revolution can be thought of as a dramatic work, then Fidel has been its director and Raúl its producer. Fidel is the visionary—the brilliant, impulsively creative, mercurial, but utterly disorganized brother. Raúl has been the manager, administrator, and rational planner—the only other truly indispensable man in the enterprise—and he is much more pragmatic."

A Change of Tack

During his first year as Cuba's provisional leader Raúl proved discreet indeed, speaking in public just nine times, four of which were simple off-the-cuff remarks at meetings. The experts' belief that he was competent in his own right and more amenable to change than his brother, and local opinion that he was a straight-talking, no-nonsense sort of guy who liked to get things done, proved true. There was a notable decline in official rhetoric, and the massive marches in front of the U.S. diplomatic mission to protest this or that action that was deemed an outrage—a cornerstone of Fidel's rule—ceased. After nearly fifty years, the constant turning upside down of people's daily lives was over. If Fidel was perhaps in deep denial over Cuba's changing reality, Raúl faced it head-on and with his eyes wide open. He sent out word to the ministries asking what they would do if Hugo Chávez was not around the next day, according to my sources, and quickly formed a commission to study socialist property relations and began polling the grass roots. Raúl focused the government's and population's attention on the country's ills. He urged the state-controlled media to be more critical of glaring domestic issues such as retail-level fraud and poor services, food production and distribution, and bureaucratic roadblocks to dealing with any number of personal needs and economic problems.

By all accounts Raúl worked methodically behind the scenes those first weeks and months to ensure the nation's security and stability while trying to shake up, rather than batter, the bureaucracy. "Raúl had a meeting with Sugar Ministry officials who immediately started saying they could do this or that if they only had more resources. Fidel would have dished out the money then and there. Raúl asked if there were reports to back up the requests. There weren't, so he announced he was leaving the meeting until reports were on his desk, then after they were studied, they could talk again," a source told me. And another said: "Raúl had a meeting with the Health Ministry, Construction Ministry, and young people renovating hospitals under Fidel's Battle of Ideas. He asked the young people how many hospitals they were working on in Havana, and they said twenty-seven. He asked how many they had finished, and they said one. 'Why don't you do them one at a time?' he asked. Then, turning to the health minister and the construction minister, he asked why the kids were in charge of renovating hospitals in the first place." And so the anecdotes kept coming those first months. True or false, they circulated through the system signaling there was indeed a new administration with the same ideology but quite a different approach.

Winds of Change

The Communist youth newspaper, *Juventud Rebelde*, published in its Sunday editions of October 2006 a scathing three-part series on graft and the dismal offerings in shops, bars, and other retail sector services, titled "The Big Old Swindle." *Juventud Rebelde* was the only paper to hit the stands on the last day of the week. The series marked a radical departure from the media's endless cheerleading and had to be approved by the highest levels of government through the Communist Party's Department of Revolutionary Orientation, which controlled all media. It was as if a flower had suddenly appeared in the desert and quickly caught everyone's attention. The articles "uncovered" what everyone already was well aware of: bartenders stealing from the state by serving less beer than stipulated or bringing in their own rum to sell, barbers overcharging clients, taxi drivers not reporting fares, cafeteria employees skimping on servings or bringing in their own supplies to prepare food for what amounted to private businesses. "The current irregularities in the country's services, in the midst of the search for a better economic model, has meant Cuba still does not have a retail and services sector that satisfies people's expectations," the newspaper said. "You don't say" was just about everyone's response, though this was the first time they learned the search was on for a better economic model.

Cuba's economy, modeled on the Soviet Communism that ultimately failed, was overwhelmingly state-controlled. There were no markets, except a few farmers' markets that opened in the 1990s and accounted for less than 10 percent of produce sales, a few home-based businesses, and of course the huge black market accounting for up to 30 percent of retail activity, according to Cuban economists. The prices of everything else were set by the state with no regard to cost, supply, and demand. The state provided supplies (though often they went missing due to poor management and theft) and set serving amounts and prices for a cup of coffee or ham sandwich, haircut, manicure, taxi ride, watch repair, or even a shoe shine, though these were regularly ignored, as higher-ups were given a cut of the take and inspectors paid off to look the other way.

"The theory that came from the Soviet Union was skewed," economist Luis Marcelo Yera of the National Economic Research Institute told *Juventud Rebelde* in the third of the three-part series. He advocated giving workers more power to decide the running of state enterprises. Marcelo was one of a number of academics quoted in the paper's October series who stated that systemic problems, including overcentralization, hampered economic development and could not be dealt with simply by more rhetoric, regulation, and discipline. This was all truly remarkable within the context of Cuba at the time and just three months after Raúl stepped in for Fidel. "We live in a society with many distortions; that's why many things have to be guaranteed through cohesion and control, but not everything can be accomplished that way," Ernesto Molina, from Cuba's top school for international relations, told the paper. "We need a scientific plan to organize society politically and economically so it works better," he said.

With the series, the public learned Raúl had established a commission of academics from various disciplines to study socialist property relations. Economists who had long advocated reform began telling me that for the first time they were being listened to and did not fear a visceral reaction from dogmatists in the Communist Party and the military. "The last such study to be undertaken by a Communist leader," Marcelo told me in early 2007, "was by Mikhail Gorbachev in 1988, but it never got off the ground before the fall of the Berlin Wall a year later." Marcelo insisted neither perestroika nor Chinese-style market Communism was on the agenda of the commission. He said forming cooperatives, increased grassroots participation, and deregulation were under discussion. He said Cuba was taking a path closer to one of his favorite Japanese sayings. "Adapt, don't adopt. We can adapt the best experiences but not adopt another's model," he said. The commission would later give way to a number of them, studying various aspects of the economy, and five years later to a comprehensive plan to overhaul the economy and a commission of one hundred full-time members, organized into eight groups, to carry out the job.

Raúl conducted two surveys as temporary head of the Communist Party that first year, to reconnoiter the terrain left by his brother, renewing long dormant forms of member participation and obtaining ammunition for the inside-the-system battles to come. It was a style of leadership that would characterize his governance. In late 2006 and again in early 2007, many sources excitedly informed me, he polled Party members on what the most pressing popular complaints were. The dual monetary system, the gap between state wages and state prices, bureaucracy, lack of transportation, high food prices, and deteriorating health care, education, and housing were the overwhelming responses, they said, and he began to demand action behind the scenes and in public.

Raúl Castro, choosing the occasion of an official Cuban trade union congress in September 2006 to deliver his first domestic speech since taking over for his brother less than two months earlier, stated that workers were the "essential force" in the fight to improve the country. He thus made clear that his brother's young troop of the Battle of Ideas was not. "There is nothing that can't be resolved if the Party, the union organization, and the administration of labor centers are working together," he said.[11]

At a closed-door session of parliament on December 24, 2006, the problems of transportation, food prices, and housing topped the agenda, with Raúl seen in video clips on television demanding that "bureaucratic red tape" end and that functionaries "tell it as it is, tell the truth, without justifications, because we are tired of justifications in this revolution."[12] Earlier in the week, Raúl told university student leaders they should "fearlessly" engage in public debate and analysis. "The first principle in constructing any armed forces is the sole command," he said. "But that doesn't mean that we cannot discuss. That way we reach decisions, and I'm talking about big decisions," he said, adding that while some people feared to disagree, differences led to better decision making.[13] At the year-end parliament meeting, Raúl termed "inexplicable" the bureaucratic hurdles that held up payments to farmers after delivery of their produce and demanded that the backlog be eliminated by the next parliament session and a system created so it did not happen again—his first reform.[14] "What's important is that the focus was on our own problems, not the outside and the U.S. blockade," a parliamentary deputy told me.

The second survey, conducted in early 2007, polled municipal and provincial Party economic commissions and Communist Party cadre of economic enterprises from factories to hotels on improving the country's performance. "He told us to be audacious and not to worry or hold back our ideas, except that the proposals could not lead to bigger budgets," a Party economist told me. "He was deluged, so much so that he said he was overwhelmed and the problem was where to start," the economist added.

Raúl's closest friends and collaborators, the military officers he had worked with for decades as defense minister, weighed in on the debate just as 2007 got under way. Raúl Castro had put them to work in the 1980s to develop a more efficient model of business administration that took into account capitalist management techniques. Led by General Julio Casas Regueiro, officers fanned out across the globe to attend business administration courses and study other models, and then fashioned their own, called *perfeccionamiento empresarial*—roughly translated as perfecting of the (state) company system.[15] Colonel Armando Pérez Betancourt, the head of the Cuban military's effort to make state-run companies in the civilian sector more efficient, said profits, wages, and productivity were raised in more than 800 companies by applying the model. "If you ask me what the most important task facing the state companies is, I would say it is better organization, and the way to do that is through perfecting the state company system," Betancourt told the Communist Party newspaper *Granma*.[16] The generals would win the day. On August 17, 2007, Raúl Castro signed a 200-page decree law mandating that all state companies adopt the military model, but even after making the decision he continued fostering discussion. By 2011 parts of the plan would be scrapped in favor of deeper reform.

Stoking the Grassroots Embers

But back to the cows, and more specifically milk. On July 26, 2007, Raúl Castro traveled to central Camagüey Province, the flatlands and the heart of cattle country, to deliver his first major speech to the nation since temporarily taking over for his ailing brother exactly a year before. July 26 is a national holiday marking Fidel Castro's failed storming of a military fort in 1953, Santiago de Cuba's Moncada Garrison, which nevertheless signaled the start of the Cuban Revolution led by his July 26th Movement. The president traditionally delivered a state-of the-nation speech to mark the Day of Rebellion. Raúl made no mention of the "you can't kill your cow law," but delved extensively into the state's often convoluted efforts to get scarce milk to consumers, calling them "absurd" and "insane." By implication, this was an indictment of the entire state system of food purchase and distribution, known as *acopio*—gathering or cornering, both translations apt descriptions of the state's monopoly.

Castro used the example of rural Mantua municipality, in westernmost Pinar del Río Province, where a few bottles of locally produced milk made a long voyage, only to return and be delivered to the children next door.

The closest pasteurizer is located in the Sandino municipality, 40 kilometers away from Mantua, the most important town in the area. Thus, in order to deliver the milk to that plant, a truck had to travel a minimum of 80 kilometers . . . each day to make the round journey. I say "a minimum" because other areas of the municipality are even farther away.

The milk that children and other consumers in Mantua receive on a regulated basis, once pasteurized at the Sandino plant, returned, shortly afterwards, on a vehicle which, as it is logical to assume, had to return to its base of operations after delivering the product. In total, it traveled 160 kilometers, a journey which, as I explained, was in fact longer.[17]

Raúl announced local producers would begin delivering milk directly to rural towns, bypassing the state pasteurization process, as the local residents usually boiled it anyhow.

And it is exactly these sorts of rules and regulations—with the layers of bureaucracy and the bizarre procedures they created, often with little if any positive result and plenty of economic and psychological damage—that the people bitterly complained about in a national discussion promoted by Raúl following his speech, and that he worked to untangle and tame while in office. It had been a year since Fidel Castro was last seen in public, and Raúl, after ridiculing milk distribution and by implication the entire system of state food distribution, was ready to outline the first hints of a new economic policy.

Wages today are clearly insufficient to satisfy all needs and have thus ceased to play a role in ensuring the socialist principle that each should contribute according to their capacity and receive according to their work. . . .

To have more, we have to begin by producing more, with a sense of rationality and efficiency, so that we may reduce imports, especially of food products that may be grown here, whose domestic production is still a long way away from meeting the needs of the population. . . .

To reach these goals, the needed structural and conceptual changes will have to be introduced.[18]

By September, some 800,000 Communist Party members and a similar number of Young Communists were studying Raúl's July 26 speech. I got hold of the guide for discussion leaders, which in part read:

A profound debate should be fostered in an atmosphere of complete freedom and sincerity around the central themes of the speech. In particular, in the organizing of the discussion, opinions and suggestions and proposals should be given on the most important subjects, especially:

- food production;
- substituting imports;
- increasing production (in particular of food), efficiency, cost cutting, and productivity;
- the concept that nobody can spend more than they earn;
- the irreversible decision to build socialism, as the only element that Cuban revolutionaries will never question;
- other opinions and suggestions concerning the economic and social situation of the country.

Within weeks the debate had moved from inside the Party to the general public, with the same guidelines. "People were expressing themselves like never before about all the problems in their lives," a Communist Party member said after attending a meeting. "Raúl is raising everyone's expectations, so he'd better have some solutions." Common complaints ranged from low salaries (which averaged about $15 a month) and poor services to restrictions on traveling, buying and selling cars and homes, and booking rooms in hotels reserved for tourists. "When the meeting started, nobody wanted to speak, but we were told to speak out frankly about the issues raised by Raúl, and everything that affects us," Angela, a Havana factory worker, said. "Grassroots debate is not new in Cuba. There was a similar debate led by Fidel in the late 1980s and again in the early 1990s as major changes began," said Rafael Hernández, editor of *Temas* (Issues), a magazine that encourages discussion among intellectuals about controversial issues from race relations to market economics. "What's new is that Fidel is less active and others need to build a new consensus, as people are not responding to current policy," Hernández said. "Cubans interpret Raúl's call for structural change to mean deep changes in the model, not just a cosmetic change."

Just over a year after the elder Castro stepped aside, government insiders said there was no doubt that Raúl was the country's new chief executive, even if Fidel, busy writing his reflections and recovering from his ordeal, was still chairman of the board. "I'm happy Fidel is getting better, but I'm more interested in the new guy, who is more active," a top advisor at the Basic Industry Ministry commented. Raúl Castro's aides were far more visible than Fidel's team of movers and shakers, introducing a no-nonsense style in the bureaucracy, my sources said. "Raúl uses existing mechanisms, demanding that people do their jobs, and if they do not, he replaces them," one Havana Communist Party activist said.

Washington was not happy at the political continuity in Cuba. Secretary of State Condoleezza Rice stated more than once that the Bush administration would not tolerate a transition from one dictator to another.

It would still be a number of years before Raúl moved to drastically overhaul the way Cuba did business and people went about their daily lives, but, in the end, the Commission on Socialist Property Relations proved a harbinger of what lay ahead and those I interviewed for my story on his seventy-fifth birthday would be proven right.

Hugo and Raúl

When Fidel Castro stepped aside in 2006, many Cuba experts and governments speculated that ties between Cuba and Venezuela might weaken with Raúl Castro at the helm, in part because the Fidel Castro–Hugo Chávez relationship was so personal and Raúl's style so different from that of the other two. Further, during his first years in office, Raúl built closer relations with a number of other oil-producing nations, such as Brazil, Russia, Algeria, and Angola. But facts are facts, and the relationship with Venezuela deepened and broadened with Raúl Castro in power. The two governments continued their joint foreign policy and appeared to see eye to eye on all international questions. Their soft-power politics to train area professionals and provide services to third countries increased, with a remarkable two million people treated free of charge for partial and complete blindness by 2012 through Plan Milagro, most of them in clinics established in their own countries.[19] Over a million mentally or physically impaired persons had been visited in the slums and jungles of member countries of the Venezuelan-led Bolivarian Alliance for the Peoples of Our America, and were receiving some medical care. Literacy programs were under way in a dozen area countries, and there was a plan to build a national health-care system in quake-struck Haiti, in collaboration with Brazil and some Western nations. In 2011, just before Chávez was diagnosed with cancer, Cuba and Venezuela announced the establishment of a joint military academy.

On December 3, 2007, Chávez narrowly lost a constitutional referendum that would have allowed for an indefinite number of presidential terms in office, his only electoral defeat. Neither government blinked. Less than three weeks after the defeat and seventeen months after Fidel took ill, the Venezuelan leader was in the southern port city of Cienfuegos, around a hundred miles southeast of Havana, to host with Raúl a PetroCaribe summit and open a joint-venture oil refinery.[20] The two men signed a number of new agreements and then staged a triumphal tour of Santiago de Cuba, standing and waving to the crowds from a jeep; Chávez's entire stay in the city was broadcast live to both nations. The visit was designed to show Cubans and the world the Communist Party's continued confidence in Chávez. Raúl's speech in Santiago was an account of the many grave setbacks the Castro brothers overcame on the way to victory. Raúl appeared to be having a great time and truly enjoying Chávez. In short, they seemed to bond. Raúl would visit Venezuela a year later, his first trip abroad after officially becoming president in 2008.

Cuba first received cash, in addition to the preferentially financed oil, after signing an agreement with Venezuela in late 2004, which included payment for health and other technical assistance that Cuba had provided for free up until then, according to both governments. Cuba's imports totaled $6 billion in 2004 and non-tourism service income was about $1.5 billion. Just two years later, in 2006, imports had nearly doubled, to $10 billion, and non-tourism service revenues had tripled, to $5 billion, mainly from payments for medical and other technical assistance to Venezuela.[21] The price of the technical assistance was pegged to the price of oil, ensuring stability in Cuba as oil prices increased. Could Fidel Castro's Cuba have survived the transition from his rule as oil spiked at $147 a barrel in 2008 without Hugo Chávez's Venezuela?

The opening of the Cienfuegos refinery symbolized a new stage in the Venezuelan-Cuban relationship under Raúl, from the trading of services for oil to joint ventures. By the time Chávez was diagnosed with cancer in 2011 and treated in Cuba, there were also around 350 Cuban-Venezuelan economic cooperation projects either planned or under way in both countries. Venezuelan banks were financing numerous manufacturing plants and more than a dozen agricultural development schemes in Cuba. Thousands of Cuban specialists, from agriculture and sugar to construction, basic industry, and waterworks, were in Venezuela, in addition to tens of thousands of health and education personnel. The two countries had signed some 30 joint ventures, most of which were sealed after Raúl Castro first stepped in for his ailing brother. Some were huge by Cuban standards: a $6 billion petrochemical complex was planned around the renovated and expanding oil refinery in Cienfuegos; another refinery was planned for Matanzas. There were an assortment of other oil-related ventures, from pipelines and refinery expansions to shipping, port renovations, and oil exploration in Gulf of Mexico waters. A nickel plant in eastern Holguín Province was receiving a $700 million upgrade to feed a joint-venture steel complex in Venezuela; a fiber-optic cable was laid between the two countries as part of a telecommunications venture; a joint fishing fleet was busy in far-off waters; and there were ventures in other sectors such as tourism, pharmaceuticals, mining, agriculture, shipbuilding, railways, and cement.

5

Fidel Steps Down

"Look, Fidel is sick now, do you think he can go on as president?"
"I don't think we need another."
"Do you think he can go on?"
"If there is going to be another, let him be just like him, with his same ideas
   and same personality."

Author's conversation with Cristina, a young hitchhiker in central Cuba

General elections are held for the single-chamber Cuban National Assembly every five years. The deputies of this parliament elect from within their ranks a thirty-one-member Council of State, including its president, first vice president, five vice presidents, and a secretary. The Council of State in turn appoints the Council of Ministers, or cabinet, which runs the country on a daily basis. The election of the Council of State is no more than the approval of a slate proposed by the Communist Party Politburo. A National Assembly election was scheduled for 2008. Would Fidel "run"? A deputy spot was a prerequisite for continuing as president.

The electoral process begins with ward-level elections every two and a half years. These were held without a hitch in late 2007, despite Fidel's absence. Neighborhood meetings nominate two or more candidates for the vote. The Communist Party insists it does not participate as an organized force in the ward elections, and in fact there is no campaigning, since other political organizations are banned, though anyone can run as an independent. Neighborhood blocks compete within the ward in hopes of getting things fixed on their street. A black-and-white mug shot of each candidate, with a biography, is posted around the barrio, and that's about it. Ward delegates meet regularly with their constituents. Party members and supporters are urged and begged to participate in their block meetings, run for office, and staff polling stations.

I have known a number of ward delegates over the years. These posts resemble the thankless job of a shop steward in a trade union, fielding the everyday problems of the population as the stewards do for workers on the shop floor, then trying to solve them through layers of bureaucracy—and, more often than not, having to explain why they failed. Most delegates and National Assembly deputies continue to work other jobs, as do shop stewards, and there are few perks at the ward level: perhaps a telephone, better or faster medical treatment, or use of your delegate ID to enter local bars and eateries, or to convince a cop not to give you a speeding ticket if you are lucky enough to own a car.

The winners of the ward elections—around 15,000 people—form the country's municipal governments and "elect" the local councils, which then "elect" the equivalents of mayors, all of whom are proposed behind the scenes by the local Communist Party. The trade unions, Women's Federation, block committees, and other groupings, also controlled by the Party, form provincial candidate committees, and a similar national commission, to draw up lists of candidates for the provincial and national assemblies. The number of candidates is always equal to the number of slots available, although the law states that there can be more candidates than positions. The ward delegates then approve the slates for a popular vote. A minimum 50 percent of the more than 600 deputies at the national level must be elected ward-level delegates, the remainder being superdeputies from the government, Party, culture, sports, and other sectors. Fidel Castro had always been nominated as a superdeputy in Santiago de Cuba. Whether he would be nominated again became an important story and the latest test of his health and political status more than a year into his vanishing act and amid still more death rumors in Miami and along Havana's diplomatic row.

Santiago and the surrounding area, known as Oriente before the Revolution and now the five provinces of Las Tunas, Holguín, Santiago de Cuba, Granma, and Guantánamo, is considered the birthplace of the Cuban nation and the cradle of its independence struggle and the Revolution. Castro's district, district 6, also is home to the national shrine to the Virgen de la Caridad del Cobre, Cuba's Lady of Charity and patron saint across all religious and political lines.[1]

On December 2, 2007, the day prior to Castro's possible nomination, I walked the hilly streets of Cuba's beautiful and legendary second city, nestled in the foothills of the Sierra Maestra as they roll down to meet the sea and form the bay. "Do you know what's happening here tomorrow?" I asked one passerby after the other. Shrugs were the only responses, or comments on the opening game of the baseball season against the archrival Havana Industriales. I informed the local residents of the nomination meeting in their city and Castro's possible candidacy. "Don't you think Fidel is too old and sick?" I asked. At that, most people awoke immediately from their political slumber and became truly indignant, even the hustlers hawking everything from cigars to *chicas*. It was obvious they identified with Castro and drew a vicarious sense of self-esteem from him and the Revolution, even if they had no idea what was going on.

At the nomination meeting—which took place at the local Communist Party School—I asked the recently elected ward delegates, who appeared to be very much from the grass roots, if they planned to nominate the Comandante. One after the other looked at me like I was an idiot, or from another planet. How could I even ask? Some people actually laughed in my face. And then Santiago nominated the ailing Castro, to cries of "Viva Fidel," leaving the door open for him to resume governing. "During his convalescence, he has continued to be actively involved in the country's most important strategic decisions," said a bio, tacked on a poster board with Castro's black-and-white photo, just like those of all the other candidates. Castro remains "intellectually active," it said, "writing about the most pressing problems facing Cuba and the survival of the human species."

A Taliban

Now imagine zipping along an eight-lane and then six-lane highway at 80 miles per hour with no other vehicle in sight and only potholes and an occasional cop or cow or horse to dodge. Well, there really is no need to imagine. Such an unreal experience is just a flight and rent-a-car away, in Cuba, as one travels a few hundred miles east from Havana to central Sancti Spíritus Province, passing through the lush green plain into the foothills of the central Escambray Mountains, their ridges topped by strings of palms, the first leg of my trip to Santiago for Castro's nomination. Rusting iron structures of various shapes litter the roadside, ready to be dragged onto the highway if enemy planes should decide to turn it into what it appears to be from the air: an endless empty runway. The highway was begun by dictator Machado in the 1930s, with graft and partying Americans—ferried over from Florida with their cars—in mind. The Revolution put an end to those plans. Years later, the collapse of the Soviet Union left the country without gas and spare parts. So much for eight lanes of highway, even if oil-rich Venezuela was now the country's main ally. The highway comes to an abrupt end in Sancti Spíritus, where work on it stopped with the Revolution. It's just three and two lanes from there on, a bit more realistic under the circumstances, because the roadway remains relatively free of traffic, except when a few vehicles get stuck behind horse-drawn carriages, bicycles, and local residents of the small towns along the way, who seem to think the road belongs to them.

In late November 2007 I went on a 1,500-mile tour of Cuba, in part to be in Santiago de Cuba for the possible nomination of the ailing Fidel Castro as a candidate for the National Assembly and to take the pulse of the land more than a year into his absence from public view and Raúl's interim presidency. I had made more or less the same trip in 2005, to see the ruins of a just-halved sugar industry, and would take it again in early 2009, 2010, 2011 and 2012 to witness reforms under Raúl. Each time that I traveled to Ciego de Ávila, Camagüey, Granma, Santiago, Guantánamo, and Holguín, also passing through Las Tunas, I visited and stayed with many of the same family and friends—from farmers, ranchers, nurses, professors, and a fighting-cock trainer and computer repairman to tourism workers and former Communist Party and government officials. These people and places served as my markers, outside of Havana and western Cuba, to measure the land's changing situation and mood. Here is what I sent my clients after my November trip:

> There is a marked improvement in the situation across the entire country. This is based on the simple fact that Cuba has billions more to spend each year and is plowing it into infrastructure. Most importantly, the place is now dotted with small, generator based, power stations. Hey, there is electricity, and that is a big deal. Daily blackouts for 15 years disorganized everyday life and economic activity. They are gone. This has improved everyone's spirits even if these same people do not realize it. Life has become more predictable, organized and comfortable, though still very hard for the majority. There are fewer interruptions in economic activity, as seen by the more than 7 percent increase in industrial output last year. Various people I witnessed cooking in their backyards with wood or charcoal, or over make-shift burners my last trip, now cook with Chinese electric burners, all-purpose electric pressure cookers called "the queen," and have brand new fridges. Few Cubans have ever had stoves with ovens, using pressure cookers to make everything from cakes and their famous flan to poultry and meat. Sorry, no microwaves yet [they would arrive a few years later]. There is plenty of water too, and with the electricity it sometimes manages, at least 50 percent of it, to reach people's homes. The campo is a lush green and not the brownish-yellow of a few years back, though adequate rainfall means there is both more grazing grass and more Marabú.[2] Public transportation has improved a bit and there is more gas available, though cars on the highway remain few and far between and bicycles far more numerous than motorcycles in cities and towns, though the motos have increased dramatically.
>
> On the negative side, there is no indication that fundamental structural issues that cause low productivity, poor quality and corruption have been addressed. Yes, early in the morning, not later than 7:00 a.m., Camaguey's streets are packed with people going to work or school on bicycles. But the question remains, do they make the best use of their

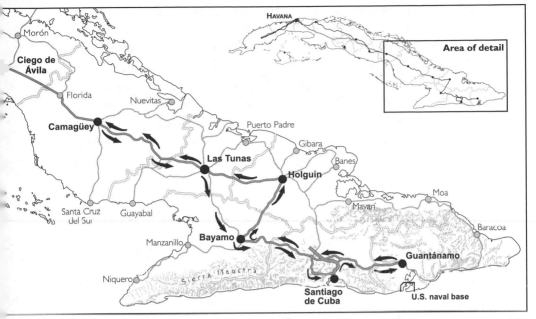

Cuba, showing my annual route through the central and eastern parts of the country. Map created by Armando Hugo Portela.

time after they arrive at their destinations? Farmers say higher prices paid by the state for their products and more fertilizer, herbicides, and other state-supplied inputs have left them feeling that more attention is being paid to their complaints and work. At the same time chronic problems related to state control of inputs and marketing continue. The feed for the pigs hasn't arrived, the cheese handed over two months earlier hasn't been paid for, the slaughterhouse won't take more cattle because they have met their plan for the year, etc. Nothing significant has been done to deal with unproductive state-owned land and farms.

I gave rides to many young people during my November 2007 trip. I found them to be well educated, articulate, and thinking about the future. Fidel's Battle of Ideas, and the art instructors, social workers, young teachers, and health care staff that came with it, were far more visible and effective in the provinces and secondary cities and small towns than in Havana. The people were impressed by new health clinics, even if they were next door to crumbling hospitals and sometimes had leaky roofs and poor plumbing. Then there were the new computers (minus Internet) and big-screen TVs in the local schools, and programs to turn high school dropouts into socially useful citizens.

I pulled into a service station in Villa Clara, about a hundred miles from

Havana, along with my dear friend Eduardo Machin who was catching a ride to Camagüey, and there picked up my first hitchhiker, a twenty-one-year-old psychology student on her way home from the province's university to Ciego de Ávila. Casually dressed, with styled hair, she flopped into the backseat, stuck her iPod plugs in her ears, and began to hum along with the tunes as if she had no cares in this world. "Ah," I thought, "she's the perfect apathetic youth to pop my Fidel questions to." I was in for a surprise. My passenger perked right up, leaned forward, and responded passionately. She proved to be a Taliban, the name journalists gave the most strident young supporters of Fidel's Battle of Ideas.

> Marc Frank. Why do you like your country?
>
> Cristina. Because it is very peaceful, there is no violence. Education is free, health care also. Education and health care are very good in my country.
>
> Marc Frank. And what do you think of Internet and things to eat and buy?
>
> Cristina. Nothing. I'm not going to think about it. I don't need that.
>
> Marc Frank. What do you need?
>
> Cristina. Peace.
>
> Marc Frank. How old are you?
>
> Cristina. Twenty-one.
>
> Marc Frank. You are studying psychology, right?
>
> Cristina. Yes.
>
> Marc Frank. What will you do after graduation?
>
> Cristina. Sports psychology.
>
> Marc Frank. What is that?
>
> Cristina. A sports psychologist is the one that takes care of a sports team as a psychologist. A baseball team, basketball, et cetera.
>
> Marc Frank. And when the baseball team loses the world championship, you will speak to them so they do not feel so bad?
>
> Cristina. The baseball team has an excellent psychologist, his name is Alvaredo.
>
> Marc Frank. Look, Fidel is sick now, do you think he can go on as president?
>
> Cristina. I don't think we need another.
>
> Marc Frank. Do you think he can go on?
>
> Cristina. If there is going to be another, let him be just like him, with his same ideas and same personality.
>
> Marc Frank. Do you think it is possible that there is another Fidel?

Cristina. Yes, and another Che and another Camilo.[3] And much better ones, too. Why not? We are being trained with all their ideas.

Marc Frank. Do you think Raúl does a good job?

Cristina. Of course, he has been educated with Fidel's same ideas.

Marc Frank. Isn't he a bit old-fashioned and stuck in his ways?

Cristina. Raúl? Not at all! He doesn't have a character like Fidel's. But I don't think he is stuck in his ways. Besides, he has known how to handle the country pretty well at this moment.

Marc Frank. What would you like for your country?

Cristina. To remain the same.

Marc Frank. But there are many problems, even Raúl says so.

Cristina. Okay, but there are problems in all countries.

Marc Frank. Many people say Cuban young people go to other countries, that they are not revolutionary.

Cristina. Actually there are problems. But I think that everyone who leaves wants to come back once they are gone. I think work could be better paid. I think salaries ought to improve. But generally speaking, everything is all right.

Marc Frank. Hey, in your university how many young people are true revolutionaries, like you? And how many are not?

Cristina. At least in my classroom, we all are. Because we discuss the issues in the [Communist] youth meetings and in all other meetings that take place, like in Raúl's debate.

Marc Frank. Do you think most of them are revolutionary, that they want to go on with socialism?

Cristina. I am not saying there are not exceptions. There must be. But most of them are revolutionary.

Marc Frank. Anything else you want to say to the world?

Cristina. That we are happy.

Marc Frank. What's your name?

Cristina. Cristina Fuentes.

Marc Frank. Do you live with your parents?

Cristina. Yes, with both of them.

Marc Frank. What do they do?

Cristina. They work.

I asked Christina how she came by the iPod. Her father, a dentist, had brought it back from Venezuela, where he had worked on a government mission. Then Cristina leaned forward and confessed that at first she thought we might be part of the counterrevolution snooping around, given our tourism plates and the fact that we were a Yankee and Cuban together, and that was why she had been so strident, although Cristina insisted that she believed everything she had said.

I was surprised at how many of the people I picked up at random answered more or less the same way, but with less conviction. When I asked them what would happen after Fidel, a blank stare, widening eyes, and a shrug were the most common responses.

Castro Resigns as President

Around 95 percent of Cuba's electorate regularly votes in general elections, though it dropped to 91 percent in 2013. Most people simply check the box for the national slate, although one can vote for specific individuals and not others from one's district, or leave the ballot blank or damaged. Some Cubans vote out of support for the Revolution or a sense of patriotic duty, others from fear of being ostracized. In any case, there are so many polling places that voting usually takes just a few minutes. While some in another land might abstain, here they end up, with a bit of encouragement from the local block organization or Women's Federation, crossing the street or walking a few blocks and casting a secret ballot. Many people do not know all the candidates they vote for; they do know that all support the Revolution or they wouldn't be on the slate. Less than 10 percent of voters leave ballots blank, damaged, or filled out improperly, according to the government.

It was a foregone conclusion that Castro, still in seclusion, would be elected to the National Assembly in January 2008. He received the second-highest percentage of votes from the districts—around 98 percent—with Raúl topping him by a fraction of a percentile, the government claimed. But would Fidel be nominated for the presidency again and accept the job? I joined a pool set up by Jordy Carasco, a diplomat friend from the European Union, and bet the local equivalent of five dollars that Castro would retire. I tripled my money the very next day, and less than a week before the opening session of the National Assembly, scheduled to elect the president and other senior members of government. Castro, in a statement published by the state-run media on February 19, 2008, wrote:

My wishes have always been to discharge my duties to my last breath. That's all I can offer.

To my dearest compatriots, who have recently honored me so much by electing me a member of the Parliament . . . I am saying that I will neither aspire to nor accept . . . the positions of President of the State Council and Commander in Chief.

. . . it would be a betrayal to my conscience to accept a responsibility requiring more mobility and dedication than I am physically able to offer.

. . .

This is not my farewell to you. My only wish is to fight as a soldier in the battle of ideas. I shall continue to write under the heading of *Reflections of Comrade Fidel*. It will be just another weapon you can count on. Perhaps my voice will be heard.[4]

Much of the world reacted to the news as if Castro would no longer be around or involved in policy making, leading to a sea change for the country. But his resignation was just one step in a long institutional transition that would continue for a number of years. Castro, as far as we knew, remained head of the Communist Party, retaining ultimate power in theory at least, although Raúl had taken over more and more of the Party's daily operations even before Fidel fell ill. Within a week of Fidel's resignation, Raúl Castro announced, to thunderous applause, his intention as Cuba's new president to consult with his brother on all important matters of state, both foreign and domestic. Fidel wrote that not only was he consulted on the composition of the new Council of State, but that he had handpicked some of its members.[5] Cubans took this all in stride. They didn't bat an eye.

6

From Clinton to Bush

One day, the good Lord will take Fidel Castro away and then . . . some will say, all that matters is stability. . . . I think we ought to be pressing hard for democracy.

President George W. Bush

Intellectuals—academics, writers, actors, musicians, and artists—staged their most significant protest under the Revolution just five months after Castro stepped aside. The spark: in January 2007 a little old man in a white guayabera, Luis Pavón Tamayo, appeared as a guest on *Impronta*, a weekly Cuban television program featuring past personalities from the world of culture. Pavón had been culture czar during perhaps the worst years of censorship, from 1971 to 1976, as Cuba moved firmly into the Soviet camp. He hounded many writers, actors, and others into obscurity or exile because of their "incorrect" views or sexual orientation. What happened following Pavón's appearance was very similar to the uproar that erupted in the United States around Republican majority leader Trent Lott's praise for Senator Strom Thurmond on his hundredth birthday in 2002. The praise came despite segregationist Thurmond's earlier and longtime support for Jim Crow during a very dark period in U.S. history, forcing Lott to step down.[1]

Pavón's victims, since restored in status and some winners of various national and international awards, began e-mailing one another that his appearance represented a threat to the more open cultural atmosphere of recent decades. They posted their e-mails on the Internet. Within a week, every academic I knew was offering me 140 pages of e-mails blasting Pavón and his activities.[2] Some of Cuba's best-known artists and writers banded together and publicly demanded an official explanation and apology from the government, which they very quickly received. An eight-hour, closed-door meeting on Pavón and his epoch, with Culture Minister Abel Prieto and 450 intellectuals and artists, took place on January 30, 2007. Pavón was never heard from again.

The firestorm of criticism and protests was not covered by the official media, but it nevertheless revealed how much Cuba had changed over the decades, and the power of the Internet. A book fair soon afterward featured an opening speech in which exiled writers were publicly mentioned for the first time as part of the country's literary heritage, as a smiling Raúl Castro looked on.[3] Soon, controversial Cuban films, previously shown only in theaters and sometimes only briefly there, were broadcast by state television. A few plays, banned from theaters for decades, were staged. The trend would continue and gain strength in the years to come.[4]

One would have expected the United States to be in the middle of the controversy, since it publicly budgets millions of dollars each year to stir up just that on the island. But the opposite proved true. In fact, even as debate raged over the Pavón incident, the State Department denied visas to key players in the protest who had been invited to a Connecticut literary conference. At the center of the uproar were a few well-known intellectuals who survived the Pavón era and had returned from obscurity, led by researcher and literary critic Desiderio Navarro, the first important figure to protest Pavón's television appearance and the organizer of the conference on the Pavón years that was held on January 30, 2007. The very next week, the U.S. State Department denied visas to Navarro and nine other intellectuals invited to a conference, hosted by the University of Connecticut, on cultural relations between Cuba and the former European Communist countries.[5] There was no better illustration of how out of touch Washington was during those critical months when Castro stepped aside. How could the State Department have missed the importance of the intellectuals' revolt—which to this day continues to open up new space in Cuba—and deny visas to some of the most prominent individuals involved? The answer explains why Uncle Sam was powerless when Castro took ill, and resorted instead to rhetorical demands for democracy and human rights, threats, and mistaken predictions that Castro was terminally ill and would die at any moment.

President Bush packed his Latin American and Cuban policy slots with the most extreme representatives and allies of Miami's Cuban American political establishment, which had played a role in his winning Florida over Al Gore in 2000. These men and women held the view that anyone who accepted living and working in Castro's Cuba, traded with Cuba, or engaged in any type of academic or cultural exchange with Cuba, was an accomplice to a cruel and brutal totalitarian regime and, therefore, as evil as Castro himself. The powerful exile political establishment's continued justification of the Batista dictatorship, and their you're-with-us-or-against-us philosophy, dovetailed nicely with Bush's worldview. They had long made Miami a strange American city where bombs exploded at the offices of companies and media outlets that advocated or participated in any contact with Cuba, paramilitary forces openly trained in the Everglades, and violence-prone exiles boasted of attacks on Cuban diplomats, a civilian airliner, hotels, and other soft targets in the fight against Castro and Communism. Cuban artists' works were trashed, eggs were thrown at those who wished to hear the island's salsa bands, books were banned from libraries, Juanes DVDs were stomped when he performed in Havana, and a little boy named Elián, after losing his mother, was held for months against his father's will, simply because he lived in Cuba.

The contrast between the Clinton administration's people-to-people Cuba policy, opposed by the Miami establishment, and the Bush administration's embrace of the latter's zero-tolerance approach was soon evident on the ground in Cuba. Clinton had broadened contacts from a few dissidents into the Grey Zone: those who were within the system but who nevertheless might favor improving or changing it. After years of crisis, the majority of Cubans were part of the Grey Zone, even if they didn't see eye to eye with Washington and Miami, and the intellectuals and artists, including those denied visas, were their most outspoken and articulate spokespersons.

During the Clinton administration, diplomats worked hard to get to know intellectuals and academics, artists, musicians, and sports figures, all of whom were encouraged to visit the United States and to reciprocate by receiving their U.S. colleagues at Cuban events. Under the 1994–95 immigration agreements, U.S. diplomats were allowed to travel throughout the country, ostensibly to ensure that rafters who were returned to the island were not persecuted—an important opportunity for the diplomats to get the lay of the land. Cuban Americans were encouraged to visit their families, and vice versa, and tens of thousands of Americans traveled in people-to-people delegations or through third countries to see Cuba, as U.S. enforcement of travel restrictions eased. Every six months, officials from the two countries met to discuss immigration issues and, off the record, other questions, the highest and most consistent public bilateral contact in decades. Cooperation on drug traffic interdiction began, and a representative of the U.S. Coast Guard was stationed in Havana. Congress passed and Clinton signed an amendment to the trade embargo allowing agricultural sales for cash, opening the way for the first such commercial transactions since the early 1960s.

The Bush administration considered just about all of Cuba a black zone, with no shades of gray and with a pure white zone composed of a handful of dissidents allied with the West and Miami-based Cuban American factions. It called off the immigration meetings, expelled more than a dozen Cuban diplomats, vigorously enforced the embargo and travel ban, drastically reduced Cuban Americans' ability to visit and send money and goods to family, and began systematically to deny Cuban professionals, athletes, and cultural figures visas to visit and attend events in the United States, and permission to their

U.S. counterparts to visit the island. Persecution was stepped up of U.S. citizens traveling through third countries to Cuba.[6] Even legal travelers were harassed at Miami International Airport, including Cuban cardinal Jaime Ortega.[7] When Bush took office, 160 U.S. nongovernmental organizations were licensed to work with Cuba. By the end of Bush's second term, their number had been drastically reduced. The Bush administration ordered its diplomats in Havana to challenge Castro openly on his own turf, and to open the U.S. Interests Section's diplomatic doors and residences, communications and mail to dissident activity. The Cuban government responded by forbidding most contact by academics, cultural figures, and others with the U.S. Interests Section and its staff. The United States restricted Cuban diplomats to a 25-mile radius around Washington and New York; Havana reciprocated, and U.S. diplomats in Havana found themselves cut off from most of the country. In short, the Bush administration destroyed the previous administration's hard work and left little in its place. U.S. diplomat after U.S. diplomat told me off the record that those in charge of Cuba policy in Washington believed that if they were not being thrown out of the country, then, as far as the policy makers were concerned, the diplomats were not doing their jobs.

I have many friends and contacts within the Grey Zone, men and women eager to talk with and learn from foreign experts in their respective fields. They expressed deep disappointment that the U.S. Interests Section no longer delivered books and other literature to them, and denied them access to U.S. academic circles. They also expressed frustration with their own government for reacting to the more aggressive tactics of U.S. diplomats by banning contact with them. As for Cardinal Ortega, he was no less than the leader of the Roman Catholic Church, the best-organized and best-financed national entity representing masses of people that espoused a different ideology than the ruling Communist Party. Many intellectuals and artists are Catholic, as can be seen by the quality of the Church's provincial magazines and web pages. Ortega had earned the Miami establishment's wrath for opposing the U.S. embargo and, after Pope John Paul's 1998 visit, adopting a more moderate approach to the government after decades of more or less open confrontation. Prepare for the future, build up the flock, the pope reportedly advised. As we shall see, the future came sooner than perhaps was expected.

The Food Trade

The United States Congress in 2000 passed an exception to the trade embargo allowing the sale of agricultural products for cash to Cuba, and President Clinton signed it before leaving office. An earlier exception also allowed the sale of medicines and other health care products for cash, but according to both the Cuban government and U.S. companies, regulations not applied to the food sales, such as one that required a report on every end-user, rendered the earlier measure commercially unviable. While Castro refused to purchase food from the United States under the Clinton administration, he reversed the policy after President Bush took office—perhaps in hopes of neutralizing Miami's growing influence at the White House. The move strengthened the anti-embargo lobby in the U.S. Congress. The Bush administration tightened the regulations, making it more difficult and expensive to sell products to Cuba, but proved powerless to stop the trade. By 2003 the United States was Cuba's biggest source of imported food and, thereafter, one of the island's top 10 trading partners, despite the embargo. Cuba moved up to become one of the top 30 to 50 export markets for U.S. agricultural products, compared with 225th place before the trade began.[8] Now imagine what would happen if sanctions were lifted entirely.

What is it with walks, mobile phones, and big news? I was taking another evening stroll on a November evening in 2001, this time through back neighborhoods of Havana's Playa municipality, when my cell phone rang. It was John Kavulich, president of the U.S.-Cuba Trade and Economic Council, tipping me off that the first commercial contracts in decades between the United States and Cuba were being signed in Havana at that very moment. John put out the weekly *Economic Eye on Cuba*, aimed at providing information on the Cuban economy and Cuba-related U.S. regulations and law. I contributed to the project for many years. The weekly became the most important source on such information for U.S. businesses and other interested parties throughout the Clinton era and the first years of the Bush administration.

"I have been doing this for more than twenty years, including opening new markets, but this was really exceptional," Terry Harris, vice president of Riceland Foods, which produces and mills 25 percent of U.S.-grown rice, told me. The company was one of a number of U.S. firms to take Cuba up on its offer to purchase food on an emergency basis after being devastated by Hurricane Michelle earlier that November. "It was really quite emotional and, for the first time in my career, drinks were brought in to toast the signing," Harris said. "You felt like it was one short moment in history, but a huge moment in the history of the United States and Cuba," he continued, describing the scene as he and Pedro Álvarez, at the time the director of Cuba's state food importer, Alimport, signed a multimillion-dollar contract involving a "significant" amount of low-grade rice. Harris said Havana and Washington made it clear that the trade deals were taking place on an emergency and humanitarian basis, and did not represent a change in their commercial relations, but he said he still held out hope for the future. "Everyone in the world believes their relations have to change, though no one is sure of the timeline," he said. Álvarez, earlier in the week, had signed contracts with representatives of Archer Daniels Midland, Cargill, and other companies to buy wheat, corn, soy, and other bulk foods.

Cuba had appealed to Washington to speed up authorization for it to buy food and medicines on a one-time basis to replenish stocks used up after its worst storm in half a century, a storm that proved but a harbinger of others that would follow later in the decade. Hurricane Michelle struck central Cuba on November 4, 2001, killing five people, wrecking tens of thousands of houses and other buildings, and severely damaging crops earmarked for both export and local consumption. Washington first offered to send humanitarian aid via nongovernment bodies, but Havana replied with a polite refusal and a counteroffer to buy food and medicines with cash, an important concession from Castro, who had repeatedly stated that he would not buy "a single grain of rice" while the embargo was still in place. The Bush administration, to its credit, and following the letter of the law, accepted the proposal. Castro said he was purchasing food on a one-time basis, but U.S. politicians, corporations, and trade organizations lobbied him hard to continue the trade. Dozens of dinners and long nights were spent by a who's who of U.S. agriculture with the Comandante, after the first contracts were signed. Sources said Castro was complaining about having to autograph so many baseballs. Marvin Leer of the USA Rice Federation, the first American to exhibit products at Havana's annual international trade fair, even before the food trade began, talked to me about the first of five meetings he attended with Fidel Castro:

Marc Frank. Flash back to the first time you met Fidel, what were you thinking?

Marvin Leer. The first time I met Fidel Castro was in 2002, just prior to the first and only American food exhibit that took place in Havana, and it was in September. I brought down a delegation of rice producers and exporters and, several days prior to that show, we were in the Hotel Nacional and were told to be down in the lobby at eleven o'clock for a special event.

Marc Frank. Eleven at night?

Marvin Leer. Yup, eleven at night. So we are down in the lobby and we had a bus waiting for us, but Pedro Álvarez, the state food buyer, took me aside and said, "Marvin, you are going to have an unforgettable evening." And so he took me in his car and the other rice guys went in a bus and we rode off to the Council of State and we were received there, and people were kind of amazed by that whole situation.

Marc Frank. Why?

Marvin Leer. Well, they were amazed at the Council of State because it's a large, a kind of stark, kind of ugly building, and getting in there we were escorted up elevators and through corridors and whatever, and then we ended up in a very small kind of room, and there was a bartender and people who went around passing out little drinks and whatever, and then he came in. And, like a lot of people, I had read a lot about him and this was 2002 and so this is a Fidel Castro in his late seventies, not the Fidel Castro of, you know, all those films and all of that, and so he was an old guy at that time. I looked at him and he had kind of a shabby green army uniform on, kind of frayed, and he was wearing black Reebok sneakers. I was looking for those army boots but I guess, like all of us when we get older, he had problems. Anyway, so we talk and drink, and welcome to Cuba, blah, blah, blah, and then from there he took us into a room adjacent to where we were and there was a long table, an oval table, and the Americans sat on one side and the Cubans on the other, and that was about two hours there. I think a hurricane had just hit or was about to hit, and he had maps brought to him instantaneously, maps brought out to him by his assistants, and so he went into the whole history of hurricanes that had hit Cuba and he had them all mapped out and what this one was going to do, that it was going to come here, so that was at least two hours. Then we went to the dining room, the place where you have dinner there, and we sat down and he was very, very charming. I was impressed by how charming he is and how obviously intelligent he is. Back at the table before dinner he was going to every one of our rice producers, asking how much land he had, what kind of tractors do you use, what kind of fertilizer do you use. I mean, he was kind of up on fertilizers, tractors, yields, and how much rice per acre, so he had lots of questions on that. Anyhow, when we went and sat down to eat, he was this gracious host, and he had a cart of wine behind him he was going to have served— and it was California wine—so we had dinner.

Marc Frank. What was for dinner?

Marvin Leer. Dinner was a lobster tail, I guess Cuban, steak and all kinds of vegetables, and I noticed he ate very little of any of this. I was sitting opposite him, next to our president. He had his translator, of course, and she was very good. I was kind of noticing, because I speak Spanish, that she was always four words ahead, so it gave me the idea that she had kind of heard all this before, like last night with the French delegation or Venezuelan, or whoever it might have been.

Marc Frank. Did he drink the wine?

Marvin Leer. He ate very little but did drink a little wine, but I have a great story about this. It is very hard to ask him questions, because it's a monologue and he doesn't breathe too much, so there is no, like, empty space to sneak in a question. It's a monologue and, of course, all our side kind of had their mouths open, thinking, "Wow, this is Fidel Castro!" and a lot of our guys were sort of older people and so we all remembered all these times. So there was a moment, and I said, "Mr. President, I wonder if it's all right if I ask a question?" He said sure, so I said, "This is a personal question, would that be all right with you?" And he said sure again, and so I said something like, "We are really honored by this invitation and this room. I am sure you have had hundreds of heads of state here over the years, you had the pope, all of these people, and we are just humble rice producers, from Arkansas and Louisiana, so, first of all, thank you for this sumptuous dinner and unforgettable evening. But I was sort of wondering, with all this wonderful food here, and with all these delegations you receive, nobody could eat like this every night, and so I wonder when—those very few times that you may find yourself alone—what's your favorite food, what do you like to eat when you're not having to entertain world leaders and so forth?" Immediately he mumbled something to some guy next to him like, "Call Eduardo," and some guy came rushing out and he talked to him and in five seconds there was a bowl of bulgur and brown rice and some kind of salad greens, and then he brings out about ten or twelve yogurt cups, and old-fashioned milk bottles, ten or twelve of those, and he said, "I also like this. This is milk made from water buffalo, and so is the yogurt, and these lemons are from Pinar del Río." Then we got forty-five minutes about buffalos, and how in 1971 he went to Thailand and Malaysia and he brought home some kind of special buffalo, and they crossed them with a famous cow they have in Cuba, and they made this super milk-producing buffalo-cow, whatever. So about thirty-five minutes into the discourse on buffalo milk—all the properties of this special milk, high protein, low fat, and so forth—he had the waiter pass around some for everybody to try. There were about fifteen of us, and eight or nine Cubans, Pedro Álvarez and different dignitaries like Ricardo Alarcón. So we are all trying this buffalo milk and we are all saying this is the best we ever had. I mean, what are we going to say, right? So then he talks about this yogurt, how it's from the buffalo milk and has this special lemon flavor. He had one of those little demitasse spoons for coffee, so he is eating as he tells us the story. And so, as he is explaining about the history of the yogurt, he hands me the yogurt with his spoon in it and asks if I want a bite. So I got the spoon of this guy inside the yogurt cup and everybody is looking at me. What am I going to do, take the spoon out and wipe it off on my shirt, or the napkin or something? What can I do? So I ate with the spoon, and as I ate the yogurt, I said something like, "Hey, this yogurt is wonderful. Once the embargo ends, you know, we will be able to sell you rice and I'm sure you will have a great market for this, for this highly nutritious, special-flavored yogurt, that's also organic." Then I took a few more little bites and I put the spoon back and I handed it back to him.

Marc Frank. Did he eat more?

Marvin Leer. Yes, he did eat more; yes, we are blood brothers. So a day or two later the U.S. show opened and, as you remember, he went around the different booths. So he came to our booth with all his bodyguards and whatever, and I'm there and the other staff is there and we have all this rice cooked up, too, and we give samples. And so we go out and hand him a sample, and all his guards, you know, are blocking the thing, and he said, "No, these guys you can trust; these guys aren't going to poison me. I've already eaten from the same spoon with this guy."

Whether it was the efforts of people like Marvin, Castro's desire to neutralize and perhaps goad the Bush administration and its Miami friends, or purely business, the food trade grew to an average of $350 million per year, reaching more than $750 million in 2008 before yet another local financial crisis and perhaps a decline in Havana's political interest resulted in the trade's precipitous decline, which came in at just under $500 million in 2012.

Canadian and other Western diplomats and merchants were not happy as they faced U.S. trade competition for the first time. The French, who sold wheat to Cuba, wondered if their trade would survive. Mike, a Canadian entrepreneur and friend who had been selling chickens to Cuba for years, said he was calling it quits. "I'm throwing in the towel and going back to selling cars in the Dominican Republic," he said. "The U.S. companies are dumping poultry on the Cuban market at ridiculously low prices, and there is no way I can compete."

University student Yusmani Arzuaga, at the Carlos Tercero shopping mall in Central Havana, bit into an apple as she left the supermarket, where she had bought the fruit with a Washington State label. "Why does something so good have to be forbidden? I sure hope they allow them to keep coming," she said, her big smile turning to a hearty laugh as she eyed the forbidden fruit and talked about Adam and Eve. The petite, brown-eyed Arzuaga could have been speaking for most of the Caribbean island's inhabitants. They were absolutely delighted over the resumption of some trade with the United States. Cubans hadn't seen apples since before the fall of the Soviet Union, when they had arrived in bulk from Bulgaria, appearing in the bodegas for just a few weeks before the year-end holiday season.

Bush Policy Takes Hold

Former U.S. president Jimmy Carter first visited Cuba in May 2002. Carter was the most important U.S. politician to set foot on the island since the 1959 revolution. (He would return a decade later.) The ripple effects of the Clinton years were still being felt, and Americans who had slipped into Cuba through third countries were waving from hotel windows and restaurant doors and yelling, "Hey, Jimmy!" and "I voted for you, Jimmy!" as he took a walking tour of the restored colonial district of Havana.

In a speech attended by Castro, broadcast live by state television, and later published by the Cuban press, Carter even managed to laud the Varela Project, a first-time-ever dissident initiative led by Christian democrats who, with the help of some priests and other laypersons, collected thousands of signatures calling for a referendum on one-party rule. Its leader, Oswaldo Paya, would die tragically in a 2012 car accident.

The Bush administration was not happy with the Carter visit and charged—while he was still in Havana—that Cuba was manufacturing or could manufacture biological weapons and had transferred the technology to Iran, a statement it later retracted. Within a few months of Carter's visit, with the arrival of a new head of the U.S. mission, James Cason—who replaced the Clinton era's Vicki Huddleston—the previous administration's policy, and many a U.S. diplomat's hard work, began to unravel.

Cason launched an open and aggressive anti-Castro campaign within Cuba itself, and by April 2003 seventy-five dissidents were behind bars, many of them Varela Project activists. They were rounded up and tried even as the U.S. invasion of Iraq got under way. The dissidents faced courts packed with government supporters, while foreign diplomats and journalists were barred. They were convicted of conspiring with the United States against the government and summarily sentenced to prison terms averaging more than twenty years. Cuba had allowed token dissent in the 1990s after the Soviet Union's demise, perhaps in hopes of improved political and economic ties with the West. A Cuban official at the Foreign Ministry told me that, while the Clinton administration was perceived to be using the dissidents as a means to rapprochement and peaceful change, Bush's government saw them as a vehicle toward violent regime change. The official pointed to Cuban Americans within the Bush administration, many of whom favored military action to overthrow Castro, and the U.S. tanks at that moment rolling into Iraq.

The Bush administration responded to the crackdown on dissent, and calls from exiles for an Iraq-style regime change in Havana, by establishing the cabinet-level Commission for Assistance to a Free Cuba, which was stacked with members and allies of the exile establishment. The commission, in a 500-page report delivered in May 2004, called for tightening the embargo further and increasing support for dissidents in order to hasten the "expeditious end of the Castro dictatorship" and Cuba's "peaceful transition to democracy." The report also called for an Iraq-style "Cuba transition coordinator." The position was quickly created and filled by Caleb McCarry, a former congressional staffer known for his militant anti-Castro stand while working for Jesse Helms, one of the most hawkish lawmakers ever to sit in the U.S. Senate. The report's recommendations were quickly approved by the U.S. president. Under the package, Cuban Americans could still send up to $1,200 a year in remittances to their hard-pressed relatives, but only to their next of kin, which eliminated support for relatives such as grandparents, uncles, aunts, and cousins. Now they could visit the island only once every three years, instead of annually, and the amount they could spend during visits was slashed by two-thirds. The measures also included provisions for a multimillion-dollar aid package for Cuban dissidents and money for an aircraft that would transmit programming from the U.S. government's Televisión Martí into Cuba. Gifts purchased and brought back from the island, with the exception of art and literature, were banned.[9]

BRUTAL ECONOMIC AND POLITICAL MEASURES, predictably screamed the red-banner headline in *Granma*, the Communist Party newspaper. Washington's new restrictions did not go down well on the streets of Havana, either. Cubans, who have particularly strong family ties despite decades of being torn apart by Cold War hostilities, reacted strongly against the Bush administration's move. "No one is going to stop my brother from keeping his ties with us, even if he has to go around the world to get here," said María Abdala, a nurse. Diana Valido, a bank employee, said that her eighty-four-year-old aunt came over every year from Miami and now could not return for two more years. "This is a humanitarian, not an economic, question. All she has left is to come here and spend some time with her sister and nieces," Valido said.

The measures were not just politically controversial, alienating ordinary Cubans, but difficult to police. Although it was relatively straightforward to monitor direct visits on charter flights from Miami, New York, and California—the only ones authorized at the time—and money sent by electronic transfers, Cuban Americans had other options, and many Americans visit Cuba illegally by traveling through third countries, such as Mexico, Canada, and the Bahamas. Airline companies in the Bahamas, Mexico, Costa Rica, and other countries quickly added flights to Cuba. Cuban immigration officials cooperated by not stamping these travelers' passports. Most remittances are sent by hand through couriers, known as *mulas*, rather than by wire transfer.

The U.S. Treasury Department's Office of Foreign Assets Control (OFAC), responsible for enforcing sanctions, was already under fire for paying more attention to Castro and Cuba than it did to Bin Laden and stopping financial flows to terrorists. A congressional report at the time found that there were just four staff members dedicated to terrorist finances and twelve to enforcing the trade embargo against Cuba. OFAC reported just 93 terrorism-related investigations from 1990 through 2003, and 10,683 Cuba-related investigations in the same period. Fines for Cuba-related offenses amounted to $8 million. Those charged with terrorism offenses paid $9,425.[10]

It wasn't long before increased tensions began manifesting themselves around the U.S. Interests Section in Havana. You had to be there to believe it!

DISPATCH: U.S.-Cuba Spat Spills into the New Year

Havana, Jan. 28, 2005 (ABC News)—With the Bush administration branding Cuba an "outpost of tyranny" and Havana yelling "fascists" back, the longtime foes seem in no mood to compromise these days.

U.S. diplomats huddle in their offices planning acts of political theater they say are aimed at drawing attention to Cuban human rights violations and getting President Fidel Castro's goat. The Caribbean island's leaders plot their counterattacks somewhere in Revolution Palace, headquarters of both the government and ruling Communist Party.

The two countries are still going at it in a bitter tit-for-tat holiday dispute that has spilled into the New Year and been marked by almost daily youth rallies and other activities in front of the U.S. diplomatic mission, a harbinger, analysts say, of the extremely tense relations expected during President Bush's second term. . . .

The Christmas quarrel erupted over the U.S. mission's traditional holiday lights display depicting Santa, Frosty and candy canes. The display also included a big 75, which symbolizes a group of pro-democracy activists serving long prison terms.

The government charged the display was provocative and demanded it come down, but the United States refused.

Cuba then erected billboards around the mission, with photographs of hooded and bloodied inmates at Iraq's Abu Ghraib prison, U.S. soldiers accosting children, and bold red swastikas and the word "fascists." Lampoons of U.S. foreign policy also went up and peace music was blared at the building.

"The U.S. is definitely not being diplomatic and the Cubans are being childish. It is like a very bad divorce that never ends," said a European diplomat of the scene.

"Who's the worse abuser in Cuba? We for protecting our country from subversion or you at Guantánamo and elsewhere?" young orators screech at events outside the mission as part of what they call "the battle of ideas" between the official ideology and what they say is U.S. imperialist thought. . . .

Frosty and the 75 came down when the holiday season ended. Cuba reciprocated by removing from a nearby apartment building a two-story lampoon of top U.S. diplomat James Cason as Santa riding a sled pulled by soldiers and dropping bombs. The music was toned down, but the U.S. Interests Section is still besieged.

A tall and thick iron fence surrounds the building. Cuban police are posted every 15 feet outside. Youth rally and stage political events at an outdoor amphitheater just a few hundred feet from the front door. Huge billboards of Iraq torture scenes face the mission and a tired-looking eagle with a big "B" for Bush is painted across the highway outside, where it is run over thousands of times each day.

A year later, Cason had been replaced by Michael Parmly, but the scene became even more bizarre when the United States turned on a Times Square–style news ticker at the Interests Section. A U.S. diplomat told me it had cost $750,000 and the pieces of the ticker had been smuggled into Cuba in the diplomatic pouch over the previous months and then assembled in secret. I was tipped off and present when the sign came to life on Martin Luther King Jr.'s birthday with his words "I have a dream that one day this nation will rise up." And at that moment—with the exception of the Coast Guard for drug and human trafficking interdiction and military coordination around the Guantánamo Naval Base turned U.S. prison camp—all bilateral contact between U.S. diplomats and the Cuban government in Havana ceased. The crimson ticker ran through twenty-five windows on the fifth floor of the six-story building. The five-foot-high ticker streamed news, political statements, and messages blaming everyday problems such as transportation shortages on the country's Communist politics and socialist economy. "Some go around in Mercedes, some in Ladas [a Russian car], but the system forces almost everyone to hitch rides," stated one message, playing on a common complaint that there were few buses and that Cubans needed the government's permission to buy a new car. "When people lose their fear, totalitarian regimes lose power," another message stated. But few Cubans could actually read the U.S. ticker. The government blocked it from view with huge black flags more than a hundred feet in the air and just a few feet from the mission's front door after digging up its parking lot.[11]

In early July 2006, just weeks before Castro stepped aside, the Commission for Assistance to a Free Cuba issued a second report, along the same lines as the previous one but even more virulent. The report said that the United States simply "would not allow" a succession to Raúl Castro or anyone else. It included a secret appendix of ideas and actions to "hasten the end of the Castro regime" and proposed even tighter enforcement of sanctions and increased funding to promote dissent. The report was branded by Cuba as a rationale and blueprint for regime change.[12]

But there was little the United States could do inside Cuba when Castro fell ill a few weeks later, and dissidents proved isolated and impotent. Uncle Sam had burned his few bridges and boxed himself out of the game. U.S. diplomats had zero contact with local authorities, the vast Grey Zone, or anyone else of importance. "The United States assures the Cuban people it will not support any effort to evict them from their homes," the crimson letters of the Interests Section ticker blared out a day after Castro stepped aside. "Everything is working normally, the consular section, the refugee program, and our two Internet centers," U.S. spokesman Drew Blakeney told me a few days later over coffee at the Riviera Hotel. "Our contacts with the Cuban Foreign Ministry remain the same," he added, but then he admitted there had been no contact since the electronic sign had been switched on that January.

Denial

It is not surprising that much of Raúl Castro's first statement, almost three weeks after temporarily replacing his brother, concerned the United States and included an olive branch for talks without conditions. Nor is it surprising that a copy of his "interview" with *Granma* on August 18, 2006, was delivered to the Associated Press well in advance of any other foreign news outlet in Havana. The Cuban government makes no important decision without taking into account its extraordinarily powerful and hostile neighbor to the north. The half-century standoff between the elephant and the mouse has had little impact on the United States since the end of the Cold War—outside of Florida and its electoral votes—but it has shaped Cuba psychologically and institutionally and has come, in part, to define its national identity. A siege mentality among Cuba's leadership, security forces, and a significant percentage of the population has been the inevitable result, a mentality put into overdrive by the Bush administration.

Raúl Castro said in the *Granma* interview that talks with the United States "would be possible only when the United States decides to negotiate with seriousness and is willing to treat us with a spirit of equality, reciprocity, and the fullest mutual respect." The State Department quickly threw cold water on the overture, disrespectfully referring to Raúl as "Fidel's baby brother." "What we want to see is a transition from the current dictatorship to a democratic government," spokesman Tom Casey said. "And we certainly don't think that a transition from Fidel to Raúl Castro fits that bill."[13]

Raúl made the offer twice more during his first year in power, and finally admitted the obvious on July 26, 2007: if there were to be talks, they would have to wait until a new administration arrived in Washington. He announced that the rolling mobilization of the military reserves, which was begun when Fidel Castro took ill, would continue until the end of the Bush administration. It is hard to believe that the Cuban government truly thought Washington was open to negotiations, but the Bush administration never bothered to call the possible bluff, and Raúl gained the higher moral ground at home and abroad.

I tell people that U.S. relations with Cuba resemble a knot in a kid's shoelaces: it will be hard to undo, no matter what. However, as any parent teaches their child, when there is a knot, you first have to loosen the laces to undo it. Pulling them, out of frustration or ignorance, just makes the knot tighter and the task that much more difficult. If you simply snap the laces, then they, and the shoe, become useless.

The Bush administration, despite the total calm and stability that prevailed on the island, apparently believed its own rhetoric—that the Cuban government was about to implode and that a handful of isolated dissidents could somehow move the Cuban masses into action—and pulled the laces still tighter. The day after Castro stepped aside, White House spokesman Tony Snow called Raúl Castro "Fidel's prison-keeper" and later characterized Cuba as a "closed society."[14] Two days into the handover, a senior U.S. government official told the *Miami Herald*: "The mandate from the president is for us to stay focused on helping the Cuban people transition to democracy. That's where the wheels of government . . . are in motion." In other words, the Bush administration would follow the second report from the Commission for a Free Cuba and tighten sanctions, increase support for dissidents and propaganda broadcasts, and carry out whatever was in the report's secret appendix, despite the dramatic change in circumstances. The administration had already established a Cuba Transition Policy Coordinating Committee, cochaired by Caleb McCarry, the State Department's Cuba transition co-ordinator, and Daniel Fisk, the National Security Council's Western Hemisphere director. "There is an interagency process focused on Cuba transition that is under way and that has been in existence before Monday," the senior U.S. government official told the *Miami Herald*. "We've clearly picked up the pace."[15]

The very day Raúl Castro's first statement appeared in *Granma*, U.S. Director of National Intelligence John Negroponte announced the appointment of an acting mission manager for Cuba and Venezuela to collect "timely and accurate intelligence." In its August 18, 2006, statement, Negroponte's office said such efforts to collect intelligence on Cuba and Venezuela are "critical today" because "policy-makers have increasingly focused on the challenges" that the countries "pose to American foreign policy." The Office of the Director said that the new acting mission manager would be "responsible for integrating collection and analysis on Cuba and Venezuela across the intelligence community, identifying and filling gaps in intelligence, and ensuring the implementation of strategies, among other duties." The agency said the U.S. intelligence community now had six mission managers to focus on various policy issues of critical concern to the United States. Besides the acting manager for Cuba and Venezuela, there were mission managers for counter-terrorism, counter-proliferation, counterintelligence, and one each for Iran and North Korea.[16] Not very comfortable company for Havana. A few days later the *Miami Herald*'s Pablo Bachelet, who did an outstanding job covering events from Washington and to whom I am deeply indebted for this chapter, reported that the Bush administration had created five interagency working groups to monitor Cuba.

> The groups, some of which operate in war-room-like settings, were quietly set up after the July 31 announcement that the ailing Cuban leader had temporarily ceded power. . . . Three of the newly created groups are headed by the State Department: diplomatic actions, strategic communications and democratic promotion. Another that coordinates humanitarian aid to Cuba is run by the Commerce Department, and a fifth, on migration issues, is run jointly by the National Security Council and the Department of Homeland Security. Many members of the groups work out of the same State Department office in what one person familiar with the operation described as a "control room."[17]

In October 2006 the Bush administration announced the creation of a new law enforcement task force that would aggressively pursue Cuban American violators of U.S. trade and travel sanctions. U.S. Attorney Alexander Acosta told a news conference in Miami that the task force would coordinate the efforts of officials from several agencies, including the Treasury and Commerce Departments and the Department of Homeland Security. Acosta promised to prosecute the import and export of goods to and from Cuba, transfers of hard currency, and unapproved visits to the Caribbean island. He urged Cuban Americans to inform on each other à la the island's Committees for the Defense of the Revolution.[18]

Exactly a year into Castro's illness, and perhaps frustrated that he was still on this earth, President Bush took an even more militant stance toward the island. Speaking at the U.S. Naval War College, Bush hinted that destabilizing Cuba and breaking those shoelaces was the way to go.

> There's only one non-democracy in our neighborhood; that's Cuba. . . . One day, the good Lord will take Fidel Castro away and then the question is, what will be the approach of the U.S. government? My attitude is that we need to use the opportunity to call the world together to promote democracy as the alternative to the form of government they have been living with. You'll see an interesting debate. Some will say, all that matters is stability, which, in my judgment, will just simply reinforce the followers of the current regime.[19]

President Bush and other members of his administration reiterated their position many times, right through Fidel Castro's resignation and the first months of Raúl Castro's presidency. There were no policy changes on either side of the Florida Straits, no bilateral diplomatic contacts in Havana, and no reduction in tension throughout the Bush administration's final year. Relations were frozen at the zero mark of the diplomatic thermometer. Raúl Castro wooed the Grey Zone; George W. Bush pushed it away. Fidel remained in seclusion, writing and working to regain some of his strength.

Cuba, through its relations with Venezuela and then China, had outflanked the Bush administration's efforts to bring down the government by tightening the embargo and travel restrictions, and a strong, if short-lived, recovery got under way during the U.S. president's second term. Havana also bested Washington in the international arena, and at a breathtaking pace, as Raúl literally routed U.S. efforts to isolate Cuba in the region.

During the summer of 2008, Michael Parmly was replaced by Jonathan Farrar as the head of the U.S. Interests Section, and on August 1, 2008, Farrar sent to Washington this cable, released by Wikileaks, which clearly demonstrates the isolation that resulted from the Bush administration's policies as it prepared to leave Washington.

Connecting with the Cuban people is extremely important, and extremely challenging.

The GOC [Government of Cuba] focuses intensely on isolating USINT [U.S. Interests Section] from Cuban society. The USINT building is isolated by the GOC police guards. There are no idle passers-by: only Cubans with appointments are able to approach the building. Only the most intrepid Cuban could catch a glimpse of the USINT billboard. . . .

The geographic travel limits are debilitating for outreach efforts, and are getting tighter. The recent transfer of an Amcit [American citizen] prisoner from Holguin means that Matanzas, a two hour drive away, is the furthest point for future consular visits.

The challenge for us at USINT is to find new ways to reach out beyond the confines of the USINT building and to reach back to Washington for information from programs that originate there. We must build our support for the democratic opposition while finding new ways to reach out to the broad spectrum of Cuban society.[20]

PART II

Raúl Castro in Power (2008–2009)

7

Conservative Reformers

I would have been happier if they included younger people with new
ideas. They might have a lot of merits, but they have a lot of years.

Ernesto, a Havana University student

Like so much that had happened since Fidel Castro took ill eighteen months
earlier, Sunday, February 24, 2008, proved anticlimactic. Cuba would have a
new president after nearly fifty years, and a new defense minister. For the first
time since the 1960s, the first vice president—the man or woman in line to succeed the president—would not have Castro as a last name, nor would anyone
at the top of the military hierarchy. Journalists arrived from around the world
for the event. Cubans, as usual, appeared to be paying little attention. Fidel
was still very much around, writing his *Reflections*, and there was no doubt that
Raúl would succeed him. Among those who did follow such matters, there
was a great deal of speculation over who would become the first vice president.
Most people put their money on Carlos Lage. He was a relatively young man,
apparently being groomed for the job, and his role for more than a decade as
the highly visible executive secretary of the Council of Ministers in many ways
resembled that of prime minister.

Journalists who gathered that Sunday at the Havana Convention Center
were herded into a room to watch the proceedings on closed-circuit television.
I was working for Thomson Reuters; my job was to find out what was up and
report back to the office before the competition. At the same time, I had a story
for the *Financial Times* ready to go on my laptop, just waiting for a few blanks
to be filled in. And then there were phone interviews with ABC television af-
filiates and radio.

The closed-circuit television signal went dead (of course) right before the
announcement of the names the Politburo proposed for president, first vice
president, and other members of the new Council of State. We got our story,
though. A few photographers had been allowed into the main hall, where the
deputies were gathered, and they heard the list and quickly passed it on. Raúl
Castro was proposed as president, and José Ramón Machado Ventura, even

older at 77, was proposed for first vice president. Four of the other five vice presidents remained the same: Juan Almeida Bosque, 80, a revolutionary commander who had fought with Fidel Castro from the very first days of the Revolution (he died a year later, in 2009); General Abelardo Colomé Ibarra, 68, the interior minister who had worked with the Castro brothers since his teens and earned his stripes in Africa; Carlos Lage, 56, executive secretary of the Council of Ministers; and Esteban Lazo Hernández, 63, a Party leader and ideologue who had come up through the ranks, serving as head of the Party in both Santiago and Havana before being promoted to the national level earlier in the decade. The only new vice president was General Julio Casas Regueiro, 72, a hero of the Angolan war, who was also appointed defense minister that day (he would pass away in September 2011), while Dr. José M. Miyar Barrueco, 75, a longtime aide to Fidel Castro, continued as secretary. Except Lage, there were no new young faces among the top eight positions. Quite the contrary, the lineup was even grayer and more conservative, if that was possible. I was so surprised that I spent thirty minutes confirming the story before Reuters ran with it, and even then I held my *Financial Times* article (could it really be true?!) until the official announcement.

The choice of Machado Ventura (the doctor who had saved Tía Paca's husband when that bomb exploded in his face during the Revolution) was a surprise to every diplomat and Cuba expert I knew, and to every Cuban I knew, as well. No one had predicted that Machado would become the third most powerful man in the land after the Castro brothers. He was a disappointment to young people, many of whom did not know who he was and who had hoped for better representation in the government. "I would have been happier if they included younger people with new ideas. They might have a lot of merits, but they have a lot of years," said Ernesto, lounging on the grass outside Havana University's elegant stone administration building. "It's just the same old story, just more of the same," added his female companion, a twenty-one-year-old economics student. Lage, in fact, received more deputy votes (609) than Machado (601) for a vice presidency spot.[1] How could Ernesto and his companion have known that the most visible young political figures and Fidel Castro protégés—Vice President Carlos Lage and Foreign Minister Felipe Pérez—were under investigation and would soon be stripped of all their posts?

Cuba's "new" Council of State signaled to governments and Cubans that there would be no radical veering from the course Fidel Castro had set over the decades. The powers that be saw the next five years as critical and no time to test younger cadre, whose time would presumably come with the next government. With Fidel fading, they had circled the wagons—12 of the 31 members had participated in the Revolution, and all active Comandantes of the

Revolution were now members. The average age of the top eight positions was over seventy, with just three members under that age. At the same time the new government was tough because the Communist Party planned to radically downsize the government and bureaucracy and lift some onerous restrictions on people's lives. It was conservative and tough to manage the changes within the system that were coming. Thirteen of the members were on the Party Politburo, including all of the top seven.

Raúl's two major promotions—of José Ramón Machado Ventura to first vice president and of General Casas to vice president and defense minister— were made because he trusted them. The two men had been his closest collaborators and friends for many years. Fidel claimed he, not Raúl, put two new military officers on the Council of State because of their tested loyalty and courage in Angola—General Leopoldo Cintra Frías, who succeeded Casas as first deputy defense minister, and General Ramón Espinosa Martín, who moved up to deputy defense minister. Fidel's new role, as very influential behind the scenes and the great legitimizer as the transition unfolded, couldn't have been clearer. He repeatedly endorsed the new government in a series of messages and reflections.[2]

Raúl soon named the same six top state officials as an executive committee of the Communist Party Politburo until the next Party congress. He took the opportunity to declare null and void the provisional organization of government responsibilities outlined by his brother in the proclamation of July 31, 2006.

A Tough Job Ahead

There was no doubt that the new openness and expectations Raúl had fostered during the eighteen months he temporarily filled his brother's big shoes would inevitably lead to some change now that he was president. The big questions were: How profound would the changes be? How quickly would those changes be implemented and where might they lead? The island's inhabitants had raised a myriad of complaints and suggestions during the debate around Raúl's July 26, 2007, speech. They fell into three general categories, according to the various sources involved in compiling them.

First there was the economy, in particular the huge breach between what Cubans earned from the state and the cost of the goods and services that the state then sold to the people, since it was in charge of just about all production and wholesale and retail trade at the time. This was often expressed in anger over Cuba's dual-currency system, with state wages largely paid in pesos and many goods and services sold by the same state in a foreign-exchange equivalent called the "convertible peso" (CUC, for Unit of Convertible Currency), pegged by the government at U.S. $1.08 or 24 pesos per CUC at its exchange offices in 2008.

In some respects Cuba resembled the old mining towns of the United States, where the mine owner also owned the only store for miles around and workers found themselves always in debt to the boss, as their wages never seemed to cover what they owed at the company store. A bottle of cooking oil sold for more than 2 convertible pesos, equivalent to 48 pesos or more than three days' work at the average wage. An apple or a bar of poor-quality soap cost 50 cents, close to a day's pay. Peso prices at farmers' and government-run produce markets also came under fire: a pound of pork cost more than a day's pay, and it would take hours of work to buy a pound of beans or rice, a head of garlic, a cucumber, a single mango, or a few onions or tomatoes. My wife, who earned around 500 pesos per month, came home from the produce market in tears more than once. She had plenty of money, thanks to my income, but she empathized with those who didn't and who faced truly exorbitant prices relative to what they earned—and vendors quick to fix the scales to their own advantage.

The government said the high prices at foreign-exchange outlets (a minimum 240 percent markup!) were to redistribute the wealth of those who could afford to shop in them to those who could not. Officials often pointed out that health care and education were free, state employees paid no taxes, and most people paid no rent, property tax, or insurance. They also received a subsidized food ration, got subsidized meals at work and school, and paid next to nothing for utilities and transportation. But these truths had long since worn thin; a good portion of the population was accustomed to them and believed they nevertheless deserved a living wage. They felt entitled to the consumer goods on display at the hard-currency stores, in the hotels, or seen in Miami or brought by visiting relatives. "Nobody remembers what they receive in subsidies and work incentives; they only calculate their monthly wage and that calculation is a bad one," Raúl Castro lamented in an interview with state-run television, marking the Revolution's fiftieth anniversary in December 2008.[3]

The second area of concern was the deterioration of those free health and education services, in large part because so many professionals were either leaving the country, migrating to more lucrative sectors such as tourism, or simply dropping out of the labor force to make a better living in the informal economy. Many doctors and health care providers were also on government missions in Venezuela and other countries, where they often earned far more than their peers at home.[4] For those who stayed, the long hours, low pay, and restrictions on travel meant that fewer top students were interested in going into medicine. Standards for entering medical school or pedagogical training declined as some of the best and brightest of Cuban youth began choosing other careers and countries. Fidel Castro, as part of the Battle of Ideas, had filled the classrooms with hastily trained high-school dropouts and video and television classes, and the hospitals with similarly semi-qualified nurses and technicians. That same approach had worked well in the 1960s when most doctors left the country and education became universal and free, but Cubans were now far healthier and better informed. Their expectations had grown by leaps and bounds. People complained these young people were often not up to their new jobs, set bad examples, and were ill mannered.

Some of Cuba's best educators were spread out across the region and the planet, conducting literacy and post-literacy campaigns. Fewer people signed up to clean the hospitals, clinics, and schools, where supplies were short and the pay even shorter. I knew a heart surgeon who made cakes on the weekends and another doctor who sold car paint from Canada between operations. I knew a teacher who made and sold pizzas and another who left the school system to tutor at home. Doctors relied on patients' gifts, and sold them to survive. Nurses began caring for the better-off at home, and dentists engaged in private practice in clinics after hours or in their homes, using stolen tools and supplies.

The other areas, more or less related, that came up in the debate involved government inefficiency, excessive bureaucracy, and onerous regulation of daily life, all of which fostered corruption. Examples were the state's domination of food distribution, which often resulted in waste, and its penchant to sit on fallow land. There were regulations banning Cubans from tourist hotels or from purchasing cell-phone service; restrictions on travel, family businesses, Internet access, satellite TV, and sales of homes and cars. The housing department was perhaps the best example: expanding one's dwelling, building a new one, or trading homes required multiple authorizations and years of waiting because it was illegal to buy or sell one's abode or rent a living unit without authorization, although by the mid-1990s it had become common practice. "I went to the municipal housing authority for final approval of my house. The local director told me flat-out that I had two choices: wait two years, or pay him six hundred CUC," Anna, a close friend, fumed in 2009 just hours after the encounter. Anna made the equivalent of just a few CUC a month and had no relatives abroad to help her out. Her boyfriend's family ended up paying the bribe.

Public criticism reached a crescendo, and perhaps crossed the line for some officials when, in April 2008, the Union of Writers and Artists of Cuba (UNEAC) held a congress and issued a critique of society that was unprecedented since the earliest years of the Revolution. Raúl had just become Cuba's new president and had begun making changes—although the Bush administration would continue to assert that reforms under Raúl were a "cruel joke" and deny visas to Cuban intellectuals and cultural figures. The congress was a sign of the times. The vanguard of the Grey Zone, Cubans who wanted change within the socialist system, did not mince words: "We must prepare for the new future of our country," the Communist Party newspaper *Granma* headlined, above historian Eusebio Leal's speech at the meeting. "We are all hopeful. Why? Because the country indeed assumes that what until yesterday was not convenient or prudent is necessary today," said Leal, one of the country's most respected intellectuals, who became famous at home and abroad for his work restoring Colonial Havana. Leal, known to be close to Cardinal Jaime Ortega and the Castro brothers, pulled out a cell phone and praised a recent measure allowing ordinary Cubans to have them. State television later broadcast the speech. "Every day, the news that reach us are encouraging. . . . At issue are things as profound as what in 1959—and even before—my generation saw as the highest aspiration: justice for the farmers, the men of the land," Leal said. The main reports at the congress denounced government efforts to block Internet access and satellite television, expressed alarm over the deterioration of education, and railed at the state's bureaucratic treatment of artists and writers.[5]

The artists and writers meeting forced me to rethink my view that the discussion and debate opened by Raúl Castro was not that different from previous ones in the early 1990s and 1980s. The previous grassroots discussions were always led by Fidel Castro, and the media focused on his criticisms. This one was much broader and bolder. The media focus was on the words of others, and there was no sign it would be cut off anytime soon. The discussion included new issues such as the status of Cubans abroad, restrictions on thought and information, and recent pet projects of Fidel himself, mainly in education, all amply covered by the media.

Fidel's Legacy

But I am getting ahead of myself. The situation left by half a century of Fidel's rule was far from desperate by area standards when Raúl officially took over—despite the longest and most comprehensive U.S. sanctions ever imposed on another country and the fall of the Soviet bloc—although high expectations, combined with low pay and day-to-day shortages and bureaucratic abuse, sometimes made it appear that way. The United Nations ranked Cuba 51st out of 177 countries for overall human development, based on official data up to 2005. Cuba came in ahead of all Caribbean and Central American countries except the Bahamas and Costa Rica, and ahead of all of the rest of the Latin American region except for Argentina, Uruguay, and Chile. The Dominican

Republic placed 79th and Jamaica 101st.[6] Transparency International, the world's leading corruption-fighting NGO, ranked Cuba 65th out of 180 countries in its 2008 Corruption Perceptions Index, ahead of all but eight nations in the region: Saint Lucia, Barbados, Chile, Uruguay, Saint Vincent and the Grenadines, Dominica, Puerto Rico, and Costa Rica.[7] Cuba continued to provide far more aid to other poor countries, in the form of medical, educational, and other technical assistance, than any other midsized developing country on the planet. At the same time, it ranked near the bottom of all indices measuring civil liberties, communications, and access to information.

Raúl Castro's acceptance speech on February 24, 2008, like his eighteen-month tenure as provisional president, generated hope for economic reform and better times to come.

> The country's priority will be to meet the basic needs of the population, both material and spiritual, based on the sustained strengthening of the national economy and its productive bases. . . . To produce more and to offer better services, we must make efforts to find the ways and means to remove any deterrent to the productive forces. . . . In many respects, local initiative can be effective and viable.

On excessive and onerous regulation of daily life, Castro pledged, "In December, I referred to the excess of prohibitions and regulations, and in the next few weeks we shall start removing the most simple of them," adding that the more complicated ones would follow sometime in the future. Cuba's new president made it clear that he heard popular complaints about bureaucracy: he promised to downsize the government and "reduce the enormous number of meetings, coordination, permissions, conciliations, provisions, rules and regulations, et cetera, et cetera." Raúl also pledged to continue fostering discussion. "There is no reason to fear discrepancies in a society such as ours. . . . The best solutions can come from a profound exchange of differing opinions, if such an exchange is guided by sensible purposes and the views are uttered with responsibility," he said.[8]

8

Computers, Cell Phones, Hotels, and More

This shows there is a change in the mentality at the top and recognition that Cuba has to move into the twenty-first century.

Eduardo, a communications engineer

Raúl Castro had differentiated himself from Fidel since the very beginning in 2006, even as he wrapped every word and measure in his brother's rhetoric and hailed him in every speech. The Castro brothers understood that, with Fidel more or less out of commission, they could no longer ignore their steady loss of command and control of the system and growing public frustration over regulation, bureaucracy, low wages, waste, and the semi-paralysis of economic activity. Fidel had approached the problem in his unique manner, Raúl in a very different fashion, but each—at least publicly—backed the other, as was their custom for more than half a century. Raúl now needed to signal quickly to the population that his words were not just rhetoric and that the public discussion he orchestrated was more than just a show, even as his aides tried to figure out how to get the country out of the multiple binds that gripped it from top to bottom.

One of my better Cuban sources handed me an internal memo from the CIMEX Corporation just a few weeks after Raúl's inauguration. CIMEX was a billion-dollar import-export company that ran hundreds of foreign-exchange stores and other businesses in the country. The document informed managers that computers and other electronic consumer goods were no longer banned from sale to the public. A document should be enough for a story, but in Cuba I felt I always needed at least one confirmation, if not two, when the information was not in the public domain. I confirmed the news through a friend who worked at a CIMEX department store. The next day I sat down to write. I messaged Mike Christie, then head of Thomson Reuters's Miami bureau, which oversaw Havana, suggesting it be put on the daily sked, or list of top stories—each with its lead paragraph and when to expect it—sent to editors and other clients so they could plan their day's work. To Mike's credit, he immediately responded that this was no ordinary story but Raúl's first measure and that it should go out as a flash and urgent. Bells rang around the world on Thomson Reuters terminals signaling clients there was an exceptional story going out on the wire that otherwise might be lost among the thousands produced every day.

The development of information technology has led to massive amounts of instant and often free news and fierce competition for clients. Wire services flash breaking news in red capital letters, usually just one line, and Thomson Reuters follows within minutes with a few paragraphs as an "URGENT." Then come six to eight paragraphs and, within an hour or so, the entire story, which is updated through the day and night as the news unfolds, and that is what one reads in the daily newspapers and on the Internet. "EXCLUSIVE" precedes the headline on the wire if the competition simply does not have the story.

EXCLUSIVE—Cuba lifts ban on computer, DVD player sales

March 13, 2008 (Reuters)—Communist Cuba has authorized the un-restricted sale of computers and DVD and video players in the first sign that its new president, Raúl Castro, is moving to improve Cubans' access to consumer goods . . .

The first official indication that the government understood that the times were changing came a few days after computer sales were authorized: telecom-munications monopoly ETECSA (a joint venture at the time with Telecom Italia) announced it would begin offering mobile phone service to the general public, although only in convertible pesos.[1] Cuba was just about the last coun-try in the world to embrace mobile phones, and its rates remain perhaps the most expensive on the planet compared with per capita earnings.[2] "This shows there is a change in the mentality at the top and recognition that Cuba has to move into the twenty-first century," said Eduardo, a Havana computer techni-cian and information technology engineer. Within a few years, more than 1.5 million mobile phones roamed Cuba's streets, with built-in cameras flashing but no Internet connectivity.

You can't win them all, and I soon blew a second scoop (and the bonus and praise that would have come with it). A friend of Marlene's, who managed a rent-a-car agency, called at around 10 p.m. on March 30, 2008, to let us know that, beginning at midnight, Cubans would be able to rent cars. I had had one whiskey too many that evening and, half asleep, told Marlene I would write it up the following morning. An hour later another friend, a hotel bartender, called my wife to say that, starting the following day, Cubans would be allowed to book rooms in tourist hotels. Given my lack of interest in the rent-a-car news, Marlene, who was deputy head of nursing at a Havana hospital and not a reporter, did not bother to wake me. By the time I got up the next morning, the story was all over the Internet. We had to settle for second or perhaps third place among the news agencies.

These changes captured headlines around the world, as they indicated some loosening of the state's control over communications and people's consumerism and intimated that Cubans would no longer be treated in some instances as second-class citizens in their own country, while other measures soon adopted and of equal, if not greater, importance for many islanders received less attention abroad.

The most far-reaching reform begun by Raúl Castro that first year was in agriculture: he decentralized some decision making; allowed private farmers a bit more space to sell produce directly and buy supplies, bypassing the state; raised the prices the state paid for most produce, meat, cheese, milk, pork, and so on; and began a massive redistribution of fallow state land to tens of thousands of individuals and cooperatives.

With the 1959 revolution and land reform, large landowners had been stripped of their property—Fidel's father's estate was the first to be confiscated—and private holdings of no more than 6.5 hectares (16 acres) were allowed. Hundreds of thousands of former farm workers were given plots. But, unlike other socialist countries, the state kept most of the land for itself. Some 70 percent of the land in Cuba is owned by the state, making it the largest unproductive landowner in Latin America when Raúl took over. *Opciones*, the official business weekly, reported in 2007 that "marabú and other weeds have become a plague in Cuba" that covered one-third of the 3.6 million hectares (9 million acres) of arable land.

Just a few days after the story broke about computers, DVDs, and domestic appliances, another source said farmers would be able to shop for some of their more rudimentary supplies such as work clothes, machetes, and fencing for the first time since the 1960s, instead of having them assigned by the state. I had more than a few good contacts among farmers, thanks to my many trips around the country. I spent two days fleshing out the story, and the bells rang again.

One story sometimes leads to another and, while confirming that stores were indeed opening in the countryside, I learned that something far more important was taking place: the government was decentralizing the state-dominated agriculture sector. At meetings across Cuba, farmers were told that decisions on issues ranging from land use to resource allocation and sales would no longer be made at the seventeen-story Agriculture Ministry in Havana, but at the local level. In addition, local municipal offices would be streamlined and were ordered to take the activities of private farmers and cooperatives into consideration on an equal footing with state farms. "They are moving decision making closer to the producers and recognizing that the private sector, with just a fraction of the land, produces 70 percent of our produce," a local agriculture expert said. The head of an agricultural cooperative in central Camagüey Province said that, under the new structure, he would only have to go to one office to take care of problems, instead of many, and officials would no longer be able simply to shrug their shoulders and say that there was no local solution and one must wait for a provincial or national government response. "The local office did little more than send our problems up the line, because it had no resources or power to solve practically anything," the cooperative chief said. "What's happening is what the farmers themselves proposed during Raúl's debate, and we feel they have listened and are responding."

Farmers soon said the government was offering them more land. Within a year, around 100,000 people would be leased plots to farm, amounting to more than a million acres of previously fallow state land.[3] The government would soon announce that housing construction was heading in the same direction: from Havana to the local level and increasingly into private hands.[4] Then domestic freight transportation was restructured and local trucking was taken over by the municipalities and provinces.[5]

Education

When people ask me about Cuba's universal and free health care and education, I use cheese as an analogy. Health and education used to be, say, a French Brie or a Camembert, but after two decades of crises they are now Swiss cheese— still absolutely delicious by developing-world standards, but with lots of holes.

Cubans raised hell during the 2007 debate over what they believed was a marked deterioration in health care and education, even though the United Nations rated the country first in the Latin American region.[6] Parents were upset about the increasing use of television classes and high-school-age teachers in elementary and junior high schools, and the need to pay teachers on the side to tutor students ahead of entrance exams for high school and college. Parents in big cities, in particular Havana, grew increasingly worried and angry that there were no longer any local high schools. They were forced to send high-school-age children to boarding schools in the countryside, where the basics (lights, water, decent meals, and adequate supervision) were no longer guaranteed and the lack of public transportation and the high cost of gasoline made visiting difficult. Some parents I knew opted to send their teenagers, especially girls, to local vocational schools instead of high school, despite what that implied for their futures.

"Can primary, secondary and prep schools properly educate children and adolescents and thus lay the foundation for the future as they are at present, governed by misconceived criteria and practices that ignore elementary pedagogical and psychological principles and violate family rights?" Alfredo Guevara, one of Cuba's best-known intellectuals and founder of Cuba's film institute in 1959, asked in a speech at the 7th Congress of the Union of Writers and Artists in April 2008. "Sound solutions cannot be built on the basis of dogmas, obstinacy, lack of knowledge of reality, or ignoring the warning messages provided by experience and coming from the people," Guevara said.[7]

Raúl's first cabinet change came only a few weeks after he took office, when Luis Ignacio Gómez, education minister for nearly two decades, was replaced by Ana Elsa Velázquez, a well-known pedagogue from Santiago de Cuba. Velázquez soon announced that there would be increased training and supervision of the young teacher-volunteers involved in Fidel Castro's program to improve education as part of his Battle of Ideas. Soon after, though, the entire program was scrapped. A year later, plans were unveiled to close the high schools in the countryside in favor of prep schools in the cities and revamp curricula to emphasize language skills and history. The high schools had always been held up by Fidel Castro as one of the revolution's most significant accomplishments, based on José Martí's axiom of combining education and work. His brother insisted they were shut down for budgetary, not ideological, reasons. New emphasis was placed on vocational schools and hard science versus liberal arts, and the courses offered by university municipal extension programs were revamped in the same direction because the government insisted that someone had to work on the land, in the factories, and in the skilled trades. Raúl called on retired teachers and those who had left (either for greener pastures or because of disagreements with policy imposed upon them) to return and teach the "new teachers" how to teach. Salaries were raised repeatedly across the board, from teachers to maintenance workers. Higher standards ensued to get into college, and once you were accepted, grading became much tougher. The number of university spots was cut almost 50 percent between 2008 and 2013, mainly in the humanities.[8]

My American daughter and Cuban stepdaughter traversed the Cuban school system from preschool through university. The core of the system, elementary school, proved remarkable indeed, even at the depths of the post-Soviet crisis (and despite the need to regularly delouse the girls). Their teachers were examples of dedication, professionalism, and concern even in the hardest of times, and the curriculum was more than adequate. There was little propaganda beyond the pledge to the flag, the Revolution, and its heroes—in particular José Martí, Che Guevara, and Camilo Cienfuegos, with Fidel Castro and his brother sneaking in through history lessons and current events—and

I liked the values the system promoted, which were similar to those of all religions: love thy neighbor, give to the less fortunate, do unto others, and so on. Besides, as I have learned in Cuba, schools can never replace the politics, the culture, and the values passed on in the family through example and daily life—no matter how hard a state may try.

Junior high was a different matter, as the 1990s drew to a close. Teachers sometimes went missing for entire semesters, along with some of the maintenance staff. I was able to fill in the holes with tutors, and my kids had access to the Internet, unlike their peers. The girls worked very hard. They were at the top of their classes and scored well on high school entrance exams. They attended the applied science high school called the Lenin, a model boarding school on Havana's outskirts where both flourished, even though they had very different personalities and interests.[9] High school students in Cuba pick their careers before attending university—be it education, economics, the hard sciences, law, or medicine—and compete for places available based on grade point average and exam scores. Dhara and Ivet studied hard for their university entrance exams. Both girls escaped by a year or two the major and often controversial changes in education under Fidel Castro's Battle of Ideas, such as teachers who provided classes in many different subjects and who followed their students through the junior high years or through high school.

Health Care

Less than a month into Raúl's presidency, the government announced it would close more than half of Cuba's family-doctor offices and boost staffing at the rest, as a major reform of Cuba's much vaunted health-care system began. During the debate the previous year, Cubans had complained that the family-doctor program had been short on staff ever since the government began sending thousands of doctors to Venezuela in 2000, and many hospitals and clinics were dirty and in disrepair and their staffs at times inattentive. Doctors, they said, sometimes paid more attention to patients bearing gifts. The new plan called for fewer family doctors, but it required that most family-doctor offices be staffed by a doctor and nurse the entire day, instead of just in the mornings. Under the new plan, the staffs at local clinics were increased to pick up the slack, although services had already been augmented under the Battle of Ideas to serve local communities better and ease pressure on hospitals. Most medical-school students now do a fifth-year residency in general medicine at a family-doctor office, then two more years of social service as family doctors before going on to further specialization.

Cuba's family-doctor program began with much fanfare in the 1980s with a doctor-and-nurse team for every 500 to 700 residents, coordinated by larger community-based clinics. The facilities were combination home-offices, designed so that the doctors would live in the community. The family doctors and nurses were given the task of preventing illness and taking pressure off the clinics and hospitals by getting to know every family under their care, searching out community health problems such as local pollutants, and identifying individual health problems early on for treatment or referral to specialists, as for example people at risk for developing diabetes or heart disease, STDs, or early pregnancy. The offices were open in the morning and closed in the afternoon so the doctors and nurses could make house calls (although people sometimes complained in those days that the family doctors disappeared on personal business). Now each family-doctor office covers up to three times as many residents, between 1,500 and 2,000.

In November 2008 I was at my friend Eduardo Machin's home, located in one of the high-rise apartment complexes in Nuevo Vedado, an area built up after the Revolution near Communist Party and government headquarters. An elderly woman came by, complaining that her family doctor had disappeared on a government mission abroad and now what was she to do? Machin walked her to the window, pointed a few blocks away and said, "What is that?"

"The health clinic," she replied.

"And that?" he asked, pointing to a complex of buildings a bit further on.

"The hospital," she said.

"And how many doctors and nurses do you know who live in this building?" he asked.

"Oh, lots," the lady replied, adding that many of them were friends.

Machin pointed out to his neighbor that she had hardly been left to fend for herself with the departure of her family doctor, and besides, there were half a dozen family-doctor home-offices within a few blocks in the densely populated area. Cuban health care professionals rarely, if ever, refuse care to anyone, especially neighbors, children, and the elderly, because all health care is free, there are no malpractice suits, there are so many doctors and nurses, and they are all paid a salary, rather than getting paid for each service they provide. My wife spent a great deal of her spare time helping family, friends, and neighbors, and I joked that my car had been converted into an ambulance as we drove people around Havana in search of solutions to whatever ailed them.

The situation was more difficult in the countryside, where the population was spread out, as were the health services, and there was little transportation. A friend ran a clinic that supervised a few dozen family doctors in Camagüey. She said that at one point, before the reorganization, 80 percent of the family doctor slots were vacant and that she and others made trips to the countryside to take up the slack as best they could.

In July 2008, two years after Fidel's first operation and ceding of power, I wrote the following analysis to my clients:

> The Cuban leadership's finesse in managing the situation has been much like a team running a crucial play in a football game. It is, after all, a life-and-death affair for them. The opposing team and spectators are still not sure where the ball is and what exactly the quarterback is up to. The hand-off, from the government's perspective, has come off without a hitch while the play continues. The secrecy around Fidel is crucial for the play to work. It empowers those in the know and keeps everyone else off balance. That they have kept the secrets of the kingdom in the face of foreign intelligence services' efforts reveals its importance and is quite amazing. So what has changed over these two years?
>
> THE FOCUS: What's most significant is the leadership's change in focus. From blaming the outside world to looking within for answers; from blaming the new rich within to blaming the bureaucracy, in effect the system; from marching hard and chanting anti-U.S. slogans to working hard and debating domestic issues; from demanding unity to criticizing unanimity; from praising equalitarianism to praising reward for individual initiative; from imposing restriction after restriction to lifting some; from "the state can do everything" to "we need a strong private sector, at least in agriculture"; from control of all decisions at the national level to granting more say at the provincial and municipal levels.
>
> THE STYLE: Raúl Castro projects a very different style than Fidel. He is discreet, not a showman; calm, not emotional; single-minded versus all over the place; disciplined and into follow-up, not jumping from one project to the other; concrete, not abstract. What he says, he does; there are no big surprises or shifts in direction. He needs and wants order and accountability, not chaos and reverence. He delegates.
>
> DOMESTIC POLICY: The strategic aim is to improve, not dismantle or erode the one-party political system and state-run economy. Raúl wants to make it all work better and become more user-friendly. The official political model is unchanged. Raúl is strengthening the Party, not manipulating a military takeover, but with more participation from others and perhaps with more grassroots participation and debate than in the past. State-run companies are to be perfected, made more autonomous in day-to-day decision making and more accountable, not privatized or joint-ventured out. This does not exclude more private initiative

around the edges in agriculture, the trades, and the retail sector, nor joint ventures when there is no choice, as in oil exploration or the building of a new port in Mariel.

FOREIGN POLICY: There is an important change in the style of Cuba's foreign policy under Raúl, though it is doubtful the brothers have major differences on grand strategy. First, it is more stable, there are no more sudden reversals or crisis as there were under Fidel. It is less provocative and confrontational, including with the United States. Second, Raúl appears ready to make some minor concessions, such as signing some international human rights agreements. Cuba's foreign policy continues to prioritize Venezuela, Latin America, China and Russia, and target the United States and European Union, while going softly with Japan and Canada. At the same time Havana's support for developing countries and solidarity work has not slowed.

9

Disaster, Man-Made and Natural

The combined action of Hurricanes Gustav and Ike ... unquestionably made them the most destructive in the history of these meteorological phenomena in Cuba.

Government report on the 2008 storms

As Raúl Castro raised expectations of better times to come and cautiously tweaked and decentralized the state-run economy, world events began to undermine his rhetoric and swamp his agenda. International prices of food and fuel, two key imports, soared by the middle of 2008, and the price of nickel, the most important commodity export, imploded. The government would report that Cuba's terms of trade (the prices of exports compared with imports) deteriorated by a staggering 38 percent in 2008.[1] Put another way, it would have taken 38 percent more exports in 2008 to purchase the same amount of goods and services Cuba imported in 2007. The first signs of the global financial crisis appeared, followed by the economic slowdown in many countries. Credit tightened and tourism slowed. Cuban vice president Carlos Lage broke the news to municipal government leaders in June 2008, in a speech published by the *Juventud Rebelde* newspaper. Hard work and greater efficiency could dampen the impact of the international trends that Cuba could not escape, Lage said, charging that "the blind laws of the market have turned the world economy into a casino." He reported the bad news that "due to the economic impact of rising fuel and food prices, and practically everything we import . . . some of the main investment projects have been reduced and further cuts will be necessary." At the time, Cuba was importing more than 50 percent of its minimum fuel requirements and 60 to 70 percent of the food it consumed. "The country spent $1.47 billion last year to import 3.423 million metric tons of food, and to import the same amount this year at current prices will cost $2.554 billion—a billion dollars more," Lage said. "The 158,000 barrels of oil per day that we consumed last year cost $8.7 million per day and this year cost 32 percent more, or $11.6 million per day."[2]

What Lage didn't say was that the price of fuel imported from Venezuela was tied to the price of technical assistance exported to the South American country, mitigating the impact of rising prices, while much of the domestic oil output was produced in conjunction with foreign companies that sold their share of output to Cuba at market prices.

Raúl began to mute his promises and warn that international events were closing in. His speech on July 26, 2008, was somber indeed compared with the previous year, and no new initiatives were announced. Instead, he told 10,000 people gathered at the Moncada army-barracks-turned-elementary-school, in the eastern city of Santiago de Cuba: "The Revolution has done and will continue to do what it can to keep advancing and reduce the inevitable consequences of the current international crisis. . . . [people] have to get accustomed to not receiving only good news."[3]

Just a month later, on August 30, Hurricane Gustav, a category 4 storm, passed directly over the Isla de la Juventud off Cuba's southwest coast and then plowed through westernmost Pinar del Río, at the Havana Province border. The hurricane, with an eye that was 40 kilometers (25 miles) wide, literally blew apart concrete buildings. A national record for hurricane winds—212 miles (340 kilometers) per hour—was registered on the Isla de la Juventud, before the recording instrument was blown away.[4] Gustav damaged just about everything on that island, home to 86,000 people, and in its path across Pinar del Río Province. The destruction was catastrophic, but limited in breadth.

Eight days after Gustav, category 3 Ike smashed into Holguín Province on Cuba's northeast coast, then churned through Las Tunas and Camagüey. Moving west just off the south central coast as a category 1 storm, Ike skirted the north coast of the Isla de la Juventud and crossed Pinar del Río into the Gulf of Mexico almost exactly where Gustav had. Ike was a huge and slow-moving hurricane and, unlike Gustav, brought heavy rains that lasted up to thirty-six hours, causing extensive flooding. The two hurricanes killed around four hundred people in the Caribbean and the United States, including seven in Cuba by Ike.

Ike was the most powerful storm ever to make landfall at Holguín, the heart of the nickel industry, a key sugar producer, and Cuba's fourth international tourism destination. And two storms within an eight-day period was also a first for Cuba, where hurricanes hit on average every other year (165 in the last three centuries). Still another storm, Paloma, caused additional, comparatively minor damage along the southern coast, in the $300 million range, before the hurricane season ended. The country, and Raúl's plans and promises, lay in ruins. The government's initial damage report stated:

Very preliminary assessments of the damage caused in the less than 10 days during which the two hurricanes impacted national territory place total losses at around five billion dollars [this was later raised to $10 billion]. Unquestionably, one of the most calamitous effects of Gustav and Ike was on housing: more than 444,000 homes damaged, a large number of them with partially or totally destroyed roofs and other impacts; and of that total, 63,249 houses completely demolished.[5]

At that very moment, Lehman Brothers went bankrupt and the international financial crisis exploded.

Raúl Castro toured the Isla de la Juventud and Pinar del Río the week after Ike and close to three weeks after Gustav. In Pinar del Río, Castro said it would now be years before the dual-currency system was abolished and insisted state salaries needed to increase, but only as productivity improved.

A month later, electricity and communications were restored to most of the country, and school was back in session (often in people's homes), but less than 20 percent of damaged housing was repaired and 180,000 people remained in shelters.[6] Fruit, vegetables, and eggs were hard to find after the hurricanes wiped out crops and poultry farms. The government diverted produce from areas spared the storms' wrath to those that suffered the most, and tapped food reserves to bolster the monthly food ration in those areas as well; It also cracked down on black-market food sales and increased imports to make sure no one went hungry. Cubans say the monthly ration usually provides enough basic food to get through no more than two weeks and must be supplemented with purchases at the farmers' markets, at state peso and foreign-exchange stores, and on the black market. The government slapped price controls on staples and limits on how many pounds of rice, for example, an individual could purchase. The government reported that sales at produce markets dropped an astonishing 80 percent in September through mid-December. Illegal but quasi-tolerated street vendors disappeared across the country. A survey of major cities and the hardest-hit provinces found that supplies of vegetables and fruits had dried up, even in the usually well-supplied black market. But starches and proteins could still be found with an effort. "The problem is, you have to be at the markets when something comes in, because supply is erratic," said Carlos Peña, a state worker in Holguín Province.

The fiftieth anniversary of the Revolution loomed on January 1, 2009, but it was no time to celebrate. Plans were scaled down to just an hour-long official ceremony, with no foreign dignitaries. "Our plans to stage a big extravaganza complete with a military parade were scrapped after the hurricanes, in favor of a more austere celebration in tune with the times," said one official involved in organizing the main event in Santiago de Cuba.

I had bet fellow journalists that Fidel Castro would put in an appearance, at least on television, to mark such an important date. This time I lost. January 1 came and went with nothing more than a sixteen-word note from Fidel congratulating "our heroic people," and a short, somber but defiant, televised evening speech delivered by Raúl before 3,000 people. "We have resisted for fifty years and are ready if needed to resist another and another," he said.

A phone survey found that most Cubans had managed to obtain the pork, rice, beans, and *vianda* (roots and tubers: yuca, malanga, sweet potato, plantain, potato) for the traditional family dinner on New Year's Eve. Havana's streets were all but deserted for the 21-gun salute to the New Year from the old Spanish fort, La Cabaña, overlooking the city, but on January 1, 2009, there were outdoor concerts and street parties in every municipality. Dinner-table cheer centered less on the Revolution's fiftieth anniversary than on the end of George Bush's presidency. His time in office had proved extremely painful for the average Cuban family with relatives in the United States, as he tightened visiting rules and restricted remittances and other support. There was also U.S. president-elect Barack Obama's pledge to review Cuba policy and lift the Bush-era family meddling, and Raúl Castro's recent promise to swap "gesture for gesture" with the new U.S. administration. The Cubans clicked their glasses—*ching-ching*—in hopes that an end to their remarkable and often excruciating half-century standoff with their all-powerful next-door neighbor was in sight. *Ojalá*, or "if it could only come true," they seemed to say in unison.

10

Obamamania

Obama is somebody we can talk to anywhere he wishes since we do not
preach violence or war. He should be reminded, though, that the stick and
carrot doctrine will have no place in our country.

Fidel Castro

The world tuned in to the United States as polls began closing on November 4,
2008, and Cuba was no exception. The scene in Havana was about as bizarre as
it gets. The annual international trade fair was under way, and U.S. politicians
and businessmen were in town drumming up agricultural sales under the 2000
exception to the U.S. embargo that made their country the island's fifth largest
trading partner at more than $700 million that year, despite the Bush adminis-
tration's hostility. The Americans were camped out to watch the returns at the
famous Hotel Nacional, where Meyer Lansky and Charles "Lucky" Luciano
once lived and the mob gathered for conferences. The U.S. government had
invited dissidents to the chief of the U.S. Interests Section's residence, where
they would be given the chance to participate in a mock vote to protest the lack
of democracy on the island. The remaining 11.2 million Cubans followed the
election returns as best they could by talking to relatives in the United States,
listening to shortwave radio, and staying in contact with family and friends
who had Internet access or worked at tourism establishments tuned to CNN.

My own first stop was the Hotel Nacional, where a delegation of officials
and businessmen from Georgia, led by Agriculture Commissioner Tommy Irvin, was holding a reception. The state of Georgia went for John McCain, and
although returns were still coming in, the mood was somber and Commissioner Irvin, a tall and lanky old-time southern politician of around seventy,
was in a dour mood. I asked Irvin how his trip was going, and he scowled.
"Fine." I asked him if he was for Obama or McCain, and he replied "McCain,"
barely holding back the "you idiot" from his thin, tight lips. I asked him how
that squared with trading with Cuba, and he said, "Just look around you: there
is plenty of trade with Bush and more will come with McCain." He strolled off
across the room to chat with four or five other somber-looking fellows in suits,
holding cocktail glasses and munching on canapés.

I was soon driving across town to the U.S. Interests Section chief's residence, where the police, as usual, were making life difficult by forcing guests to park a good fifteen minutes' walk away, a practice begun as relations deteriorated under President Bush. The U.S. government still owns a beautiful mansion in the diplomatic enclave called Cubanacán, on the western outskirts of Havana, complete with a swimming pool, tennis courts, and an elevator to the second floor, reportedly installed for Harry Truman. The sprawling backyard and garden feature a huge bronze American eagle that was toppled by a hurricane from a Havana monument to the victims of the battleship *Maine*, whose fates— when the ship blew up just off Havana Bay—led to U.S. intervention and the end of Spanish rule. The head of a second eagle erected atop the monument after the storm, and somehow rescued when it fell victim to the first days of Fidel Castro's Revolution, presides over the Interests Section's Eagle Bar. The mansion was the residence of U.S. ambassadors until diplomatic relations broke off in 1961, and it once more became the residence of the top U.S. diplomat on the island, the chief of the Interests Section, after the lower-level diplomatic rapprochement was accomplished under President Carter in 1977.

Some 150 dissidents, accompanied by a few dozen U.S. and other Western and Eastern European diplomats, had gathered at the residence on election night to drink, eat, and watch the returns. The "exercise in democracy," as U.S. diplomats billed it, had begun with the previous presidential election, when Castro's opponents overwhelmingly "voted" for then-president Bush. Pictures were soon splashed across the Cuban media of dissidents placing their symbolic ballots in the voting box for perhaps the most unpopular U.S. head of state in Cuban history. The event proved a no-brainer for Cuban government propagandists, who painted all opponents as U.S. mercenaries who represented no one. This time around, no cameras were allowed as the dissidents "voted" for John McCain. Their "vote" was again featured in the state-run media a few days later, this time without graphics.[1]

I left the residence sometime around 11 p.m. to watch the returns with Cuban staff at the Comodoro Hotel, another piece of mob-owned Havana real estate before the Revolution. The scene at the Comodoro bar, where a group of a dozen employees and a lone hooker had gathered to watch CNN, was very different from the one I had left at the U.S. residence. Everyone except the hooker was young to middle-aged, and mulatto to black, and the pride of both the men and the women was unmistakable. Hope glittered in their eyes as they watched the victorious Obamas proclaim victory in Chicago. They asked me if this meant that fifty years of hostility would end and that big-tipping Americans would soon arrive. I said I wouldn't be surprised. I asked them whether they were so enthusiastic about Obama because he was African American, young, intelligent, progressive, or just not George W. Bush. Their reply: "All of the above." The hooker, in her late thirties, sat down at my table to join the conversation and hit me up for at least one drink. I obliged, and she beamed and toasted Obama, "To a brand new day."

I have no doubt most Cubans felt the same way as those gathered at the Comodoro bar, while their "future leaders" who voted for McCain at the U.S. residence obviously did not, and their current leaders no doubt understood that they faced a completely new situation after their fifty-year standoff with Washington, and a unique, if daunting, challenge in Barack Obama.

On election eve a still all-but-invisible Fidel Castro weighed in with one of his reflections, repeatedly broadcast on state-run television and radio, which set the tone for the coming months.

> Tomorrow will be of great significance. The world will be following the elections in the United States. It is the most powerful nation on Earth. . . . He [Obama] supports the system and will be supported by it. The pressing problems of the world are not really a major source of concern for Obama.[2]

Fidel Castro would set to work trying to dampen his people's expectations, even as Obama, as he had promised during his campaign, made some changes in policy aimed at the Cuban regime's soft underbelly, while strengthening enforcement of economic sanctions. Castro argued in his writings that no matter how attractive and sincere Obama might be, he was now president of "the empire" that would tie his hands and that, besides, the new U.S. president wasn't all he was made out to be. "Somebody had to offer a calm and serene response even though this will have to swim up the powerful stream of hopes raised by Obama in the international public opinion," Castro wrote, at the end of a scathing criticism of Obama soon after he was elected.[3]

Perhaps Fidel Castro wanted to undermine any hope of improved relations, but it is far more likely that he really believed a single man could do little to change U.S. foreign policy and the internal dynamics of the U.S. political and economic system. "Obama is somebody we can talk to anywhere he wishes since we do not preach violence or war. He should be reminded, though, that the stick and carrot doctrine will have no place in our country," Castro wrote in the same column.[4] A few days after Obama took office, on January 22, Castro said, in another reflection:

> No one could doubt the sincerity of his [Obama's] words as he stated that he would turn his country into a model of freedom and respect for human rights in the world and for the independence of other peoples. . . . How-

ever, . . . Obama has not taken the main test: What will he do when the immense power he now has proves to be absolutely useless to overcome the insoluble antagonist contradictions posed by the system?[5]

The Cuba Lobby

The Bush administration, which owed a great deal to Florida's Cuban American political and economic establishment and shared a similar ideology, managed to repress majority sentiment in the business community and the U.S. Congress for loosening the embargo. Bush threatened to veto any measures loosening sanctions, and instead tightened them through executive orders and more aggressive enforcement. That all seemed to change overnight with Obama's election. He won the country and Florida without kowtowing to exiles to whom, in fact, he owed little. The anti-embargo Cuba lobby inside and outside Congress sprang back to life. Amendments tweaking Bush-era travel and other restrictions on Cuban Americans and amendments making the food trade a bit less difficult were swiftly attached to a larger spending bill and signed by Obama.[6] Bills were introduced to remove all travel restrictions on Americans, loosen food-trade regulations, and lift the embargo completely, and congressional committees were soon holding hearings on Cuba policy. Think tanks and policy groups quickly issued reports on the best way to approach Havana and untangle fifty years of enmity and sanctions, as they had to no avail after the collapse of European Communism in the early 1990s and would again in 2013 as Obama began his second term. Dozens of business groups, from the Chamber of Commerce and Business Round Table to the Farm Bureau and trade organizations such as the American Travel Association and the Rice, Wheat, and Poultry Associations, quickly joined the rising chorus for a new Cuba policy.[7]

But it was the dramatic changes under way in Latin America well before Obama took office that were the decisive factor at work as a new era apparently dawned in U.S.-Cuba relations. Country after country had elected left-of-center presidents who called for regional unity and greater independence from the United States. These men and women viewed Cuba as a symbol both of resistance to U.S. domination and of their nations' independent aspirations—despite the island's different political, social, and economic system to which almost all, to varying degrees, took exception.

Raúl Castro traveled to Venezuela and then Brazil in December 2008, his first trip abroad since officially taking over for his brother earlier in the year. Castro's destination was a Latin American and Caribbean summit on integration and development, hosted by Brazil, where regional history was made. The summit voted unanimously to admit Cuba to the Rio Group of area countries, a far weaker version of the Organization of American States, but without the United States and Canada. The Rio Group became the Community of Latin American and Caribbean States in 2011, comprised of all thirty-three Latin American and Caribbean nations, and with Raúl Castro again present voted to hold its 2012 annual meeting in Chile and the next year's in Cuba.

The heads of state gathered in Brazil, including those most closely allied with Washington at the time—Mexico, Colombia, Peru, El Salvador, and Costa Rica—wished Fidel Castro well and lamented that he was not present for the occasion. The summit called on the incoming Obama administration to end unilaterally all sanctions against the island and normalize relations. It was an historic and emotional moment, a stunning diplomatic victory for Havana and a unanimous show of support for the island as it faced the incoming U.S. administration. Fourteen Caribbean heads of state had met in Santiago de Cuba less than two weeks before to prepare for the summit, discuss cooperation, make similar demands on Washington, and bestow their highest honor on Fidel Castro.[8]

Democracies are taking hold in the Latin American region after more than a century of alternating in many countries with military coups and dictatorships, violent revolutions and counterrevolutions. The revolutions often had the support of Cuba, and the counterrevolutions were invariably in alliance with local oligarchies and Washington to squash the nationalism and demands for social justice that arise in the most polarized region (in terms of wealth) on the planet, which some referred to at the time as the United States' backyard. It was ironic and, no doubt for many in the West, bizarre, that an increasingly democratic Latin America and Caribbean would welcome Cuba back into the fold and hail the area's only remaining and most famous dictator. Then again, Cuba had long since renounced armed revolution; Cuba had denounced the extraordinarily bloody dictatorships from which some countries were still emerging even as the United States supported them; Cuba had backed local opposition to the dictatorships and provided refuge for thousands of the men and women fleeing imprisonment, torture, and being disappeared; Cuba had vigorously supported the emergence of Caribbean nations from colonial rule; Cuba had given refuge to many of the friends of now-sitting heads of state; Cuba had achieved much in terms of health, education, civil defense, and general social security and peace, and was sharing those gains with its neighbors.

Spain's domination of Cuba, and efforts by other European colonial powers to wrest the "always-loyal island" from the Spanish crown, had more to do with the riches of the region than those of the largest of the Antilles itself. The size and location of the island make it the natural gatekeeper between Europe and the Americas and an ideal way station for shipping between them. The United States' relations with Cuba had never been a purely bilateral affair either, but multilateral, tied to the Monroe Doctrine that viewed the region as an exclusive U.S. domain (much as Russia had always viewed its neighbors).

Raúl Castro, speaking to the press in Brasilia after the summit, said the embargo was finished, and he outlined Cuba's position for future talks with the Obama administration.

> It's been almost fifty years now; it's time for it to end, it's dying. . . . It's time to start getting ready, because the blockade has no perspective. The gentleman, the president of the United States said during his election campaign that he will ease the blockade, but if it's maintained, that is the carrot and the stick.[9]

With the end of Fidel Castro's rule, and his death apparently near, the United States' main allies—from Canada and Europe to Japan, India, Mexico, and Brazil—were all doubling their efforts to engage Havana. The European Union in 2008 dropped all the political and economic sanctions it had imposed after the 2003 crackdown on dissent, although it maintained the "common position" adopted in 1996, which set political reform as a condition for joint economic cooperation. The position was adopted in exchange for a U.S. pledge not to apply to EU companies the extraterritorial sanctions contained in the Cuban Liberty and Democratic Solidarity (Libertad) Act of 1996, better known as the Helms-Burton Act. For decades many European and Latin American leaders, under pressure from Washington, had insisted on meeting with dissidents whenever those leaders happened to be in Cuba. No more. The mix of brave souls, government agents, and charlatans looking for money and visas had proved impotent when Fidel Castro stepped aside in 2006. According to a number of Havana-based diplomats, a series of factors combined to leave them out of the diplomatic loop: Cuban government pressure; the dissidents' inability to influence events when Castro stepped aside; the rise of a new generation of cyber dissidents, led by pioneer blogger Yoani Sánchez; and the realization that Cubans within the Grey Zone and institutions such as the Roman Catholic Church would prove far more important to Cuba's future, even if they did not openly ally themselves with the United States.

Read My Lips

A parade of Latin American presidents traveled to Cuba soon after the Brazil summit to meet physically with and demonstrate their respect for the Castro brothers, to affirm their friendship with Cuba, and to denounce—from Havana—U.S. policy toward the island even as Obama settled into the White House. None met with dissidents. The presidents of Panama and Ecuador came in December; Argentina's president arrived in Cuba at the very time Barack Obama was taking his oath of office in Washington; the Guatemalan and Chilean presidents followed in February; Honduras's and the Dominican Republic's presidents came calling in March; and the president of Trinidad and Tobago visited in April, just days before that country hosted the Summit of the Americas, as would Colombia's before hosting another such summit in April 2012. Paraguay's president arrived in June; Brazil's president had visited twice in 2008, preparing for the regional summit in his country; and Uruguay's president had visited once. Revolutionaries such as Venezuela's Hugo Chávez, Nicaragua's Daniel Ortega, and Bolivia's Evo Morales were already frequent guests, as were Haitian president René Préval and a number of other Caribbean leaders.[10] The center-left then won the presidency in El Salvador in March 2009 and immediately announced plans to normalize relations with Cuba. Costa Rica, the last holdout in the hemisphere besides the United States, quickly restored relations as well.

Soon after the Cuban Revolution, all the area's governments except Mexico and Canada had cut diplomatic ties with Havana and had backed sanctions, along with Cuba's suspension from the Organization of American States. Now the region was welcoming Cuba back and making the embargo the signature issue of its newfound integration and sense of independence. U.S.-Cuban relations in the larger context of the region had come full circle. Washington now stood alone against the hemisphere and at a 2012 Organization of American States summit in Colombia was informed by many area heads of state that they would simply not attend another without Cuba present.[11]

For all intents and purposes, the Brazil summit appeared to signal that the United States' siege of Cuba was over, no matter how much rhetoric flew on both sides and how long it would take for relations to be fully restored. There was no dancing in the streets of Cuba, no fireworks. Those who paid close attention to such matters understood the summit's significance, and the Communist Party–controlled media did play it up. But the island had just been wrecked by two hurricanes and, like humble people around the world, the Cubans were bracing for the inevitable repercussions of the unfolding international financial crisis on their already difficult lives. Besides, the Cubans were just plain tired. Many were completely exhausted by their fifty-year fight with the United States and the terrible crisis of the 1990s. And they were becoming increasingly frustrated by bureaucracy and the daily stupidities of a system that seemed at times to be deliberately making their lives miserable. The more tired and exasperated they were, the more hope they placed in Obama. Most families were now divided geographically, if not ideologically, with some members living abroad, and the man who had led them for half a century was ailing and no longer in charge. The Cubans wanted peace and to be left alone; they wanted space and support, not sanctions, to work out the many political and economic problems they faced domestically, and to safeguard what they had built since the Revolution, now that those who made it would soon be in their graves. It was not to be.

11

Old Foes Get Reacquainted

Now, we're facing an almost united front against the United States regarding Cuba. Every country, even those with whom we are closest, is just saying you've got to change, you can't keep doing what you're doing.

U.S. Secretary of State Hillary Clinton

The Obama administration inherited a slew of grave problems ranging from international terrorism, the wars in Iraq and Afghanistan, climate change, and Russian and Chinese relations, to the financial crisis, deepening recession at home, huge budget deficits, soaring health-care costs, mass immigration, and political polarization. As it settled in, the new U.S. administration had little time for Latin America and the Caribbean—let alone Cuba. Key players during the Bush administration, such as career diplomat Tom Shannon, undersecretary of state for Latin American affairs, stayed in position for months. Slots such as assistant secretary of state for Latin American affairs remained empty, and staff at the State Department's Cuba desk and the Treasury department responsible for enforcing the trade embargo went unchanged. The head of the U.S. Interests Section, Jonathan Farrar, appointed under Bush, continued at his post for another two and a half years. The one major exception was the Bush era's Commission for Assistance to a Free Cuba, which was quickly and quietly closed.

The administration reiterated Obama's campaign promise to free Cuban Americans from all regulations that limited their interaction with family on the island, and pledged to engage Havana while maintaining the embargo as leverage to pry open its Communist system. "We have a two-pronged approach. There are a series of issues we want to move forward on unilaterally because they are in our interest, and a series we will hold on to, as bargaining chips," a U.S. diplomat told me six months into the new administration. That sure sounded to me like the carrot and stick, I responded, and I pointed out the Castros were probably serious when they both warned against taking such an approach.

As the December summit unfolded in Brazil, Barack Obama was naming his cabinet and Hillary Clinton, his choice for secretary of state, was preparing a hundred pages of answers to questions posed by Richard Lugar, the ranking Republican on the Senate Foreign Relations Committee, a few pages of which were dedicated to Cuba. She pledged to review Cuba policy and reiterated Obama's position during the campaign that lifting the embargo and normalizing relations would require changes in Cuba's political and economic system.[1]

Lugar, apparently more aware than Clinton of what the Brazil summit meant for U.S. policy toward the region and Cuba, did not wait for Obama and Clinton to take office. He sent the Senate committee's senior staff member for Latin America, Carl Meacham, to Cuba on January 11–14, 2009, accompanied by his House committee counterpart, Peter Quilter. The two men met with Cuban government officials, ambassadors, members of the Catholic Church hierarchy, United Nations representatives, foreign journalists, and ordinary Cubans, and then issued a report on February 23, 2009, calling for sweeping changes in U.S. policy.[2]

The report said a new approach was needed because of the region's and Europe's changed stance toward Cuba, U.S. security interests (such as drug interdiction and immigration), and Fidel Castro's use of the embargo to legitimize his regime. The United States, it said, had become "a powerless bystander" as historic events unfolded in Havana. The report recommended building trust by replacing a policy of "conditionality" with "sequenced engagement" in areas such as drug interdiction, human smuggling, and immigration. "The U.S. embargo has not served a national security agenda since Cuba ceased to be an effective threat to the security of the United States" with the end of the Cold War, it stated. Senator Lugar followed up the report with a letter to President Obama calling for a special envoy to carry out its recommendations, because the embargo "undermines our broader security and political interests in the Western Hemisphere." The senator said that the upcoming Summit of the Americas in Trinidad and Tobago in April 2009 would present a "unique opportunity for you to build a more hospitable climate to advance U.S. interests in the region through a change in our posture regarding Cuba policy."[3]

Lugar was one of four senators who introduced bipartisan legislation on March 31, 2009, to end restrictions on U.S. citizens traveling to Cuba. A similar bill was introduced in the House a few days later by 121 members. The never-ending debate over the troubling island next door was heating up once again in Congress. Senator Byron Dorgan, the bill's chief sponsor and a Democrat from North Dakota, said Americans should be allowed to visit Cuba, as they were free to travel to other Communist lands such as China and Vietnam. He said U.S. citizens were the nation's best ambassadors and their travels the best way to promote American ideals. Dorgan said Cuba policy "has done nothing to weaken the Castro regime. It's long past time to change this ill-advised policy."[4] Republican senator Mel Martinez, a Cuban American from Florida, shot back for the pro-embargo lobby in a statement issued by his office: "This is the time to support pro-democracy activists in Cuba, not provide the Castro regime with a resource windfall. Changing travel restrictions for U.S. citizens will simply allow Americans to contribute to the resources available to the Castro regime to perpetuate its repression."[5]

A seven-member delegation from the U.S. Congressional Black Caucus arrived in Havana the first week in April 2009 and, before their trip was through, met with Raúl Castro for six hours and more briefly with Fidel. They promised to present President Obama with their findings. The lawmakers were the first U.S. officials to meet with Raúl since he had stepped in for his brother in 2006, and the first to see Fidel since he became ill.[6] California representative Barbara Lee, chairwoman of the caucus, was all business as she held daily press conferences at the Hotel Nacional at the ungodly hour (for journalists) of 7:30 a.m. Lee put forth a novel proposal for change: President Obama should simply normalize relations, and then, if he so chose, work to untangle all the bilateral issues between the two countries, following in the footsteps of every other nation in the hemisphere and all but a handful on the planet.

The Obama administration avoided focusing on the region during its first few months in office, but by April 2009 there was no choice but to tackle the area and the Cuba issue in particular. The Fifth Summit of the Americas, initiated by the United States through the Organization of American States (OAS), was scheduled for April 17 in Trinidad and Tobago, and an annual OAS foreign ministers meeting was set for the first week in June, for which a push was already under way to lift Cuba's forty-seven-year-old suspension from that body.

The Obama administration was forewarned that it could not escape the Cuba issue by Brazilian president Luiz Inácio Lula da Silva's senior foreign policy advisor, Marco Aurélio Garcia, according to a Wikileaks cable describing a January 22, 2009, meeting with the U.S. ambassador to Brazil, Clifford M. Sobel.

The Ambassador asked how central discussion of Cuba would be, in Garcia's view, to establishing relations with the region. "You can't talk about Latin America," he responded, "without talking about Cuba." It has become a "sign" for the region. Garcia urged a "strong" U.S. overture to Cuba "without conditions," such as removing the embargo. It would be, he said, a small price to pay for a large gain. On the one hand, he said, the Cubans would be astounded and embarrassed, and the United States would gain the moral high ground. On the other, he stressed that, on the basis of his long relationship with Cuba and knowledge of Cuban history, he was certain the Cubans would never agree to a proposal that had explicit conditions attached.[7]

The Obama administration would soon learn that much had changed in the region since the first Summit of the Americas in Miami back in 1994, when an isolated Fidel Castro waited on the tarmac at Havana's José Martí International Airport to greet the recently imprisoned and equally shunned Hugo Chávez. Chávez had let the genie—Castro and Cuba—out of the bottle. Besides, the world and the region looked little like they did in the 1960s when Cuba was suspended from the OAS for being "Marxist-Leninist." Cuba was not invited to the 2009 Summit or the OAS meeting, but would nevertheless take center stage at both, as just about every head of state present insisted that Washington bury the hatchet without preconditions.

The Obama administration, in the period leading up to the summit, tried to avoid the unavoidable, arguing that the Cuba issue should not be an obstacle to addressing more pressing multinational issues such as the economic crisis and drug trafficking. The new U.S. administration took its first step to change U.S. policy in hopes of blunting the debate when on April 13—only four days before the summit—it lifted all restrictions on Cuban Americans visiting their homeland and sending money and goods to relatives and friends. Communications companies were given the green light to explore business opportunities on the island, and airline companies to look at establishing regular commercial flights.[8]

The lifting of restrictions on Cuban Americans was indeed an historic act, going much further than the Clinton administration had. In 1993 Cuba had lifted bans on most of its citizens' communicating with, receiving money from, and traveling to see relatives and friends in capitalist countries, including the United States, though one still needed government permission to leave the country.[9] For the first time since 1963, neither government was interfering in a big way with the divided Cuban family.

Cuban dissidents and official economists, state workers and private entrepreneurs, the man on the street and foreign businessmen, and even Fidel Castro grudgingly praised the measures. "I'm planning to fix the place up, make it more comfortable, a better environment for family fiestas," said Teresita, the owner of a small family restaurant that bears her name on the outskirts of Havana. Similar to many small businesses off the beaten tourist track in and around Havana, La Doña Teresa in Fontanar—Cuba's closest approximation to a leafy suburb with street after street of single-family homes in relatively good condition—catered to Cubans who were often supported and visited by family abroad. "There will be more people and money coming in and, logically, more business," Teresita said as she looked at the empty tables nestled in her quaint back patio and garden. "Cubans like to take their families and friends out for a meal when they visit." Fidel Castro allowed that the new U.S. policy was "positive, although minimal," in one of two essays on the subject. In the other he demanded that Obama lift the "cruel" and "genocidal" blockade completely.[10]

The Obama administration then tried to take the offensive by repeatedly insisting throughout the summit that if Cuba was serious about a rapprochement, it should make some sort of gesture in response. The position was disingenuous, to say the least, as the administration itself admitted that lifting restrictions on Cuban Americans and allowing communications companies to explore business with Cuba was aimed at undermining Cuba's government while keeping all other sanctions in place. A State Department official involved in Cuba policy agreed with me in private that letting Cuban Americans loose on the island was like setting a swarm of termites on a wooden shack. "That was the idea; what we need are more termites," he said, with a devilish grin.

The week of the summit, Obama wrote an opinion piece for Latin American newspapers, which also appeared in the *Miami Herald* and a few other U.S. dailies, calling for a new beginning in relations with the region. In it he devoted three paragraphs to Cuba.

> This week, we amended a Cuba policy that has failed for decades to advance liberty or opportunity for the Cuban people. . . . The U.S.-Cuba relationship is one example of a debate in the Americas that is too often dragged back to the 20th century. To confront our economic crisis, we don't need a debate about whether to have a rigid, state-run economy or unbridled and unregulated capitalism—we need pragmatic and responsible action that advances our common prosperity.[11]

Obama, in Mexico on the eve of the summit, told the press: "Having taken the first step, I think it is very much in our interest to see whether Cuba is also ready to change."[12]

Secretary of State Clinton, before going on to the summit, was in Haiti, where hundreds of Cuban doctors and other health care workers had toiled for a decade alongside Cuban-trained Haitian colleagues. The country's president was receiving regular medical care in Cuba. "We stand ready to discuss with Cuba additional steps that could be taken, but we do expect Cuba to reciprocate," she said. "We would like to see Cuba open up its society, release political prisoners, open up to outside opinions and media, have the kind of society that we all know would improve the opportunities for the Cuban people and for their nation."[13]

While Obama was in Mexico and Clinton in Haiti, Raúl Castro was in Venezuela at a summit of the left-leaning Bolivarian Alliance for the Peoples of Our America (ALBA) in preparation for the broader one in Trinidad and Tobago that he could not attend. Heads of state from Bolivia, Nicaragua, Honduras, and Dominica also participated in the meeting, while the leader of Paraguay and a lesser official from Ecuador attended as observers. Raúl reiterated Cuba's position: "We have sent word to the U.S. government in private and in public that we are willing to discuss everything—human rights, freedom of the press, political prisoners, everything."[14]

The ALBA nations at the time—Bolivia, Cuba, Dominica, Honduras, Nicaragua, and Venezuela—announced they would not sign the final Summit of the Americas declaration because "it unjustifiably excludes Cuba, without mentioning the general consensus that exists in the region for condemning the embargo and the attempts at isolation to which its people and government have constantly been subjected in the most criminal way."[15]

Obama discovered in private meetings at the summit that the Cuba issue would not go away. An administration source told the press that 20 percent of a meeting with South American leaders dealt with the island. "I think it's clear that, at least speaking of this meeting this morning . . . I think all of the presidents there would like to see us move expeditiously to lift the embargo."[16]

First Contacts

A few weeks earlier, during the last week of March 2009, cultural diplomacy between the two countries resumed with the opening of an art show in Havana. *Chelsea Visits Havana*, the first important group exhibit of American art since the 1980s, featured works of more than thirty artists representing New York City's Chelsea district and included paintings, photographs, sculptures, installations, and videos. Artists from both countries mingled behind the scenes, and a who's who of Cuban art accepted invitations to attend a reception at the residence of the U.S. mission chief, thus breaking the ice that had formed during the Bush administration. Dance, music, and more art flowed back and forth in the following months and years. The artists and intellectuals mingled and, at times, so did the diplomats. The American and Cuban public simply enjoyed.

Speaking to a town hall meeting at the State Department on May 1, 2009, Clinton seemed to drop her demands that Cuba dump its political and economic system in favor of a more diplomatic tone. "Now, we're facing an almost united front against the United States regarding Cuba. Every country, even those with whom we are closest, is just saying you've got to change, you can't keep doing what you're doing. We would like to see some reciprocity from the Castros on political prisoners, human rights, and other matters," she said.[17]

The Obama administration found itself fighting a losing battle against that united front a month later at the annual meeting of the Organization of American States (OAS) in Honduras, where the 1962 suspension of Cuba was unanimously lifted. The United States opted to support the motion at the last minute, after insertion of a vague paragraph stating that Cuba would have to request, and then discuss, rejoining the group.

> Recognizing the shared interest in the full participation of all the member states the Organization of American States resolves that Resolution VI, adopted on January 31, 1962 . . . which excluded the Government of Cuba from its participation in the Inter-American System, hereby ceases to have effect . . . and that the participation of the Republic of Cuba in the OAS will be the result of a process of dialogue initiated at the request of the Government of Cuba, and in accordance with the practices, purposes and principles of the OAS.

But after the measure was passed, both Fidel and Raúl Castro scoffed at the idea of ever rejoining what they said was an instrument of U.S. domination that was gradually falling apart.

Much had already happened between the Summit of the Americas and the OAS meeting. The Undersecretary of State for Latin American Affairs, Tom Shannon, and Jorge Bolaños, the head of the Cuban Interests Section in Washington and one of Cuba's most senior diplomats, held a series of talks in April and May. Those first contacts were most likely designed to inform Havana about upcoming administration decisions and to feel out Cuban authorities to make sure the Castro brothers would not blow those decisions out of the water. Neither side leaked the content of the talks—a sign that both wanted them to continue.

On May 31, just as Secretary of State Clinton prepared to leave Washington for the OAS meeting, the State Department announced that the immigration talks between the United States and Cuba, halted by President Bush, would resume, along with efforts to establish direct mail service, which was suspended soon after the 1959 Revolution. The first immigration meeting took place in New York in July 2009. The first round of postal talks was held in Havana in September. Both sides emerged from the discussions praising their tone and content and stating they were looking forward to the next round. The State Department said Cuba also expressed an interest in improving cooperation in areas such as terrorism, drug trafficking, and hurricane preparedness. "We've made more progress in four months than has been made in a number of years," Clinton told the press as she prepared to leave for the OAS meeting in Honduras.[18]

The Times Square–style ticker mounted on the U.S. Interests Section in Havana went dark in June 2009, opening the way for resumed diplomatic contact in Havana. The Cubans had refused to meet with U.S. diplomats inside the country ever since the "news stream" lights went on in 2006. The flip of the switch followed Cuba's removal of offensive billboards around the mission. The big black flags that had blocked the view followed; they were replaced by just a handful of smaller ones, which later disappeared as well, although larger Cuban flags still sporadically appeared for events and important national dates. The Demodrome remained, but unused except for occasional concerts and school graduations. But it took a month for anyone except the two governments to notice the ticker lights were off.

Phil Peters, a Cuba expert at the Virginia-based Lexington Institute and author of the invaluable blog *The Cuban Triangle* (Washington-Miami-Havana), sent me an e-mail in late July asking if there was anything to the rumors in Washington that the ticker was no longer ticking. I happened to be invited that week to a farewell reception for the U.S. Interests Section's two press and cultural attachés and a few other U.S. diplomats whose tours were ending. Much to my surprise, the usually tight-lipped U.S. personnel seemed more than eager to confirm some news. "Oh yeah, we turned it off around a month ago," one said, and another, "I do not think there are any plans for it to go back on." For those who followed U.S.-Cuba relations, it was an important story and quite remarkable that it had gone unnoticed. Peters blogged:

> Depending on your point of view, the scrolling electronic signboard that the U.S. Interests Section in Havana turned on in 2006 was a vital source of information for the Cuban people, or it was an ineffective attempt to disseminate opinion and information, or it was a silly use of a diplomatic building. The State Department acknowledged yesterday that it was turned off in June, which means at least three-and-a-half weeks ago. Until yesterday when the news broke in the *Financial Times*, no one outside Cuba knew. More important, during that time there's no indication that any Cuban batted an eye. There's no report from any dissident, not a single story on Cubanet or elsewhere from Cuba's independent journalists, and nothing from any Cuban blogger. . . . There's more reaction in Miami-Dade than in all of Cuba. Pull the plug on TV Martí, and I'll bet the same thing happens.

Bisa Williams, head of the Cuba desk at the State Department during the final months of the Bush administration and the first few months of the Obama administration, and then named temporarily as U.S. deputy assistant secretary of state for Western Hemisphere affairs, traveled to Havana on September 16, 2009, for postal talks the next day. Unbeknownst to the public, however, Williams stayed on for five more days. She held private conversations with Raúl Castro's new point man for U.S. relations, Deputy Foreign Minister Dagoberto Rodríguez; she traveled beyond the twenty-five-mile limit imposed by both countries on the other's diplomats, to tour hurricane-damaged areas in Pinar del Río; she visited dual-citizenship Cuban Americans in Cuban prisons; she met with dissidents, Western diplomats, and others; and she attended, as just another spectator among a million Cubans, the Juanes "Peace Without Borders" concert in Revolution Square.

Under President Clinton, officials at a similar level had done much the same, although the visit to a prison was a novelty. Havana had always insisted that Cuban Americans were Cuban citizens and had denied U.S. diplomats access to those in prison. Given the moment, Williams's meeting with Rodríguez was of obvious importance, although it was never reported in the Cuban media and was downplayed as "technical" in Washington.[19] Williams's visit proved to be the end of the short one-year warming trend between the old foes during Obama's first term as discussed in part III, although cultural exchanges, some talks, and security cooperation continued.

As for the Juanes concert, Cubans expressed their disagreement with its characterization by some media as a great gift to a poor, repressed, and isolated people. They dubbed Juanes the Christopher Columbus of the twenty-first century for "discovering" the island long since inhabited by Indians, ignoring the fact that Juanes's Sunday-afternoon spectacular was not all that different from those by many other international stars who had performed in Cuba, including at night in Revolution Square before tens of thousands of people.

The concert was special in its timing, size, global transmission, and because so many Cubans, on the island and elsewhere, enjoyed the experience on television together. An important event took place in Miami even as Juanes and his troupe were winding up theirs in Havana. Before the concert, a few dozen exiles had smashed his CDs with sledgehammers in front of the Versailles Cafe and Restaurant on Calle Ocho, a gathering place for Cuban American hardliners. Now they planned to use a mini-steamroller to do the same at 7 p.m., when the concert ended. But for the first time since the Cubans began filling up and developing Miami and dominating local government, media, and business, a much larger crowd of young Cuban Americans—who had watched the live feed in Miami—also came out to Calle Ocho shouting "Juanes! Juanes!"

and drove the CD-smashers across the street, stealing their publicity stunt. For this to take place on Calle Ocho, in front of the Versailles, a symbol of exile politics, was remarkable. The incident revealed a significant challenge emerging to Miami's stubborn refusal to move on from the hatred and rage of those who lost everything to Castro in the first days and months and years of the Revolution to the more moderate tone of those who immigrated later. The Grey Zone was growing, not just in Cuba, but across the Florida Straits as well. Cuban bands such as Los Van Van and Habana Charanga were soon playing local venues without major incidents.[20]

The U.S. Interests Section in Havana held a reception to welcome its new press and cultural attachés in October 2009, and numerous personalities from the world of Cuban culture accepted the invitation to attend. The former press and cultural attachés' farewell, months earlier, was attended only by dissidents, a few journalists, and diplomats. Under Clinton, such events had always been filled with the elite of the island's musicians and artists. Under Bush, dissidents with no cultural standing at all had been invited, which meant that everyone else stayed away, for a variety of reasons including fear of official reprisals. Now they were back, just about all of them, in a flash, and the dissidents had to content themselves with meeting the new arrivals at a separate event.

A good barometer of the state of any country's bilateral relations with the Cuban government is whether Cuban officials, the Castro brothers' relatives, and personalities from the world of culture attend that country's diplomatic receptions. At the dozens of U.S.-hosted receptions I attended over the years, a Cuban foreign ministry official (and a low-level one, at that) showed up just once if my memory serves me right, during the early years of the Clinton administration. I'm still waiting for an encore.

12

Shock and Awe, Raúl Style

These changes demonstrate once and for all that
Raúl is the pilot, not the copilot, of this plane.

Rafael Hernández, editor of Temas *magazine*

Cubans, and Cuba watchers the world over, were taken by complete surprise on Monday, March 2, 2009, when the midday newscast delivered the broadside that Raúl Castro had sacked two men believed to be headed toward the heights of power in post-Castro Cuba. Along with Vice President Carlos Lage Dávila, executive secretary of the Council of Ministers, and Foreign Minister Felipe Pérez Roque, another ten ministers, almost all with economic portfolios, were also dismissed. José M. Miyar Barrueco, secretary of the Council of State and longtime Fidel Castro troubleshooter and handler of his megaprojects, was moved from the center of power to become minister of science, technology, and environment. The post of vice president of the Council of Ministers for the Battle of Ideas was abolished, and its programs were merged into other ministries. The vice president of the Council of Ministers for the Battle of Ideas, Otto Rivero Torres, of Elián fame, was canned from his last position of influence. The Fishing Ministry was merged into the Food-Processing Ministry and the Foreign Investment and Cooperation Ministry into the Foreign Trade Ministry and their ministers let go.[1] The dramatic cabinet sweep appeared intended to shock and awe the economic bureaucracy that resembled a huge mountain of Jell-O, absorbing every push with a ripple, but refusing to budge. It also served to muffle the fall from grace of Lage and Pérez Roque for other reasons.

There was no explanation in the communiqué announcing the seismic shift in the political landscape. It simply referred to Raúl's inaugural speech where he stated, "Today we require a more compact and functional structure, with a smaller number of organizations in the central administration of the State and a better distribution of the functions they perform."[2]

Castro's new cabinet now included two more generals with long experience in the military's efforts to improve economic efficiency, and several former officers and middle-aged Party cadre who had risen through the provinces and worked closely with him for years. Raúl's former chief of staff at the Defense Ministry, General José Amado Ricardo Guerra, was named secretary of the Executive Committee of the Council of Ministers, taking Lage's place; and Internal Trade Minister Marino Alberto Murillo Jorge, who would later emerge as point man in Raúl's efforts to reform the economy, was moved to the key post of economy and planning minister and was also named a vice president of the Council of Ministers. Murillo was joined by a new first deputy minister, Adel Yzquierdo Rodríguez, former head of the military's economic department (later named economy minister). Both men would soon take seats on the Politburo. The new minister of the Steel and Mechanical Industry, General Salvador Pardo Cruz, up until his appointment, ran the military companies that supplied the armed forces. He would become industry minister in 2012 when chemicals and light industry were brought under his command. All the military men had participated in the armed forces project to improve state company management.[3]

The government statement said that the cabinet changes and ministerial restructuring would not be the last, and indeed, within a few months, Central Bank president Francisco Soberón Valdés, who had served for fifteen years, would resign and be replaced by career banker Ernesto Medina. On August 1 a new Comptroller General's Office, attached to the Council of State, replaced the lower-level Ministry of Auditing and Control. Its mission: fighting white-collar crime. The Sugar Ministry was abolished in 2011, followed in 2012 by the merging of the Light Industry and Steel and Mechanical Ministries into a new Industry Ministry, which also absorbed the Basic Industry Ministry's chemical union, among other productive spin-offs from various ministries. The Basic Industry Ministry would become the Energy and Mining Ministry in 2012.

It certainly is normal for a new president to name his cabinet. What wasn't normal was that there hadn't been a new president for nearly fifty years until Raúl took over. He was Fidel's brother, and second in the government and the Communist Party during Fidel's long rule. Further, Raúl waited more than two years after first stepping in for his brother, and a year after being named president, to take decisive action. That action, at least temporarily, militarized parts of the government and economy even as military-run businesses took control of most hard-currency shops and moved into tourism and other areas of the civilian economy, eventually controlling some 30 to 40 percent of foreign exchange flows, according to local economists.[4]

Cuba's economy performed poorly in 2008, Raúl Castro's first year in office. True, the island was battered by three hurricanes, wild spikes in commodity prices, and the global financial crisis, but Castro clearly was not impressed with the old cabinet's handling of the situation. The economy grew 4 percent during 2008, but the trade deficit soared a startling 70 percent, fueled by a 43 percent increase in imports. Exports of goods totaled $4 billion, similar to 2007, while imports increased to $15.4 billion, the National Statistics Office reported, leaving a deficit of $11.4 billion. Service exports, including tourism and communications, but mainly the export of professionals to Venezuela and other countries, topped $9 billion for the first time but could not fully offset the expenditures. The balance of payments, which measures the flow of foreign exchange into and out of a country, went from a $400 million surplus to a $2.3 billion deficit, leaving the country little choice but to block hard-currency bank accounts and negotiate new payment terms with foreign creditors, investors, and suppliers. Only a freeze on the exchange rate avoided further deterioration in the peso's value as domestic production made little progress, the budget deficit jumped 121 percent, and pesos in the hands of the population increased 21 percent.[5]

Local analysts told me that the new cabinet removed any doubt that Raúl, not his brother, was in charge. "For those who still had doubts, these changes demonstrate once and for all that Raúl is the pilot, not the copilot, of this plane," said Rafael Hernández, editor of *Temas* magazine. "The fundamental changes were in the economic realm, indicating the intention to institute a new economic policy. In other words: reform."

But those ousted on March 2, 2009, also included the head of the cabinet, Carlos Lage, 57, and Foreign Minister Felipe Pérez Roque, 43, both Fidel Castro protégés believed to be headed toward future leadership of the country. Another up-and-coming cadre, Fernando Remírez de Estenoz, 57, who headed the Communist Party's Foreign Relations Department and sat on its Secretariat, was dismissed at the same time, though it was never mentioned in the official media. Fidel Castro protégé Otto Rivero, who had held the ministerial post for the Battle of Ideas, was fired too. Fidel Castro's personal secretary and a member of the Council of State, Carlos Valenciaga, who first announced to the world that the iconic figure was ill, had been sacked in late 2008 without any public explanation. Finally, Fidel Castro's secretary of the Council of State, José M. Miyar Barrueco, had been pushed aside. No one identified as a Fidel Castro protégé or minister—with the exception of Culture Minister Abel Prieto and Central Bank president Soberón, soon to be replaced as well—remained in any position of importance within the government on March 2, 2009. Was this further proof of a serious rift between the Castro brothers? Perhaps, but the leaders of the Communist Party Politburo and Council of State were all Fidel Castro loyalists who rose to prominence while he was in power. Adding to the mystery were reports that Fidel Castro had staged a dramatic recovery from whatever ailed him and was walking around the Siboney neighborhood where he lived.

Fidel Castro called the speculation ridiculous in a March 4 reflection:

On the occasion of the changes in the heart of the executive branch, there are some cable agencies that are throwing up their hands in grief. Several of them are talking about or spreading the "rumors on the street" about how "Fidel's men" have been replaced by "Raúl's men." Most of those who have been replaced . . . arrived at their positions by being proposed by other comrades in the Party or state leadership. I never devoted myself to that job.

As for Lage and Pérez Roque, Fidel wrote:

No injustice of any kind has been committed with specific cadres. . . . The sweet nectar of power for which they hadn't experienced any type of sacrifice awoke ambitions in them that led them to play out a disgraceful role. The enemy outside built up their hopes with them.[6]

A few months later a video of a March 2 meeting, where the protégés were stripped of their positions and the ministerial changes were announced, would clear up some of the mystery. But at the time, the changes skewed further in the military's favor the seven-man leadership of the powerful Politburo of the Communist Party and the Council of State, of which Lage had been one of only three civilian members and by far the youngest of the group. Ten active and inactive generals were now top government officials, and other officers were in key civilian economic positions. Nevertheless, all my good academic and government sources urged me to view the new cabinet not as "Raúlista" versus "Fidelista," or military versus civilian, but as the replacement of those with an old style of doing business with representatives of a new style.

During the summer of 2009, more than a million Communist Party and Union of Young Communists members were invited to view a three-and-a-half-hour presentation on the inside story of Raúl's shakeup. It was complete with spies, foreigners softening up ministers with gifts and meals, and various officials who expressed their lack of confidence in elder leaders, abused their positions, and broke Communist Party discipline. Security was tight, and the theaters were swept for any recording devices before the presentation, as the government successfully kept the material off Miami TV and YouTube. Viewers were not permitted to bring with them even a pen or a lipstick.

The following is my reconstruction of the event, gleaned during evening rooftop meetings in the dark, meals with sources more nervous than usual, and eventually, as more and more people saw the material, casual conversations with friends at my home about the presentation and its message. Everyone agreed that the show had riveted their attention better than any soap opera from Brazil or Mexico, crime drama from home, or baseball game ever did.

The presentation consisted of four DVDS. The first covered an investigation of an Italian businessman. The message: that the former economic cabinet, headed by Lage, was lax with foreign businessmen bearing gifts and meal tickets, leading to economic loss and security breaches. The second featured Raúl as he relieved the cabinet of its duties and engaged in a fairly pleasant back-and-forth with the new members. The third again featured Raúl as he fired the Castro protégés, and the fourth covered investigations into the protégés' activities.

Ministers Replaced

The show started with a state security video. The surveillance material flashed before viewers fairly rapidly and was a combination of photos, taped conversations (some with a written transcript, as they are hard to understand), a few video clips, and a narrator in the background tying it all together and drawing conclusions. The collage told the tale of Italian businessman Alfonso Lavarello, a joint-venture partner in Cuba's cruise ship terminals, who the narrator charged liked to spread gifts and hospitality around and engaged in other business activities such as importing duty-free goods for foreign-currency shops (including outdated food), and negotiating the renovation of various Cuban ports. The former transport, investment, and trade ministers admitted in the video that they did not follow procedures when authorizing contracts drawn up by Lavarello, and they blamed Lage, who they said authorized the various deals. "He is one of us," former foreign investment minister Marta Lomas said Lage told her.

Lavarello, the narrator stated, pretended he represented Italian investors but really got his seed money from a woman partner with an office at a U.S. Air Force base and then used the profits to fund other business operations, all the while taking cash out of Cuba. The woman was not identified or seen. The video implied that Lavarello passed on information about port facilities to the CIA through the female associate, and the narrator stated that he escaped after being tipped off that he was under investigation. The DVD ends with a view of CIA headquarters in Langley, Virginia.

The star of the second DVD was a calm, wry-witted Raúl Castro as he sacked most of the cabinet inherited from his ailing brother. Castro was in uniform and sat alone at a table facing the gathering. The video begins with Castro taking a first group of papers, carefully removing the staple or clip, and then reading a resolution replacing all the ministers except for Lage and Pérez Roque; he names their replacements, as well as new leadership for the Council of Ministers, engaging in a back-and-forth with a few about their new duties. For example, Raúl talks with Agriculture Minister General Ulises Rosales del Toro about what sectors he is responsible for as a new vice president of the Council of Ministers and of plans eventually to merge various ministries. Raúl tells José M. Miyar Barrueco, secretary of the Council of State, that his transfer to become minister of science, technology, and environment is not a demotion but a promotion, and that he and his staff will have more, not less, work. Then Raúl talks some about accountability and following the law. He holds up a copy of the Cuban Constitution and talks about how it should be respected, and that ministers should know their duties and carry them out without waiting for his or other higher-ups' permission. Castro repeatedly states that institutions must be real functioning bodies and their rules and regulations respected, and indicates that the constitution might need changing.

Fidel's Protégés

The third DVD featured Castro doing in his brother's protégés for unwittingly collaborating with Spanish intelligence, talking disrespectfully about older leaders, and lusting for power. "I am now going to speak of some painful matters," he reportedly states, looking around the room. Raúl announces that Conrado Hernández, the Cuban representative of the Basque government's business operations on the island, was arrested on February 14 on charges of treason as he prepared to fly to Spain. Raúl reads Hernández's confession in which he admits he was an informer for Spain's National Intelligence Centre (CNI) and used his friendship with Carlos Lage, Felipe Pérez Roque, Fernando Remírez de Estenoz, and Otto Rivero to obtain information. Cuba and Spain at the time had open intelligence agents in each other's countries, supposedly to build trust. I had many chats with them over the years. Conrado Hernández's wife, also a doctor, was a lieutenant colonel in the Ministry of the Interior and director of hygiene at Cimeq Hospital, the facility at which the top leadership was attended.

Raúl asks each protégé if he has anything to say about Hernández. Lage says he has been a close friend of Hernández's since his youth. The others say they know him and are friends. Raúl continues reading from Hernández's confession as he fingers each of the four protégés for providing him with secret information and favors. Raúl again asks the four in turn if they have anything to say. Lage recounts his long friendship with Hernández and says he had no idea that Hernández was working for Spanish intelligence. Remírez de Estenoz says much the same. Rivero, sacked earlier in the day by Raúl, says nothing, and Pérez Roque protests he should have been warned that Hernández was under investigation.

Raúl next asks Lage if he knows a man named Dr. Raúl Castellanos Lage. Lage responds he is his cousin and like a brother to him. Raúl asks, "Is that all, how about his wedding party?" He asks the same of Pérez Roque. Lage says he was there, and Pérez Roque has a fuzzy memory. Raúl explains that the party was really to celebrate Lage's expected appointment by the Politburo as first vice president of the Council of State. He accuses Lage of telling people at the party that Machado Ventura was named instead for the post, despite an order to tell no one. Raúl tells Lage and Pérez Roque to stop lying, that he has surveillance proof of all their activities. He says Castellanos, who worked at the heart center where leaders are treated, was put under investigation in 2006 after making counterrevolutionary statements. Raúl charges that at one point Castellanos said that a stent placement for Machado Ventura should have been botched for the good of the nation, and that future ones for aging leaders could be. "Don't worry," Raúl quips to those present who might be in line for such a procedure, "Castellanos was arrested this morning."

There is a back-and-forth with the protégés, who claim they can't recall much, provoking Raúl, who is now seventy-eight, to respond that while people say he and others are too old for their jobs, it appears that "you are the ones who are losing your memories." He suggests they take Sipina, a local remedy for memory loss. He shows the surveillance proof. (In the presentation, this came later.) Lage and Pérez Roque are seen being stripped of all their posts, and they sign resignation letters.

The fourth and final DVD provided the surveillance backup for booting the protégés. Like the first, it was a collage of footage and taped conversations, photos, and a video of Hernández's confession, tied together by a narrator. One scene opened with Dr. Castellanos's wedding party at the Ambos Mundos Hotel in Havana. The celebration took place February 23, 2008, the day the Politburo would approve a new president, first vice president, and other members of the Council of State for their "election" the following day by the Cuban parliament. Raúl Castro was sure to be named president, and most believed Lage a shoo-in for first vice president—the real reason, accused spy Hernández confesses, for picking the party's date. Lage arrives from the Politburo meeting to tell Pérez Roque and others on a hotel balcony the news—that seventy-seven-year-old José Ramón Machado Ventura is to be named first vice president—violating an order by Raúl Castro a few hours earlier to keep it secret. What viewers saw was a photo of them talking, along with their taped conversation. An infuriated Pérez Roque swears, promises to protest, and states that

Machado will ruin the country. The party mood evaporates, the narrator states, and Hernández runs off to inform Spain's intelligence service of the decision, according to his confession.

Another scene in the fourth DVD shows Hernández in 2007 meeting at the Templete restaurant in Havana with two open agents from Spain's National Intelligence Centre (CNI). They ask him for information on Fidel Castro's and other leaders' health, the economy and foreign policy, offer him money, and state he should provide the information in writing, not verbally. A history of the CNI's activities in Cuba since 1994 follows, with photos of some of its agents, including an active undercover operative.

The fourth DVD traces requests from the undercover agent, a diplomat who quickly packed his bags, to the CNI open agents and then to Hernández. The latter then is taped approaching Lage, Pérez Roque, Remírez de Estenoz, and Rivero to obtain the information—ranging from the decision-making structure of the government to investment plans and Cuba's view of Basque elections. The narrator notes that the CNI has a cooperation agreement with the CIA.

The surveillance material also reinforced accusations of Lage's and others' indiscretions and lack of respect for elder leaders. A taped conversation between Dr. Castellanos and Lage had them referring to the country's leaders as "living fossils" and Machado Ventura as a "dinosaur." Photos of weekend gatherings at Hernández's country ranch showed Lage, Pérez Roque, and others feasting, drinking, and smoking cigars as surveillance tape caught them trashing older leaders as stuck in their ways. The narrator points out that Hernández illegally bought the place for $30,000. Other surveillance materials covered Party International Secretary Remírez de Estenoz providing confidential information to Hernández and hanging out with the group and talking disrespectfully, Otto Rivero building a canal to divert water from a river to cross Hernández's property and providing Hernández with investment plans, and Pérez Roque obtaining a diplomatic passport for Hernández. There are a number of other examples portraying a very high-level and disgruntled clique infiltrated by Spain through Hernández. There is a recording of a long-distance phone conversation between Rivero and a Spanish businessman in which the latter says Rivero's traveling wife is with him and he just gave his credit card to her and his own wife to go shopping. "You know how women are when they have your credit card. Anything you need, Otto?" he reportedly says. Finally, there is a photo of Carlos Valenciaga, Fidel Castro's trusted personal aide for almost a decade, who was fired the previous year, as he celebrated his thirty-fourth birthday in September 2006. The party was thrown at government and Party headquarters a few floors above where Castro, the narrator states, fights for his life. Valenciaga, who was the first to inform Cubans and the world that the iconic figure was gravely ill, sports a Castro cap, apparently mocking his boss, with a bandana around his neck and is caught engaged in lewd dancing. "I have more photographs if anyone wants to see them after the meeting," Castro reportedly states.

There were at least three investigations that came together to do in the protégés: one after Valenciaga's party in 2006, another that started with Castellanos's statements about killing off leaders, also in 2006, and a third around Hernández because of his contacts with Spain's agents. Viewers said the presentation left no doubt about the protégés' political errors, lack of respect for Party leaders, and breach of secrecy within the context of Cuban Communist Party rules, particularly for high-ranking officials. Except in the case of Hernández and Castellanos, though, there was no proof of criminal activity, just insinuation. No one expressed sympathy for the sacking of Fidel's economic cabinet. Less-educated viewers emerged feeling betrayed by Lage, whom they had viewed as squeaky-clean and modest. "He was an example for the people of sacrifice and a man who one day could be president of the country," one viewer said. "He betrayed Fidel, the Party, and all of us." They blamed Lage for bringing the group of disloyal officials together: his cousin Castellanos, his close friend Hernández, and his followers Pérez Roque, Remírez de Estenoz, and Rivero.

Hernández was presumably sent to prison for treason and Dr. Castellanos for commenting about the possibility of killing off Machado Ventura and other elderly leaders with heart problems, though there was no mention of their fates in the official media. The Castro protégés remained free. Raúl stated in the third part of the presentation that they did not commit treason or desertion and should work at jobs in line with their formal education to redeem themselves. Lage began working at a Havana hospital, Pérez Roque at an electronics factory, and Valenciaga at the national library.

The Communist Party, with Fidel Castro in retirement, decided future young leaders must come up through the trenches, not the president's office, after being leaders of the University Students Federation and Union of Young Communists. They now must work in their fields for a minimum five years before promotion in Party and government ranks. The presentation's hidden script: Cuba's aging revolutionary leadership had failed to renovate its ranks, something Raúl would publically admit at the Sixth Communist Party Congress in 2011.

PART III

The Road to Reform (2009–2010)

13

Blueprint for Survival

State-run socialist companies must be efficient and what they need for their optimal performance must be guaranteed. The remainder of the economy must adapt to a form of ownership better suited to the resources available.

Government report

Raúl Castro's new cabinet was given just thirty days to get its bearings. The members gathered for a Council of Ministers meeting on April 9, 2009, amid the worst financial crisis to hit Cuba since the fall of the Soviet Union. The ministers threw out their predecessors' plans and made a somber appraisal of the economic situation facing the country, which was unable to pay its foreign debts, suppliers, and joint venture partners, and needed fresh funds even as the international financial crisis weighed in. Economy and Planning Minister Marino Murillo, who would emerge as a driving force of reform, said the country was short 30 percent of the resources needed to meet the 6 percent growth figure projected for 2009 by the old cabinet. A big, heavyset man in his late forties, Murillo hailed from Santiago and was an economist with a domineering, aggressive style. He had moved up almost unnoticed through the bureaucracy over the years, serving in various posts, including in the Food Processing Ministry and Economy Ministry and as internal trade minister. Murillo declared there was no option except better use of what was available, savings, and hard work, according to a source who viewed a video of the cabinet meeting.[1] Central Bank president Francisco Soberón delivered the sobering news that some 600 foreign companies had hundreds of millions in foreign exchange frozen in state banks and were unable to withdraw or transfer it out of the country because there was no money to back up the accounts.[2]

Cuba, heavily indebted and dependent on imports, had gone from a trade surplus to a huge trade deficit almost overnight. The country's current account of foreign exchange fell from a $400 million surplus in 2007 to a $2.3 billion deficit in 2008. The domestic budget deficit had doubled, and pesos in circulation were up 21 percent, which was undercutting efforts to strengthen the local currency, because there were more pesos on the street but without a corresponding increase in local production to absorb them.[3] Economic growth the year before had been based mainly on an expansion of the free health and education services, which Cuba—unlike any other country in the world—included in the gross domestic product, even though no money changed hands.[4] In short, the economy had gone from a brief recovery to a rapid deterioration of just about all economic indicators.

The new government proceeded to take apart the old cabinet's plans for the year. It slashed the budget by 6 percent and declared an energy emergency. Power consumption at all state buildings, companies, and other entities was reduced 12 percent. The government warned the public to prepare for hard times and said it could avoid the much-dreaded *apagones*, or blackouts, of the past only through a voluntary reduction in energy use. Electricity rates were soon increased for everyone except low-end users. Rising expectations, fostered by Raúl after he came to power and already deflated by the hurricanes of 2008 and mushrooming international economic woes, took another hit.

The new cabinet cut the year's economic growth estimate from 6 percent to 2.5 percent and drastically slashed the import budget by 22.2 percent, or some $3.4 billion, compared with an increase of nearly $1 billion projected by the former ministers. The new Council of Ministers forecast a decline of $500 million in export revenues, compared with the old cabinet's projection of a $600 million increase.[5] Pie-in-the-sky was out, a new realism was in. Paternalism had to be replaced by austerity, perhaps the real reason behind the sacking of the previous cabinet.

Local analysts said the island had not faced such a dire situation since the early 1990s, when the fall of the Soviet Union forced a 75 percent cut in imports. They said growth would be less than 2.5 percent. The government adjusted its forecast down to 1.7 percent by July, after making new cuts in the budget and imports.[6] Growth for 2009 came in at 1.4 percent, the lowest in a decade, and imports fell a staggering 37 percent, or by around $5.3 billion. At the same time, the current account deficit was all but eliminated, and would show a significant surplus through 2012.

While the situation was serious, a look at import figures shows that it really did not compare with the 1990s, when the gross domestic product fell 35 percent in three years and imports averaged less than $5 billion. Imports would still total $8.9 billion in 2009, compared with $9.5 billion in 2006 and $7.6 billion in 2005, and in part reflected lower oil and food prices, rather than volume. They had fully recovered, once more reaching 14.8 billion by 2012.[7] Fuel continued arriving from Venezuela and Algeria; credits came from the latter two countries and from China, Russia, Brazil, and Iran; goods and machinery came from China and Brazil, military spare parts from Russia, chicken from the United States, wheat from France, rice and coffee from Vietnam, and around 2.5 million tourists from Canada, Europe, and to a lesser extent other countries. The sale of medical and other technical services brought in billions from Venezuela, but also from Angola, where more than 3,000 Cubans worked,[8] and from Algeria, China, South Africa, Portugal, and even Qatar, where a small hospital, staffed by 150 Cubans, opened in the desert. On Cuba's streets, food services and retail establishments in general held their own in 2009, and the hurricanes' impact on produce markets gradually disappeared. The Cubans' all-important bananas and plantains, a must in the local cuisine, be they served as fruit, fried, boiled, or as chips, trickled back to market.

Raúl's rhetoric and various laws decreed during his first few years in office had come up against the entrenched bureaucracy, rigid ideology, vested interests, inflated payrolls, low wages, pilfering, and slovenly management and work habits that had formed over decades and had become especially glaring after the collapse of the Soviet Union. Raúl Castro expected his new cabinet to deal effectively with it all, and he replaced a number of its members over the next few years when they proved not up to the task—transport, construction, agriculture, and basic industry, among others.

Raúl's efforts to reform wage policy are a good example of the challenges the new ministers faced. In May 2009, more than a year after the government pushed through a wage reform aimed at rewarding productive workers, most state-run companies had yet to implement the measure. The decree eliminated wage caps and replaced a collective five-tier salary system with a piecework system as the heart of Castro's program to raise productivity. Raúl signed Decree Law 9 on the piecework system in February 2008, under the old cabinet; it was due to take effect in August 2008, but was postponed until December. *Bohemia* magazine reported in its May 2009 edition that a Labor Ministry inspection found that "only 25 percent of the companies visited used some variation of the piecework system." *Bohemia* reporters had fanned out to a number of provinces, where they discovered that many managers and workers had only vague notions about the law. There had been little if any discussion of the wage plan despite a mandate from on high to do just that. "Today, the use of wage formulas more in tune with the results of one's work is still in diapers," *Bohemia* said. Managers claimed that they did not have the technical expertise to implement the system, lacked adequate resources, or simply were waiting for orders from their superiors. Some said they were implementing the new wage system, but their workers said they were not. Carlos Mateu, deputy minister of labor, told *Bohemia*, "The majority of companies can adjust their system immediately . . . by simply making the decision to go along with what's been established."

Blueprint for Survival

Raúl Castro and his new cabinet and advisors soon settled on the outlines of a plan that would reengineer Cuban socialism and end its paternalistic practices and the state's monopoly of the retail sector and agriculture. They supported decentralizing small- and medium-scale economic activity and shedding many secondary state retail services and minor construction and production in favor of new forms of administration—such as leasing and cooperatives—and of property, by allowing more private small business, euphemistically termed "working on one's own account," and cooperatives. Egalitarianism was out. They wanted to prioritize individual rewards over social spending—and thus more individual choice over state-imposed consumption—although it would still be almost two years before the plan was approved by the Communist Party and government and began to be implemented in earnest.

In June 2009 the Economy and Planning Ministry, now headquarters for carrying out Raúl's vision, delivered to a closed-door meeting of accountants a PowerPoint presentation on the economic situation and the government's plans, a copy of which I obtained.[9] It revealed much about the Castro administration's economic thinking and thus what was behind its public discourse and actions throughout the remainder of 2009 and thereafter. The presentation turned out to be the skeletal structure around which the administration would flesh out its plans to overhaul the economy, announced in November 2010 and ratified by a Party congress in April 2011.

Following a litany of the usual Cuban culprits for the country's economic woes (the world economic crisis, embargo, and hurricanes), came the heading "Why the Adjustments" and this list, which went much further than any other document I had seen.

1. Low efficiency of the economic model
2. Excessive state protection of the population's consumption
3. Subsidies that do not lead to an increase in productivity
4. A labor structure that does not correspond to the generation of earnings
5. Accumulated decapitalization of the economy and need to reinsert Cuba into the world economy

The report listed, under the heading "Medium-Term Causes" of Cuba's economic woes, "Cuba's aging population, with a life expectancy approaching 80, a low birth rate, and scant immigration, which means there are fewer people working in proportion to those retired, and this will become critical by 2015–2020."[10]

Then came the heading "Structural Changes in the Economy" and the statement "more than three-quarters, or 76 percent, of the gross domestic product came from services in 2007, compared to 57 percent in 1989, while 64 percent of export earnings in 2007 were from services, compared with 10 percent in 1989." In other words, there was less and less domestic production of goods in proportion to services, some of which—for example, the export of health care services—generated few new secondary jobs, unlike tourism, which required two jobs in related services and supplies for each in the sector. The report pointed to medium-term challenges ahead: "Income from medical services provided to Venezuela will decline by the end of the current five-year period, as Venezuelan personnel (trained by Cuba and now concluding their preparation) gradually replace Cubans, and no new source has been found to make up for the loss of revenue." The report also included these observations and recommendations:

1. We must eliminate problems of the management model that create obstacles to the smooth functioning of the economy.
2. The lack of an industrial policy has resulted in certain activities continuing that should have been shut down due to obsolescence or impossibility of fitting into industrial development plans.
3. Production of food is not sufficient and agriculture exports are extremely low, resulting in a too-high and increasing level of food imports.
4. Labor incentives are not sufficient, and as a result the demand for workers in various sectors of the economy is not being filled.
5. Labor productivity in some key sectors is extremely low.
6. The number of people choosing not to work remains high, and people are not attracted to jobs in key sectors.
7. There is a negative work incentive due to a wage system that does not correspond with the cost of living.
8. Demand for goods and services is extremely high because of various factors, such as earnings not related to work [remittances]; supply does not include all the goods and services that people require according to their level of education and culture; and the excessive segmentation of markets [convertible peso and peso] makes a solution more difficult.

The report then outlined policies to meet the challenges facing the country.

- Adjust spending to the resources available.
- Increase exports and replace imports.
- State-run socialist companies must be efficient and what they need for their optimal performance must be guaranteed. The remainder of the economy must adapt to a form of ownership better suited to the resources available.
- Invest to guarantee development in the medium and long term.

- Wages must stimulate collective work.
- Every sector has particularities that must be considered.
- Strengthen municipal-level authority and local production, especially of food.

Under the subhead "Goals" came the following.

- Balance external finances [the flow of foreign exchange entering and leaving the country].
- Obtain the foreign financing needed for the country's development.
- Increase the amount of savings from economic activity to guarantee middle- and long-term development.
- Balance the domestic budget.
- Eliminate the dual-currency system.
- Increase labor productivity and economic efficiency.
- All plans must take into account the worsening demographics of the country.

By July 2009 the official media were taking up the report's refrain, in particular the newspaper *Juventud Rebelde* and the country's most visible economic commentator, Ariel Terrero, through his position as economic editor of *Bohemia* magazine and his twice-weekly commentaries on the government's *Good Morning* television show. Cash-strapped Cuba should consider putting more of its state-run economy in the hands of producers, as President Raúl Castro has done with agriculture, Terrero said, suggesting that sectors such as food and other retail services could perform better if they were run in a new way. "In the Cuban economy, there's a need to look for formulas that are more dynamic, more intelligent about understanding property, about running a business, about running a cafeteria," he said. Terrero pointed to reforms in the island's agriculture that included decentralization of decision making, greater emphasis on private cooperatives and farms, and the leasing of state lands to some 100,000 individuals at the time. "The leasing of state lands, which in the end is the placing of state property in the hands of producers, could be applied in other sectors, for example food services, retail trade, and other areas where it is really impossible, given the diversity and breadth, for the state to administer directly," he said.

Juventud Rebelde joined the debate. "Why should there be cooperatives only in agriculture? It is an organizational principle that is valid for other sectors," economist Omar Everleny told the newspaper. Everleny gave the example of informal groups of men who did bodywork on cars and split the profits. "They already work as a cooperative, why not legalize their business and tax them," he said.[11]

A communiqué issued after the July 29, 2009, meeting of the Communist Party Central Committee stated, "Marino Murillo Jorge, vice president of the Council of Ministers and minister of economy and planning . . . listed the premises to be met by economic activity up until the end of the year and particularly in 2010, which will be equally difficult. These include . . . the search for innovative formulas that will release productive potential." It also said, "Raúl stated that we have not as yet managed to extend the solidness of our national defense to the equally important economic front, which is also essential to national security, given that while ideas chart the course, the reality of figures is decisive."[12] This was a remarkable statement in a land where ideology and politics always trumped economics.

Raúl Castro next delivered a speech to the National Assembly on August 1, 2009, in which he once more laid out his short-term economic program in advance of what he implied would be his and other older leaders' last Communist Party congress. The importance of this speech became evident when it was then used for a second public discussion along the same lines as the one that followed Castro's July 26 speech in 2007.

Castro told the National Assembly that the Party congress would define "the socialist society that we want to build and can build under the present and future conditions of Cuba, and the economic model that will rule the life of the nation." But then Raúl said the congress, already more than five years overdue, would once more be postponed. It was "urgent" to inject fresh blood into the Party's leadership, he said, and a Party conference would be called to elect a new Central Committee, which would then presumably name a new Politburo and the first and second secretaries of the Party. The conference too was later put off, despite the "urgency" expressed by the Cuban president.

Raúl said that his proposal for a Comptroller General of the Republic (approved during that session) would "provide a resolute response to any manifestation of corruption, as well as the causes and conditions that could open the way to a negligent or criminal behavior by any leader or government employee." It later became apparent the Comptroller General's Office was established with an eye to the economic reforms that would soon follow and that had generated increased corruption in other Communist countries when they moved to mixed economies.

Castro then delved into the economy and, as on each previous occasion, was a bit clearer and tougher than before.

We have been consistent about the need to adjust spending to earnings. . . . no one, neither a person nor country, can endlessly spend more than they earn. Two plus two always make four, not five. As I said three days ago during the Central Committee Plenary meeting, in the conditions of our imperfect socialism, due to our own shortcomings, quite often two plus two make three. . . . We should definitely put an end to the irresponsible attitude of consuming while no one, or very few, care to think of how much the country pays to ensure it and, foremost, if it can really do it.[13]

Before Raúl took over, statements such as "State-run socialist companies must be efficient and what they need for their optimal performance must be guaranteed. The remainder of the economy must adapt to a form of ownership better suited to the resources available" would have come only from the mouths of the most reform-minded Cuban economists, in private! Then similar statements began appearing in the official press. It was clear Cuba was moving along the slippery slope of reform from agriculture to the retail sector. Slippery, because when initial measures fell short of expectations, deeper reforms would become inevitable—for example in agriculture, where eventually market forces, based on supply and demand, would need to be introduced.

A Symbolic Reform

My sources told me in September 2009 that the government would close work-center lunchrooms and increase wages to make up for the lost meals, as long as an employee regularly showed up for work. Just as Raúl Castro's taking milk distribution to task as "absurd" in 2007 signaled that the entire food distribution system needed reorganization, the closing of workplace cafeterias was a harbinger of what was to come as Raúl moved to replace social, across-the-board subsidies with individual reward and targeted welfare—or, as he put it in a speech a year later, "replace subsidizing goods and services with subsidizing people."

Granma soon announced that lunchrooms at the Ministries of Economy and Planning, Labor and Social Security, Finance, and Internal Trade would close on October 1, and that employees would receive 15 pesos per day in compensation. The newspaper reported that after the plan was "perfected," some of the other 3.5 million Cubans who ate meals at work could expect many of their 24,700 lunchrooms to close as well, and the lunch money (equivalent to around $0.60 per day) would go into the workers' pockets. *Granma* said the lunchrooms were costing the country $350 million per year in imported bulk foods (rice, beans, cooking oil, and chicken) alone, plus transportation and storage and other related costs.[14] Within a year, 250,000 workers were included in the program.

The measure was symbolically important. Since the very start of the Revolution, there had been a tactical back-and-forth between policies promoting social reward and those aimed at individual reward, but this was a strategic, long-term, and perhaps irreversible decision. It marked the beginning of the end of a half-century effort to form "the new man," as Che Guevara put it, by suppressing individual reward and consumption and promoting social labor and collective consumption. Furthermore, the new plan was bound to fuel demand for food services provided by private vendors and state-run outlets. Given the Economy and Planning Ministry's PowerPoint report, the Communist Party communiqué, and Raúl's speech to the parliament, this measure could only mean that reform of the food service sector was close at hand.

A Party economist said the lunchrooms were a major source of black-market activity, with at least 20 percent of the tons of imported food allocated daily being stolen. Waste was rampant, and shifting the supplies to other state-run food services would simply shift the problems, not eliminate them. Another economist, Omar Everleny, told me the plan killed numerous birds with one stone, from worker theft and employee grumbling over poor lunchroom meals to the need to transport supplies and supervise the lunchrooms. What still needed working out, though, was how the new demand for food on the street would be met. "The daily lunch stipend represents almost a doubling of Cuba's average base pay of just over 400 pesos per month and will greatly increase demand on the street for state- and family-based food service providers," he said. Everleny added that many employees were expected to bring a box lunch to work, or go home for lunch, especially in the provinces where they lived closer to work, but that others would buy the sandwiches, pizzas, or box lunches of rice, beans, and pork or chicken typically offered by private vendors and state-run food services for 10 to 20 pesos per meal.

On October 2, 2009, Armelia emerged from the Finance Ministry onto always bustling Obispo Street in the Colonial district of Havana, after eating a lunch of chicken breast and mashed malanga that she had brought from home. "No workplace in the world, no country, capitalist or socialist, subsidizes meals like in Cuba," she said. But fellow worker Ogdalys was not pleased with the turn of events, stating with a bit of anger that a hot meal was a hot meal, and 15 pesos would fetch only a bun with a slice of ham in the middle, at best. "It is not good for people's health and workers' peace of mind," she said. Minerva, who had the good fortune to be running a pizzeria and sandwich shop from the door of her home at 201 Obispo, right next door to the Finance Ministry, said sales were picking up. She and a friend, helping out during the now-busier lunch hour, nearly rolled on the floor with laughter at the suggestion that it might be the moment to nail down a McDonald's or Pizza Hut franchise. *Granma* had said that *gastronomía*, as the infamous state-run food services were called, would largely fill the lunchtime void for the moment. I told Minerva, who sold a small plate-sized circle of pizza dough topped with a bit of tomato sauce and cheese and a glass of fruit-flavored sugar water for 15 pesos, that one alternative under discussion at the highest levels of government would allow cooperatives in the food-service sector and perhaps increase the highly restricted licenses for the self-employed. "I doubt they will allow it," Minerva said with a smirk, recalling all the trials and tribulations she had gone through just to stay open since 1997, as thousands of her compatriots were closed down. Individuals holding self-employment licenses in Cuba—many of whom actually ran small family businesses—had dropped from close to 200,000 in the latter part of the 1990s to fewer than 150,000. "The state hates competition," Minerva said, her smirk turning into a scowl.

The Second Debate

Raúl Castro was determined to force through changes in how the economy ran and people lived: he decentralized economic decisions, called for "new forms of production," and repeatedly stated that Cuba must learn to live within its means. That message, the lunchrooms, the monthly food ration, and the entire scheme of things were being debated in workplaces and block associations across the island at that very moment in response to Castro's August 2009 speech that, in essence, called on the population to work harder and expect less in exchange for higher wages and a socialist system that would be more user friendly in the future. Some Cubans began saying they wanted the more paternalistic Fidel back.

The discussion guide for the second public debate in less than three years, which I got hold of, termed Raúl's August speech "transcendental." The guide included most of the speech and was broken down into mainly economic questions. The guide called on participants to apply its concepts to their daily lives and work. Under point 3—food production and distribution—it included excerpts from Castro's July 26 speech that year, in which, while pounding the podium, he said that reversing the country's dependence on food imports was "not a question of yelling 'Fatherland or Death! Down with Imperialism! The blockade is hurting us,'" but of working harder and overcoming poor organization.

The first debate in 2007, soon after Raúl Castro took over from his ailing brother Fidel, had created a great deal of enthusiasm: it took place at a time of economic recovery and sought input on the society's problems and what residents wanted from a state that oversaw most aspects of daily life and administered almost all economic activity. But that was before the 2008 hurricanes devastated much of the island and before the financial crisis broke. The guide for the second debate said:

> This time, the idea is not to solicit critical demands, suggestions, and recommendations for higher bodies . . . but to stimulate a response in each workplace and community to confront and solve existing problems. . . . The main goal of every meeting will be to reflect on the ideas, concepts, and policy implications of the speeches, look at what really occurs in each locality; that is to say, an inward-looking analysis of every community, work center, or school or other place, in such a way that the reflection leads to identifying existing problems and determining concrete ways to solve them.

Participants in the second debate said it quickly became bogged down because of the complexity of the agenda, the Cubans' well-known tendency to be defensive and rarely introspective, the growing anger directed at the bureaucracy, and resistance to eliminating such customs as the food ration without a clear idea of what would follow.

"He's Paternalistic, You're Paternalistic, I'm Paternalistic," the Communist Party newspaper *Granma* soon screeched as the debate unfolded, in a column by editor Lázaro Barredo Medina, which appeared to signal official frustration with the grass roots. Barredo said that most Cubans suffered in varying degrees from four syndromes that were holding back the very progress they desired:

1. The young-pigeon syndrome: We walk around with our mouths open because a large part of the systems we have developed are conceived to give us everything . . .
2. The volleyball syndrome: We have become accustomed to throwing and hitting the ball to the other side of the net . . .
3. The ostrich syndrome: We have developed the habit of sticking our heads in a hole, almost always so as not to see the problems . . .
4. The obstacle syndrome: You cannot transform the economy and satisfy basic needs in one month. But some people think you can, and when they encounter the first obstacle, they stop and wait for someone else to remove it or get around it for them.[15]

Most Cubans appeared to support Raúl Castro's efforts but believed that they were not at fault and were at the mercy of a state bureaucracy that they expected him to tame. Many were insulted by the editorial. "Our ability to do a good job doesn't depend on us, but on guidelines from the ministry. I can't plan anything, because they decide the factory's work and supplies and that's where the problems are and continue," said Carlos, an industrial worker. An overweight employee of a dark and dingy state-run cafeteria in Central Havana, which sold cold hot dogs, flavored sugar water, and dangerous-looking pastries from a fly-infested counter, blamed the lack of supplies and low wages for the dismal merchandise on offer. She frowned at the suggestion that she might be able to improve it. Many farmers had a hard time criticizing themselves for the country's poor agricultural performance, because the state was only then beginning to lease millions of acres of fallow land that it had sat on for years and recognizing that a monopoly on farm supplies and sales often led to lost crops. "Farmers have never wanted the state to give them anything. What we want is that the state sells us what we need to produce and then not waste it because of poor planning, transportation, and other problems," a farmer friend in Camagüey said.

Another friend, responsible for organizing more than a dozen block-organization discussions in eastern Cuba, said that in the end the official agenda was scrapped in favor of a discussion about how to improve their daily work, a theme already discussed numerous times over the years. "It's too bad the material was so extensive and did not allow for an analysis of every point," said Lidia, a Havana teacher. A Havana retiree said that his community Party organization called it quits after three hours, having discussed just the first three items of the ten-point agenda.

A phone survey of people who were either involved in or had knowledge of dozens of meetings held across Cuba indicated there was near-unanimous opposition to eliminating the food ration without a clear explanation of what would replace it and how those who really needed help would eat. "I know the ration has to go, but you have to study carefully how you do it, because many people depend on it to eat, most of all those who don't receive any foreign currency from somewhere," Guantánamo retiree Pedro de la Fuente said in a telephone interview. Over the next year, the potatoes, chickpeas, one of five pounds of sugar per individual per month, and the cigarettes would be removed from the subsidized ration, while still available at state shops at higher prices. Then soap, detergent, and toothpaste were removed, as the government opted for a gradual approach to elimination. The coffee allotment was diluted in 2011 when roasted chickpeas were mixed in. Nothing further was eliminated in 2012 and the first months of 2013.

Cubans would again be called to discuss the economy (for the third time in four years) in early 2011, but this time it was a 32-page, 291-point plan to revamp both the economy and society that was up for debate at the Communist Party congress, finally called for that April. Meanwhile, *Granma* had instituted a Letters to the Editor section in its Friday editions that featured for-and-against views on Raúl's economic program, in particular his reform of retail services and specific examples of bureaucratic ineptitude and abuse, in a fascinating debate that will provide raw material for scholars of Communism for years to come.

"We have to shake off the stereotype, developed over many years, that private property is always evil," González de la Cruz wrote in one of hundreds of published letters backing reform. "Property, state or private, is valid when it serves a social purpose," he said.

The opposing view was expressed in *Granma* by Guerra González, in another letter: "The solution of creating new owners and co-operatives and making current employees into supposed collective owners (in the retail sector) will only lead to uncontrolled free competition and capitalism," he wrote, adding, "This would represent not only an economic step backward but a political, social and ideological one."[16] González de la Cruz would win the debate hands down.

14

Stealth Reform

> For a long time, when you picked fruit from your yard and went to sell it on the highway, the police would appear ... and take it away. ... You can imagine what it means to be able to bring our fruit here and not have that struggle.
>
> *Edilberto Fernández, a young man working a fruit stand in the mountains*

Havana is not Cuba; in fact, many of the island's residents refer to the capital as Little Miami. The head of the Party in Havana sits on the Politburo, and since the early 1990s the Communist Party and government have fielded a special commission to keep the lid on the city of 2.2 million people. In contrast, provincial capitals are relatively small places with just a few hundred thousand residents, where the streets remain immaculately clean and the slightest change, for better or for worse, is quickly noted by all. Official speeches and policies often make little sense within the context of Havana because they are directed at the rest of the nation, where eight of every ten Cubans dwell. Raúl Castro is no showman, and he is a man of the provinces. His reforms, I figured, would not be televised or focused on the capital.

In January 2010 I decided it was time to take another look at the lay of the land. I left Havana, where there was a sense that the country was in crisis, the military taking over, reforms stalled, and people complaining that there were fewer goods in the dollar shops and peso markets. In Ciego de Ávila, Camagüey, Granma, Guantánamo, Holguín, and especially Santiago, I was greeted by the news that more peso eateries and shops were opening and there was more food to be had, not less.

Retail service outlets, selling everything in Cuban pesos, were popping up across the country, in a reversal of the two-decades-old policy that priced most goods and services in dollars and then in the dollar-linked convertible peso. "They have opened restaurants, pizzerias, cafeterias, and pastry shops and set up areas across the city where they sell sandwiches, snacks, and soda," said Pedro de la Fuente from Guantánamo, the capital city of Cuba's easternmost province. "The population has welcomed this because, before, these things were available only in convertible pesos," he said. The "they" was the state, but it wouldn't be long before "they" would be outnumbered by budding entrepreneurs.

The dual monetary system was one of the population's biggest beefs, but eliminating it would take time. The government wanted to strengthen the value of the peso first, and for that it needed, among other things, to improve local production and increase the peso-denominated offerings to absorb the excess amounts of local currency in circulation.

The epicenter of the new policy was Santiago de Cuba, the island's second-largest city (with a population of 426,000), where far more peso outlets had opened than in other cities. "There is a special plan, in which the Party and government allocated a budget for Santiago to remodel dozens of establishments and open new ones," said a Communist Party cadre and administrator of various eateries. "The idea is for the people to feel good, to have the services they deserve, to be able to sit down in any restaurant, cafeteria, or what-have-you and pay in pesos," she said. For the 50 percent of the population with some dollar income from family remittances, state bonuses, tips, or other sources, the prices were often a steal, but they were also occasionally accessible to those not so fortunate. "At least I can go out to eat a few times a month with the money I'm paid in," said my friend the professor of nursing in the central city of Camagüey, where she earned around 500 pesos per month.

A daylong look around Santiago de Cuba found that some of the wares in the convertible-peso supermarkets could be had at new (peso-only) Ideal supermarkets for a price that would be equivalent to up to 20 pesos per convertible peso, still very expensive but a bit more affordable than the 24:1 official exchange rate. Local seafood stores sold a kilogram (2.2 pounds) of shelled oysters for 60 pesos, lobster meat for 50 pesos, crabmeat for 15 pesos, and salted fish for 50 pesos. At the restaurant Las Americas, a meal of pork, rice and beans, salad, and a local beer or soda cost about 35 pesos, and in the evening the place was packed. The pizzeria down the street sold its medium-sized pie-and-beverage combo for 20 pesos to a full house, adding on up to 10 pesos for a topping of lobster, chicken, sausage, or shrimp. A few doors away, a fish restaurant did a brisk business offering a variety of grilled and fried dishes for 30 to 50 pesos. The peso establishments were well lit, clean, and air-conditioned, luxuries that had been reserved for CUC-priced eateries since the 1990s. The government soon announced that it would continue the trend and transform some 6,000 peso eateries across the island.

Private Food Sales

In the days before Raúl began eliminating true stupidities, wherever you traveled in Cuba you would be offered some kind of local produce by roadside hawkers. In the western part of the country, men darted out from behind lush foliage brandishing garlands of garlic and onions. In the central plains, they leaped from the sugarcane fields bearing white cheese and guava paste (a typical Cuban dessert), while in the eastern Sierra Maestra, they emerged from the woods and thick underbrush holding up fruit and live fowl. These stealthy men often risked the wrath of the Cuban police, who guarded the state's monopoly on food distribution. As the vendors haggled over price with passersby, they kept a close eye out for the highway patrol. The cops in their green jeeps were usually easy to spot, since the roadways boast little traffic.

But about thirty miles outside Santiago de Cuba, in the Sierra Maestra, the scene was different this time around. There were a few dozen small stands offering tangerines, grapes, bananas, and tropical fruits with exotic names like *mamey*, *guanábana*, and *níspero*, and the cat-and-mouse game had suddenly ended. The stands were government sanctioned. The "criminals," as the vendors had been known, now proudly sold their fruit and other produce, and customers happily munched while enjoying the spectacular view. The highway patrol attended to what one hoped were more important matters, and the government collected taxes from those it used to persecute at a cost.

Lázaro Expósito Canto, soon after he took over the Santiago de Cuba Communist Party in 2009, ordered the roadside stands built and allowed local residents to sell what they produced in their often extensive yards. "I thank God for this opportunity and also Comrade Expósito," said a passionate Edilberto Fernández, one of a group of young men working a stand. "For a long time, when you picked fruit from your yard and went to sell it on the highway, the police would appear, jump all over you, and take it away, when really we were doing nothing wrong," he said. "You can imagine what it means to be able to bring our fruit here and not have that struggle. The fruit no longer rots on the trees; the animals no longer eat it; we Cubans eat it." Fernández said his stand was open twenty-four hours a day, and demand was so high that he and his neighbors were planting as many fruit trees as they could.

And the idea was catching on. A former Party official in neighboring Granma Province said a similar measure had recently been implemented in the mountains there, and Holguín Province followed. Farmers in the lowlands of central Cuba said plans were afoot to set up kiosks along roadways around Cuba's fourth-largest city, Camagüey, where the farmers could sell their produce directly to consumers. The Santiago plan became the law of the land in August 2010, and kiosks loaded with tempting fruit, garlands of onions and garlic, and other produce soon appeared along highways and secondary roads across the country. The stands were manned mainly by former peddlers and members of private farm cooperatives and were both a tourist attraction and a source for local consumption, as well as providing economic relief for the Cubans who grew the food in the mountains and on the plains.

I found similar breakthroughs were occurring in the cities. In a further concession to individual initiative and consumer complaints about the state's monopoly on food distribution, the authorities had granted licenses to street vendors of fruits and vegetables who had previously risked fines and confiscation of their wares. Unlicensed men and women still prowled Camagüey's side streets on foot and bicycle selling products, but there were now licensed vendors as well, hawking pineapples, squash, onions, tomatoes, and other produce from carts along quaint colonial avenues and streets, where bicycles and horse-drawn carriages still easily outnumbered the cars.

In Santiago de Cuba, local authorities had begun accepting license applications from the *carretilleros*: owners of mainly horse-drawn wagons. These men in wagons, and others pulling smaller carts and pushing wheelbarrows, all laden with produce, had plied the city's hilly streets for centuries. "The police were always all over us; they didn't let us work," said Rubén, his wagon loaded with oranges. "Now, we are at peace. We can sell more without any problems." Retired parliament deputy Yolanda said: "These measures allow me to buy root and garden vegetables at my door, without walking to the market, which is far away." By 2011 there were 48 kiosks in the mountains and 200 licensed *carretilleros* in Santiago de Cuba Province, according to a May 31 article in *Granma*, and thousands of people were hawking produce from carts on street corners across the island.

Suburban Farming

After spending a week in Oriente, I returned to Camagüey, site of the pilot project for Raúl's suburban agriculture program. It was a five-year plan to make the country's food supply low-cost and environmentally friendly by surrounding urban areas with tens of thousands of organic farms (the one big exception being Havana). Castro had prioritized agricultural production in part because it was a sector where improved performance and thus lower imports and a greater peso supply were attainable, including through food services and processing into canned goods. His various agriculture reforms all came together in the government's strategy to surround 150 cities and towns with ten kilometers of organic farms, backed up by cooperatives and reorganized state farms farther away. Adolfo Rodríguez Nodal, head of the program and the man who led the widely acclaimed urban-gardens program, had called for the elimination of bureaucratic mechanisms so that produce arrived fresh and in good condition to consumers. This meant more direct sales by farmers to the population.

The plan was clearly designed to bring together various reforms, from decentralization and land leasing to allowing more direct sales to consumers and cutting back on imports of farm supplies such as fuel and fertilizer. Authorities also hoped that small-scale farming close to urban areas would entice city residents, soon to be laid off from jobs in Cuba's bloated bureaucracy and state employment rolls, back to the land. Farming in Cuba has suffered a labor shortage for years, with a state-run television program on agriculture reporting in 2010 that the average age of those working the land was over fifty. The plan also sought to save on the cost of transporting goods to market, rely less on expensive and fuel-consuming machinery, and ensure a greater variety of fresh produce. The biggest obstacle to its success was water. As of 2012, only 10 percent of the land allocated to the plan was irrigated.

As the sun came up over the beltway surrounding Camagüey in late January 2010, men and women were plowing the fields with oxen, building protective coverings for crops, hoeing the earth, and putting up fencing. The quaint city, where the 320,000 inhabitants take their time going about their daily lives, will eventually have 1,400 plots and small farms covering 130,000 acres, according to the Agriculture Ministry, producing 75 percent of the city's food. "They gave this land to us, the private farmers. I have four hectares [ten acres], and now they have leased me eight more," said Camilo Mendoza, a farmer with a Florida cap on his head. Mendoza said he grew fruit-tree saplings on his farm, but his new plot would be sown with yuca, a root vegetable that is a Cuban favorite when boiled and topped with a garlic-based sauce called *mojo*. Fried yuca is a delight as well.

A year earlier, marabú had covered the area for as far as the eye could see, rendering it useless even for the area's traditional cattle ranching. It's just a few minutes from the city, and Mendoza said that urban residents had joined the farmers to clear the brush. He pointed around the fields: "Look, on this side and the other side are other plots, and over there, another. They have given quite a bit of land and support to private farmers here," he said. For the first time, farmers could sell part of what they produced directly to licensed street vendors and consumers at stands set up every mile or so along the beltway.

On the other side of Camagüey and a few miles up the central highway, Armando said his cattle cooperative was persuaded to join the plan when the state offered the co-op more land to raise garden and root vegetables and the chance to sell some of what was produced directly to the population. "In December we produced about five tons. We had to sell the root vegetables to the state, but we were free to sell the garden vegetables directly," he said, adding that growing and selling produce was a first for his cooperative. "In the case of the suburban plan, there are no chemicals or anything else that can damage the environment," Armando said.

Plans in Cuba are made to be broken, a local saying goes. While some foreign and local experts applauded the project, others said it harked back to feudal times, and many voiced skepticism that it could meet its goals without the establishment of free markets where farmers could buy their supplies and sell their produce. "It will take a lot of seed. Let's see if the state can provide it on a timely basis," a local farmer said. The government had opened shops where farmers, for the first time, were buying work clothes and basics such as fencing, machetes, and plows; but fuel, seed, irrigation systems, fertilizer, tractors, and the like were still centrally allocated—although plans adopted by the Communist Party and government in 2011 called for them eventually to be sold directly to farmers as well.

Murillo Sounds the Retreat

I returned to Havana in early February 2010 and to friends who were once more going to the movies. This time the video featured Economy Minister Marino Murillo speaking to Party, government, military, and Interior Ministry officials about the need for the state to pull back from minor economic activity and end its paternalistic practices.

"The gigantic paternalistic state can no longer be, because there is no longer any way to maintain it," Murillo said, according to a Communist Party source who attended a showing of the video. Murillo said the Caribbean nation could no longer afford, for example, to pay tens of thousands of people to control state barber shops, beauty parlors, and service outlets to repair such items as shoes, appliances, and watches. He suggested they could be administered differently by leasing them to workers, according to two other people who also saw the video of his speech. Speaking to the National Assembly at the close of 2009, Murrillo had said, "We have begun experiments and are working on others to ease the burden on the state of some of the services it provides," but he did not elaborate further. I would have to dig and dig to find them.

The CubaTaxi office on Palatino Street in the Cerro municipality of the capital was home to one such experiment. Thirty of the more than 2,000 state taxi drivers in the capital began leasing their vehicles in January 2010, rather than working for a salary, a small percentage of the tips, and whatever they could pocket on the sly. "You pay 595 CUC [convertible pesos] for the car and then, after a month, a 39 CUC leasing fee plus 40 pesos for gas per day," said Elio, one of the drivers. "You are responsible for maintaining the taxi and paying for any gas you use beyond the 40 CUC, but you can buy parts and services from the state. Overall, the drivers are happy. There is still control over what we charge, but we are freer and earning more," said Elio, who began driving a cab in 1986. "I think this system is also better for the state, which is guaranteed a net income with few headaches," he added. By 2012 many taxis outside the capital were going over to the new system, but with some tweaks depending on the province, although some drivers, especially in Havana and the pilot project, complained that they were overtaxed and still couldn't make a decent living without working massive amounts of overtime.

I asked my network across the country, which had proved so helpful in tracking agricultural reform, to do the same with the retail sector, and alert me of any changes, no matter how small. In April 2010, the phone rang off the hook as the government began leasing small barber shops and beauty parlors to the people who worked in them and until then had been employees of the state.

The first call was from Pedro in Guantánamo. He said a cardboard sign had appeared on the door of a barber shop: "This barber shop now rented. A haircut costs five pesos. We apologize for the inconvenience." (The state price had been just a single peso.) The state was handing over hundreds of barber shops and beauty parlors that had three or fewer chairs to the employees, who would now pay rent and taxes and maintain the facilities. Barbers and hairdressers across the country said they would now be able to rent the space where they worked, charge their customers for services, and pay taxes, instead of receiving a monthly wage from the government.

In a radio interview in early 2011, First Deputy Minister of Domestic Trade Mary Blanca Ortega Barrero said there were 1,669 state-run barber shops and beauty parlors in the country, 1,358 of which had from one to three chairs. The new measure set a monthly fee to be paid by each barber or beautician, based on 15 percent of the average revenue generated by haircutting and styling in each area. The new "owners" could charge whatever the market would bear, and were expected to make good money by Cuban standards. The policy represented the first reform of the retail sector under Raúl Castro, and the first time that the state had given up control of a single retail shop since all small businesses—some 58,000—had been taken over in 1968. By 2012 the larger establishments were also leased, and all operated under new regulations for a booming small business sector.

"You have to pay rent for the shop, and costs such as water, electricity, materials, and the wages of anyone you hire, for example a receptionist or someone to clean up," hairdresser Rosita said in a telephone interview from Holguín. "You can charge whatever price, on the basis of supply and demand, and you have to pay taxes on your profits," she added. State-subsidized materials had arrived sporadically at the parlors, and services cost anywhere from 5 pesos (the equivalent of $0.20) for a shampoo to between 25 and 50 pesos ($1 and $2) for hair dyeing. "We buy shampoo, conditioner, dye, or what-have-you at state foreign-exchange shops [with a 240 percent markup] or get our friends to bring them in from Miami or Madrid," another beautician said. "Then we tell our clients there are no state supplies, but we bought them ourselves and will have to charge accordingly and then give something to the inspectors to leave us alone," she said, adding that some clients simply brought in their own materials for a make over.

It was a Castro stealth reform. The government made no announcement, and the official media breathed not a word for months.

Obama versus Raúl

*It's like the hurricanes. Every time we get somewhere, one comes
along to wreck it all and there is almost nothing you can do.*

Pepe, a used-book vendor, on relations with the United States

John Kavulich, president of the U.S.-Cuba Trade and Economic Council in
New York, back in the 1990s as he worked to promote trade between the
seemingly intractable foes, used to say that trying to get anything constructive
done was like walking through terrain mined by both parties. "You never know
when or where one or more of them will go off," he would say. A young Cuban
once told me that U.S.-Cuba relations were like a bowl of spaghetti: it would
be difficult to untangle even if both parties so desired.

I proved way too optimistic with the staff at the Comodoro Hotel on election night in 2008, visiting businessmen, and my friends the used-book sellers in the Plaza de Armas during the first weeks and months of the Obama
administration. I believed relations would slowly, but steadily, improve and
the United States might well lift its ban on travel to the island, a step that
would quickly undermine the embargo and in my view Cuba's rationale for
the one-party system. But Havana still considered itself a revolutionary force
for social and economic justice in the region and the world and saw the United
States as the main obstacle to Latin American and Caribbean independence,
integration, and development. And Washington still insisted it was the "good
neighbor" and believed Cuba's political, social, and economic regime punished
its people and was a threat to regional stability and democracy.

In early 2010, U.S. Secretary of State Hillary Clinton appointed Chilean academic Arturo Valenzuela to head up Western Hemisphere Affairs at the State
Department, and by summer, career diplomat Peter Brennan would become
director of Cuban affairs. Around the same time, Caribbean expert Daniel P.
Erikson, a senior associate with the Inter-American Dialogue think tank in
Washington and author of a book on U.S.-Cuban relations,[1] was named senior
advisor to Valenzuela. Clinton's Cuba team was finally in place, more than a
year after her taking over at the State Department, but by then a U.S. citizen

who had been working for Washington was behind bars in Havana and the Tea Party and throw-the-bums-out movement were sweeping through the United States. Valenzuela would resign less than eighteen months after taking the job.

The Castro brothers repeatedly stated that they were ready to talk with the Obama administration, but there was to be no interference in Cuba's internal affairs; they would talk as equals, without the "carrot and stick"—a position they had held from the first days of the Revolution. Obama, Secretary of State Clinton, and others in the new U.S. administration repeatedly stated that they wanted to make progress with Cuba, but Havana would first have to change its political, if not economic, ways. They planned to maintain sanctions, and to continue both open and covert support for the regime's opponents, until there was a fundamental shift in Cuba's domestic policies, a position similar to those of past administrations.

The cautious series of contacts during the first months of the Obama administration served to convince both parties that the other's position was not mere posturing. Given the mountain of issues, grievances, and mistrust built up over half a century, only a major shift in attitude and position by one side or the other could lead to a significant breakthrough. The bowl of spaghetti remained a bowl of spaghetti, even after a few strands were removed.

Obama's domestic agenda met tough resistance, as did Castro's, and perhaps neither side believed rapprochement served their domestic interests at the moment. Obama's signature issue, health care reform, became bogged down in Congress. Senator Bob Menendez from New Jersey, head of Democratic Party fundraising, and South Florida congresswoman and Democrat National Committee chair Debbie Wasserman Schultz, became ever more vocal and intransigent both in public and behind closed doors when it came to changing policy toward Cuba, a U.S. diplomat told me. Perhaps a combination of horse-trading for votes on health care and the need to protect their right flank had led to a hardening of the U.S. administration's position, anti-embargo advocates speculated. In addition, a new election cycle in 2010 and possibilities of inroads in Florida soon seduced Obama into fundraising and other activities involving the powerful Cuban American establishment.

Raúl Castro's efforts at economic reform were also slowed by bureaucratic tangles and interests and the ideological dogmatism of some officials, and, in addition, the island nation was entering its own electoral cycle. Local elections were held in late April 2010, under the usual banners of a show of unity against the empire. Perhaps a hardening position toward the United States and the European Union helped cover Raúl's left flank.

A series of events and incidents (Kavulich's mines) soon put an end to my earlier optimism. On June 28, 2009, a bloodless coup, if one does not count those killed and injured in the ensuing protests, toppled Honduran president Manuel "Mel" Zelaya, who just a few months earlier had hosted the OAS meeting that lifted Cuba's suspension from that body. Zelaya was a strong backer of Cuba's and Venezuela's Bolivarian Alliance for the Peoples of Our America (ALBA). His downfall was the first major setback for the Alliance and, what was far more important, for the democratic trend that was taking hold in the region. A similar "legal" coup in 2012 would take out another progressive head of state in Paraguay. Honduras was the home of an important U.S. military base which Zelaya might well have closed in the future, as another ALBA member, Ecuador, was in the process of shutting down a U.S. base in its territory. That country would successfully weather a police rebellion and attempt on president Rafael Correa's life in 2010. Fidel Castro charged that the Honduran coup—the first in the region in more than two decades, not counting a failed attempt against Venezuelan president Hugo Chávez—was openly backed by conservative elements in the United States and treated with kid gloves by the Obama administration. Fidel Castro suspected that the CIA and the Pentagon had played a role.[2] In August 2009 the United States and Colombia updated a previous agreement giving the Pentagon increased access to seven military bases in the South American country that bordered on Cuban allies Venezuela and Ecuador, and soon agreements were struck with Panama and Costa Rica for an increased U.S. military presence in those countries as well. Fidel Castro lashed out at Obama, accusing the U.S. leader of attempting to roll back progressive movements and governments in Latin America, and of putting a "friendly smile and African-American face" on "imperial policies of force."[3]

Cuba's most prominent dissident blogger, Yoani Sánchez, was stopped by plainclothes security agents on November 6, 2009, as she and her live-in companion and fellow blogger Orlando Luis Pardo Lazo headed on foot to a student peace march. The two bloggers claimed that they were roughed up when they resisted being forced into an unmarked car. Sánchez and her partner said they were warned off their activities and left brutalized on the street about twenty minutes later, but they refused to show journalists any bruises. The Obama administration deplored the incident, and then upped the ante when the president himself responded in writing a few days later to questions submitted to him by Sánchez. (A cable published by Wikileaks would later reveal that the answers were prepared by the U.S Interests Section.)[4]

"Your blog provides the world a unique window into the realities of daily life in Cuba. It is telling that the Internet has provided you and other courageous Cuban bloggers with an outlet to express yourself so freely, and I applaud your collective efforts to empower fellow Cubans to express themselves through the use of technology," Obama "wrote," before "answering" Sánchez's questions.[5]

The move angered Cuban authorities, who regard such high-level recognition of opponents as provocative and disrespectful. They viewed Sánchez's repeated winning of European and United States awards (more than any other of the region's journalists, writers, or intellectuals ever in such a brief period of time) and the translation of her blog into eighteen languages as proof that she was part of the United States' effort to use the Internet to discredit and subvert its enemies. A round of immigration talks set for December was postponed by the Cubans soon after Obama "answered" Sánchez's questions, and then they struck back at the heart of a covert U.S. program designed to support her and a new generation of cyber dissidents.

U.S. citizen Alan Gross was arrested on December 3, 2009, as he prepared to leave Cuba. Washington insisted that Gross was simply working for a Maryland-based aid organization called Development Alternatives Inc., on contract with the U.S. Agency for International Development to promote democracy in Cuba. Development Alternatives president James Boomgard said Gross was in Cuba to "strengthen civil society in support of just and democratic governance in Cuba." Gross's wife said her husband was helping the island's "tiny Jewish community set up an Intranet so that they could communicate amongst themselves and with other Jewish communities abroad, and providing them the ability to access the Internet." Secretary of State Clinton characterized Gross, who was contracted at around $300,000 per year, as a kindly man helping some senior citizens get connected. The State Department, Development Alternatives, and the Gross family insisted that the contractor was no spy, but simply a good-hearted former social worker. They did admit the obvious: that Gross was working for a U.S.-funded program aimed at subverting the Cuban government and that he had posed as a tourist to enter the country under false pretenses on many different occasions.[6] In the end, it would be revealed that Gross had traveled to Cuba six times, the first time in 2004, well before Obama took office, to deliver video equipment to José Manuel Collera Vento, head of the Freemasons fraternal organization in Cuba, who was actually working for Cuban counterintelligence. Gross was arrested a day after he met again with the Masons about a project to set up Internet platforms in their lodges.[7] His trip reports, which the Associated Press eventually got hold of, made clear he was well aware of the illegal nature of his activities and had smuggled in a classified chip that made it impossible to pinpoint the location of Internet transmissions, and in 2013 other documents detailing what he was really up to would emerge during a legal battle between his wife and his former employers.[8]

Gross's arrest effectively threw ice water on the slow but sure improvement in relations during Obama's first year in office. A Cuban official countered that it was the new administration's continued efforts to topple the government that chilled the atmosphere. "After all, what were we supposed to do? Sit back in hopes of further improvements even as the United States tried to overthrow us," he said in an off-the-record chat.

The Cubans had demonstrated before that their national security and their own agenda trumped improved relations with the United States. In the 1970s they had marched off to Africa, putting a halt to improved relations with the Carter administration when they increased their deployment in Angola while he was in office. In 1996 they had shot down two exile-piloted planes, ending a thaw with the Clinton administration and resulting in the Cuban Liberty and Democratic Solidarity (Libertad) Act, or Helms-Burton Act, which strengthened the embargo and codified it into law. The common wisdom within Havana's Western diplomatic circle was that the Cubans did not want improved relations. But there is no question that the Cubans played an important role in ending apartheid and that before the 1996 shoot-down they repeatedly asked the Clinton administration to stop exiles from flying their planes, not only in Cuban airspace, but over the capital within seconds of government headquarters and right by my apartment on two occasions.[9] Now Raúl Castro was preparing to introduce reforms that were inherently destabilizing, and the last thing he wanted was the United States mucking about.

It was left to Raúl Castro to inform the Cubans of Gross's arrest, which he did during a speech to the National Assembly on December 21, 2009, thus highlighting its importance to the Cuban government and his understanding that improved relations with the United States would be set back.

> Despite the enormous propaganda campaign staged to confuse the world about an apparent willingness to make a turn in the bilateral differences, alleging the repeal of the restrictions on the trips of Cuban émigrés and remittances to their relatives, the truth is that the instruments for the policy of aggression to Cuba remain intact and the U.S. government does not renounce its efforts to destroy the Revolution and generate a change in our economic and social regime. . . . The enemy is as active as ever. Proof of that is the detention in recent days of a U.S. citizen, euphemistically described by State Department spokesmen as a government "contractor," who engaged in the illegal distribution of sophisticated means of communications via satellite to groups in the so called "civilian society" that aspire to join ranks against our people.[10]

Just a few days later, Cuba's eleven-year legal effort to bring back its five agents arrested in Miami—where, according to thousands of pages of their communications with Havana presented at their trial and read by the author, they were mainly keeping an eye on and trying to disrupt Cuban American exile groups and seeking with little success to monitor traffic at local military bases—all but came to an end as three of the five's long sentences were reduced, one from life to thirty years, but the others by insignificant amounts.

If the arrest of the Cubans had signaled that the United States would no longer tolerate Havana's sending its undeclared agents to Florida, and that long prison terms would be the penalty, the arrest of Gross signaled that Havana would no longer tolerate the United States' sending its agents to gather information and support dissent on the island, and that, likewise, long prison terms awaited them. Gross was sentenced to fifteen years in 2011.

In December 2009, Fidel Castro and other officials launched a blistering rhetorical assault on Obama's efforts to salvage talks at the December World Summit on Climate Change in Copenhagen. They charged his methods were undemocratic and aimed at blocking real progress by shielding Western countries from taking responsibility. They called the final, nonbinding agreement that Obama had brokered a farce. Cuban foreign minister Bruno Rodríguez said in a televised press conference that Obama had lied in Copenhagen. "He lies all the time, deceives with demagogic words, with profound cynicism," Rodríguez told reporters. "In this summit there was only an imperial, arrogant Obama who doesn't listen, who imposes positions that threaten developing countries," he said.[11]

As 2009 came to a close, and just a year into the Obama presidency, the mood at Cuba's Foreign Ministry was grim. "We expect nothing more during Obama's first term," said one official involved in U.S. relations. "We invited them to discuss a series of substantive issues, and they responded with trifles, sanctions, and subversion." A Havana-based U.S. diplomat said, "I don't know why the Cubans are so upset. We are trying to treat them like any other dictatorship."

Cubans were mobilized in community and workplace rallies to denounce a U.S. decision in January 2010 to include Cuba on a list—along with thirteen Middle Eastern and African nations—of countries from which all airline passengers would be required to pass through extra screening before flying to the United States. The attempted Christmas bombing of a U.S. airliner (for which a Yemeni branch of al-Qaeda claimed responsibility) triggered the new security measures, but when asked what Cuba had to do with that, the U.S. State Department had no response except to repeatedly brand the Communist-run island as a state sponsor of terrorism. This was guaranteed to infuriate the Cubans, as the label seriously affected their financial operations around the world, in addition to the embargo, and because they believed that the numerous violent attacks by exiles on soft targets over the years, including the bombing of a commercial airliner, belonged in the same category.[12] The anti-U.S. rallies were the first of their kind since Fidel Castro became ill in 2006, when perhaps the most noticeable change in Cubans' daily lives was the disappearance of anti-American mobilizations and the accompanying round-the-clock anti-U.S. rhetoric that characterized his long rule. The rallies were now back, in workplaces and parks across the land, although not in front of the U.S. diplomatic mission.

The mobilization slowed with the Haiti earthquake as Cuba focused on providing medical assistance to its neighbor, and some cooperation began between Cuba and the United States in that Caribbean country. By April 2010 the U.S.-required extra screening of travelers flying to the United States from Cuba and the thirteen Middle Eastern and African countries was simply dropped.[13] Here is what the United States mission in Havana had to say about the deteriorating situation in a cable sent at the close of 2009, published by Wikileaks and titled "U.S.-Cuba Chill Exaggerated, but Old Ways Threaten Progress":

> Over the course of the last month, the tone coming out of Havana seems a regression to the hostile language that kept U.S.-Cuba relations on ice for much of the last 50 years. . . .
>
> ### HEATED WORDS OVER CLIMATE CHANGE
>
> The language coming out of Havana after the Climate Summit was as incendiary as it has been over the last year and a half. Communist Party boss and former President Fidel Castro railed about the U.S. "deceit" and "arrogance" and his foreign minister, upon his return from Copenhagen, duly repeated the charges at a press conference. . . .
>
> ### THE INFLUENCE OF THE CASTRO GERONTOCRACY
>
> The former president is widely blamed in the island for the regime's obstinate refusal to change its old ways. According to many of our contacts, the political and policy paralysis in Cuba is a reflection of the sway that Castro and his generation of "históricos" (including his brother and current President Raúl) have over the GOC. . . .
>
> ### EXPLAINING THE ARREST
>
> President Raúl Castro himself was the first Cuban official to have acknowledged the arrest [of Gross]. . . . Theories about the arrest abound, from an attempt to force high-level attention from Washington à la North Korea, to a move to counter the blogger movement. . . . However, at his National Assembly speech on December 20, President Castro linked the detention to U.S. democracy programs on the island, deriding the very notion of a Cuban "civil society." Whether that was Castro's intent or not, the arrest has chilled the atmosphere for democracy programs in Cuba, especially those that hinged on unfettered and hassle-free travel to the island. . . .

BLOGGER BOGEYMAN

The conventional wisdom in Havana is that the GOC sees the bloggers as its most serious challenge, and one that it has trouble containing in the way that it has dealt with traditional opposition groups. The "old guard" dissidents mostly have been isolated from the rest of the island. The GOC doesn't pay much attention to their articles or manifestos because they have no island-wide resonance and limited international heft. For a while, ignoring the bloggers too seemed to work. But the bloggers' mushrooming international popularity and their ability to stay one tech-step ahead of the authorities are causing serious headaches in the regime. The attention that the United States bestowed on superstar blogger Yoani Sanchez first by publicly complaining when she was detained and roughed up . . . and later by having the President respond to her questions, further fanned the fears that the blogger problem had gotten out of control. . . . [14]

A U.S. delegation led by Craig Kelly, temporary assistant secretary of state for Western Hemisphere affairs, traveled to Cuba for a second round of immigration talks on February 19, 2010, but unlike the previous round of discussions, they were followed not by praise but by hostile rhetoric. According to both Cuban and U.S. sources, these talks usually included more than immigration, and this time around, the subject of Alan Gross topped the U.S. agenda. After the meeting Kelly met with a few dozen dissidents, drawing a furious response from the Cuban Foreign Ministry, though U.S. diplomats said their hosts were well aware the meeting would take place. That action, a ministry statement front-paged in *Granma* said, "once again demonstrates that their priorities are rather linked to support for the counterrevolution and promoting subversion to overthrow the Cuban Revolution than providing a framework for a true solution of bilateral problems."[15] A senior State Department official told interested media that it was standard operating procedure under the Obama administration for visiting delegations to seek out nongovernment players. "Worldwide, we have a policy of reaching out," the official said in a conference call with reporters. "We're not inclined to make exceptions to that."[16] The talks, and those around mail service, were soon suspended.

A mid-level U.S. official, involved with Cuba on a daily basis, said that Obama's agenda had become more complicated by the day and Cuba policy was not a priority, especially given that it was just too much of an effort to move forward due to resistance on Capitol Hill and in Miami, unless the Cubans cooperated. This official was in Havana for a few days to attend the immigration talks, and we chatted over coffee at a hotel in Miramar. "I think there still might be some progress around the edges, but substantial change? I doubt it unless something significant happens here," he said.

Four days after my chat with that official, imprisoned dissident Orlando Zapata Tamayo died after an eighty-five-day hunger strike, the first such death in forty years. His tragic fate, like the deaths of twenty-six patients from undernourishment, the cold, and related illnesses at a Havana psychiatric hospital a few months earlier,[17] also the first such incident at a Cuban institution in decades, was further indication that the central government's command and control was breaking down. Low wages led to lack of interest by administrators and employees at state institutions and the hatching of schemes to steal supplies and shake down inmates and patients rather than care for them.

Zapata's jailers in Camagüey Province denied him water and waited far too long to send him to the hospital. The higher authorities' efforts to save him came too late. Zapata became a martyr, and the incident sparked protests from Western governments and became a rallying point for exile organizations and dissidents. Another government opponent, Guillermo Fariñas, who was not behind bars, went on a hunger strike demanding better treatment of political prisoners. Fariñas—who had used the tactic numerous times in the past—was soon admitted into a local hospital in Villa Clara to be fed intravenously, from where he continued to denounce the regime by mobile phone from his free hospital bed in intermediate care.

Dissidents were energized by the publicity. Protests by female relatives of imprisoned Castro opponents and their supporters received new attention when they were mobbed by government supporters. Obama, reacting to the death of Zapata and the harassment of the political prisoners' relatives, known as the Damas de Blanco, or Ladies in White, issued a statement on March 24, 2010, which read in part:

> Recent events in Cuba, including the tragic death of Orlando Zapata Tamayo, the repression visited upon Las Damas de Blanco, and the intensified harassment of those who dare to give voice to the desires of their fellow Cubans, are deeply disturbing. These events underscore that instead of embracing an opportunity to enter a new era, Cuban authorities continue to respond to the aspirations of the Cuban people with a clenched fist.[18]

The message was timed to coincide with a Miami rally the following day, led by the exile establishment's cultural icon, Gloria Estefan, in support of the Ladies in White. A few weeks later, on April 15, Obama attended a $15,000-per-person cocktail party at Estefan's mansion for the Democratic National Committee.[19]

The same day that Obama issued his statement, Fidel Castro issued one of his reflections, ostensibly praising the passage of Obama's healthcare reform, but which began as follows.

> Barack Obama is a zealous believer in the imperialist capitalist system imposed by the United States to the world. . . . The warmongering policy and the plundering of natural resources, as well as the unequal terms of trade of the current administration toward the poor countries of the Third World are no different from those of his predecessors, most of them from the far-right, with few exceptions throughout the past century.[20]

Obama, in his statement, said:

> During the course of the past year, I have taken steps to reach out to the Cuban people and to signal my desire to seek a new era in relations between the governments of the United States and Cuba. I remain committed to supporting the simple desire of the Cuban people to freely determine their future and to enjoy the rights and freedoms that define the Americas, and that should be universal to all human beings.[21]

Castro, in his reflection, said: "I hope the foolish remarks [Obama] sometimes makes about Cuba do not cloud his mind."[22]

During the first eight months of 2010, as bilateral relations took a turn for the worse, smaller mines were also going off, as they always do on a monthly, if not weekly, basis, adding to that tangled bowl of spaghetti. Among them: Walter Kendall Myers, 72, a former State Department employee, and his wife, Gwendolyn Steingraber Myers, 71, were arrested in the United States on charges of spying for Havana over a period of no less than thirty years. They confessed and were convicted. Three nuisance lawsuits—one involving relatives of an imprisoned dissident, another by relatives of a man shot down while flying over Cuba in the early 1960s, and still another by the wife of a Cuban agent who returned to Havana—went uncontested and resulted in tens of millions of dollars in judgments against Cuba, as Havana refused to defend itself in the "enemy's" courts. The U.S. Treasury Department fined Philips Electronics of North America $128,750 in July of 2010 for "an employee's travel to Cuba in connection with the sale of medical equipment by a foreign affiliate." And in August of that year, the Treasury fined an Australian bank 7 million Australian dollars for trade-financing operations connected to transactions with Cuba and other countries subject to U.S. sanctions.[23]

The most intransigent political players on both sides of the Florida Straits no doubt breathed long sighs of relief as tensions mounted in 2010, casting a chill on the improved bilateral climate that they opposed and that would only worsen in 2011 and 2012 as both sides took a break from their immigration and mail talks and the presidential election campaign unfolded in the United States. Those who hoped for improved relations with the Obama administration fretted. Efforts to lift the travel ban on Americans visiting Cuba found the going tougher than it already was. Havana announced that in the future the Ladies in White would need a permit when they marched, and the government mobilized supporters who mobbed them every time they did. Rallies across the island denounced European Union and U.S. condemnations of Cuba's human rights policies, along with the Western media's coverage of events, as a biased assault aimed at discrediting the Revolution. Cubans resigned themselves to more of the same-old, same-old as accusations were traded back and forth in the political stratosphere, while at the same time they enjoyed increased contact on the ground with their visiting relatives and friends from abroad.

Elections for ward delegates in Cuba went off without a hitch on April 25, 2010, as the usual 95-percent-plus of eligible voters cast their ballots for "the motherland and the Revolution" and, by implication, against the latest assault and abuse by "the empire" and its European allies. The Republican Party trounced the Democrats in November's midterm elections in the United States, and one of the most visceral Cuban American opponents of rapprochement rode the Republican wave into a key position in Congress. "It's like the hurricanes. Every time we get somewhere, one comes along to wreck it all and there is almost nothing you can do," said Pepe, my friend the used-book seller in Havana's Old Town, with a shrug.

Congresswoman Ileana Ros-Lehtinen, a Cuban American from Miami and a fierce Castro foe, became chair of the House Foreign Affairs Committee in 2011 and all but declared war not only on Cuba, Venezuela, Bolivia, Ecuador, and Nicaragua but also on the Organization of American States.[24] Another staunch anti-Castro politician from Florida, Connie Mack, took over the Foreign Affairs Committee's subcommittee on the Western Hemisphere. "When dealing with a committee chair it becomes a question of relative priorities, and Ileana Ros has a hearts-and-minds commitment to the Cuba issue that overrides a rather lukewarm one by Obama," said Robert Muse, a Miami-based attorney who specialized in such thorny issues as commerce with Cuba and old property claims. Marco Rubio, a staunchly pro-embargo Cuban American Republican from Florida, was elected to the U.S. Senate. Rubio, a rising star in the Republican Party, would now join forces with the man most credited for slowing Obama's Cuba policy—fellow Cuban American and Democratic senator from New Jersey, Bob Menendez—and block the president's Latin American diplomatic appointments in protest over the administration's handling of the island. They were buttressed by David Rivera, a third Cuban American

Republican of similar stripe in the House of Representatives, while a number of key embargo critics in Congress retired or lost their seats.[25]

The bill that sought to abolish the decades-old ban on travel by Americans to Cuba was declared dead in the water. "It is going to be difficult. It is a big damper, of course. Any talk of lifting the travel ban or normalization is out the door for the next couple of years," Wayne Smith, who opened the U.S. Interests Section in Havana under President Jimmy Carter, told me. Smith, like others who had worked to improve relations, expressed frustration that Obama had not done more when he had the chance, but he still held out hope that Obama would reverse restrictions on academic and other specialized travel imposed by former president George W. Bush. Obama could not lift the whole embargo without congressional approval, but he could still use his executive authority to relax parts of it. "The president can remove restrictions on academic and other people-to-people travel at the stroke of a pen; so let's see: will he do it, will he face up to Ileana and do it?" Smith said.

On December 16, 2010, State Department spokesman Phillip J. Crowley, responding to a Wikileaks revelation that Raúl Castro had sought — through Spain—a direct line of communications with the White House in 2009, only to be rebuffed, had this to say: "We have made clear to Cuba that, first and foremost, before we would envision any fundamental change in our relationship, it is Cuba that has to fundamentally change . . . fundamentally change its political system. . . . That remains our position."[26]

Raúl Castro, speaking to the National Assembly a few days later on December 18, said: "Sometimes it seems that their most heartfelt wishes prevent them from seeing the reality. In making their true desires evident, they blatantly demand that we dismantle the economic and social system that we created, just as if this Revolution were willing to submit to the most humiliating surrender."[27]

Ironically, by 2011 the big changes that might have moved the Obama administration and Congress to act, before the arrest of Alan Gross and the midterm election changed Washington's political landscape, were getting under way in earnest in Cuba, although "surrender" was not on the agenda. Obama did loosen the sanctions a bit more. On January 14, 2011, by executive action, Obama once more allowed religious, academic, and other professional (people to people) travel to Cuba, which had been stopped by Bush, and he went further than the Clinton administration had. Obama authorized all international airports to service charter flights and removed a cap on the number of Cuba-travel providers and charter companies. Obama also added a new provision: any U.S. citizen could send up to $500 every three months to just about anyone on the island, to "stimulate small business." More termites were headed toward

Cuba, but perhaps they would also learn much about the island and go home to eat away at the rhetorical structures that justified U.S. policy.

Havana belittled the new regulations. "Although the measures are positive . . . their reach is very limited and they do not modify U.S. policy against Cuba," a Foreign Ministry statement said. Havana credited public pressure within the United States for the decision and charged that Obama, like his predecessors, sought to dominate Cuba. "It is also an expression of recognition that the U.S. policy towards Cuba has failed and new ways to accomplish the historic objective of dominating our people are being sought," the Cuban government concluded.[28]

Bilateral relations continued to deteriorate in 2011 and 2012, even as more and more Cuban Americans and American citizens visited Cuba. Gross's conviction was upheld by the Cuban Supreme Court; U.S. funding for the programs Gross worked for was renewed; $245 million in Cuban assets were seized in 2011 due to the country's status as a state sponsor of terrorism, and embargo sanctions resulted in numerous fines against foreign companies and banks who did business with the island; the Obama administration actively opposed efforts by lawyers for the five Cuban agents for even such minor leniency as allowing one of the five, released in October after perfect behavior behind bars, to return to Cuba instead of serving three years of probation in the United States. Efforts by the Cuban agents' lawyers to obtain U.S. satellite footage of the 1996 shooting down of the exile planes, so as to settle the question of whether it took place over Cuban or international waters, were energetically opposed by the Obama administration. In 2010 the head of the Senate Foreign Relations Committee, John Kerry, who would be named secretary of state in 2013, met in New York with Cuban foreign minister Bruno Rodríguez to discuss the Gross case, but to no avail. Former president Jimmy Carter and former New Mexico governor Bill Richardson traveled separately to Cuba in 2011 to negotiate Gross's release but returned empty-handed, as did a delegation of U.S. senators and representatives in early 2012 and again in February 2013. The charges and countercharges became ever more strident.

On April 14 and 15, 2012, Obama attended the 6th Summit of the Americas in Cartagena, Colombia. The United States and Canada blocked the unanimous demand by all the Latin American and Caribbean heads of state in attendance that Cuba be included in the seventh, scheduled for 2014. They proceeded to deliver their own ultimatum as various heads of state announced they would not attend another Americas summit without the Cubans.

16

Wired

If only this will allow Internet to arrive in Cuban homes, because
I think it's the only place in the world without this service.

Yurislaidi, a Cuban programmer living in Chile to further her education

The Caribbean Basin teems with underwater fiber-optic cables, but not a one
touched the largest island in the Antilles until February 2011. The *Île de Batz*, a
cable ship flying the French flag, arrived in eastern Cuba with a line laid from
Venezuela. It was a rags-to-riches story, sure to greatly improve the efficiency
of the government and the state-run economy, while provoking great expectations among Cuba's Internet-starved population. "From what I understand,
this will improve communications and lower the cost. I think there will be
many more options to have Internet, which is almost impossible right now,"
teacher Pedro Estrada said, voicing the view of the faithful.

I, for one, was thrilled. "Broadband, my God, at last," I thought. I enjoyed
the luxury of Internet at home and in the office, but it was so slow I never
bothered to upload pictures or download videos. Opening a web page or e-
mail took minutes, sometimes many of them. E-mail in Cuba was like snail
mail everywhere else. It was almost as frustrating as being stuck in traffic on the
Brooklyn Bridge when I lived in New York.

The cable, owned by a Cuban Venezuelan state venture, Telecomunicaciones Gran Caribe, increased data transmission speed 3,000 times and could
handle 10 million international calls simultaneously. A Chinese subsidiary of
the French company Alcatel-Lucent provided the $63.4 million connection
(it contained less than 10 percent U.S. product, in order to meet U.S. embargo
specifications) that finally overcame a U.S. measure that cut Cuba off from U.S.
telecommunications networks. The company dubbed the line ALBA-1, implying there would be more.

"I have no doubt that, at least in the short term, this will do more to modernize the economy and improve our efficiency than the measures we are taking
to shed excess labor and grant companies more autonomy," said a local Cuban
economist who was a consultant to state-run firms. "It also opens up new pos-

sibilities for online business," he said. Antonio, a telecommunications engineer involved in the sector since the 1980s, agreed. "This is very, very important in terms of connectivity. It will be a change like night and day," he said when the cable arrived. "Now, using videos, photos, teleconferencing, and other facilities will work; without a doubt it will be magnificent."

International tourism was just getting off the ground back in 1992—in partnership with foreign firms such as Spain-based Sol Meliá and French hospitality company Accor—but Cuba's communications systems, even before the fall of the Soviet Union and the advent of the Internet, were abysmal. There were few land lines, no mobile phones, the last directory dated to the early 1980s, and the system was 100 percent analog. The Cuban Democracy Act, often referred to as the Torricelli Bill, further tightened the embargo in hopes of pushing the country over the edge after the demise of European Communism. In terms of telecommunications, it denied Cuba access to U.S. communications cables and technology to undermine the future tourism industry and other business.

By 1996 the Cuban telecommunications monopoly, Empresa de Telecomunicaciones de Cuba, S.A. (ETECSA), had partnered with Telecom Italia to digitize the system, and with Canadian firm Sherritt International to develop a mobile phone service for tourists, diplomats, foreign businessmen, expats, and select Cuban officials and personnel. The country finally connected to the Internet in 1996, through an expensive and agonizingly slow Russian satellite link that had limited capacity and, again, was only for the privileged. A decade-long project got under way to lay an underground fiber-optic system connecting the country's provincial capitals and then the main urban centers of all 169 municipalities. Today Cuba's telecommunications system is completely digitized. The Italians and Canadians no longer own a stake in the company.

Computers and computer-science courses were introduced from kindergarten on up in the late 1990s, and computer clubs were established across the country. A computer science university opened in Havana—where the famous Lourdes Soviet listening post, used to spy on Cold War foe the United States, once stood—and then three other computer science schools in the provinces. A Cuban intranet was developed, and the Cuban government, businesses, and media debuted on the World Wide Web. Special web-based libraries and knowledge-sharing systems for professionals appeared, such as INFOMED for the public health sector. Doctors I knew, who used to beg foreign colleagues for copies of medical journals, even if months and years old, now had access to real-time literature in their fields.

According to the government, at the close of 2010 there were around 725,000 computers in the country, 600 computer clubs, and 1.7 million users of the government-run intranet, of which analysts said an estimated 450,000 had some official Internet access. Cuban media sported 136 web pages, and there were more than 200 blogs and 10,000 students of computer science.[1] Yet when the cable finally arrived, and despite these advances, communications remained the worst in Latin America and the Caribbean, lowering the island's standing in the United Nation's Human Development Index.

How can one explain that arguably the region's most advanced nation in terms of health, education, social peace, and civil defense has the area's worst communications? The Cuban government blames the embargo for this dismal state of affairs, while its critics charge that the authorities fear the Internet and too much communication among local residents and with the world. The average Cuban blames both for keeping them from cyberspace.

Dashed Expectations

When the cable finally arrived, a computer engineer, who was part of a special government group pulled together to build infrastructure and manage the country's new digital resources, told me that priority would go to improving the connectivity of the government, business, computer clubs, and social service networks in health and education. Deputy Communications Minister Jorge Luis Perdomo, speaking a day before the cable arrived, warned that it was not a "magic solution" and that getting most Cubans online would involve large investments in infrastructure. Perdomo said there were no "political obstacles" to Internet use, just economic ones, but implied that, for most Cubans, getting connected was still a long way off.[2] "The underwater cable will provide higher quality communications, but not necessarily mean a broader extension of the same," the Communist Party daily *Granma* warned in late 2010. *Granma* opined that priority would go to those who already had access.[3] In other words, broadband would debut for the government, state and foreign companies, tourists, expats, some Cuban professionals, and individuals who bought online time at hotels, or account numbers and passwords on the black market. The cable was finally up and running in 2013, without any explanation as to the delay, but an official announcement once more cautioned that due to the expense of getting the nation online, it would be a long time coming.

"There won't be general access for the population to the Internet. Limits are more ideological than economic, so we'll have to keep connecting through the black market," said Alberto, a Santiago de Cuba resident in his early twenties. During a trip around the country in January 2012, I could not find a single person with home-based Internet access, though a few academics and other professionals were said to enjoy a few hours a week on the Web.

Young Cubans looking to leave the island often point to poor communications and isolation from modern life as a motive, along with low wages and a sense that they will never be able to adequately support a family. "At last we will have a good and less expensive connection to the world," thirty-two-year-old computer programmer Yurislaidi gushed in an interview from Chile when the cable arrived. She had moved there in 2009 to learn more about her profession after becoming frustrated with the lack of technology and limited Internet access in Cuba. "If only this will allow the Internet to arrive in Cuban homes, because I think it's the only place in the world without this service," she said.

Tunisia, Egypt, and other North African and Middle Eastern kingdoms and autocracies were swept by social-media-fueled revolts in 2011. The information revolution is forcing all politicians and governments—democratic, autocratic, or somewhere in between—to change how they operate, and of course Cuba is no exception. You can love the place or hate it, but there is no question that secrecy, the control of information flowing into and out of the country, and poor domestic communications have helped sustain the government in the face of fierce pressure from the United States. Those days are clearly numbered, and I have no doubt that coping with the Internet is one of the greatest political challenges Cuban authorities have ever faced. So far, the powers that be have been stalling for time as they ponder how their Revolution should manage the telecommunications revolution that is already well under way. An analogy would be using rags to stop rising floodwaters from seeping in under the front door as one's belongings are moved to the higher floors. But the Internet has arrived; cell phones and their cameras are everywhere; flash drives hang on lanyards around more and more people's necks. Blogs and Twitter appeared at the end of the last decade, though extraordinarily few residents are aware of them. The water is already at the authorities' knees. Complicating matters for the Cubans, the United States, both unintentionally and by design, uses the Internet to promote its own international political and economic agenda, values, and culture and to attack its enemies.

Cyber War

Around the same time that the fiber-optic cable arrived, another video made its appearance, this time from the Interior Ministry. The film featured a briefing by a young official in June 2010 on the United States' use of the Internet to undermine the government. The video was posted on the Web by someone using the screen name Black Coral, and its existence was first brought to the attention of pioneer blogger Yoani Sánchez as if to say, "Okay, you might have been just about the lone Cuban voice in cyberspace up to now, but we have decided to join you."[4]

The video, which appeared to have been leaked to Sánchez in an in-your-face manner, amounted to a declaration of war against what Cuba's secret services viewed as Washington's latest efforts to overturn the existing political and economic order on the island, this time through the use of Internet and telecommunications, and in no uncertain terms it branded imprisoned U.S. contractor Alan Gross as part of the plot, even as the Cuban government prepared to bring him to trial.

The video provided a unique and fascinating view into the thinking of Cuban officials as they struggled to come to terms with the inevitable, in one of the last countries in the world to require government authorization to access the Internet. With later events in Tunisia, Egypt, Bahrain, and then other Middle Eastern and North African countries still more than six months away, the presenter charged that the Obama administration was carrying out a four-point program aimed at fomenting civil unrest in Cuba and toppling the government: First, Washington was smuggling in sophisticated technology to set up an underground Wi-Fi system capable of allowing government opponents to communicate with each other inside the country and abroad, and with U.S. secret services and their proxies. Second, the United States was organizing, financing, and promoting bloggers opposed to the government. Third, Cuba's archenemy was establishing organizations outside the country to promote the bloggers and interact with young people through social networks. Finally, it was working to develop future leaders of the coming Internet-driven social unrest.

The presenter, speaking before a group of uniformed men and women, insisted that the Internet should be viewed not only as a threat but also as an opportunity. He said the government should take the offensive. "The technology in itself is not a threat, the threat is what someone does or could do from behind this technology, in the same way it is an opportunity because of what we are able to do with it," he said. He then charged that the United States had turned the Internet into a battlefield, and Twitter into a political weapon.

> It's a dynamic of permanent combat, and we cannot lose the perspective that the Internet is the battlefield, and that the enemy has their troops ready. We cannot step off the battlefield; we must enter the field with the strength and knowledge of our people so we can fight.... That, comrades, is what they mean to say that this is a tool that even though it was created by the enemy, we must also use it to fight.

The official in the video then charged that the United States was smuggling satellite-linked Wi-Fi systems, known as BGAN, into the country with an additional transmitter that could connect up to twenty-five people within a one-mile radius simultaneously to the Internet. The plan, he said, was to create enough of these links to establish a clandestine Internet platform that, via satellite, would circumvent government controls.

> What does a BGAN module bring, that is, this thing they are distributing in Cuba? What does it include? It comes with a video camera, five Blackberries . . . a notebook—which is a very small computer that guarantees the connection—the BGAN itself, and that's it: we're on the Internet.

The presenter explained that the program was first developed during the last years of the Bush administration and then actively pursued by the Obama administration, which was also trying to recruit technicians in Cuba to maintain it on the ground.

> Anyway, the idea, comrades, is to distribute this equipment and to establish national networks, and they want to supply members of these networks with cell phones with text-messaging service. The modules we've operatively detected have mostly been high-performance Blackberry phones with satellite connectivity, which is paid for outside Cuba, so they do not depend on our networks, nor do they pass through our supervision mechanisms. And of course they pay for this service, and they send emissaries to contact and finance these networks, which are made up of about five to ten members. They train them, establish and maintain contact with them from the outside.

The presenter went on to say that the main objective of the program was to use the Internet to foster social unrest, but cautioned that it could have a parallel purpose: to transmit intelligence.

> But if we put ourselves in the enemy's place, it also gives us the confidence that any intelligence transmission of any kind, I don't know, sitting there on that corner, I can open my laptop and have a secure connection which the Cuban authorities cannot control.

The official said that Alan Gross had been helping to set up the illegal network.

> This man we have up there [pointing to his PowerPoint presentation on the screen] is Alan Philip Gross, an American who is a prisoner in Cuba, a mercenary—now we can't say "mercenary," in modern discussion he is a "contractor," those are the terms of modern language—for the DAI, Development Alternative Initiative, that is, an agency subcontracted by USAID to create subversion in Cuba. Comrades, since I was a little boy,

those whom they pay to fight, to battle in a foreign land, that is a mercenary. And that is what this man was doing. The very same as in Playa Girón [the Cuban name for the Bay of Pigs invasion in 1961], but this guy came with other arms. He didn't come on a boat and didn't disembark with a gun in his hand, but it's the same story.

The presenter then delved into U.S. support for bloggers in Cuba who opposed the government.

In parallel, it is articulating and organizing a virtual network of mercenaries, of counterrevolutionaries, who are not the traditional counterrevolutionaries. . . . We're talking about young people, people who may have an appealing spiel, guys who live with our children, our brothers and can seem like normal people.

The presenter insisted the United States was out to paint the island black, as being anti-blogger, just as it did when it charged that there was no democracy or civil society in Cuba. Cuba had responded by promoting its own form of democracy and civil society, he said, and it must do the same on the Internet and not cede space to the enemy. "Being a blogger is not a bad thing. However, they are already presenting them as part of the same counter-revolutionary group. . . . They have their bloggers and we will have ours. And we're going to battle to see which group is stronger," he said. (Indeed, less than a year later there were dozens of "revolutionary" bloggers crossing swords in cyberspace with "counterrevolutionary" bloggers, and even Fidel Castro boasted a Twitter account.)

The official in the video moved on to charge that the United States was conducting Internet-based leadership classes inside its diplomatic mission in Havana, and setting up new organizations abroad.

The creation of a group of organizations that are different from the ones we're used to seeing. It's no longer the Cuban American National Foundation [the most powerful exile organization], no. They are there, but these do not resemble the Foundation. . . . No, now they appear with names a little more interesting: CubaVibra [Cuba Vibes], on the web, of course; Raíces de Esperanza [Roots of Hope]; Red Hispánica [Hispanic Network]. . . . What is their discourse? "I am not my dad, I did not leave Cuba, I was born here and I want to reconnect with my roots. And my roots are the same as yours, you are my same age, and you are there. It doesn't matter to me if you're part of the Juventud [Union of Young Communists]. . . . Let's talk, young person to young person, professional to professional." And with these dynamics they try to give the U.S. Cuban community a new face with which to engage with their counterparts, our nation's youth.

The official concluded the presentation by explaining the new breakdown of the $20 million in annual U.S. funding earmarked for promoting democracy, human rights, and civil society in Cuba. He stated that, in the past, most of those funds went to support traditional dissident activity, while in the latest funding, 80 percent went to support Internet-related activity.[5]

Dissidents, Western diplomats, and others scoffed at the video, arguing that in today's world access to the Internet is considered part of daily life and the sinister plot existed only because the country was one of the few on the planet where government authorization was required.

A week after the video appeared, the Cuban government stopped blocking dissident blogs inside the country. The battle in cyberspace—aimed more at the international audience than the Cuban, which had little access—was on. Then, as Alan Gross went to trial in March 2011, the Cuban government surfaced five of its double agents who had operated within ever more connected dissident circles. A documentary series was broadcast on Cuban television, featuring the undercover operatives as they told their stories. A few were seen and heard in hidden-camera videos interacting with U.S. diplomats and U.S. emissaries who were bringing in equipment and discussing their Internet plans.[6] Two of the agents testified at Gross's trial. One, the head of the Freemasons, had been the recipient of Gross's first package in 2004.

17

Castro, the Cardinal, and the Damas

Our country is in a very difficult situation, probably the most difficult we have experienced in the twenty-first century. . . . There is a need in Cuba to make the necessary changes promptly to remedy the situation.

Cardinal Jaime Ortega

During the short spring of 2003, a handful of women gathered on a Sunday morning at the Church of Santa Rita in the upscale Miramar district of Havana—a church attended by Cubans, but also by diplomats and other foreigners, and named after the patron saint of desperate, seemingly lost causes. The church also houses the Conference of Bishops offices. The women wore white and, after Mass, with pink gladioli in hand, they left the church at 26th Street, posing for pictures on the steps for a few moments. They walked, two abreast, two blocks to the right along Fifth Avenue, the most luxurious avenue in Havana, lined with mansions-turned-embassies, government buildings, foreign companies, and bank headquarters. The women stopped at 30th Street, crossed the avenue, and then walked silently twelve blocks to the left along the broad, leafy center divide, and then ten blocks back again to Santa Rita, where they chanted "Libertad! Libertad!" They entered a park alongside the church for a brief rally and press conference. The park hosts a monument to India's Mahatma Gandhi.

The women—relatives of seventy-five dissidents who, except one, were all men imprisoned for long terms in a just-concluded crackdown on the opposition—marched every Sunday for months under the watchful eyes of diplomats, foreign journalists, and state security agents, but were otherwise undisturbed. Their protests were the first such street demonstrations allowed since the earliest days of the revolution.

The female relatives of the imprisoned dissidents, who came to be known as the Damas de Blanco, or Ladies in White, had only a few dozen members across the country, plus a similar number of women supporters without imprisoned relatives, called the Damas de Apoyo, or Ladies in Support. The women were ignored by the Cuban media and the public, including passersby on Fifth Avenue. No one ever spontaneously joined their ranks as they marched week after week, month after month, year after year. The women, around thirty in number and reaching close to fifty on important dates such as Father's Day or the anniversary of their loved ones' arrests, returned Sunday after Sunday to stage their quiet demonstration.

A few times a year, the Damas would break from their pattern and march to state buildings, usually harassed by a few hundred government-organized hecklers. In 2005 they staged a sit-in near the offices of Fidel Castro, only to be dragged onto a bus and driven home. None of the ladies was ever placed behind bars during their protests, beaten with clubs, handcuffed, or tear- or pepper-gassed in Havana. There were no heavily protected and armed riot police, cops on horses, or water cannons. Because there were so few Ladies, the mob—and the policewomen pulling and pushing them onto buses to take them home after a sit-in—served the same purpose.

I worked Sundays for Thomson Reuters and so became a regular observer of the Damas and the various incidents that occurred over the years. Through their struggle, leaders Berta Soler and Laura Pollán grew into seasoned government opponents.[1] Over time, 23 of the original 75 imprisoned dissidents (including the only woman) were paroled for health reasons.

And so it went until March 2010, when—energized by the international coverage of the death of hunger striker Orlando Zapata Tamayo, Guillermo Fariñas's hunger strike demanding that sick prisoners be released, and the West's condemnation of the Cuban government in response—the women staged a week of daily marches and sit-ins throughout Havana to mark the anniversary of their loved ones' arrests. The Damas were met by government supporters, pushed and shoved, and so they once again captured international headlines and sympathy. President Obama praised them, and a huge rally of Cuban Americans in Miami supported them. The Cuban government declared that the Damas would need a permit to march in the future, even in front of Santa Rita on Sundays, and for the first time, state security agents stopped the support group from going to the Sunday protests, leaving just the handful of prisoners' relatives to stand alone. For three Sundays in April 2010, as they left the church, the women—never more than six in number—were met by authorities who said they needed a permit for their silent march. The women stood their ground, but each time they began their walk, they were surrounded by government supporters, and grueling *actos de repudio* (demonstrations of repudiation) followed. On the last Sunday in April, the counterdemonstration lasted seven hours: a mob pushed the handful of women into the nearby park and, directed by state security agents, shouted obscenities, tormented them, and refused to let them leave. "We will be back," Laura Pollán said as dusk fell and the Ladies in White were finally escorted by security agents to a bus that took them home.

The Damas would be back, but not the mob. The Damas could not be broken, and well-known Cuban artists and intellectuals, including iconic musicians Pablo Milanés and Carlos Varela, publicly criticized the *actos de repudio*. Many more cultural figures and intellectuals questioned the repression in private. Fariñas, still on his hunger strike in the hospital, weakened, adding to the international human rights clamor and pressure on the government.

Cardinal Ortega Enters the Fray

Cuban Cardinal Jaime Ortega entered the political fray through a remarkable interview in the April 2010 issue of the Havana archdiocese's monthly magazine, *Palabra Nueva* (New Word), which captured the moment perfectly and would catapult him and his church into a new role in Cuban society. He began:

> Our country is in a very difficult situation, probably the most difficult we have experienced in the twenty-first century. In the Cuban media there appear all kinds of opinions on how to find solutions for economic and social difficulties at this time. . . . But there is a fundamental common denominator among almost everyone in the discussion: there is a need in Cuba to promptly make the necessary changes to remedy the situation.

The cardinal did not mince words; he charged that the international media were distorting Cuban reality by turning hunger striker Zapata's death into a "violent" campaign against the country. At the same time, he more diplomatically took the U.S.-Cuba conflict to task, deliberately beginning with the Obama administration.

> At the beginning of his administration, President Raúl Castro suggested to the United States dialogue without conditions, and on all issues, including human rights, and has repeated his proposal in more than one occasion. In his presidential political campaign, Barack Obama also said he would change the style used so far and will seek above all to talk directly to Cuba. At that time there were growing expectations about a possible meeting between the two countries. However, after coming to power, the new American president has repeated the old pattern of previous governments: if Cuba makes changes regarding human rights, then the United States will lift the embargo and open up space for further dialogue. While important steps were taken to modify some unwise measures imposed by the previous administration, in time the pre-election proposals were altered. Once again the old politics prevailed: start at the end.

The cardinal next tackled government repression.

> In recent weeks, the situation has worsened, specifically from the death of the prisoner Orlando Zapata Tamayo due to a hunger strike. At least one Cuban citizen [Guillermo Fariñas] has joined this kind of protest, the wives and mothers of political prisoners are demonstrating on the streets for their loved ones, to which the Cuban government responds with firmness. . . . All of this further thinning the environment. Is it possible to have a dialogue in these conditions? . . . That is why it is so sad to see the acts of repudiation to mothers and wives of several prisoners, which are now joined by another group of women, all known as the Ladies in White. . . . Such verbal and even physical intolerance should not continue in our history as a people, as a characteristic of the Cuban person.[2]

More than 90 percent of Cubans believe in the supernatural. Compared with other parts of the Latin American region, relatively few are practicing Roman Catholics. Nevertheless, hundreds of thousands of Cubans attend church, at least once in a while. Others claim the label simply because they were baptized and never joined another religion.[3] Cuba is more of a magical, gay place than somber Roman Catholicism would seem to allow. Few Cubans I ever met were prone to guilt or much introspection, always believing they are victims of outside forces, both natural and man-made. "If you get the chance, enjoy yourself: who knows what will happen tomorrow?" is the popular attitude. Artists, from Wilfredo Lam to Nelson Domínguez, José Fuster, and Manuel Mendive, offer a window on the colorful and abstract Cuban psyche. And Cuban music does spring up like magic from every corner of the island, generation after generation, bathing an often suffering people in song and dance, then spreading like a gift around the world—the rumba, cha-cha-cha, salsa, and Compay Segundo.

Cardinal Ortega was never a great fan of Communism, nor were the Castro brothers fans of his. Cuba's Council of Churches and the Jewish community had worked closely with the government and had more or less come to support the national revolutionary process under way. The Council of Churches' leaders even served as deputies in the National Assembly. Not the Catholic Church, though. Throughout most of their respective careers—which in Ortega's case included a stint in a "reeducation" labor camp in the late 1960s—the Castros and the cardinal had been embroiled in confrontation. The thaw began around the time of the fall of the Soviet Union and picked up with Pope John Paul's visit in 1998, but it is still safe to say that the Roman Catholic Church is the largest organization in Cuba that has a different ideology from the Communist Party. It is also its most powerful domestic critic, which makes what followed the cardinal's interview even more remarkable.

The Prisoner Release

According to the Havana Archdiocese, on April 26, 2010—a day after the Damas were subjected to the grueling seven-hour *acto de repudio*—the cardinal sent a letter to Raúl Castro lamenting the incident and asking that it not be repeated. A series of meetings followed between the Church and the government, and the Church and the Damas, and the following Sunday the cardinal himself served Mass at Santa Rita and announced that he was present to guarantee that the Damas could resume their Sunday strolls unmolested—which they did.

The cardinal's shuttle diplomacy continued, and on May 19 he and Bishop Dionisio García of Santiago de Cuba, the head of the Conference of Bishops, met with Castro. The official media headlined the talks the following day, complete with a photo of a smiling Raúl Castro standing with the prelates and a statement that they had discussed "the favorable development" of Church-state relations and the "current national and international situation."

Cardinal Ortega told the press that same afternoon that the Wednesday meeting was a "magnificent beginning of an ongoing process . . . recognition of the role of the Church as an interlocutor; of overcoming any old grievances that may have existed, so that we may walk along a new path." Ortega said that, unlike past meetings with officials, including one with Fidel Castro in 2005, the four-hour discussion had not focused on Church complaints and petitions, but on Cuban society and how to improve it.

Cardinal Ortega and Bishop García said that the plight of political prisoners was discussed. "I believe that there is willingness on both sides. I hope it will be resolved. . . . I believe it will be," Bishop García said.[4]

So why was the good cardinal so optimistic after the meeting? And, more important, why did he then put his reputation on the line both at home and abroad by praising Raúl Castro's intentions and braving the wrath of Washington, the exile establishment, and dissidents aligned with them? Here is a paraphrased account of what a Cuban friend of mine said Ortega told him about that first meeting.

> The cardinal said: "Raúl met us at the Central Committee building and walked us to his offices. On the way, he stopped and opened a door to a large office. 'This is my brother's office. No one uses it. It is exactly the way it was that night when he became ill,' Raúl said. He then opened another door, into a large room with many tables and computers. 'This was the headquarters of the Battle of Ideas,' Raúl said."

The cardinal told my friend that he was impressed by Raúl's sincerity, candor, and understanding of the need to reform Cuba's economy, strengthen its social and moral fabric, and lift many restrictions on personal freedoms. Besides, he saw no viable nonviolent alternative to Raúl on the Cuban horizon.

> The cardinal said: "Raúl said he had run into an economy and bureaucracy that was like a brick wall. It had to be demolished, but he had decided to do it brick by brick, not all at once." The cardinal asked Raúl why he had appointed so many military men to his government. Raúl said simply that the country was in crisis and he had turned to men he knew and trusted, and that this would change over time.

The cardinal told my friend that Castro said that Cubans should be free to come and go as they please, as in any other country. Castro asked the cardinal—and, through him, the Damas—to draw up a list of all the political prisoners in the country who had not committed violent crimes, and indicated he wanted to release them all.[5]

The cardinal, Bishop García, Castro, and visiting Vatican foreign minister Dominique Mamberti met in Havana on June 21, 2010. Government officials and Church leaders stood smiling together and gave speeches praising one another and government-Church relations at the farewell reception for Mamberti. The beaming cardinal walked around like a peacock in the barnyard, with tail feathers on full display. Apparently something big was up, and I told a U.S. diplomat that our government was about to be outflanked. The diplomat appeared puzzled by the scene.

Spanish foreign minister Miguel Ángel Moratinos arrived in Cuba on July 5, 2010, as his country's soccer team went to the World Cup finals in South Africa. That Sunday, the seventh, after watching the game in Raúl's home, Moratinos met with Castro and the cardinal, and it was announced that all 52 dissidents still behind bars from the 2003 crackdown would be released, and that Spain would accept any of them, and their families, who wished to leave the country. My sources said Castro planned to release not just the 52 dissidents but many more viewed by human rights advocates as political prisoners. In the end, 13 of the 52 prisoners went to their homes in Cuba and Amnesty International's 53rd prisoner of conscience to the United States. In April 2011 the Spanish government announced that a total of 115 prisoners had arrived, along with 647 relatives, and the process had come to an end.[6] Many would later move to the United States.

Raúl Castro has zero sympathy for those whom he views as wishing to return Cuba to the pre-Revolution days and once more become a U.S. dependency. And, although not forced, the prisoners were clearly pressured to trade their jail cells for exile in Spain. "It is worth reiterating that there will be no impunity for the enemies of the homeland, for those who attempt to endanger our independence. Let nobody be deceived. The defense of our sacred achievements, of our streets and plazas, will continue being the prime duty of revolutionaries whom we cannot deprive of that right," Castro told the National Assembly in August.[7]

The Damas kept marching along Fifth Avenue, gladiolas in hand, though few remained from the original group or had relatives behind bars. Their demands continued to include freedom for those they considered political prisoners, but now the women also condemned political harassment and repression in the form of temporary detentions and demanded the right to freely protest on Cuba's streets. Attempts to spread the tiny bit of space they had carved out in front of Santa Rita to other provinces and churches were met by the mob and temporary detentions.

Human Rights

Raúl Castro had already taken a number of steps signaling that he might be more willing than his brother to make some concessions to international criticism of Cuba's human rights record—criticism also voiced more and more openly and importantly by Cuban intellectuals, academics, musicians, and artists. When he first took over for his brother in 2006, and with no fanfare or publicity, Castro gradually began reducing the number of common and political prisoners. According to local human rights advocates, between 2006 and July 2010 the number of political prisoners declined from more than 300 to 167, while Amnesty International listed only 53 prisoners of conscience.[8]

Four days after Raúl became president, Cuba signed the International Covenant on Civil and Political Rights and the International Covenant on Economic, Social and Cultural Rights, two U.N. human rights pacts that Fidel Castro had refused to endorse for more than three decades.[9]

Raúl Castro announced on April 28, 2008, that all death sentences had been commuted to prison terms of thirty years to life, with the exception of two Salvadorans convicted of bombing hotels, including the Capri and the Nacional, and a Cuban exile convicted of terrorism after he stormed ashore in 1994, heavily armed, and killed a policeman. "The Council of State decided to commute the death penalty imposed on a group of prisoners," Castro announced at a Communist Party Central Committee meeting, in a speech broadcast by state-run television. "This does not mean we have eliminated the death penalty from the penal code," he said.[10] By the close of 2010, the sentences of the three remaining inmates on death row had been commuted to thirty-year terms.

Castro also loosened regulations on outdoor religious processions and lifted a ban on priests visiting prisoners on Sundays and ministering to the faithful.

The Caridad del Cobre would soon emerge from her shrine in Santiago de Cuba (in the form of a replica) in 2011 to be marched across the entire country for five months in preparation for the four-hundredth anniversary of her discovery by fishermen in the Bay of Nipe. Then the Vatican announced Pope Benedict XVI would visit in March 2012 to commemorate the anniversary.

As 2011 drew to a close, and with the visit of Pope Benedict looming in March, Castro announced that more than 2,900 common prisoners would be freed under a government amnesty. He said the amnesty was a "humanitarian gesture" that had "taken into account" the upcoming papal visit and requests by relatives of the prisoners and various religious organizations in Cuba. The amnesty covered prisoners over sixty years of age, prisoners who were ill, women, and some young inmates who had no previous criminal history, as well as a few who had been convicted of crimes against "the security of the state." The Cuban president said that 86 foreigners, from twenty-five countries, were also on the amnesty list. U.S. contractor Alan Gross, who began serving a fifteen-year prison term that year, was not among them. The government would soon announce that 10,000 common prisoners were released over a six-month period, leaving some 57,000 behind bars.[11]

The United States and Cuba have fought a fierce propaganda war in the international arena since Fidel Castro and his band of rebels first took to the mountains. After the fall of European Communism, the United States focused on the lack of civil rights and political and economic freedoms on the island, and Cuba on Washington's incessant pummeling of the country. Cuba has always justified its one-party political system and its repression of political opponents as legitimate defenses against a far-more-powerful United States out to destroy at all costs the region's most important dissident leader and nation, while the United States insists that its efforts to change the island's political, social, and economic way of life seek only to promote democracy and protect Cubans' human rights in the face of a cruel totalitarian regime. It's a bit of a chicken-and-egg situation. Which came first, the U.S. repression of dissident Cuba at a time when Washington engineered and supported many military dictatorships in the region? Or Fidel Castro's repression of dissent, followed by Washington's efforts to rescue the island's inhabitants? From the very start of his career, the debate has swirled around the person of Fidel Castro and his well-known intolerance of those who disagree, and the U.S. embargo, and Washington's well-known intolerance of any serious challenge to its dominance over the region. Does the Cuban Communist Party repress its opponents? Without a doubt! Does the U.S. embargo aim at making Cubans suffer to the point where, it is hoped, they desperately topple the government? No question about it! Organizations such as Amnesty International regularly con-

demn both parties for the mess, as do the vast majority of the world's governments, including the United States' closest allies, with the exception of Israel.

Then there are the small, isolated groups of individuals within Cuba who
challenge the government and almost inevitably become allied with and openly
and/or covertly supported by the United States or other Western powers and
exile organizations. The dissidents, like the Cubans on both sides of the Florida
Straits, are caught in the middle of an undeclared war and the propaganda
that goes with it.[12] The United States and its allies openly and covertly provide
Cuban dissidents with funds and resources. When the dissidents are inevitably
repressed, the unlucky individuals become the excuse to paint the island as a
tropical gulag and justify external sanctions. The Cuban government gives opponents little choice but to turn to Washington and exiles for survival, then
blasts them as mercenaries and agents of an enemy foreign power, and as proof
of the need for single-party rule and remaining ever vigilant in the barrios and
on the streets.

I have known all the main dissident players for years; I have covered their
activities, chatted with them at diplomatic cocktail parties, interviewed them,
and witnessed them being mobbed and shoved around by government supporters in acts of repudiation. Discontent runs deep in Cuba, where no one
has made a living wage for two decades, but most Cubans are seeking change
through reform and evolution of the system, not in open alliance with Washington and Miami's political establishment which seeks regime change. Most
Cubans are dissidents, just not "dissidents" as they are known abroad.

All politics are local, even in Cuba, and Raúl's remarkable tip of his hat
to the cardinal and the subsequent prisoner release were no exception. Big
changes were in store for the Cubans, and Raúl was hoping to get the Church
publicly on board as those changes began. Castro wanted to do far more than
release political prisoners. He was ready at last to move ahead with his reforms,
and he wanted to build a coalition to push them through and ensure stability,
in which the Church could play an important role. Castro apparently wanted
his big brother's visible support as well.

18

Fidel, Born Again

A distinguished visitor gives Fidel a rare turtle for the zoo. Castro holds up the animal with his usual curiosity.

"How long do these turtles live?" he asks.

"Oh, a very long time, maybe even two hundred years," his visitor replies.

Castro hands the animal back.

"I'm sorry. I don't want to become too fond of it only to be around when it dies," he says.

A Cuban joke

Talk about a dramatic entrance! On Monday, July 12, 2010, one month shy of his eighty-fourth birthday and after being absent from public life for four years, Fidel Castro went on television to warn that the world was on the brink of a nuclear holocaust. The first of the political prisoners released by his brother were preparing to board a plane for Madrid even as the previously taped, hour-long interview aired.[1] Fidel stole the international coverage. The previous Wednesday, he had gone to the National Scientific Research Center to chat with its directors. This first public appearance in four years did not become known until a few days later when it was mentioned in a pro-government blog.[2] There would be many more visits around and about Havana as the "Historic Leader of the Revolution" came out of seclusion to once more dominate the domestic news cycle and impact international coverage throughout the summer with his doomsday message.

State-run media reported all during the day that television and radio would transmit a "special roundtable with Comandante Fidel Castro Ruz to evaluate the dangerous events taking place in the Middle East." There was no mention of the prisoners preparing to leave for Madrid, nor would there be, as they trickled out of jail over the coming months. Castro, in a blue track suit and answering questions put to him by a reporter, appeared in far better condition than he had in August 2009, when a twenty-minute video was broadcast of him talking to Venezuelan law students (the new guerrillas of democratic revolution).

Castro had penned a series of opinion columns over the preceding weeks, forecasting that new U.N. sanctions against Iran—and subsequent movements by U.S. and Israeli warships in that area—would presage a shooting war if Iran's merchant ships were boarded, and the war could quickly escalate into a nuclear conflagration. Raúl Castro and other government officials remained quiet on the subject, but Fidel lamented that Russia and China had backed U.N. sanctions on Iran, saying that while they sought peace, they paved the way for war. "Russia and China are armed . . . but are trying to preserve the peace, so they could have vetoed the sanctions, but didn't," he said. "The United States does not play fair and never tells the truth."

Castro, who was sitting behind a desk and shuffling papers as he answered questions from his interviewer, warned that Iran would not give in to international pressure. In a column published the previous evening, Castro had said the "main purpose" of his writings on the Middle East was to "warn international public opinion about what was occurring."[3] The columns had attracted little attention internationally, while his appearance and message now did.

Fidel Castro, who retained his parliamentary seat and at least symbolically the post of First Secretary of the Communist Party, was next spotted at the National Aquarium, watching the dolphin show, and then meeting with economists, whom he ordered to study what the region should do after the nuclear war; a few days later he was preaching his apocalyptic views to Cuban diplomats, and then to war veterans, intellectuals, and artists.[4] His recorded activities were broadcast repeatedly by state-run media, leading up to a live speech before a special meeting of the National Assembly in early August 2010.

The Cuban public, by and large, welcomed their Comandante back after four years of seclusion, with the warmth and sympathy one might bestow on an ailing and wise grandfather, home after a prolonged hospital stay but in no position any longer to be the real head of the household. Some paid attention, some didn't. Some raised their eyebrows and then tilted their heads to the sky as if to say, "¿Hasta cuando?" (How long will we have to put up with him?) Others furrowed their brows in concentration over his every word. "I think Fidel is acting intelligently, as he always has," housewife Gladys Ulloa said in a telephone interview from eastern Santiago de Cuba. "He has an important role to play, alerting the world to tragedies ahead while his brother governs. I do not believe that one role contradicts the other."

Most young people in Havana shrugged Castro off as they enjoyed their summer vacation. Some of his critics, such as dissident blogger Yoani Sánchez in the *Washington Post*, heaped scorn upon him. "The stuttering old man with quivering hands was a shadow of the Greek-profiled military leader who, while a million voices chanted his name in the plaza, pardoned lives, announced executions, proclaimed laws that no one had been consulted on and declared the right of revolutionaries to make revolution," she wrote.[5]

Other Cubans, with their wry sense of humor, weighed in. One of many jokes making the rounds at the time opened with Castro lying on his deathbed, with his brother Raúl at his side and a crowd of Cubans at the window chanting, "Fidel! Fidel!"

"What are those people doing outside?" Fidel asks.

"Saying farewell," Raúl responds.

"Oh, where are they all going?" asks Fidel.

Another yarn had a distinguished visitor giving Fidel a rare turtle for the zoo. Castro holds up the animal with his usual curiosity.

"How long do these turtles live?" he asks.

"Oh, a very long time, maybe even two hundred years," his visitor replies.

Castro hands the animal back.

"I'm sorry. I don't want to become too fond of it only to be around when it dies," he says.

On August 7, 2010, Fidel Castro convened a special session of the government. "I can't believe it," said Havana resident Diana as she stared at the television set in her living room. There was the Comandante, who would turn eighty-four on August 13, back from the dead in his olive-drab military pants and untucked shirt, rather than formal uniform, as he spoke from a podium to the National Assembly. Fidel Castro's appearance that Saturday—before parliamentary deputies, the diplomatic corps, and foreign journalists—marked the first time the Cubans, and all of us, had been offered a live glimpse of the iconic bearded figure since he underwent surgery in July 2006. Castro walked slowly, bent over, and with the help of aides and his wife. His speech lasted eleven minutes, rather than hours, and after an hour of back-and-forth with deputies, he tired and the special session was ended.

The elder Castro used the expected publicity to deliver a message that was hardly reassuring to people like Diana, who considered him a prophet. Fidel warned that the most recent U.N. sanctions on Iran would trigger a nuclear holocaust if, come September, the United States inspected the country's ships, as called for in the United Nations' June sanctions on Iran. Only world pressure on U.S. president Barack Obama, he said, could avert a conflagration that would bring all leading economies to a standstill. "Does anyone believe that the powerful empire will back away from the sanctions' demand that Iranian merchant vessels be inspected?" Fidel asked rhetorically, as he defended his doomsday forecast that had raised eyebrows at home and abroad. "Does anyone think the Iranians—a people with a culture of thousands of years and which is much more intertwined with death than ours—will lack the courage we have shown in resisting the demands of the United States?" He predicted that Iran would respond by sinking the U.S. fleet and that events would then spiral out of control.[6]

"I doubt Fidel believes what he is saying. He is being dramatic, trying to stay relevant," a European diplomat said. "The question we all have is what this means in terms of Cuba's domestic politics," he added. Indeed, ever since Castro became ill and resigned the presidency in favor of his brother Raúl, there had been speculation over who was really calling the shots in Havana and whether the slow progress of Raúl Castro's efforts to reform the state-dominated economy was a sign of opposition by his brother. Fidel Castro's sudden reappearance and the leadership's penchant for secrecy only added to the fog.

But it had been eighteen months since Fidel Castro had strayed from international issues and uttered or written a word about Cuba's domestic situation—with one exception, which indicated, I believed, that the brothers were working together and had divided up the public turf. That one exception was in a reflection earlier in the year when Fidel had stuck in a few lines—which everyone seemed to have missed—backing his brother's economic plans, outlined on April 4, 2010, at a Congress of Young Communists where Raúl said:

Without a sound and dynamic economy and without the removal of superfluous expenses and waste, it will neither be possible to improve the living standard of the population nor to preserve and improve the high levels of education and healthcare ensured to every citizen free of charge. . . . If the people do not feel the need to work for a living because they are covered by extremely paternalistic and irrational state regulations, we will never be able to stimulate love for work or resolve the chronic lack of construction, farming and industrial workers; teachers; police agents and other indispensable trades that have steadily been disappearing. If we do not build a firm and systematic social rejection of illegal activities and different expressions of corruption, more than a few will continue to make fortunes at the expense of the majority's labors while disseminating attitudes that crash into the essence of socialism. If we keep the inflated payrolls in nearly every sector of national life and pay salaries that fail to correspond with the result of work, thus raising the amount of money in circulation, we cannot expect the prices to cease climbing constantly or prevent the deterioration of the people's purchasing power. We know that the budgeted and entrepreneurial sectors have hundreds of thousands of workers in excess; some analysts estimate that the surplus of people in work positions exceeds one million.[7]

Fidel Castro, in a reflection four days later, termed Raúl's speech "short, profound and precise . . . especially the need to overcome everything that works against the healthy development of our economy."[8] That sure sounded like an endorsement to me.

So why, then, wasn't Fidel vocally backing his brother by repeating his words every chance he got? And why, later in the year, when the historic measures became public, did he continue to speak and write only about international issues? Perhaps doing otherwise would indeed have undermined Raúl's presidency.

Fidel Castro once again began granting interviews to foreign journalists in August 2010, first to the editor of the Mexican paper *La Jornada*, in which he talked about being near death and wishing his ordeal was over; and then to American journalist Jeffrey Goldberg, accompanied by Julia Sweig, senior fellow at the Washington-based Council on Foreign Relations in charge of Latin America and author of a number of books on Cuba. Goldberg and Sweig would soon make headlines when they publicized a brief comment by Castro during a lunch at his home.

Goldberg, a Middle East expert, had written a few months earlier in a piece in the *Atlantic* that Israel would almost inevitably have to act against Iran if its nuclear program was not halted and, while not warning of nuclear war, Goldberg did point out that Iran's geopolitical position, along strategic oil-shipping lanes and bordering Russia, meant that such an action could have huge international repercussions.

As August gave way to September, Fidel Castro lured Goldberg to Havana with the promise of an exclusive interview. He came in the company of Julia Sweig, who knew the island and Fidel. Goldberg soon blogged a statement by Fidel that reverberated around the world: "The Cuban model doesn't even work for us anymore," Castro had shot back when asked about exporting revolution. This was interpreted by much of the world's media as an admission that socialism was a failure and that even Fidel Castro thought so. Not really. Castro was exploring a theme he'd visited before. He garnered similar headlines back in 2005 when he stated, "Among all the errors we may have committed, the greatest of them all was that we believed that someone really knew something about socialism."[9]

The Cuban model had changed little since 2005, and it was clearly on the eighty-four-year-old semiretired leader's mind as his brother prepared to announce plans to overhaul the economy. Nevertheless, as word filtered onto Cuban streets—from CNN and Miami television headlines picked up in hotels and on illegal satellite dishes—that the man referred to as the Historic Leader of the Revolution wanted to dump Communism, Castro publicly scolded Goldberg and Sweig for misinterpreting him. The statement was a dodge, Castro said in September 2010, as he launched the second volume of his memoirs of the revolutionary war at Havana University. The journalists' question—whether the Cuban model was still worth exporting—was a trick to get him to admit that Cuba had been exporting revolution. Fidel had offered up the nine words with great irony, he said. "My idea, as the whole world knows, is that the capitalist system doesn't work now either for the United States or the world, driving it from crisis to crisis, which are each time more serious."[10]

PART IV

Brave New World (2010–2013)

19

Pink Slips and Permits

> We have to permanently erase the notion that Cuba is the only
> country in the world where people can live without working.
>
> *Raúl Castro*

In early September 2010, even as the Church-brokered prisoner release proceeded and with Fidel still out and about, a source handed me the Communist Party presentation "Information about the Reorganization of the Labor
Force," used to prepare officials for another Raúl Castro shock-and-awe event.
"No wonder Raúl wants some backing," I said to myself, thinking of the cardinal and Fidel. The long-awaited reform of retail services had begun, but with it
came massive layoffs and deep cuts in unemployment benefits.

Just as I was preparing my scoop, the official Cuban Federation of Trade
Unions beat me to it, announcing on September 13 that the government would
lay off 500,000 employees over six months—some 10 percent of the state labor
force—and another 500,000 thereafter. The statement said workers deemed
"available" could look to "new forms of non-state employment, among them
leasing land, cooperatives and self-employment, absorbing hundreds of thousands of workers in the coming years."[1]

The Party document I acquired said that laid-off employees would no longer
receive unemployment benefits until they obtained another job. They would
be eligible for up to five months of unemployment benefits, beginning with just
one month for ten years' service and increasing to five months for twenty-five
years or more. Equally harsh conditions would now apply to workers whose
jobs were temporarily or permanently lost due to natural phenomena—for
example, hurricanes—or not-so-natural ones, such as lost markets, mechanical breakdowns, or a lack of spare parts and raw materials to keep a factory
running. For a long time, workers who were let go had received their most recent average pay at their subsequent jobs, but this practice too was eliminated.
And while workers who were laid off temporarily due to work stoppages not
under their control, but who did not permanently lose their jobs, had previously been guaranteed unemployment payments indefinitely until they were

called back, they would now come under the formula for laid-off employees and could be fired if they refused temporary work. The new unemployment regulations were not mentioned in the trade union statement. A good example of those affected was tourism workers. Some 35 percent of the labor force was laid off from May into October as tourism dropped. According to a family member, who cleaned hotel rooms in the idyllic key of Cayo Guillermo off the northern coast of Ciego de Ávila, most employees received just one month's unemployment benefits beginning in 2011 and then were left on their own until they were called back. Some were offered temporary employment—in this person's case, a cleaning job at a local hospital. She turned down the job without repercussions.

"Our state cannot and should not continue maintaining companies, productive entities, services, and budgeted sectors with bloated payrolls [and] losses that hurt the economy," the trade union federation statement said.[2] Economic commentator Ariel Terrero commented "traumatic but inevitable" during his morning television spot the next day.

The Communist Party document gave me an advantage over other journalists, at least for the few days until it surfaced on the Internet, because the story was as much about creating a private sector as it was about the layoffs. The much-awaited transformation of retail services had finally begun—the most important economic restructuring since the earliest days of the Revolution. Many restrictions on self-employment (often a euphemism for small businesses) were lifted, and many of the 500,000 state jobs would be moved to the "non-state sector," which barely existed at the time. The Party document said that 250,000 new self-employment licenses would be issued through 2011, and 215,000 jobs would shift from state services and small state-owned manufacturing workshops to leasing arrangements, cooperatives, and other "new forms of administration." The government reported that, at the close of 2009, more than 85 percent of the Cuban labor force—about 5 million people—worked for the state. There were 591,000 workers in the private sector, most of them farmers and 143,000 self-employed, and the remaining 5 percent went unaccounted for.[3]

All this was quite a shock in a land where job security was a way of life guaranteed by the Constitution, along with a minimum income and free social services. For the first time since the 1960s, Cuba would have the beginnings of a labor market. Raúl Castro had warned in April and again in August 2010 that the shoe was about to drop. "We have to permanently erase the notion that Cuba is the only country in the world where people can live without working," Castro said in his August 2010 speech to the National Assembly.[4] Further, the "non-state" sector had officially been viewed with suspicion—if not contempt—under Fidel Castro, and, despite Raúl Castro's efforts to change that perception, and countless letters to *Granma*, it was still seen that way by many.

Cuba's streets were soon abuzz with talk of pink slips raining down and the once all-but-forbidden self-employment permits being issued with few questions asked. It seemed workers were being laid off everywhere, from the Party Central Committee apparatus and much-touted sports training centers to hospitals and hotels. Employees at the state-owned Special Protection Services Company (SEPSA) were told they would be let go. "We were offered jobs in the prison system, police, and traffic," said a disgruntled neighbor, who worked for SEPSA. "Security guards were told they would be hired by the companies they protected." SEPSA later backtracked. Communist Party officials had to be brought in to calm workers down at the Havana Libre Hotel (the former Hilton), where a large number of jobs were eliminated, a friend who worked there said. Those who lost these positions, highly prized because of the tips and other benefits, appealed twice on the grounds that they were let go arbitrarily; but they lost their case.

The plan to lay off 500,000 workers quickly became bogged down due to worker resistance and caution in implementing new forms of administration such as leasing and cooperatives. Raúl's point man for reform, Marino Murillo, would say a year after the announcement that only 127,000 state jobs were eliminated.[5] The state payroll was reduced another 5.7 percent in 2012, Economy Minister Adel Yzquierdo said in his year-end speech to the National Assembly, or by 228,000 jobs.[6]

It is always a psychological and an economic shock to lose one's job. Diplomats, other foreigners, and some Cubans fretted about potential unrest and a crime wave. But Cuba's new unemployed would not be left totally out in the cold. All citizens still received free health care and education, subsidized utilities, subsidized food rations, and an automatic adjustment of mortgages to no more than 10 percent of the top breadwinner's income. Further, there were no private pensions at stake, and on-the-job benefits—from a month's vacation to lengthy maternity leave—were automatic, at least at state jobs, and did not depend on seniority. The self-employed, their employees, and agriculture workers would now also receive some state benefits, as they began contributing to social security. In addition, many Cubans received remittances from relatives abroad, worth far more than the average monthly salary (which was equivalent to around $18), or did something on the side to make ends meet. Still, as my neighbor Fifi pointed out, Cubans were now facing a lack of security that most had never experienced. "I understand the need to improve the economy, but it's hard to take after fifty years of job security," she said. "It will be hard to get another state job, because they are cutting everywhere, and many older workers are used to a desk job and might have a hard time adjusting to doing something else."

Adding to the confusion and sense of injustice was that the layoffs were not based on seniority, but were the top manager's prerogative after taking into account an evaluation of each employee's job performance by workplace committees. The committees, made up of administrators and Communist Party and trade union members, helped decide workers' fates in a process that was viewed by some as open to the vagaries of office politics. "Ability means friends and interests," one friend remarked. An immediate consequence of the new policy was that many workers, suddenly fearful of losing jobs they once took for granted and often carried out with little interest, began to take their work more seriously. "People used to stay home if they or their kid had a sniffle, and now they are going to work and school even if they are really sick, spreading their colds around," my daughter, the family doctor, said.

Local economists said the cuts were long overdue, in spite of the accompanying unease and pain. The Cuban system, modeled after the Soviet Union, was based on each employee's doing a single task and refusing to do more, even if it meant sitting around all day. One economist said that each ambulance, with its driver and two medics per twelve-hour shift, boasted an additional dozen or more support staff, from mechanics to cleaners! And he said that the Construction Ministry had 20,000 security guards and just 8,000 bricklayers, yet theft of bricks went on unabated. "Workers will now be expected to do more, but will also receive a higher salary," he said. "There is no reason for a state-hired mechanic or cleaner to sit around waiting for an ambulance to break down, or for it to return in the evening to get cleaned. Private contractors could do that," he said.

Old habits die hard. During Spain's domination of the island, government jobs were viewed as a way to fleece the treasury, both for the king and for oneself. Phantom posts were created and distributed more or less at will to friends and "business associates" for four centuries, with some of the more lucrative positions, such as those in customs, staying within the family or going to close friends. The practice continued, although in a slightly less outrageous fashion, during the years of U.S. tutelage and after that, under the Revolution, in the form of inflated payrolls and "indirect" jobs. For example, in 2011 Havana Province was divided into two new provinces, Artemisa and Mayabeque, both tasked as pilot projects to design more efficient government at the provincial and municipal levels, with plans for the outcome to go nationwide in 2014. In January 2013, the weekly *Opciones* newspaper ran an interview with the president of Mayabeque's provincial government, Tamara Valido Benítez, during which she stated, "Here, the experiment has led to a considerable rationalization of the human and material resources used for public administration to carry out its functions. There has been a reduction of 3,135 leadership posts, 25,540 additional jobs, and the elimination of 111 buildings."[7]

Retail Sector Reform

My standard line to visitors interested in knowing more about self-employment in Cuba was that they really meant small businesses, because just about everyone in the country was "self-employed" in some capacity to make even bare-bones ends meet. All Cubans worked for the state and also for themselves. And by 2010 many people had small underground businesses, for example car body shops or making pastries, or worked full-time without a license in the building trades. When Cuba first authorized self-employment in 1994, Fidel Castro called it a temporary concession to capitalism, and the *cuentapropistas*—literally those who worked on their own account—were overregulated and overtaxed, which forced many to operate quasi-legally, go completely underground, or close up shop. The issuing of new licenses for many types of work was soon frozen, including home-based restaurants, taxis, and snack shops. *Granma*, in a September story, said that this time would be different, and that the aim of this new opening to small business was to "distance ourselves from those conceptions that condemned working for oneself almost to extinction and stigmatized those who decided to join it, legally, in the 1990s."[8]

The freeze on granting new licenses was lifted, as were regulations that limited who could apply for licenses and that restricted the activity to the municipality where the license was issued. The self-employed were now authorized to hold more than one license: renting rooms to tourists and also running a home-based eatery, for example, or running more than one restaurant. For the first time there was a veiled admission that self-employment often translated into operating a small business, because those with licenses would now be able to hire employees in 83 out of the 178 authorized categories of work instead of being restricted to using family members. The self-employed were authorized to do business as contractors with the state, open bank accounts in their business's name, not their individual name as they had in the past, and apply for bank loans, though it would be a year before these regulations went into effect. They could now rent storefront space, while before they had to operate out of their homes. Private restaurants, known as *paladares*, were authorized to seat up to twenty instead of twelve customers at a time, and could serve previously banned shellfish, beef, and potatoes, which were often scarce on the island. Cubans could now rent out their entire homes and apartments, whereas previously they could rent out only a room or two and had to remain on the premises, and when they traveled or lived abroad for extended periods, they could now hire an agent to manage their rented property.

All of this was a huge step in the right direction within the national context. Yet limiting self-employment to 178 categories (of which only 83 could hire other employees) instead of simply allowing people to engage in any type of business they liked, and limiting seating at private and mostly home-based restaurants to twenty instead of eliminating the seat restrictions altogether, was evidence that the state was still far from ready to relinquish its hold. Many inspectors would still have useless jobs where they could look the other way for a price. Six months later, in a demonstration of what by local standards was remarkable flexibility, the government authorized all types of self-employed licensees to hire employees and allowed the *paladares* to have up to fifty seats— an important signal that it was open to ongoing review and correction of policy as the country moved into uncharted waters.

One of the biggest obstacles to starting small businesses was that supplies had to be purchased from state-run retail outlets at huge markups, but only 10 percent of costs could be deducted for income-tax purposes. Economy Minister Marino Murillo did admit to *Granma*, a month into the opening to small business, that wholesale markets for the self-employed were needed, but he also said it would be a number of years before they were established. Income taxes for the non-state sector remained the same, at 15 to 50 percent depending on one's earnings, but the self-employed now had to pay sales tax and a labor tax and a 25 percent social security tax for themselves and each of their workers. On the positive side, these taxes were deductible at the end of the year, and in many cases the 10 percent deduction for costs was increased to up to 40 percent of income. But most striking was the new payroll tax, on a sliding scale from one to "more than fifteen employees," along with regulations governing the hiring of labor by private farmers. This represented a small revolution in a country where article 21 of the Constitution stated that one's property and instruments of work "cannot be used to obtain earnings from the exploitation of the labor of others."

The government reported that it had issued 200,000 new licenses through March 2011—more than 1,000 licenses per day—most of them to people who said they were not employed, although one can assume that many were already working on the side. By the close of 2012 it said there were more than 390,000 self-employed, a number that included 60,000 employees of small businesses. Between 20 and 30 percent of all new small businesses folded within the first year, according to government insiders, a reasonable rate by international standards.

Cristina, a licensed hair stylist, said she welcomed the chance to start a beauty parlor for her clientele, many of whom were diplomats, diplomats' wives, and better-off Cubans. "I'm already planning to rent a storefront and hire staff, although I bet it will be a lot of work and time before it all comes together," she said.

"Those who continue working on their own without documentation, or do not pay the required taxes, will feel the weight of the law imposed upon them by those mandated to enforce it: the National Tax Office," *Granma* warned upon announcing the liberalization of self-employment.[9] Pedro, a carpenter who had worked for years without a license, gave up trying to get a copy of the regulations. "I'll hear about it and then decide what to do. As long as the taxes are not too bad, I'll get a license to avoid all the hassles with police and inspectors," he said. Pedro also said that he and two carpenter friends shared four machine tools sent by relatives in Miami. "Who knows? Maybe we'll get a bit more help from over there, rent a place, and go into business someday," he mused.

Cooperatives and Leasing

The word "cooperative" began appearing in conversations with my sources in the summer of 2010. "Cooperatives are not something on the horizon; they are already approved by the Havana Provincial Assembly in hopes of restoring local production and improving morale and competitiveness," said one government insider. "There are already local workshops that have received approval to move to a cooperative form of production and administration," he said, listing furniture making and garment workshops as good candidates. The state would still own most cooperatives' premises, as it did most things in Cuba, but the workers would run them, pay operating costs and taxes, and keep the profits. "Thirty of our restaurants, some with a good image and others less so, have already been selected to become cooperatives. They should begin the process soon," a mid-level administrator in Havana's food-service industry said in late 2010. An economist involved in drafting rules for nonagricultural cooperatives said that the degree to which the cooperatives would be allowed to function through market mechanisms was still under debate.

Raúl Castro, earlier in the year, had taken a first step toward bringing local and provincial governments into the task of economic development. They were ordered to come up with projects to stimulate economic activity and create new jobs under a program called the Municipal Initiative for Local Development. According to the document announcing the program and read by the author, the reason for the initiative was that "the scarcity of local development plans has created a complicated and unfavorable situation in a number of municipalities. . . . Centralization has left big empty spaces at the local level that must be filled—for example, in food production, services, transport, and trade." A mid-level Communist Party member in Granma Province said: "Raúl wants us to study what to do at the local level. It doesn't have to be the same in Havana as, say, Las Tunas or Camagüey, nor purely state initiatives. Cooperatives are fine." But in the end it would take almost two years for the first nonagricultural cooperatives to appear on an experimental basis and three years before a significant number of state establishments began switching to cooperative forms of business.

And there was little doubt that leasing of minor services, like the taxis and barbershops, would soon take off as well. The official trade-union weekly, *Trabajadores*, ran a story on September 13, just below the labor federation's front-page shock announcement of the layoffs, about a meeting of transportation officials. Buried in this article were a few paragraphs with the astounding news that productivity at the pilot Palatino taxi garage was up, not by 55 percent, but by 55 times its previous level, and that the state's yearly take from each taxi was estimated at the local equivalent of $18,360, compared with $580 in the past.[10] It was time for me to go back to the nondescript taxi garage on Palatino Street in the Cerro municipality of Havana for a glimpse into the past, present, and future. The past—as even the government admitted—was characterized by suffocating bureaucracy, massive pilfering, and slovenly work habits. The present still was, but it was also characterized by the recognition that one of the world's last Soviet-style economies must change. More and more, open controversy over who gets what piece of the pie, and anger at the tax man, would replace paternalism, passivity, and pilfering.

The thirty-car garage opened for business on an experimental basis in January 2010. Unlike other state garages, which had three support staff for every vehicle, the pilot project's garage had one administrator, a bookkeeper, a mechanic, and a custodian manning the fort. The drivers did not work for a state wage, but leased the cars on a daily basis and paid for their gas and vehicle maintenance. They would now also have to pay social security and income tax at the end of the year. "It's no mistake," bookkeeper Cristina said of the startling statistics in *Trabajadores* as she sat with me on a bench outside the Palatino garage. "No one hangs around here anymore doing nothing for a few dollars, stealing, and taking the family to the beach in a company cab, all expenses paid." The drivers were not as enthusiastic as when I had first visited the garage earlier in the year; now they were saying that the fantastic statistics were coming out of their hides. "It's slavery. We don't have a minute for the family," said Roberto, one of the drivers. "We have to work day and night and seven days a week to pay the lease and tax office," he growled.

Transportation officials met with the drivers in June to discuss the project and, according to Roberto, got an earful. The officials promised to hold another meeting in December to announce "adjustments" before the experiment went nationwide. Four drivers soon quit, while Roberto said the rest had adopted a wait-and-see attitude. Bookkeeper Cristina confirmed all this, but with a scoff, as if to say things were not all that bad, although she admitted that given the spectacular results, perhaps a bit more of the pie could be shared.

Havana drivers and the government negotiated throughout 2011 and 2012, the drivers raising hell at garage meetings, the officials promising to get back to them. Meanwhile, of the dozens of state taxis I took when my car repeatedly broke down, just one driver turned on the meter. And this even as they all swore that the government wanted to take them to the cleaners.

The government announced in August 2011 that there were now two pilot taxi projects in Havana, another in Varadero, and ten more being readied in the provinces. The government then agreed to allow the drivers to deduct 40 percent in costs and the daily rental fee from their income tax.[11] By the time I traveled back to eastern Cuba in January 2012, most taxis in the area were going over to the leasing system.

20

Requiem for the Command Economy

Damn, at last there is recognition at the highest level of what we have been saying for years. They have never thought like this before; at last they recognize the need for reform.

Cuban economist

Raúl Castro and Venezuelan president Hugo Chávez presided over a ceremony in Havana on Monday, November 8, 2010, televised to viewers in both nations. The event marked the tenth anniversary of the first cooperation agreement between the two countries. The two men appeared relaxed on the podium and in jovial moods as they joked with each other and the audience. They declared the first decade of cooperation a resounding success and an example for the region. Castro and Chávez said they had spent the day with their ministers and other functionaries hammering out plans for the next ten years. "We are directing our efforts at the economic union of Cuba and Venezuela within a new kind of relationship . . . toward the objective of achieving genuine economic complementariness," Castro declared. Chávez hailed the new agreement, which he said included oil exploration in Cuba's Gulf of Mexico waters. "I am convinced that both our peoples and Revolutions will continue mutually supporting each other; that we will continue to consolidate," he said, after detailing Cuba's health and other technical assistance over the years. So much for speculation that the two leaders did not get along and that the bilateral relationship was on the ropes, or that Chávez would lose his next bid for president in October 2012, or that Cuba would throw in the revolutionary towel. No one would have guessed that Fidel and Raúl Castro would be at the Venezuelan president's bedside in Havana just a few months later, as he fought for his life—and his and their Revolutions—in an ironic reversal of Chávez's role when the elder of the Castro brothers had taken ill five years earlier. Fidel Castro didn't suffer from cancer, but Hugo Chávez did.

Cuba's rulers do love surprises—although not the kind that Chávez's health would soon deliver—and Raúl Castro certainly pulled one out of his sleeve at this November event. He announced that the repeatedly postponed 6th

Communist Party Congress would finally take place in April 2011 and would focus only on "updating" Cuban socialism. The much-ballyhooed conference to chart a political course, he said, would now follow the congress. The Cuban president announced that the overall social and economic direction of the country through 2015 would be the only theme at the Party summit, and said that a 32-page, 291-point road map to modernize the economy would be distributed to the public for discussion leading up to the event, the third orchestrated by Castro in just four years. "The 6th Congress will concentrate on the solution of problems within the economy and on the fundamental decisions involved in the updating the Cuban economic model, and will adopt the economic and social policy development project of the Party and the Revolution," he said. And lest anyone think that Fidel was not on board, or that Chávez might not be happy with the revamping of Cuban socialism: "We have already presented the leader of the Cuban Revolution, compañero Fidel Castro Ruz, the first copy of the Policy Development project. To you, compañero Hugo Chávez Fries, Comandante of the Bolivarian Revolution and President of that sister Republic, I am presenting the second copy," Raúl said. Chávez hailed the Castro brothers for trying to improve Cuba's economic model, stating that that was what his "Socialism of the 21st Century" was all about. "Raúl's courage in modernizing socialism must be recognized," he said, adding that his government would "accompany" the island on all fronts, political and economic, going forward.[1]

The Road Map

The Party congress's blueprint for reform said that "in the updating of the economic model, planning will be paramount, not the market," making it clear that Communist authorities wanted to reform the socialist system, not junk it. At the same time, given that there were virtually no markets in the country at the time, it implied that there would be more, as in fact did much of the document. But it would be planning of a new type, the document added, regulating and taxing state businesses, not administering them, and taking into account a growing private sector and supply and demand in retail and agriculture. State companies would continue to dominate the economy, but "mixed-capital companies, cooperatives, farmers with the right to use idle land, landlords of rental properties, self-employed workers and other forms that contribute to raise the efficiency of social labor" would not only be recognized but encouraged.

The document also highlighted Cuba's "strategic" relations with the Latin American region and, in particular, Venezuela and other socialist-minded governments, stating they would continue to have priority.

Expectations had run high that Raúl Castro would open up the country to more Western investment, and this proposed five-year plan seemed, at least partially, to justify them. It called for the development of "special economic zones to promote development," perhaps similar to those in Vietnam and China; joint ventures in non-hotel tourism-related activities such as golf courses, amusement parks, and marinas; and more industry partnering with foreign companies.

The five-year plan was long on generalities and short on details, although several themes ran through all the proposals. First and foremost, the state should get out of administering the economy and regulate it instead through taxes and other financial tools. State-run businesses were to be granted more autonomy to make day-to-day and personnel decisions and reinvest a percentage of their profits, although still under guidelines imposed by the government. "Control of state-business activity will be based principally on economic-financial mechanisms instead of administrative mechanisms," it stated. Bankrupt businesses would be considered just that and "liquidated" instead of being endlessly subsidized.

Second, there was an emphasis on decentralization of economic decision making to the provinces and municipalities, along with the creation of new revenue streams to strengthen local governments. Municipalities were called on to become self-sufficient in food production, to promote small-scale manufacturing and food processing, and to participate more directly in investment decisions, while state businesses would pay a new local tax to the governments of the areas where they were located, as would small private businesses. As part of the process of strengthening local governance, and to eliminate inefficiencies, they would be reorganized and streamlined along the lines of the provinces of Artemisa and Mayabeque discussed in the previous chapter.

Third, the document repeatedly referred to small private businesses and farms, cooperatives, and other forms of "non-state activities," and said that they should be supported, while making it clear that the "non-state" sector would continue to play a secondary role in the economy. "In the new forms of non-state economic activity, a concentration of ownership by businesses and individuals will not be permitted," it warned. Nevertheless, a wholesale system would be established to meet the needs of private entrepreneurs and farmers, while authorities in charge of foreign trade were instructed to take those same needs into account when importing machinery and supplies.

When it came to international financial relations, Raúl Castro had repeatedly stated that "two plus two equals four; never five." The document endorsed ongoing efforts to reduce imports and increase exports with an eye to creating a foreign exchange surplus, both to pay back creditors and to fund development projects. "Work with the maximum rigor to increase the country's credibility in international economic relations through the strict fulfillment of contractual obligations," it stated. That was good news for governments, joint venture partners, and suppliers, who had repeatedly seen payments postponed and rescheduled debt agreements broken over the years.

There was less good news for those Cubans who had become accustomed to living in a paternalistic society. The document endorsed the layoff of hundreds of thousands of state employees and a drastic reduction in unemployment benefits—cutbacks that had already begun in October. While free health care, education, and social security were still guaranteed, as were low-cost sports and cultural activities, they were to be reorganized with an eye toward greater efficiency. The World War II–style food ration would be phased out, the prices of utilities increased, and, in general, all other state subsidies and freebies gradually eliminated and replaced by targeted welfare for the truly needy. Governments around the world were put on notice that the days of free Cuban health, education, and other technical assistance were also coming to an end, and that, wherever possible, the governments on the receiving end of the aid would be expected, at a minimum, to cover the costs of that aid.[2] There was some good news for Cubans at the end of the document, where it called for "review [of] current prohibitions that limit internal trade," referring, among other matters, to the ban on buying and selling cars and homes.[3]

The Third Debate

The document was soon up for discussion in workplaces and barrios. I attended one of the discussions on a Monday evening in early December at the José Martí cigar factory in the Vedado district of Havana. "The problem is that farmers are paid a miserable amount for their products and so are we for our work," Ariel Izis said to resounding applause. "It shows a complete lack of respect," he added, addressing the podium where Communist Party and trade union functionaries sat, took notes, and explained the need for more discipline and efficiency to meet the workers' complaints. Izis had the last word at the often contentious two-hour debate. Only a few of the proposals were discussed, as workers focused attention on low state wages and high state prices. The 120 workers gathered in the cafeteria voted unanimously to endorse the 291 economic and social policies. Increased productivity and less state waste would allow the government to pay workers more for their labor and bring down prices, said Raúl Fernández Sierra, the provincial Communist Party representative at the meeting. "Everyone thinks, fine, but how will these plans be carried out by the same people who got us into this situation? They have their interests," a worker told me after the meeting.

The debate I witnessed played out in more or less the same fashion across the land over the next three months, as people expressed their concerns about low salaries, high prices, and cuts in state subsidies, according to sources involved in compiling the results. "People are very concerned about rising prices, about the lack of balance between wages and prices, and about what will happen to the most vulnerable, for example if the food ration is cut," one source said. Cubans repeatedly demanded that the government improve its performance in exchange for their tightening their belts. "Many people asked why, after the government repeatedly complained about the waste generated by its monopoly on food distribution, most produce was still under its control and food was rotting in fields and on trucks," said a retired Party official in Granma. All in all, "the discussions generated an enormous amount of information about how the people look at and understand the main problems facing the country," said my Party friend in central Camagüey Province. "And this puts enormous pressure on the government to respond appropriately."

Behind the Scenes

A series of high-level conferences were held in November 2010 to prepare Party leaders and government officials for the public discussion of the plan that followed. The first conference took place the same week as the announcement of the congress and was chaired by Raúl Castro and attended by five hundred top officials. It featured then–Economy Minister Marino Murillo, who explained the 32-page economic road map, which he said had been prepared by ten working groups and had gone through four previous drafts. A series of three-day conferences for mid- to upper-level officials took place through the remainder of the month and featured a video of the original conference chaired by the president. The video made clear there would be no turning back, according to more than one of my sources who saw it.

Murillo, as was his style, did not mince words, even speaking to the powers of the land, as he stated that growing foreign indebtedness and dismal domestic economic performance were the driving forces behind "modernization, which should not be mistaken with reform." Murillo explained "reform" implied ceding property to private hands, which he said was not on the agenda. The economy minister said that Cuba simply could not meet its debt principal and service charges over the coming five years and therefore had no choice but to renegotiate its debts for the umpteenth time. Further, unlike the Soviet Union, new creditors such as China, Brazil, and Russia wanted their money repaid. He said Cuba would need to borrow billions more in the coming years to carry out its plans to develop oil refineries, power generation plants, ports, railways, waterworks, tourism, and the nickel industry. Murillo added that if the country succeeded in renegotiating what it owed, it would be for the last time, and therefore it had to get the economy to a point where it generated a large surplus.

Under the U.S. embargo and thus excluded from most international lending organizations, Cuba could not turn to the International Monetary Fund or the World Bank to bail it out and provide it with fresh funds. The government had last reported its foreign debt at $17.8 billion in 2007.[4] Most analysts agreed that by 2013 it exceeded $23 billion, or around 50 percent of gross domestic product and 30 percent more than its annual foreign-exchange revenue. China had become the island's lender of last resort, providing billions in loans and becoming Cuba's largest creditor, holding a debt of more than $5 billion by 2011, according to my sources. Murillo specifically talked about the need to repay China on time and said that the first thing he did every month was to cut the Asian powerhouse a check. Chinese, Russian, Brazilian, Canadian, and Vietnamese officials had repeatedly "suggested" that Cuba modernize and offered their assistance, according to diplomats in Havana. A diplomatic cable, released by Wikileaks, describes a U.S. diplomat's breakfast meeting with the commercial attachés from Cuba's most important trading partners. "Even China admitted to having problems with getting paid on time," the cable reported, adding that French and Canadian officials "responded with 'welcome to the club.'"[5]

Murillo, Castro's point man for economic reform, who would be promoted in March 2011 from economy minister to overseeing modernization efforts, reportedly argued in the video that, given its international obligations and development plans, the government had no choice but to become—along with state businesses—more efficient and productive, and that in order to reach that goal it had to get out of administering the companies, eliminate bloated payrolls, cede minor economic activity to the "non-state" sector, and end most subsidies for companies and the population. The plan was similar in some respects to International Monetary Fund adjustment programs, except that the IMF also called for the selling-off of businesses and services to private foreign and domestic companies.[6]

Murillo termed the recentralization of the economy over the previous decade a "disaster" that "killed" domestic production, said my sources. "Over the last ten years, our investment plans were never met," Murillo said, "not once." Murillo said there was a need to modify the military-inspired "Perfecting of the State Company System," which had been held up as a model for twenty-five years and which sought to improve government administration of the companies through the ministries, while the proposals went further and called for making the state companies independent of the ministries.

The approximately 3,700 state companies managed just about all of the Cuban economy, from hotels and the nickel, oil, and cigar industries, to utilities, agriculture, transportation, banks, international and domestic trade, and sugar mills. "I estimate thirty-five to forty percent of the businesses are critical to the economy and more than fifty percent of all the companies operate at a loss," a local expert on state business administration said. The companies were managed by government ministries through clusters of firms attached to them called unions. Ministers and the Communist Party reviewed all plans, set salaries and prices, controlled imports and exports, managed partnerships with foreign firms, and conducted endless inspections.

Murillo said the unions of companies would be eliminated in favor of public holding companies operating outside the government and that some ministries whose sole function was administering businesses would disappear. The holding companies would be responsible for the profitability of subsidiaries and overall management and, as a rule, would not be eligible for state subsidies, he said. "We have to stop leading the companies by the hand," he said. Murillo gave the example of the Food Processing Ministry, which boasted a number of unions of companies, saying that, in the future, they would operate independently and simply sell their goods to the state and non-state sector, eliminating an entire layer of bureaucracy. "Thirty-five percent of their employees are not directly involved in production, and the ratio should never be more than twenty percent," he said.

Murillo defended plans to move more of the agriculture and retail sectors from state to non-state hands, stating that by 2015 about 35 percent of the labor force—1.8 million people—would work in the non-state sector, compared with 600,000 reported at the close of 2009. "We can't be scared of cooperatives; we have cooperatives in agriculture," Murillo said, adding that plans called for transforming small state service and production companies with more than six employees into co-ops. "We are going to do it, especially in services. The state doesn't lose, it simply rents the property to the cooperative and collects taxes," he reportedly said. More and more construction would be in the hands of private contractors and cooperatives, and by 2015, he projected, 60 percent of home building and repair would be in private hands, compared to the current 20 percent.

As for the new emphasis on private-sector farming, Murillo said that the farming sector employed 18 percent of the workforce and contributed only 4 percent to the national product, while food accounted for 16 percent of imports. Asked about the fate of the state system known as *acopio*, under which supplies were provided in exchange for produce, Murillo responded that fourteen out of sixteen companies within the system—one for each province, one for Havana city, and another for the Isla de la Juventud—had operated at a loss for years, and that this was no longer acceptable.

Murillo also delved into plans to decentralize government activity and eliminate subsidies. He said the ration alone cost the equivalent of 25 billion pesos a year, of which the population paid just 12.3 percent and the state the remainder. Murillo said local governments needed to be empowered to meet local needs, and for this to happen, local revenue streams had to be established. "The local governments are not sustainable because they get nothing," he reportedly stated. Murillo said that, of 169 municipalities, 97 were rural and agriculture-based, yet they consumed $280 million of the $860 million spent abroad in 2010 for rice, beans, meat, and vegetable oil, all of which could be produced locally if the resources were at hand.

As for health care and education, they would remain free and universal, he said, but they needed to become much more efficient and would be restructured. There was little discussion about self-employment. Murillo was asked why there was a list of authorized types of self-employment. He replied simply that it was just the first and that there would be others. "Damn, at last there is recognition at the highest level of what we have been saying for years," said a Cuban economist. "They have never thought like this before; at last they recognize the need for reform."

Why the Reforms

Raúl Castro's presidency had been marked by both continuity and insistence on the need for reform, but very little had changed except in official rhetoric, the fostering of more public criticism, and scattered pilot projects. The balance would now shift decisively as economic reform moved forward at a much quicker pace.

Raúl Castro continued to meet with the cardinal and the head of the Bishops' Conference on a fairly regular basis, and they now supported his efforts. "This celebration today includes also a prayer that this renovation process goes well," Cardinal Ortega said during New Year's Day Mass in 2011.

The idealistic, paternalistic, and personalized revolutionary project of Fidel Castro was to be replaced by a more realistic vision, a systematic approach, decentralization, and acceptance of self-interest. "I am not announcing any new discovery when I state that improvisation in general, particularly when it comes to the economy, leads to a sure failure, regardless of the lofty ends one intends to attain," Raúl told the National Assembly in December 2010.[7]

A number of factors had come together to push forward change.

1. After twenty years of crisis and the stratification of Cuban society, the old model simply no longer fit the new social realities.
2. The government's command and control had steadily deteriorated, along with health care and education, in part because of low wages.
3. The population was increasingly critical of blatant stupidities, general incompetence, waste, and overregulation.
4. Young people continued to vote with their feet.
5. The country faced a debt crisis and insolvency, as new creditors, such as China, Brazil, Algeria, Qatar, Iran, and Russia, wanted assurances that they would be paid back, especially as Cuba sought new funds for its development projects.
6. With Fidel no longer around to work his rhetorical magic, the country had to be put on a sounder footing.
7. Changes in Latin America and the Caribbean and their relations with Cuba and the United States provided more space to carry out reforms.

21

On the Road Again

It isn't easy. The future is bleak, more uncertain, but I have my health to face it with and, with health, you can deal with anything.

Maria, a laid-off Santiago bookkeeper

The daylong drive from Havana to central Camagüey in February 2011, and then the following day to eastern Santiago de Cuba, was different this time around. The roads remained all but empty, but those produce-filled kiosks had moved from the Santiago mountains to—well, just about everywhere. They were now joined by mom-and-pop home-based restaurants, snack shops, and snack food and beverage carts along the route to catch whatever traffic there was and cater to the clusters of people waiting for rides at crossroads or under bridges to escape the sun and occasional tropical downpours.

I usually toured the central and eastern parts of the country every two years, but had changed the routine to an annual trip as reform began. The layoffs were under way, some retail services were finally moving into private hands, the discussion of Raúl's economic and social plans was winding down, and the Communist Party congress was just around the corner. How all this was playing out in the provinces would be ample raw material for a series of good stories. Besides, I was after a scoop that could only be fleshed out in the countryside, where my contacts were better informed than in the capital—or at least more willing to talk.

I was surprised the previous year by how upbeat many of my friends and acquaintances were. This time around, some were in dour moods indeed. One couldn't blame them, as they were repeatedly being told life would get worse before it got better—and for some it already had. Take, for example, a December 12, 2010, *Juventud Rebelde* interview with Joaquín Infante, one of the country's top economists: "There will be an impact in 2011 and part of 2012," he said of Castro's plans, when asked about rising prices, layoffs, and other negative consequences of the reforms. "But we have no alternative but to straighten out so many things. If we don't do it, then we'll lose the socialism that has cost us so much and that we have given so much for. But in 2013 we will start to see the benefits, of this I have no doubt."[1] And Raúl Castro also had far-from-encouraging words for my friends in his December 2010 speech to the National Assembly.

> It is necessary to change the mentality of the cadres and of all other compatriots in facing up to the new scenario which is beginning to be sketched out. It is just about transforming the erroneous and unsustainable concepts about socialism, that have been very deeply rooted in broad sectors of the population over the years, as a result of the excessively paternalistic, idealistic and egalitarian approach instituted by the Revolution in the interest of social justice.[2]

No wonder dread and hope were mingled across the countryside as the congress approached!

"The plan brings with it changes in daily life that in some cases will be painful. Logically, this worries you and creates a certain insecurity and fear, but what keeps people's faith is the promise to safeguard our main achievements, like health care and education, and that no one will be left completely alone," said Raúl Castañera, a Santiago de Cuba retiree. A longtime acquaintance, Castañera had recently taken up driving people around in his thirty-year-old Russian Lada to make ends meet. He was not happy about rising gas and parts prices, nor that there were no tires to be had in the city. "There is going to be a transition period of a few years, and it is going to hurt," he said, "but then, hopefully, things will get better."

Life was already improving for farmers and some of the newly self-employed, who saw a way forward through hard work, but state employees and pensioners—at least those without substantial family remittances—felt left behind and complained about job insecurity and about their pockets being picked by both the state and the new private vendors. Prices were rising as the government cut subsidies, loosened controls on small businesses and market forces at the retail level, tripled what it paid for produce, and passed some of the increased cost on to consumers. State salaries and pensions stagnated. Layoffs, or the threat of them, haunted every workplace. "Chico, I don't know, because where I work they still have not said who is staying and who has to go. They do say a lot of people will go," said Roberto in Holguín. And another friend complained, "Everything is going up, except wages and pensions."

A friend in Camagüey, with whom I stayed my first night on the road, set the tone for much of the trip. She did the same the previous year when she talked enthusiastically about the new state-run peso eateries. This time around, the first thing out of her mouth was that there was no bread—or, at least, no soft rolls for her grandson's school snack—because the newly self-employed were buying it all up for their *negocios*, or businesses. Other family members and acquaintances griped as well: the government didn't know what it was doing, they said, and taxes were so high that many self-employed people had already gone out of business. Further, a recent decision to take a pound of sugar off the ration and sell it on the market at a higher price had boosted the cost of soft drinks and sweets. Camagüey city and province were falling behind neighboring Ciego de Ávila, they said, and suburban farming—even though Camagüey was Raúl's pilot project—had made little progress.

All this was not exactly so, as bread vendors bicycled by early the next morning. (It was true that they had only hard-crusted bread on offer—preferred by many Cubans anyway, although not that grandson.) And the following week, as I made my way back toward Havana a few days earlier than planned for the trial of American contractor Alan Gross, a walk down Camagüey's splendid Avenida de la Libertad, just a block from my friend's home, revealed droves of the newly self-employed. The four-lane avenue—with little traffic except motorcycles, bicycles, *bicitaxis*, and horse-drawn carts and carriages—has wide sidewalks shaded by awnings and is lined with magnificent homes and buildings, boasting huge living-room windows and tall colonial-style verandas leading to times-gone-by carriage houses. Just about every living room and veranda facing the sidewalk was now rented out by the owners—at 25 pesos on up per day—to a hodgepodge of vendors selling everything from basic household supplies and clothing to services such as computer, cell phone, handbag, and shoe repair. Snack foods, drinks, and sweets were everywhere. "My God, what has happened to my lovely avenue?" I asked myself. I was impressed a year earlier because a few bicycle-pedaling produce vendors had been allowed to sell their goods on the street. Now they were lost in the crowd.

Twenty-eight-year-old Amelia ran a sandwich and snack shop from her front porch just off the avenue. She had been a temporary employee of Gastronomía before the state food-service industry let go all its temporarily contracted employees in December 2010. Her husband, thirty-four-year-old Roberto, a food-service manager in the city, was relieved of his post when Amelia started her business, because it was seen as a conflict of interest. The couple now worked their small business together, Roberto getting up before dawn to buy bread and other supplies and both of them cleaning up and shutting down at about 9 p.m. They were taking in 3,000 to 4,000 pesos per month after expenses, Amelia said, but then they had to pay a 400-peso license fee, 10 percent sales tax, social security tax, and so forth, leaving them about 2,000 to 3,000 per month—the equivalent of perhaps $100. "With that we can live, but it's a lot of work and the inspectors come by three or four times a week," she said. By

2012 the couple had switched to selling ice cream, because of what they said was excessive competition from their neighbors.

A tour of the suburban farms revealed that there had, indeed, been little progress from the previous year. There was far more brown than green along the two-lane beltway that circled the city. There hadn't been a drop of rain since mid-November, and few plots were irrigated. The fruit and vegetable stands were largely empty. An exception was the suburban garden belonging to my friend who headed up a cattle cooperative. They had agreed to grow vegetables and raise some livestock as part of the new plan. The plot was doing quite nicely, including the yuca or cassava patch, thanks to a well that never ran dry and a windmill and irrigation system that the cooperative had purchased from the state on credit. The organic produce was sold fresh each day by vendors on bicycles, and the yuca was sold to the state. My friend was now raising rabbits, guinea pigs and hens, and trying his hand at breeding pheasants. I realized that suburban farming would go nowhere without irrigation, an expensive proposition that would take a number of years to develop.[3] My friend said that fifty new irrigation systems were available for the Camagüey area in 2011, a drop in the bucket for a plan that envisaged 1,400 farms.

Santiago de Cuba

By late afternoon on the second day of my trip, I was once more in the foothills of Santiago de Cuba and once more surprised by what I discovered. This time it wasn't the fruit stands but the lush farms that had sprung up along the two-lane road wherever the hilly terrain permitted—benefited no doubt by the ample rainfall in the area over the previous year. A few days later, during an interview with the province's administrative council vice president, Ruperto Arias Radu, I asked why, despite Raúl's reforms in agriculture, food production fell 2.5 percent in 2010. "We had a seventeen percent increase in sales last year over 2009, and in terms of volume an eleven percent increase," he replied, with that particular pride characteristic of the area. The people of Santiago insist they make the best rum and coffee, sing and dance better than other Cubans, and boast the most beautiful women and toughest men in the land.

According to the government, by February 2011 more than 128,000 plots of land covering 1.2 million hectares (2.9 million acres) had been distributed across the country under the land-lease program begun in 2008. But critics said that was still only half the land available and that new farmers did not have access to the financing and supplies they needed to become productive. Eastern Santiago de Cuba was apparently an exception. It had about 77,000 hectares

(190,000 acres) of vacant land, and most was already leased, Arias claimed, with 90 percent of that in production.

Much to my surprise, the International Press Center had actually organized interviews for me in Granma, Santiago, and Camagüey with relatively high-ranking provincial officials, for the first time outside Havana since I arrived in December 1993, a mere—what?—seventeen years before! I had requested the interviews because I was interested in the decentralization of revenue and local responsibility that was implicit in Raúl's plans, and the progress of the municipal economic initiative he had ordered the previous year. I was disappointed, though: my vision of a new Cuba, where the local governments took the initiative in a big way, was still far off. The provincial vice presidents in charge of such matters in Granma and Santiago appeared to have given it little thought, or—perhaps better put—their thinking simply hadn't moved on from appeasing the national government to new possibilities. Both men simply stated that new revenues would cover local budget deficits with the national government and the surplus after that would go to health and education.

I asked them, "How about local development and jobs?" Between the two provinces there were around 150 local development projects under consideration, but only a dozen were nearing approval and, from what I could tell, all but one (in Santiago, involving a cooperative to process surplus produce) were state, not private, initiatives. In addition, although they were local projects, they had all been sent up to the national level for final approval because they needed some sort of financing, perhaps because the new local revenue streams had yet to come on line. In Granma, rice husks were to be used as fish feed; in Santiago, some state and Party guesthouses were to be turned into tourism hostels; and both areas had projects to turn marabú into coal for export.[4]

The officials said that in their provinces the national plan to eliminate 500,000 jobs by April had barely gotten off the ground. Some 3,000 jobs had been slashed in Granma Province since November, a similar number in Santiago de Cuba, and 1,000 in Camagüey, the local officials said. That was just 10 percent of the 70,000 jobs they said were slated to be cut in their provinces during the first six months of the reorganization of the labor force. The officials said they were scrambling to provide alternative employment and deal with the inevitable unease, hurt feelings, and anger that the layoffs caused. Castro announced, even as I tooled around the island, that the six-month deadline to carry out the plan was scrapped. Meanwhile, nationwide, some 180,000 people had taken out licenses to work on their own, including some 15,000 in these three provinces. I asked Marta Adán Hernández, the director of labor and social security in Camagüey Province, how the city of Camagüey could absorb more people working on their own with its main streets already crowded with vendors. "There is no limit. Many services still need to be provided to the population," she insisted.

The officials I met with in the three provinces said that there was no choice but to keep trimming the job rolls if the economy was to move forward, but the process was now open-ended. Granma's provincial vice president for economic affairs, Raúl López Rodríguez, insisted the reorganization would go forward, but admitted that only 10 percent of those laid off could be absorbed by a shrinking state sector. The remainder had little choice but to return to the land or strike out on their own. "You are going to see a reorganization of the labor force to improve efficiency, and those who remain must be paid much more," he said, estimating that the average monthly wage of 440 pesos (equivalent to just over $18) would need to double in the short term to motivate workers.

Granma's López Rodríguez provided me with a glimpse of how Raúl Castro was running the country. He said he had just come from a two-day meeting with the president. "In Havana?" I asked. No, he had participated in the meeting via teleconference. Castro had initiated what he called an expanded meeting of the Council of Ministers at the end of each month that included members of the Politburo and the Council of State, the first secretaries of the provincial Party organizations, the heads of provincial assemblies of people's power (the equivalent of governors), and select others. Lesser officials, gathered in the provinces and municipalities, joined the meeting by teleconference and, in an effort to circumvent bureaucratic distortions of reality on the ground, had the right to comment and ask questions. At the just-concluded meeting, the decision had been made to scrap the six-month timeline for the layoffs.

The New Unemployed

The program was called the "reorganization of the labor force" because, in theory, when workers on bloated state payrolls were declared "available" (meaning they were going to be laid off), they were offered at least one job on a different state payroll. During my visit to Camagüey, twenty-nine nurses at one of nine community health clinics in the city were declared "available" and offered jobs at local hospitals. "Some are taking the offer and others are going home, because at the clinic you work eight-hour days, while in hospitals you work a twelve-hour day, plus night shifts, and it often turns into twenty-four hours when your relief doesn't show up," said my friend the nursing supervisor and professor.

That wasn't the case for bookkeepers at twenty restaurants in Santiago de Cuba run by the Tourism Ministry's Palmares chain. The job classification was simply eliminated; all twenty were let go in early January and their four supervisors took over the work. "They declared me 'available' on January fourth and sent me home with a month's salary, and then seventy percent of my salary for another month," forty-year-old María said. "They haven't offered me anything. They haven't even called me or any of the others," she said. "It wasn't fair at all. I spent five years studying at the University, worked sixteen years in the same restaurant and never had any problems," she added bitterly. María said that, for now, she was simply taking the time off to supervise work on the home she had moved into a few years back, which needed extensive repair. Her husband had a decent job and a skill that brought in some extra money on the side to support their two children. "Being laid off was more of a psychological shock than an economic one, because I wasn't paid much. It hurts your self-esteem. You feel you did something wrong, even if you worked for many years without any problems and you know it isn't your fault," she said. "It isn't easy. The future is bleak, more uncertain, but I have my health to face it with and, with health, you can deal with anything. We Cubans are a very optimistic people." By year's end, María had used her newly acquired Spanish passport to fly to the Bahamas and then to Miami to work with a relative for three months to earn some cash, which she then turned into goods, brought back, and sold. She went on to also sell ice cream from her door, and her husband established an electronics repair business.[5]

My last night in Santiago fell on a Saturday. Party boss Expósito had long since declared Saturday night to be party night for the city's youth, thousands of whom filled the streets to listen to local bands and recorded music and dance the night away. Popular movements were sweeping North Africa and the Middle East, and the uprisings against aging autocracies were being covered by the official media, though often as sinister U.S. plots. Some outside observers wondered if the Cubans might not be far behind. Dissidents promised an Arab spring was just around the corner. I sat at a cafe overlooking Victoriano Garzón Avenue and watched the city's youth frolic in the moonlight. These young people could have turned their fiesta into a *protesta* in a matter of minutes. They didn't. "No one is desperate here," one reveler said, when I asked why they hadn't. "Our leaders are not demented, brutal, and greedy fools; they know how to appease the masses," his Spandex-outfitted female companion remarked. Indeed, since the city was founded some five centuries earlier, Santiago residents had suffered from water problems, with the precious liquid coming for only a few hours every few days—or even every few weeks—to be stored in people's tanks. A water megaproject was just then in its final phase, and most of the city, for the first time in its history, was finally enjoying running water 24/7.

Fidel and the Party

Now for that big story I was chasing. Provincial and municipal Communist Party organizations were in the process of electing delegates to the congress and, according to media reports, pre-candidates to the Central Committee. That caught my attention because Raúl Castro had said in 2009 that the Central Committee would be elected at a "conference" and more recently that the coming congress would focus only on economic and social reform. And since the Central Committee would in turn elect a new Politburo and Secretariat, Fidel would presumably resign from his final post. So why was the Party electing pre-candidates for the congress, I asked my friends. "Someone read the Party rules," they only half-jokingly replied, pulling out copies of the statutes from cabinet drawers. The rules were crystal clear. A conference could replace and appoint individuals, but only a congress could elect the Central Committee, which in turn had to elect the top leadership.

DISPATCH: FIDEL CASTRO EXPECTED TO RESIGN
AS CUBAN PARTY CHIEF

Holguín, Feb 28, 2011 (Reuters)—The Cuban Communist Party has moved forward the election of new leadership to a Congress in April, where longtime Party leader Fidel Castro is expected to step down, sources close to the Party said over the weekend.

Castro, 84, previously handed over most of the responsibilities as first secretary, but kept the title. His official departure from his last leadership position would be a symbolically important step toward a new era for the island he ruled for 49 years. . . .

As first and second secretaries, the Castro brothers led the Party's guiding Central Committee, for which elections originally were expected to be held at a Party conference at the end of this year. But sources said the vote has been moved to April because Party statutes say it must be done at a formal Congress.

It was not long before Fidel responded to the confusion and rumors—especially in diplomatic circles—that were caused, at least in part, by my article on the Party's election plans. On March 23, as Japan struggled with the aftermath of the tsunami, missiles and bombs rained down on Libya, and Obama visited South America, Fidel issued a reflection on the U.S. president's trip and, in an aside that had nothing to do with Obama, wrote:

In truth, I gave my services to the Revolution for a long time, but I never eluded risks nor violated constitutional, ideological or ethical principles; I regret not having better health so that I could carry on serving the Revolution. I resigned, without hesitation, all my state and political positions, including that of First Secretary of the Party, when I became ill, and I never tried to exercise them after the Proclamation of July 31, 2006, even when I partially recovered my health more than a year later, although everyone continued to affectionately address me in that manner.[6]

My *Financial Times* editor, John Paul Rathbone, e-mailed what everyone was thinking: "So is this a resignation after the fact?" I replied, "Fidel temporarily stepped down from all posts in 2006, using same wording for all positions. Fidel resigned as president in 2008, never resigned as Party chief. This is his way of signaling he won't accept post at Congress; a roundabout way of saying he is resigning. That in fact he doesn't run the Party and won't in future." So, did Fidel resign in 2006 or was he doing so in 2011 as the congress neared? Who knows! What is important, though, is that he and his brother kept the world guessing and off balance as the transition from his rule unfolded. The congress finally forced their hand. The quarterback had indeed deftly handed off the football, and at least most of the opposing team finally understood that Raúl Castro had it firmly in his grasp.

22

Forward March

It is advisable to recommend limiting the time of service in high
political and state positions to a maximum of two five-year terms.

Raúl Castro

Politics is often all about symbolism, with events carefully staged as theater.
The military parade and massive march through Revolution Square on April
16, 2011, the curtain-raiser for the many-times-postponed Sixth Communist
Party Congress that opened later in the day, was loaded with both. April 16
marked the fiftieth anniversary of Fidel Castro's proclamation that the Revolution was indeed socialist, not capitalist and democratic in the Western sense,
as some of his supporters (no doubt including my grandfather's critic Sylvia
Cannon, from the introduction) were led to believe. The date also marked the
fiftieth anniversary of the start of the botched U.S.-organized exile invasion at
the Bay of Pigs. The congress would close four days later, the time it took for
Fidel Castro's forces to achieve victory in what he dubbed "the first defeat of
U.S. imperialism in the Americas."

The carefully choreographed march was a show of force, a tribute to an absent Fidel Castro, and a promise to remain faithful to his legacy. Raúl Castro
presided from on high, at the base of the statue of José Martí, with stories-high
likenesses of deceased revolutionary commanders Che Guevara and Camilo
Cienfuegos looking on from the facades of the Interior and Communications
Ministries on the other side of the square. A huge banner read: "This revolution is of the humble, by the humble, and for the humble," a quote from Fidel's
proclamation of fifty years earlier. Flag-waving uniformed children, students,
and young adults marched by the reviewing stand, surrounding floats carrying
such symbols of more glorious days as the yacht *Granma* that brought Fidel
Castro back to Cuba from Mexico to begin his revolution, and the tank from
which he reportedly fired at U.S. ships during the Bay of Pigs. But this was no
Macy's Thanksgiving Day parade. There were young troops marching in lock-
step with all sorts of light weaponry and refurbished Soviet weapons. MiG-21
and MiG-23 fighters and helicopters swooped overhead, all "ready to protect

the fatherland no matter what the difficulties" and "to resist any imperialist aggression," according to the script read by a young narrator and booming over loudspeakers. "This is a clear message to imperialism. The young people will not waver," said the only speaker at the event dedicated to the country's youth, Maydel Gómez, president of the University Students Federation. The spectacle was a defiant blast from the past even as the Party struggled to find its footing in the present and a very different path into an uncertain future.

Raúl Castro, in a speech to the National Assembly a few months earlier, had said:

> I, for one, remember an idea expressed by a Soviet award-winning scientist who about a half-century ago . . . was thinking that even though the possibility of a manned flight into space had been theoretically documented, it was still a journey into the unknown, the undiscovered. While we have counted on the theoretical Marxist-Leninist legacy, according to which there is scientific evidence of the feasibility of socialism and the practical experience of the attempts to build it in other countries, the construction of a new society from an economic point of view is, in my modest opinion, also a journey into the unknown—the undiscovered. . . . We do not intend to copy from anyone again; that brought about enough problems to us because, in addition to that, many a time we also copied badly. . . . However we shall not ignore others experiences and we will learn from them, even from the positive experience of capitalists.[1]

The Cuban Constitution defines the Communist Party as the "highest directing force" of the Cuban state and society. All top-level government and military officials are Party members, as are almost all lower-level functionaries, the leaders of labor and other mass organizations, and some 800,000 of the country's 11.2 million residents. The Communist Party was formed in 1965 from various revolutionary organizations, including the old Communist Party under Soviet leadership, which Fidel Castro shunned to make his Revolution. Fidel Castro was first secretary from the start of the new Party until he became ill and stepped down, and Raúl Castro was second secretary until he took over for his brother. All other political parties are banned. The Communist Party's highest authoritative body, at least in theory, is its congress, which is supposed to convene every five years and which elects a Central Committee—that is, it ratifies a slate that a Party candidate commission has proposed, taken from a larger number of nominees proposed by members—and then ratifies that body's election of a Politburo and Secretariat, proposed by the Party leaders themselves. The Communist Party's members are organized into committees in most workplaces and communities. The committees form municipal and provincial organizations. In theory, it is the members of the Party from the base on up who decide who leads the organization and the country, but in practice Realpolitik prevails: the higher bodies "recommend" and the lower ones ratify, with some discussion and give-and-take behind the scenes. The Party runs the Union of Young Communists, with a membership approaching that of its parent organization in number, and from which the Party recruits many members.

The congress was indeed a watershed moment and crowned Raúl Castro's relentless five-year effort to prepare the land for what was, in local terms, fundamental economic and social change. The thousand delegates would adopt the essence of his program, despite the questions and misgivings expressed by some during the three-month public discussion that preceded it: the third and last debate on the economy that Castro would orchestrate before moving forward in earnest.

"The discussions extended for three months, from December 1, 2010 to February 28 of this year," Castro said in his opening report to the congress. "Every opinion, without exception, was incorporated to the analysis, which helped to enhance the Draft submitted to the consideration of the delegates to this Congress," he said. Maybe so, but the final 311-point version, in essence, was indistinguishable from the pre-congress draft discussed in chapter 20.[2]

Castro then made it clear that the food-rationing system would still have to go, and layoffs would continue: the two main popular concerns expressed during the preceding months.

> Undoubtedly, the ration book and its removal spurred most of the contributions of the participants in the debates, and it is only natural. Two generations of Cubans have spent their lives under this ration system that, despite its harmful egalitarian quality, has for four decades ensured every citizen access to basic food at highly subsidized derisory prices. . . . This principle is absolutely valid for the restructuring of the work force—an ongoing process—streamlining the bloated payrolls in the public sector . . . its pace determined by our capacity to create the necessary conditions for its full implementation.

Castro sweetened the news by announcing that progress was being made toward making the bureaucracy more responsive and allowing citizens to buy and sell property. He also assured all Cubans that no one would be left out in the cold. "The Revolution will not leave any Cuban helpless. The social welfare system is being reorganized to ensure a rational and deferential support to those who really need it. Instead of massively subsidizing products as we do now, we shall gradually provide for those people lacking other support."[3]

The "new" fifteen-member Politburo included Castro, five other active-duty generals, retired officer Adel Yzquierdo, and Comandante of the Revolution Ramiro Valdés Menéndez—so it made good sense to think in military terms when analyzing the congress. A "strategic retreat" quickly came to mind, which the University of Colorado's Conflict Research Consortium defines as follows:

> When confronted with a losing situation, the losing party accepts defeat in a way which allows them to preserve as much of their resources (both moral and physical) as possible. . . . Classically, this term refers to military retreats and the regrouping of forces. Since military confrontations are commonly thought of as consisting of a series of battles, it is generally considered to be good planning to retreat before one is completely defeated. The concept applies equally well, however, to political and economic struggles.[4]

That sure sounded like Raúl Castro's explanation of his economic policy in the main report to the congress:

> The growth of the non-public sector of the economy, far from an alleged privatization of the social property . . . is to become an active element facilitating the construction of socialism in Cuba since it will allow the State to focus on rising the efficiency of the basic means of production, which are the property of the entire people, while relieving itself from those management activities that are not strategic for the country. This, on the other hand, will make it easier for the State to continue ensuring healthcare and education services free of charge and on equal footing to all of the people and their adequate protection through the Social Welfare System.[5]

The congress called for establishment of a Party commission to supervise implementation of the reforms, led by former economy minister Marino Murillo, who was elected by the congress to the Politburo. The commission would report regularly to the Politburo, the Central Committee, the Council of Ministers, and the National Assembly, where it would have first place on all agendas, in hopes that the reform package would not meet the fate of past Party economic decisions, which at best were only partially implemented.

It had been almost four years since Raúl Castro, in his first speech to the nation in July 2007, suggested that there was a better way to distribute milk and, by implication, food in general. Now a makeover of the entire economy and how Cubans lived, though still within socialist parameters, was before the highest political body of the land, where it would undoubtedly be ratified.

Castro had long since replaced his brother's cabinet and advisors with more reform-minded technocrats, many from the military. Now, despite the fanfare, apparently it was the Communist Party's turn for turnover. Fewer than 50 percent of the incumbent members of the Central Committee were nominated as candidates for the new Central Committee that would be elected by the delegates at the congress, and the new candidates appeared to be much younger and more diverse in gender and race than the top Party leaders. Those leaders were still not ready to give up the reins of power, and the Party "election" for the Politburo was a repeat of the election of the Council of State three years earlier. Aging conservatives would lead the reform.

Raúl Castro, 79, as first secretary, replaced his brother, and José Machado Ventura, 80, first vice president of the Council of State, was named Party second secretary. Ramiro Valdés Menéndez, 78, who was now thought by many observers to be number three in the hierarchy, joined the body, and five generals retained their seats: Defense Minister Julio Casas Regueiro, 75 (who passed away a few months later, in September 2011); Interior Minister Abelardo Colomé Ibarra, 71; First Deputy Defense Minister Leopoldo Cintras Frías, 69; Deputy Defense Minister Ramón Espinosa Martín, 72; and Alvaro López Miera, 62, head of the Joint Chiefs of Staff. Other members who maintained their seats were Ricardo Alarcón de Quesada, 73, president of the National Assembly; Juan Esteban Lazo Hernández, 66, longtime Party ideologue and former provincial Party leader; Salvador Valdés Mesa, 62, head of the official trade union federation and longtime Party functionary; and Miguel Mario Díaz-Canel Bermúdez, 51, minister of higher education and former Party leader in Villa Clara and then Holguín. The new members were Marino Murillo, 50, recently promoted to lead the implementation of economic reforms; Adel Yzquierdo Rodríguez, 65, economy minister, a former military officer and close aide to Raúl Castro when the latter was defense minister; and Mercedes López Acea, 46, first secretary of the Party in the capital.

Political Reform

The youthful message of the military parade contrasted so starkly with the aging leadership's decision to stay in power that Raúl Castro felt compelled to address it in his televised report to the congress as it opened on April 16, even before the "new" Political Bureau, with an average age of 69, was announced. Having consolidated his drive to reform the economy, he now opened a similar debate on reforming Cuba's political culture, admitting it had failed to renovate the country's leadership in terms of gender, race, and age.

> In this regard, I think that the Party leadership, at all levels, should be self-critical and adopt the necessary measures to secure the promotion of

women, black people and people of mixed race, and youths to decision-making positions on the basis of their merits and personal qualifications. It's really embarrassing that we have not solved this problem in more than half a century. . . . Although we kept on trying to promote young people to senior positions, life proved that we did not always make the best choice. Today, we are faced with the consequences of not having a reserve of well-trained replacements with sufficient experience and maturity to undertake the new and complex leadership responsibilities in the Party, the State and the Government, a problem we should solve gradually, in the course of five years, avoiding hasty actions and improvisations but starting as soon as the Congress is over.

Within two years, in February 2013, a new National Assembly and Council of State would reflect Castro's words and a young presidential successor would emerge.

I have not delved into racism and sexism in this book because discrimination in Cuba is so markedly different and benign compared with the United States and many other countries. Racism and sexism certainly exist, but they are impossible to address in a few paragraphs, pages, or even chapters. Cuba's superstructure remains disproportionately white and male, and the opening up of the country to family remittances has greatly increased inequality, as the vast majority of Cubans living abroad are "white." Prejudices about one's own race and others' remain and are reproduced through the culture and family. At the same time, the country has made remarkable progress in eliminating structural inequality in education, health care, and social milieu. Racism does not take a violent, aggressive form in Cuba. Domestic violence continues, but it is regularly condemned and fought in the media and the barrios. Multiracial coupling is trending toward the rule, not the exception, among Cuban youth.

Castro next dropped the political bombshell of the congress. "We have reached the conclusion that it is advisable to recommend limiting the time of service in high political and State positions to a maximum of two five-year terms," he said. Castro did not blame Cuba's one-party political system for its failure to generate new leaders. Nor did he blame his brother Fidel—in power for almost half a century until illness forced him to step aside in 2006—but said that times had changed and the system had to change with them. "This [term limits] is possible and necessary under the present circumstances, quite different from those prevailing in the first decades of the Revolution that was not yet consolidated when it had already become the target of continuous threats and aggressions," he said.

Now back to the University of Colorado Conflict Research Consortium's definition of strategic retreat. After stating, "When confronted with a losing situation, the losing party accepts defeat in a way which allows them to preserve as much of their resources (both moral and physical) as possible," it continued:

> They then set about the task of building their power base so that they can raise the issue more successfully in the future. This may involve the development of efforts to expand their coalition of supporters, define the moral justifications underlying their goals, build enthusiasm among their current supporters, and strengthen their resource base.[6]

The only real surprises at the congress dedicated to the economy were in fact political, and they fit quite nicely into the above on coalition-building. Raúl Castro spoke extensively about faith in his opening remarks.

> It is necessary to continue eradicating any prejudice that prevents bringing all Cubans together, like brothers and sisters, in virtue and in the defense of our Revolution, be them believers or not, members of Christian churches; including the Catholic Church, the Russian and Greek Orthodox Churches, the evangelicals and protestant churches; the same as the Cuban religions originated in Africa, the Spiritualist, Jewish, Islamic and Buddhist communities, and fraternal associations, among others.[7]

Castro then went on to praise improved relations with the Roman Catholic Church and the prisoner release. "With this action, we have favored the consolidation of the most precious legacy of our history and the revolutionary process: the unity of our nation," he said.

Castro all but called for affirmative action in his closing speech, a policy shunned in the past as divisive in the face of the "enemy." He said the new Central Committee was made up of 115 members, of which 48 were women, or 41.7 percent, more than three times the number of the previous one. There were 36 blacks and mestizos, 10 percent more than the old body, or 31.3 percent.[8]

Castro called for getting the Party out of administering the government and economy, putting forth a vision for society much like that in the armed forces, where he said the Party gave its opinion but the officers made the decisions. This was an old refrain that had always failed because all top- and middle-level functionaries and military officers were Party members. Castro did state there was no need for that to be the case. Finally, the congress called for the decentralization and reform of government with an eye to improving its efficiency.

Fidel Castro repeatedly endorsed the congress proceedings and the call for term limits—writing that he was consulted beforehand—and he showed up for the closing session, just in case someone didn't get the message.[9] Photos appeared of him looking over the list of proposed Central Committee members. He did not speak.

The Party Conference

On January 28, 2012, José Martí's birthday, the two-day Communist Party conference finally opened. There were no surprises. I had toured the country earlier in the month and talked with a number of Communist Party contacts about what to expect. Term limits, they said, were nothing new at the provincial level, where leaders were already rotated around; they would now be applied at the national level. Separating the Party from the government meant there was no longer any reason for the head of the Party, for example, to also be head of the government and armed forces, but it did not mean the latter posts would now go to non-Party members. Nor was it necessary for government officials in the provinces to also run local state businesses, which in the future would be separated. But the conference, they insisted, would mainly be about ridding the country's only political organization of bureaucracy, opportunism, and corruption in an effort to better lead the masses.

The conference ratified Cuba's one-party system and called for more democracy within the organization and improved relations with nonmembers. The meeting approved term limits for top officials and other proposals first outlined by Raúl at the congress. There were no changes in leadership, though a motion allowing the Central Committee to co-opt up to 20 percent more members was approved. Political continuity and economic change would be the mantra for the coming years. "Renouncing the principle of one sole party would simply be equivalent to legalizing the party or parties of imperialism in our homeland," Raúl said, insisting that critics, and even some friends, did not take into account U.S. pressure on the country.[10]

23

Cheers and Jeers

In the end, all the controls end up controlling nothing. Many are just absurd. What they do is foster corruption, and a lot of people make money off them.

Havana housewife

Most Cubans had adapted to an overregulated society through the decades. They believed that unity and discipline were prerequisites for development, social justice, and defense of their country and revolution, even as they found ways around a myriad of prohibitions and complained constantly to one another about them. Others simply left town. The population accepted the status quo and tolerated the bureaucracy as long as life steadily improved and their children lived in peace and were better fed and educated and healthier than they had been. Many took pride in the Revolution's successes, the fame brought to their land by Fidel Castro, and the country's aid to the even less fortunate. Few residents openly fought abuses on the ground as they believed that doing so would aid and abet the enemy. As their old world fell apart during the post-Soviet crisis, the Cubans seemed to hope that with Fidel still at the helm, life as it was in the 1980s—the years of the *vaca gorda*, or fat cow—would somehow return. But the times they were a-changin', and recovery proved difficult. Inequality and stratification grew year by year even as the country came into increased contact with the developed capitalist world. Two decades of crisis degraded the infrastructure and services. A tighter U.S. embargo made matters even worse. Millions of tourists arrived and more and more Cuban Americans. Cubans traveled to capitalist countries in record numbers. The telecommunications revolution dramatically increased interaction with loved ones and friends living abroad, and between Cubans within the country, despite local restrictions. Fidel's ceding of power, the three grassroots discussions orchestrated by his brother over the next five years, and Raúl Castro's and the official media's relentless critique of the status quo reset the population's thinking about the bureaucracy and, by implication, the Soviet-style system. The past, for better or for worse, became just that, the past, even if the future was uncertain.

After the Party congress, the pace and scope of reform picked up. But the Cubans reacted not only with cheers but also with jeers and demands for more. When the old ways of governing reared their ugly head—such as a drastic hike in customs duties in 2012 to protect state dollar shops—the Cubans howled bloody murder, sending forty pages of criticism to the official Cubadebate web page.[1] It had slowly dawned on the population that they had suffered under any number of mistaken policies, especially those that had allowed a parasitic and indifferent state bureaucracy to develop, and it was now their patriotic duty to criticize, though through official channels. Debate and reform proved a consciousness-raising and empowering experience. Many functionaries suddenly appeared incompetent at best, corrupt at worst. A local economist said that managing the timing of the reforms was critical to their success. Moving too quickly might tumble all that was positive in the Revolution, while going too slowly would frustrate rising expectations and do the same. "Reforms are necessary, but dangerous, as they are bound to open people's eyes and minds and lead them to demand further deregulation," he said. And that certainly was the case as the government eliminated bureaucratic and financial obstacles to travel and living abroad, threw out decades-old bans on the sale and purchase of automobiles and homes, loosed businesses from ministerial administration, and moved forward with the privatization of agriculture and retail services.

In August 2011, less than four months after the Communist Party congress—and to no one's surprise—the National Assembly unanimously approved the 311-point plan to update the economy. Raúl Castro and the man charged with the day-to-day implementation of the reforms, Marino Murillo, made clear they had not been twiddling their thumbs, and that the plans should not be taken lightly.

Murillo said that the Permanent Commission to Oversee the Development and Implementation of the Economic and Social Guidelines had been legally constituted and consisted of 98 members, including himself as chairman, General Leonardo Andollo Valdés as vice chairman, and a secretary, along with an additional 66 people who would work closely with the commission. By September it was to deliver a secret timeline through 2015 for putting the measures approved by the Party congress into practice, from the simplest, which required few resources and legal changes—for example, the cars and dwellings—to the most complex, such as decentralization, eliminating the two-currency system, and reorganizing the government, state companies, and the planning process. Murillo said the commission was organized into eight working groups, including one for each section of the Party's plan to modernize the economy, and others to develop the theoretical architecture of the new economic model, its legal underpinnings, and the planning and coordination needed as the reforms were put in place. As each measure was rolled out, it would be closely monitored, and the commission would recommend adjustments and new measures as experience dictated. A year later various government and university think tanks were recruited into an advisory committee for implementation of the reforms.

Cuba's president was merciless as he closed the August National Assembly meeting.

> The greatest obstacle which we face in terms of fulfilling the decisions of the 6th Congress is the psychological barrier created by inertia, resistance to change, simulation or double standards, indifference and insensitivity. . . . I warn that any bureaucratic resistance to the strict fulfillment of the Congress agreements, massively supported by the people, is useless. . . . Let us clear our minds of stupidities of all kinds, don't forget that the first decade of the 21st century has already ended.[2]

Even as the National Assembly met, a crackdown on corruption that began with the establishment of the Comptroller General's Office in 2009 was gaining momentum. Establishment of the Comptroller General's Office was one of Castro's earliest measures as he sought to clean house in hopes of avoiding the tide of corruption that often followed reforms in other Communist countries. Over the previous two years, organized corruption in the Food Processing Ministry, civil aviation, the nickel industry, and the export of cigars was brought to light, and high-ranking officials, including a minister and number of deputy ministers, were jailed. Major scandals in telecommunications, agriculture, and the import business followed in 2011, bringing down more officials and civilian and military businessmen. When foreign companies were involved, they were closed and their top executives arrested.[3]

Castro, closing the December 2011 National Assembly meeting, had declared that the fight against corruption was "strategic" and said that a meeting of the Communist Party Central Committee had resolved "to do away with that parasitical plague." Corrupt bureaucrats, "with posts obtained through simulation and opportunism, who are utilizing the positions that they still occupy to accumulate fortunes, betting on the possible defeat of the Revolution," were warned that the government would "combat this scourge with all the severity that our laws permit," because, Castro declared, "I am convinced that corruption is currently one of the principal enemies of the Revolution, far more damaging than the subversive and interventionist activity of the United States government and its allies within and outside the country."[4] He would use part of his speech closing the Communist Party conference a month later to repeat his warning. Videos, with the results of various corruption investigations and featuring confessions by former top government officials, foreign businessmen, and their Cuban aides, began making the top Party rounds in early 2012.

Cars, Homes, and Travel

The long-awaited "you can buy and sell your car law" was announced on September 28, 2011, and took effect October 1.[5] The far more important "you can buy and sell your home law" followed a month later.[6] These were the first two of three reforms during the latter part of 2011—in response to popular complaints raised during Raúl's three debates—involving personal liberties and aimed at the Grey Zone, citizens who were not directly opposed to, or somewhat supported, the socialist system, but who were tiring of its abuses. The third was the lifting of restrictions on migration from the provinces to the capital, imposed in the 1990s as country folk streamed into Havana during the crisis of the 1990s, straining its infrastructure.[7]

Plumbing supply salesman Luis Miguel, sitting at his kitchen table, said that he would finally be able to sell his Havana apartment and buy another. But he expressed anger over the months he had spent struggling with restrictive regulations and labyrinthine bureaucracy as he tried to trade his property under the previous housing regulations. "I have been trying for months to *permutar* [trade homes], and it's been one bureaucratic runaround after another," the forty-five-year-old said with disgust, getting up and dumping a stack of papers relating to the *permuta* into the garbage. "Now I'm looking for a buyer without so many useless restrictions or having to pay anyone under the table and bribe everyone."

Across town, maintenance worker Jorge expressed similar emotions. He asked why, previously, he'd had to break the law in order to get rid of his old Russian Lada. "I needed to sell my car. Since I wasn't allowed to, I 'loaned' it to someone. Now I have to figure out how I'm going to fix the papers to transfer ownership legally and pay tax on a car I actually sold more than three years ago," he said.

Havana housewife Margarita Rojas summed up the general sentiment in the land soon after the Party congress and before the new series of reforms were implemented: "In the end, all the controls end up controlling nothing. Many are just absurd. What they do is foster corruption, and a lot of people make money off them," she said.

The reforms covering cars and homes tended to bring above ground the massive black-market sales of property that had developed with the stratification of the society that followed the Soviet Union's demise, and to undercut the corrupt bureaucracy that fed off it. They would, in particular, benefit better-off Cubans and those with family abroad, as well as the state through taxes. The laws also allowed Cubans moving to other countries to sell their property or give it to family members, instead of having their homes and cars confiscated by the state—just the first of a series of measures that would be taken in the coming years to make leaving and returning to the country easier and less expensive. Resident foreigners, when they moved on, could give their property to Cuban members of their families, instead of only selling it to other foreigners or the state. Permanent foreign residents could now purchase a new car every five years, and a home, while those with temporary resident status (including me) could not buy residential real estate but could purchase two new cars during their stay, albeit with a 100 percent tax slapped on, and still only with permission from their state sponsor, in my case the International Press Center. The two measures also created incentives to work, so as to buy and care for what in all lands are the most important and expensive investments one makes. They brought the nation and the diaspora closer together and drew in capital from abroad as relatives invested through family, but they also tended to consolidate and make more visible the stratification of society and to reward those who had family outside the country or had previously bought homes through the underground residential real-estate market.

The law allowing private used-car sales paled in its impact compared with the housing regulations soon to follow, but it did mark a step forward in a land where such a simple transaction was forbidden for half a century except for those on the road before the 1959 revolution. The procedure was relatively simple (as was that for selling a home), requiring nothing more than a notary, a bank account for the transaction, proper ownership documents, a 4 percent sales tax paid by the buyer, and a 4 percent capital-gains-like tax paid by the seller. If the purchaser already owned one car or more—for example, a fleet of old vehicles rented out as taxis—the tax was higher. One had to pledge in writing that the money used to purchase a car or home was legally obtained, and be able to prove it if requested to do so by the authorities. And all transactions had to be in pesos, as part of the government's plan to eliminate the dual-currency system.

Raúl's point man for reform, Marino Murillo, in a September 2011 closed-door speech opening a new government and business administration school for top officials, a copy of which I obtained, said there were 600,000 cars in the country, and 300,000 of them were owned by the state. Of the other 300,000 in private hands (one for every thirty-seven inhabitants), most had been in use for more than fifteen years, and 79,000 dated to before 1959. The ban on purchasing or importing new cars without the government's permission went unchanged, making the old vehicles the only ones available for most people and therefore—despite their often deplorable condition—precious indeed. An old Russian Lada, for example, went for as much as $15,000. Owning a new car in Cuba remained akin to owning a mega-yacht anywhere else.

Cuba, and just about every Cuban's life, changed for the better on November 10, 2011, when a decree decriminalizing the sale and purchase of residential real estate took effect. To be sure, an underground housing market had existed since the early 1990s and would simply come above ground now. And another regulation, this one limiting home ownership to a single urban dwelling plus one rural or beach "vacation" home, went unchanged. Foreigners, including Cuban Americans, remained banned from the housing market. Those interested in large-scale real estate development and rental properties no doubt were disappointed, but most Cubans rejoiced over this particular measure, including those living abroad who simply purchased homes through family still on the island. There were few, if any, jeers.

According to the government, 3.7 million dwellings existed in the country, 80 percent of which were owned by the residents, although more than 50 percent were classified as in poor condition. The vast majority of Cubans, in the blink of an eye, were now able to buy and sell their residences easily after half a century, and thus owners of something that could be turned into cash legally. A mansion in the Varadero beach resort, which had somehow remained in private hands, went on sale for a cool million dollars (24 million pesos) and another, in Havana's upscale Miramar district, for $500,000 (12 million pesos). A friend figured his spacious apartment in avant-garde Vedado would fetch the equivalent of $70,000 or more, although most apartments in the district were selling for around $50,000. There were tens of thousands of homes and apartments belonging to the pre-Revolution middle and upper classes that despite depreciation were worth respectable sums of money, but there were hundreds of thousands more that were worth more modest amounts, and the majority of dwellings on the island were worth hardly anything at all. Small apartments in housing projects sold for the equivalent of anywhere from a few thousand dollars to $15,000 if they were relatively close to the center of Havana, while prices in the provinces tended to be lower. Residents in apartment buildings—some because they wanted to sell their homes, others to rent, and all because their apartments now represented an investment—began forming committees to spruce up and maintain their buildings.

During my look around the country in January 2012, I found that "For Sale" signs had gone up on doors and windows in the provinces and buyers walked the streets looking at homes the whereabouts of which were passed along by word of mouth. Prices varied from the equivalent of a few thousand dollars to much more, depending on size, condition, and location. Few people appeared to be speculating. Most sellers said they wanted to move for personal reasons. Camagüey bicitaxi driver Roberto Sosa said "no problem" when asked to pedal around town for a look at what was on the market. An hour and five homes later, one place caught my eye on Virgin Street. The neighborhood needed a plaster and paint job and the road needed paving, but the half-block-deep five-bedroom single-story house, freshly painted and with new tile floors, was splendid. "We want $35,000 and have a possible buyer, but she is checking with her family in Miami," said the owner's son, who gave his name only as Santiago. Sosa wasn't surprised. "Most of the houses are bought with the help of family abroad. If not, it wouldn't be possible, because their value is going up a lot now," he said.

Emilio Morales in Miami wasn't surprised either. "A number of law firms, mainly here in the United States and Spain, have already called asking about the law for clients who want to know how they can buy property in Cuba," said the former marketing strategist for CIMEX, the largest state-run trading and retail corporation on the island. Morales, founder and head of the Havana Consulting Group, a start-up company specializing in potential Cuban markets, including residential real estate, said there was plenty of interest. "Here in Miami there are a lot of people interested in buying property in Cuba for diverse reasons, some to start restaurants, cafeterias, or other businesses, and others to have a place to retire and live out their old age," he said.

Travel

Raúl Castro pulled a rabbit from his hat during his August 2011 speech to parliament, announcing out of the blue that the government was reviewing policies governing residents wishing to leave the country temporarily or permanently and Cubans living temporarily abroad or who wished to visit their homeland—another popular beef brought up repeatedly during the three grassroots discussions. Like every other aspect of daily life, leaving and returning to the island had become completely tangled up with the United States' efforts over more than fifty years to undermine "the Castro regime," the bureaucracy's quest for control and income, and the Communist Party's efforts to defend the "Revolution and independence." I will spare the reader the long and tragic history of this particular field of battle, as countless books and articles have been written on the subject. What is certain is that, unlike any other illegal immigrants, Cubans were, and still are as of this writing, treated as heroes rather than villains upon their arrival in the United States, and immediately given legal status and financial support, while Havana for decades was tightly controlling Cubans' travel.

Cuba lifted most travel restriction soon after the demise of the Soviet Union, the big exceptions being for medical and security personnel and most dissidents. At the same time, the category of leaving the island "definitively" stayed in place, along with confiscation of the property of those in that category until the new housing and car laws of 2011. Regulations governing taking minors out of the country without both parents' permission, or leaving before completing one's military service (in the case of boys) or social service (in the case of university graduates) remained, and the government's permission, an exit visa, was still required each time one traveled. New bureaucratic procedures cost people a great deal of time and a relative fortune and, along with the need for permission to leave, occasioned the bulk of the travel-related complaints during Raúl's three grassroots discussions.

For decades, Cubans who left the island—especially for the United States—were considered traitors who were joining a foreign power's attempts to overthrow the Cuban government and reestablish U.S. dominance over the nation. This began to change by the 1980s, and especially after the disappearance of the Soviet Union. Cubans began departing more for economic reasons than political ones, and as part of family survival strategies. In addition, their government welcomed and heavily taxed the money they sent home or spent on visits to the island. Now Cubans leaving the country, even for short visits abroad and even after obtaining a passport for $55, paid another $150 for permission to leave, known as a *permiso de salida* or *carta blanca*. In addition, they needed a letter of invitation from a relative or friend in their destination country, the price of which had to be paid to the Cuban embassy in that country and varied depending on the location but, for Western countries, was usually between $200 and $300. This did not include the fee charged by destination countries for a visa: around 100 euros for most European countries and $160 just to apply for a visa to the United States. Cubans leaving permanently, most on their way to the United States, had to pay Cuba $400 for an affidavit and another $400 for a medical exam. Once abroad, Cubans would pay a monthly fee to the local embassy to avoid the label of "definitive departure" (for example, 40 euros in Spain and $150 in the United States) and had to return home every eleven months to maintain their temporary status abroad, in exchange for which they were still entitled to free health care and other benefits. Cubans moving abroad permanently had to pay the Cuban government $450 for a passport and exit visa—and every two years they had to pay to update their passport and pay a new visa fee.

In August 2011, Castro said times were changing, and that most Cubans were now leaving for economic, not political, reasons.

> We are currently working on updating the emigration policy in force, in the function of which we have been advancing in reformulating and drafting a series of regulations in this sphere, adjusting them to present and foreseeable future conditions. We are taking this step as a contribution to increased links between the nation and the émigré community, whose composition has changed radically in relation to the initial decades of the Revolution, during which the government of the United States gave shelter to criminals from the Batista dictatorship, to terrorists and traitors of all kinds.... Today, the overwhelming majority of Cubans are émigrés for economic reasons.... What is a fact is that almost all of them maintain their love for the family and homeland of their birth and, in different ways, demonstrate solidarity toward their compatriots.[8]

In October 2012, Castro proved as good as his word when he told Cardinal Ortega during their first meeting in 2010 that he saw no reason why Cubans shouldn't be free to travel like people in other countries. A series of changes to Cuba's travel laws were announced, effective January 14, 2013, which eliminated almost all restrictions. At the same time, the measures made it much easier to stay abroad for extended periods of time and for Cubans living in other countries to visit. A ban on allowing Cubans living abroad to move home was tweaked to take more into consideration humanitarian issues.

By 2013 a passport would do to leave, and in the case of those working in the public health sector who previously needed the permission of a minister, a simple nod from one's supervisor. Cubans could now travel anywhere. Blogger Yoani Sánchez, denied permission to leave more than twenty times, was soon touring the Americas and Europe, followed by other well-known dissidents. Most Americans were still banned by their government from visiting Cuba. Further, Cubans who left the country illegally after 1984 and were considered defectors, including personalities such as sports figures and musicians, could return after eight years. A resounding chorus of cheers followed in Cuba and abroad. There were few jeers, except at foreign embassies where some Cubans seemed finally to discover that one still needed a visa and money to travel to another country.[9]

"This is the best news I could receive. Now I'll look for the details, but what I heard on the radio this morning is enough to make me happy," government employee Isabel Martinez said as she made coffee and prepared to go to work the morning the new regulations were announced.

"I'm getting ready for a trip abroad, and it appears that at least I've been saved from the famous Carta Blanca [exit permit]. At last Cuba is becoming more like other countries," the Havana bookkeeper said.

As always, Cuba's foes, claiming Cubans had not previously been allowed to travel, speculated the reforms would lead to a massive stampede to Havana-based foreign embassies and a further bleeding of the country's youth, as they opted not to return from their travels abroad. The government thought otherwise and released previously secret migration statistics to explain why.

Homero Acosta, secretary of the Council of State, appearing on television on October 24, 2012, to explain the new rules, said that from 2000 through August 2012 the government had approved 99.4 percent of all requests to travel. During this time, 941,953 Cubans went abroad for personal reasons, he said, of which 12.8 percent, or 120,705, did not return.[10] At one fell stroke, hundreds of bureaucrats who processed and enforced travel regulations, most employees of the Interior Ministry, had to find something else to do. The Health Ministry discovered it had far more time to improve services instead of handling thousands of travel requests.

"Many doctors and nurses decided not to return because of all the travel restrictions, so now that they can come and go more easily, I think fewer will move abroad," said my wife Marlene, who was a deputy head of nursing at a Havana hospital, and who over more than thirty years on the job had come to know hundreds of doctors and nurses, including many living in Miami. But there was a catch. The Cuban American establishment by 2013 had begun calling for changes in U.S. policy that welcomed illegal Cuban immigrants, after a majority of Cuban Americans in Florida voted for Obama and not Romney, their preferred candidate. Acquaintances began asking me if the United States was going to stop allowing them in, no questions asked. Cuban Americans began urging family members to get to the United States one way or another before 2013 drew to a close, as fears grew that the Cuban Adjustment Act, which gave them automatic entry, would be eliminated under a new comprehensive U.S. immigration law.[11]

Meanwhile, just a year after liberalizing the regulations governing small businesses in the retail services sector and three years into the land-lease program, the government moved to further strengthen the "non-state" sector, confirming that it viewed the opening to private initiative as a permanent or strategic, not temporary or tactical, decision.

Agriculture

A September 2011 telephone survey of farmers found that they were becoming increasingly frustrated with the pace of change, blaming bureaucratic bungling and self-interest for undercutting efforts to increase production. The farmers said that some of the hallmark reforms they applauded, such as the land-lease program, decentralization of agricultural management, and freedom from the state's monopoly on supplies and the sale of produce, were turning out to be woefully insufficient in practice. Decentralization had become a double-edged sword, as some local officials were taking advantage of it to protect their own interests, the farmers said.

Ninety-seven of Cuba's 169 municipalities were rural, and the officials who controlled the state's monopoly on agricultural supplies and food sales in these areas controlled the only significant business and money flow in town. The farmers charged that Castro's reforms were being sabotaged by local power structures built up around the state's agricultural monopoly. "Agriculture officials at the intermediary levels think that if they apply these reforms, they will lose their positions and power, and the advantages and privileges they now enjoy," said a retired president and still-active member of a cooperative in central Camagüey. "That's why they keep looking for ways to limit reform," he said. Arsenio, a farmer in Oriente, agreed: "They have to take the tough decisions from the top on down, without wavering or backing off, or the changes we need won't happen," he said. Arsenio ripped into the state's food-contracting system, which still dominated the countryside.

> It is a diabolical system that will drive you crazy. First you sign a contract covering when and what you are going to plant, in exchange for supplies. Later, you have to confirm and ratify how much you will produce—something that's just about impossible. And if you come up short, they demand compensation; and if you produce more, they don't come get your product because it wasn't contracted for and their plans didn't include the extra fuel.

In 2011 the state still owned more than 70 percent of the arable land, of which huge tracts remained fallow and the rest produced less than the private sector did. According to the Agriculture Ministry, some 1.4 million hectares (3.5 million acres) of land had been leased to more than 150,000 farmers and would-be farmers since the land-lease program began in October 2008—around 60 percent of what was available at the time. Under the program, plots of no more than 13.42 hectares (33 acres) were leased to new farmers for ten-year periods, with the option to renew—but building "permanent structures" such as homes on the land was prohibited. Under the land reform put in place after the Revolution, farmers could not sell their farms either, but they could own up to 67 hectares (165 acres) of land, five times the amount offered under the land-lease program, and could pass it on to relatives and build as they pleased. "Only someone sitting in an office in Havana with no idea what goes on in the countryside would lease land for just ten years and prohibit building permanent structures on it," said a Camagüey farm leader named Jorge. The government, he said, should authorize building homes on the land, increase the size of the leased plots, and make the leases indefinite. Alfredo in Guantanamo said, "It's ridiculous to try to work a plot of land during the day and, when night falls, to have to go away and leave it until the following day. Who is going to protect your animals and crops? What were those people in Havana thinking?"

Practical experience and rising expectations weighed in, pushing agriculture reform forward, as they were bound to do in every aspect of the economy and society over the coming years. The government moved in 2012 to meet the farmers' frustrations in hopes of boosting production, which continued to stagnate. It began to dramatically alter the land-lease program in Camagüey and a few other areas, apparently as pilot projects. Farmers who demonstrated the ability to produce could now lease up to 67 hectares from the state, compared with the 13.42 hectares mandated in the program begun in 2008. Leases could be passed on to family members and, in some cases, to laborers. And for the first time, the farmers were allowed to build homes on the land they leased and make other improvements under a regulation that guaranteed state reimbursement if their lease was terminated.[12] By July 2012, Murillo, the point man for reform, would announce that the pilot project had become the law of the land.[13] New measures also became law as 2011 drew to a close, making it easier for farmers to obtain bank loans and allowing them to sell produce directly to the tourism sector, bypassing the state. By the close of 2012, Units of Basic Agricultural Production—quasi-cooperatives that worked 30 percent of the state's land and remained under the thumb of state companies—were given the same rights as private cooperatives and small farmers, except that they did not own the land.[14]

"These measures deal with many of the problems we face and give us security in terms of our work," said Anselmo Hernández from eastern Cuba. Oscar Palacios, president of the Antonio Briones Montoto agricultural service and credit cooperative in the town of Florida, Camagüey, said the measures were "of enormous importance." He was head of a group of 114 private farmers who received services and loans collectively from the state, including 68 who had leased land. "Now producers will feel much more motivated and secure that the fruit of their labor will be theirs," he said. "These measures bring farmers and their families closer to the land they work, and make them feel the land is really theirs." At the same time, he complained the state still would not allow his group of farmers to buy a tractor. A new tax code, which went into effect in 2013, gave farmers a tax holiday of up to four years to clear and put into production fallow land and preferential treatment in general.

Retail Services

Regulations authorizing state banks to grant loans to small businesses and farms took effect in December 2011, as did another allowing the state to do business with the private sector and small businesses to open commercial accounts and use other banking instruments for this and other purposes. Local monetary expert Pavel Vidal said the measures would stimulate the economy, lead to stronger small-sized and perhaps medium-sized private businesses, and apply to nonagricultural cooperatives when they made their appearance in the future. "It is very positive for the development of the non-state sector that it now has at its disposal new financial instruments that before were available only to state companies and joint ventures with foreign companies," he said, adding that the measures opened a huge market for the private sector—the state, as in most countries. My sources said the government would begin contracting out some services to the private sector in 2012. They said food and cleaning services, construction, and some freight transportation were at the top of the list.[15] During my January 2012 tour of the country I met a private landscaper who had just signed a contract with the Santiago de Cuba government and a truck owner who had contracted to haul freight for local authorities. The state's media began running stories about private contractors, for example electricians working for the ministries, landscapers pruning public arteries, and private construction businesses renovating state properties and building public housing.

Then on December 26, 2011, the government announced that in the coming year some 2,000 state-run workshops and businesses, which had 7,000 employees and provided more than twenty types of domestic and personal services such as carpentry, photography, and appliance, watch, clothing, and other repairs—would go over to the same leasing system as the small barber shops and beauty parlors had beginning in 2010. The shops' workers, in effect, would become self-employed and be governed under the same regulations and tax system.[16] During my 2012 trip I discovered that most taxis in Oriente were going over to leasing, as were larger beauty parlors and barber shops and some 200 small coffee and snack shops in Holguín province, these last apparently a pilot project.[17] By 2013 more than 1,000 similar establishments across the country were also moving to the leasing system, and if employees were not interested, they were rented out to anyone who was.[18]

A group of people on a corner in Havana's Cerro municipality, not far from

Party and government headquarters, were discussing the leasing system the day after Christmas in 2011 when I happened upon them. "It's too early to have an opinion on this. We have to see how they deal with the problems it will cause. For example, where will they get spare parts and supplies? Without them, there will be no work," said Manuel, a thirty-five-year-old television and radio repairman. Retiree Zoila Armenteros fretted about prices: "I have been preparing for a while for the increases in prices this will cause, like the hairdressers and barbers. Now, any type of haircut costs more than twenty pesos." Junior high school teacher Julio Fernández, aged thirty-eight, said the measure was too little and too late: "They have to keep making these necessary adjustments, but this is like a single fruit falling from the tree. Now is the time for the state to let go of all these minor matters and begin to concentrate on what's important, which it hasn't done."

Decoupling Business

On a grander scale, the once all-powerful Sugar Ministry was abolished in November 2011 in favor of a state-run national corporation called the Grupo Empresarial de la Agroindustria Azucarera (Sugar Industry Group).[19] The ministry's demise symbolized the end of an era of Soviet-style management of what had been the most important sector of the economy and the beginning of another that promised more flexibility and—at least in theory—efficiency. The new holding company was composed of 26 subsidiaries, compared with the ministry's 139 companies, having shed secondary tasks such as farming and rail transportation. Thirteen provincial subsidiaries would manage 56 mills. The group would keep a percentage of the profits instead of handing over all earnings to the government and then waiting for funds to be allocated to it. Under Decree Law 287, which closed the ministry, the Council of Ministers would still appoint the new sugar group's director, who would then be responsible for hiring and firing the remaining executives and staff. In the future, if the Party's plans became reality, management would have more say over investment, hiring and firing, wages, the prices it paid to farmers for sugarcane, and everyday business decisions in general. Forming significant joint ventures would still be in the hands of the highest authorities in the land, and exports and imports would remain the domain of the Foreign Trade and Investment Ministry. At the same time, there would be no more state subsidies.

The sugar industry had been nationalized with the Revolution and then built up as part of the Soviet-style command economy, directly under the government's, and in the end Fidel Castro's, control. With European Communism's demise, the Cuban sugar industry began a long twenty-year decline, from an output of 8 million metric tons of raw sugar to 1.1 million metric tons, the lowest in a century and just 20 percent of its pre-Revolution production. The number of mills had fallen from 156 to 56, and land under its control dropped from 2 million hectares (5 million acres) to 700,000 hectares (2 million acres). Just eight of the mills were built after the 1959 Revolution, the last in the 1980s. These mills could now partner with foreign firms without risking the wrath of previous owners or violating U.S. sanctions. In 2013 a Brazilian firm began managing a sugar mill, the first foreign firm to do so since the Revolution. Around 50 percent of the industry's 400,000 manual laborers and office workers had lost their jobs since 2003, along with many more in secondary industries that depended on sugar, such as tire manufacture and machine building. The Communist Party and the government hoped the ministry's demise represented the beginning of a new era, and not just for sugar but for the economy and the country as a whole. A new sugar industry was being born, they said, out of the ashes of the old. It would be a model to follow as state companies were separated from government ministries and given more autonomy. Local government-run businesses would go the same route, becoming provincial and municipal holding companies outside the direct administration of the People's Power provincial and municipal governments.[20]

Sugar Ministry spokesperson Liobel Pérez told the press that sugar was the first sector to complete its "economic reorganization." Ariel Terrero, during his October 13 early-morning TV spot on the economy, said the move did not represent just a change in name, but a change in how the entire sector functioned. "It is part of the general reorganization of the state, and we may see, in the future, the reorganization of other ministries to reduce their size, make them more efficient and as they let go of business activities that these ministries are often involved in," Terrero said. The 2011–12 harvest would be the first test, with plans to increase raw sugar output by 19 percent, from 1.2 million to 1.45 million metric tons. The new company hoped to produce 2.5 million metric tons by 2015, and eventually 3.7 million. Output did increase to 1.4 million metric tons of raw sugar during the company's first harvest, but efficiency still lagged behind expectations as mills and harvesting and transportation equipment broke down and management and labor problems persisted.

What *Granma* and Terrero did not report was that the closing of the Sugar Ministry was just the beginning of a broader reorganization adopted at the September 2011 Council of Ministers meeting, as authorities acted more quickly than I expected to move business out of government. The Basic Industry Ministry's chemical union was spun off into holding companies under other jurisdictions. The Light Industry Ministry and Steel and Metallurgy Ministry were soon merged. Basic Industry was then renamed the Energy and

Mining Ministry. "If a ministry is left with no state function, it will be closed," a source told me. A spate of articles in the official media indicated that most ministries had shed their businesses, and by 2013 a second experimental state company with dozens of subsidiaries, this one manufacturing pharmaceuticals, began operations.[21]

Reform czar Murillo, speaking before the National Assembly in July 2012, announced that regulations on a number of other companies would be loosened in 2013. Murillo said state companies would determine the eventual success of reforms, as they would continue to play the dominant role in the economy. "We can't keep doing things for the non-state sector and not do the same for state companies," he said, referring to their autonomy in decision making. The companies would no longer be micromanaged by government officials, and their annual plans would largely be their responsibility, he said. The government would monitor company performance through four or five indicators, such as "fulfillment of state contracts, profits, the relation between the average salary and productivity, and that's it," Murillo said. The companies, previously part of various ministries, would be able to make day-to-day business decisions without waiting for government approval, manage their labor relations, and set prices. After meeting state contracts, they could sell excess production on the open market. "You shouldn't think of a wholesale system as a building where you go to buy something. If a state company fulfills its obligations and goes to market with the excess production, this is also a wholesale market," he said. The companies would be self-financed, including through bank credits, and expected to cover their losses, as opposed to handing over all profit to the state and receiving financing and subsidies from the treasury.[22]

The long-awaited nonagricultural cooperatives would finally get off the ground in 2013 as well. Murillo announced at the December 2012 parliament meeting that 222 small- to medium-sized state businesses, ranging from restaurants and produce markets to shrimp breeding and transportation, had been selected to become cooperatives. Since cooperatives were a more social form of production than private businesses, in that an owner did not exploit others' labor, with decisions taken collectively and profits shared among members, they would be treated in a preferential manner when it came to taxes and other fees. "They are preferable to other non-state solutions," Murillo had said a few months earlier. The cooperatives would lease state property and equipment at ten-year renewable intervals, operate on a market basis, and divide profits among members, who would then be taxed on their income. The cooperatives would operate "horizontally, not vertically," Murillo said, independently from the government and state businesses, but could not be sold.[23]

The Tax Man Cometh

Most Cubans had not paid taxes or contributed to social security for half a century, but that began to change under a new code that took effect on January 1, 2013, the first comprehensive tax legislation since the Revolution. The landmark measure signaled a dramatic shift in the relationship between Cubans and their government on the horizon and was a further indication that market-oriented reforms were permanent. In the 1990s, after the collapse of the Soviet Union, the government had established the National Tax Office and imposed a few scattered taxes, but mostly preferred to maintain low wages in exchange for across-the-board subsidized goods and services. The new code included nineteen taxes—for example, inheritance, environment, sales, transportation, and farmland—various license fees, and three contributions, including social security. A sliding-scale income tax, from 15 percent on earnings of more than 10,000 pesos annually to 50 percent on earnings of more than 50,000 pesos, adopted in 1994, remained for the self-employed, small businesses, and farms, but the code also included a series of new deductions to stimulate their work. Farmers could deduct up to 70 percent of income as costs, and small businessmen, who were taxed on income rather than on profit, up to 40 percent, plus various fees and secondary taxes they paid. A labor tax of 20 percent would gradually be reduced to 5 percent by 2017, and small businesses with five employees or fewer were exempt. Eventually all Cubans would pay income taxes as well as a new 2 percent property tax if they owned their homes, but both measures were suspended until "conditions permit." Taxes on start-up farms and small businesses were waived in exchange for clearing the land and initial investment. Companies would pay a 35 percent tax on their profits, but could take advantage of a myriad of deductions ranging from amortization and travel to sales taxes, insurance, and environmental protection.

The new code was not etched in stone—it could be amended each year as part of the annual budget passed by the National Assembly and temporarily modified for various reasons by the executive branches of government.[24]

"They collect taxes for all these things around the world, it is normal," said Havana economist Isabel Fernández. "But here we face two problems. On the one hand, we are not used to paying for anything, and on the other, our wages are so low we can't spare a single peso," she said.

A Western banker who worked in Cuba said: "Like the reforms, the tax code is a work in progress, a work that has barely begun and will take time to put in place." But, he added, "this is of course a major step forward toward the twenty-first century and a modern state."

Conclusion

Life is a book. We simply turned the page and moved on.

*A Vietnamese official, on coming to terms with those who
had sided with the United States during the war*

I bid farewell to 2011 and welcomed in the new year in Camagüey. Bicitaxis
and pickup trucks hauled carcasses of hundred-pound pigs around town on
New Year's Eve. The animals, upon reaching their final destinations, were un-
ceremoniously run through from rear to mouth with long hardwood tree limbs
and then slowly turned over coals by men on sidewalks and in yards. The rum
flowed and music blared as dominoes slapped down on tables. The smell of
roasting pork filled the air as children played and women prepared rice, beans,
yuca, salad, and sweets. Rent-a-cars parked on just about every block attested
to the presence of family and friends visiting from abroad for the fiesta. My
friends and I spent hours slowly turning our porker over the coals, and then
around thirty of us feasted. Like most Cubans, they were common folk, three
generations just getting by with the help of one another and a few relatives
abroad. But they managed quite a party as the local family doctor and some
neighbors joined us. We quickly devoured our pig.

Cuba, as always, was a land of contrasts as 2012 got under way. The scenery
was as spectacular as ever, and its people just as joyful, complicated, and ob-
stinate. If anything, there was even less traffic on the roads. The vast stretch of
empty highway to Sancti Spíritus and beyond remained a stark testament to
just how impoverished the country was and how out-of-reach the legal price of
gasoline, at $4.00 per gallon on up, proved for most residents even if they could
now buy and sell their cars. There were great expectations as the New Year began and a huge deepwater drilling rig moved into position within sight from
Havana's seaside drive to begin the search for offshore oil and gas. There was
also much trepidation as Venezuelan president Hugo Chávez's cancer returned
and he spent much of the first months of the year being treated in Havana, a
scene that would be repeated in 2013 after he won a third presidential term
and then underwent a fourth operation, to no avail. There was no end in sight

to devastating U.S. sanctions. Quite the contrary: the Obama administration, furious over the fate of Alan Gross and harassed by a pro-embargo lobby that had become emboldened by the rise of the conservative movement, was tightening them once more. The future remained a roll of the dice.

In Camagüey, the university professor I always visited had finally repaired and actually painted the interior of her home after twenty long years, perhaps with some help from her daughter, a dentist who had recently "defected" in Venezuela and was now living in Miami. The professor's daughter may have opted out, but my friend now rented two rooms to Latin American medical students thankful for the opportunity to become doctors. Five thousand foreign students would graduate in 2012 from Cuban medical schools. The mid-level Party member I always stayed with had "traded" up her home to a second-story apartment a few blocks away facing the lovely Casino Park. The place, an old two-story house with high ceilings and a huge front balcony overlooking the park, was spectacular, though in need of a serious plastering, paint job, and much more, as it boasted disastrous wiring and plumbing from well before the Revolution. "We will fix it up little by little," she cheerily proclaimed while watching her New Year's gift from a farmer friend, three chickens, pecking away in the small backyard. There were four generations in the home. My friend's daughter, a physical therapist, was on a mission in Venezuela earning some money, while my friend took care of her eight-year-old grandson, not to mention an aging mother. The grandchild's father, a descendent of a Cuban sugar baron, had long since left for the United States. My friend's brother drove a tow truck in Miami and helped as much as he could. The mother, who spent much of her time watching television, now had a very large flat-screen variety in her bedroom. A year later the place had been rewired, plastered, and painted. The plumbing still leaked.

On New Year's Day I visited my friends at the cattle cooperative a few miles outside the city. President Armando said everyone had all the roast pork they could eat the night before, even the farm workers, unlike the previous year when some settled for fowl. The co-op was now selling produce directly to schools and hospitals at the same price as the state-run monopoly Acopio did. Before, they sold the produce to the state, which then sold it to the institutions. Now the produce arrived fresh and the cooperative kept the 21 percent profit that previously went to Acopio. Marino Murillo would tell parliament deputies in July 2012 that just 53 percent of farm output was contracted by the state that year and the other 47 percent sold on the market or consumed by farmers, compared with more than 80 percent sold to the state just a few years earlier. The ranchers said some bureaucrats at the state's local produce monopoly saw the writing on the wall and were jumping ship for other jobs.

The cooperative had just leased a large tract of land along the beltway around the city to grow produce as part of the suburban agriculture plan and was to be the beneficiary of a cooperation project with a European Union country. Armando's wife was expecting their first child, a girl born six months later, and by 2013 the cooperative had purchased two rebuilt trucks on credit to deliver produce to hotels, schools, and hospitals. The ranchers, turned quasi-farmers, scoffed when I said the 2.5 percent decline in food production reported in 2010, and 2 percent increase in 2011, meant that the agricultural reforms that began in 2008 were a failure. They insisted the data was based on old reporting that did not accurately take into account the growing amount of food being sold directly to consumers, bypassing the state and sometimes its antiquated reporting system. Maybe so, I said, but how to explain the 20 percent increase in food prices in 2011? Market economics and the end of subsidies, they replied without hesitation. Food production continued to stagnate in 2012, according to government figures, even as a visibly increasing supply streamed into the cities, where vendors, it seemed, staked out every corner and pulled their carts down every street shouting, "Tomatoes, onions, yuca, malanga, garlic," or what have you.

I spent a day in neighboring Ciego de Ávila visiting friends and then left Camagüey on January 4 for Oriente. I picked up a teenaged farm girl on my way to Bayamo, the capital of Granma Province, for lunch with some Party friends. She was hitching back to a boarding school. I asked numerous young people on this particular trip about the Internet, only to be met by scowls, howls of laughter, and resignation. There simply was none, came the unanimous reply. The farm girl said she had never surfed the World Wide Web. Over lunch my Party friends blamed the embargo for her plight. I protested that Cuba had been the first in the region to boast a fully literate population and now it was the last when it came to the new literacy. By late afternoon I was on my way to Santiago.

Driving around downtown Santiago was always a harrowing experience. Cars and motorcycles zipped through narrow, hilly streets with even narrower sidewalks loaded with pedestrians spilling onto the roads. The locals had little patience for cautious tourists. *Cocomóviles* and *bicitaxis* are rare in Santiago due to the hilly terrain. Motorcycles perform the same service, horns blaring. I quickly noticed that no one was furiously protesting on my tail. "Ah, I've finally come to manage this place," I proudly said to myself, but I soon realized that the traffic was perhaps half of what it had been on previous visits. The government had shut down the black market for the fuel that the locals depended upon, I learned from friends. "Another pilot project," I said to myself, thinking of Havana where thousands of old gas-guzzling U.S. cars served as group taxis and not a one was ever spotted at a gas station. The car museum on wheels surely consumed tons of black market gasoline and diesel fuel every day, but without them the capital would all but grind to a halt, and if fares went up, few residents could afford them. "How will Castro manage that?" I wondered. A year later he hadn't.

A friend who owned an eight-ton 1950s Ford truck said he was privately hauling produce for farmers and the state. "The cops used to treat me like a terrorist," he said. "I never drove on the main roads, because I was stopped every five minutes, and I even parked the truck for a while because I feared they would confiscate it. No one has bothered me for seven months. Things are definitely loosening up," he said.

I always rented a room in a once upper-middle-class Santiago neighborhood just minutes from downtown—and, in the other direction, from San Juan Hill of Theodore Roosevelt's Rough Riders' fame—where most homes had gone over to revolutionaries in the 1960s. Now in their seventies on up, the owners rented out rooms at $20 to $25 a night to tourists. Alfredo, one of their children, who was around forty years of age and ran a private landscaping business, was in very good humor. The local Communist Party and government planned to convert more than a hundred of their guesthouses to hostels, and he had landed a contract for landscaping work. Alfredo said couples would live in the hostels in exchange for managing them, and in addition to receiving a wage and some supplies, they could also provide other services to guests on demand and keep that income. "They want to put us out of business," my host said. Reform czar Murillo announced a few months later that more than 1,900 Party and government guesthouses left over from better days across the country, with a potential of 23,000 beds, would go the same way.

In October 2012, Hurricane Sandy would seriously damage just about everything built in Santiago over the previous five years under Raúl and local Party boss Lázaro Expósito Canto, from the new ice cream parlor and peso eateries to the airport and those mountain kiosks. The storm ripped roofing off tens of thousands of dwellings and other buildings in Cuba's second city and took down just about every tree. Surrounding fruit orchards and coffee plantations were flattened, the crops of old and new farmers decimated. Eleven local residents died.

The Grey Zone

Driving back to Havana from my 2012 visit to the central and eastern provinces, I thought about my latest tour of the island. The streets of Cuba's provincial capitals were all but barren a few years earlier, let alone the small towns' along the way. Much of the land lay fallow and overrun by brush. There were few people working the fields. The state began leasing land, decentralizing agricultural decision making, and allowing farmers to sell more of what they produced directly to consumers. Then the produce kiosks in the mountains, vendors on street corners, and peso-priced restaurants and shops appeared. The mom-and-pop business boom began a year later, even as the state moved to shed thousands of retail outlets and leave them to compete within the growing non-state sector. Now more people were working the land and building and fixing up their homes. The Party's strategic retreat from controlling everything through the state was already proving a big step forward on the street and in the countryside. It was as if someone was methodically filling out a barren landscape on a computer. First one layer, then another and another, as the scene slowly came to life. The nonagricultural cooperatives would appear in 2013.

In the old Cuba it was illegal to buy and sell one's dwelling, and it could take years for permission simply to improve upon where one lived. Now one's home was really and truly one's home. There were "For Sale" signs everywhere. The *trámites*, or formalities, took only a few weeks, and bureaucrats and office workers, under pressure not to sabotage reform, scrambled to get out the paperwork and made every effort to avoid unnecessary delays, for fear they would be denounced in the letters to the Communist Party's *Granma* and other official media and then quickly and publicly sanctioned. In the old Cuba the government sold building materials at a 240 percent markup at the dollar stores and subsidized the remaining building materials and assigned them. Now all building materials were sold in pesos on the open market, and state manufacturers and distributors were under intense pressure in the state-run media to improve the quantity and quality of their offerings. Money from relatives abroad freely trickled in for upgrades. By January 2012 the state banks were offering home improvement loans, issuing around 90,000 that year. The sale of building materials tripled, the government reported, but was still far short of meeting demand. This was an example of across-the-board subsidies being replaced by targeted welfare. Local governments—using 40 percent of the profit from the building materials sales in their province—now issued small grants to the less fortunate to buy construction materials and employ builders.

I talked with countless people during my two weeks in the provinces, many for the first time. The Grey Zone was far from satisfied, but also far from hitting the streets. There was Sosa, the Camagüey bicitaxi driver, convinced the new competition was driving down eatery prices and improving what was on offer in his city. And Tomás Mayedo Fernández, a young man in the backwater town of Guiamaro in central Cuba who, with his wife Yaima López, had opened the Magno cafeteria, and then a restaurant, and planned to build a small motel on the empty plot behind the place on the central highway. "I thank the government for giving us the opportunity to demonstrate to ourselves that we are capable of doing this well," Mayedo told me. "No state can subsidize an entire population, it is impossible. Furthermore, we provide jobs, pay taxes, and help the economy in a big way," he said. By the close of 2012 the government would report there were more than 1,700 private restaurants and 5,000 private bed-and-breakfasts in the country, compared with no more than a few hundred *paladares* and a thousand private rentals a few years earlier. Then there were the people I met in Ciego de Ávila and Camagüey as I went knocking on doors with "Se Vende" or "For Sale" signs tacked on them, and all the people I chatted up at bars and eateries across the land. There were the hitchhikers, the ranchers and farmers, the acquaintances of acquaintances—the list went on and on. They were all, it appeared, going about their business as usual. They had plenty of gripes, especially about rising prices and the slow pace of reform, but no one whispered in my ear that they were preparing to revolt or criticized the increased presence of the Cuban Americans and their money. Some young people did say they would leave for greener pastures and the modern world the first chance they got. My farmer friends said they were worried when Raúl first took over because of his reputation as a "hard-line extremist," but they said he had proved quite the opposite and was doing a fairly good job. "Fidel tried to fix the world, while Raúl is trying to fix Cuba. Too bad he is so old," one of three women doctors I picked up outside Camagüey said.

My favorite bar at the time was attached to the Tocororo restaurant at the corner of Third Avenue and 18th Street in Miramar. Named after a colorful midsized bird native to the island and anointed its national bird, the bar boasted a great mix of Cubans, diplomats, and foreign businessmen and a free-flowing atmosphere after 10 p.m. that is often hard to come by in Cuba, though that now is also changing. I met a group of Eastern European diplomats at the Tocororo during the summer of 2011. We talked politics Sunday nights and compared Cuba with the former Eastern European Communist countries where all had been anti-Communist activists and a few still were, but this time in Havana! My new friends understood that nationalism and U.S. policy worked against "liberation" on the island, while in their countries these factors had helped drive the revolt against the Russian-imposed system. And they conceded my point that Cuba was neither a Muslim land nor a medieval kingdom, à la the Arab Spring. Nevertheless, the four of them insisted, autocracy was autocracy and Communism was Communism and besides, they said, there were more dissidents in Cuba than there had been in some of their own countries before the fall of the Berlin Wall. Trouble was surely brewing right below the surface. Millions in the Grey Zone could turn against the system at any moment, they believed. I had bet Juraj (Slovakia), František (Czech Republic), Piotr (Poland), and Zsolt (Hungary) each a steak dinner at the Tocororo restaurant that there would be absolutely no social unrest in the country through July 2013, not a peep for two years. I thought of my steak dinners and upon return to Havana assured my diplomat friends over drinks that they most certainly would lose our bet.

Cuba's Future

I was soon invited to present my views on Cuba's future to a meeting of European Union member diplomats. Much had changed since Fidel Castro first stepped aside in 2006 and his brother quickly established a commission to study socialist property relations, telling university students to speak their minds because different points of view, not imposed unanimity, led to better decision making. Yet the country was just beginning to enter the post-Castro era with Fidel and Raúl still very much around. There was much more in store as Raúl's reforms took shape on the ground and within the superstructure, a new leadership emerged, and the United States sparred with its unruly neighbor, still looking for that elusive knockout punch even as the region embraced the island. "A new Cuba is being born, but it is far too early to forecast how the *criatura*, what they call infants here, will turn out. As with life itself, there are far too many unknowns," I told my hosts. At the same time, what the Cuban leadership wanted to accomplish over the coming years was clear enough. "The 311-point reform plan adopted by the Communist Party and government is not just a piece of paper. It is a life-or-death blueprint to save their revolution and will be carried out with military precision," I said. To be sure, it might take longer than forecast and be changed some along the way, but the sketch of things to come was clear enough. "Then, perhaps five years from now, when the results are not as positive as expected, they will open up further under a new leadership, as the Vietnamese did in the 1980s," I said.

My hosts fretted that the reforms were halfway measures and coming down far too slowly. I pointed out that Raúl's plans amounted to a profound—and potentially destabilizing—remaking of the economy and society. "Vested interests and out-of-date thought patterns slow change here, like everywhere else," I said, using the example of the developed world's foot-dragging on climate change. "There will be winners and losers; in fact, there already are, as some take the initiative to get ahead and others fall victim to layoffs and inflation."

I told my distinguished audience that over the next few years most retail services—with the exception of the bus service, gas stations, large company outlets such as the telephone company, foreign exchange stores, and some restaurants—would pass over to private and semiprivate (leasing and cooperative) hands and operate on a market basis. So would the bulk of housing and other minor construction and production. The state would contract out to the private sector more and more maintenance and other minor services and tasks. Agriculture would also become increasingly privatized as the state's monopoly on wholesale purchases and retail sales eroded. The non-state sector would purchase most of its supplies from wholesale, not retail, outlets and would compete, develop, and pay taxes. Big state companies would become more independent, and since the new mantra was sink or swim, they would push for permission to import and export directly, partner with foreign firms, and who knows what else to survive. There would be more advertising, but not the overwhelming commercialization one found in other lands. More revenues and decision-making powers would move from the national level to the provinces and municipalities, where the local governments would be reorganized and downsized. Local elections would take on new importance as their revenues and responsibilities increased. Over a million people would move from state to non-state jobs, the ration would indeed finally disappear, and state salaries and pensions would gradually increase. People would be freer to travel and live abroad. The owners of cattle might even be allowed to kill and eat them, I joked. Someday the land would have a single currency, the peso. Drugs and drug trafficking, and the crime that came with them, would remain well under control. There would be fewer and fewer subsidies and more and more taxes, fundamentally changing the relationship between the state and the people. I mentioned a state-run radio talk show I happened upon while driving to work the week before. The commentators said that under a paternalistic system the people had no right to complain and demand more of their government, but that was now changing and they should do just that. I told my hosts:

> Raúl's plans are strategic, not tactical, and have been sold to the public over the last few years through the admission of mistakes and through confessions that the Party has been way too slow at adopting new policies for new realities. External factors, from the discovery of oil or gas offshore to the loss of Venezuelan largesse may slow or accelerate reform, but the direction toward a more mixed economy and personal freedoms is irreversible. There is no turning back.

And what of Cuba paying back its debts and opening up to foreign investment? My distinguished European interlocutors wanted to know. Raúl Castro had imposed austerity measures and managed to pile up a foreign exchange surplus since taking office, but it would be years before there was any real drawing down on the debt, I believed. Priority would go to improving work incentives, repair of dilapidated infrastructure, and development. There would be more foreign investment, but not necessarily Western investment, I cautioned.

As for Cuba's one-party political system, I said its years, but not days, might be numbered. I pointed out that single-party Vietnam bordered single-party China, while Cuba was in the Western Hemisphere where all nations now had multiparty democracies, albeit with some backtracking in Honduras and Paraguay. "Just as economies stagnate without some level of competition, so do political systems, but as long as a country's leaders are viewed as legitimate, few seriously question the system, let alone consider bringing it down," I said. "After the Castro brothers are no longer around, we will see whom the Party comes up with and if a crisis of political legitimacy erupts sometime in the future." I could imagine only four scenarios that might significantly alter that political timetable. A reversal of the democratic process and integration under way in the Latin American region would lead the Cubans to hunker down. A big oil or gas find offshore would certainly improve the chances of future leaders. There might be a series of catastrophic external economic shocks that sped up the political agenda—for example, the fall of Chávez and his political party, a major hurricane hitting Havana, and a worsening of the international economic crisis. Finally, the United States might unilaterally lift all sanctions. Such a dramatic shift in U.S. policy appeared unlikely, but it would strip the government of its principal justification inside and outside the country for one-party rule. "I have no doubt a now more democratic and ever more integrated Latin American region would help Cuba transition without having to surrender to Washington and Miami," I said.

My hosts were curious about who might replace the Castro brothers. "I have no idea," I replied. How about the military or another Castro? they asked. "Cuba may have had the Castros on top for more than half a century, but there is an institutional process in place, and it is inconceivable to me that it would be violated in favor of a dynastic succession. These people are simply not that stupid," I said. "The Politburo and Council of State boast no Castro kids or other relatives, prerequisites for top leadership posts." As for the military, historically it had developed with the Revolution, maintained close ties with the population, and thus was very different from some other militaries in the region. The question was how opportunist and corrupt had it become. Was the military taking control of more and more of the economy as a patriotic and revolutionary duty because it could actually do a better job, as Raúl claimed, or not? Only time would tell, but there was certainly reason for concern. Any one of the generals on the Politburo, or all of them, could conceivably take over, though I doubted that option, because open military regimes were simply out of fashion in the region. "I certainly would look at Marino Murillo and who's who in his reform commission, as they are the ones fashioning Cuba's future," I said. "Then there are the younger people sitting on leading Party and government bodies and the provincial Party leadership." I urged patience. "Perhaps in a few years we might have a better idea of who is moving into position," I said.

The changes under way in Cuba attracted new investor interest. Was the island finally opening up? Was this the moment to get in before the crowd and make a killing? Was that tsunami of money across the Florida Straits about to wash over the island? Would a McDonalds open on Havana's seaside drive? Scouts representing very big bucks, some open as to who they were and others masquerading as tourists or cigar buffs, looked me up for a chat. There were the Russians, the Hong Kong crowd, Europeans, and of course Cuban Americans and Americans. "There is no question the country has gotten off the dime and is moving in a more market-friendly direction," I told them. "But the process is just getting started, and the Cubans are still reorganizing how they govern and do business. They are not ready for massive investment. Perhaps in a year or two, but even then there will be no sell-off of the country or free-for-all, but a careful vetting of partners and projects," I said. There were real risks on the horizon, as my new acquaintances were quick to point out. Hurricanes aside, there was cancer-stricken Hugo Chávez, and while the newly reelected Obama included in his cabinet John Kerry as secretary of state and Chuck Hagel at the Pentagon—both critics of U.S. Cuba policy—this did not necessarily mean a big breakthrough in relations, given the continued imprisonment of Alan Gross and the Cuban Five and the power of pro-embargo lawmakers. The three deepwater oil wells drilled by various foreign companies in 2012 proved a bust, with no plans for further exploration in 2013. But a less sophisticated drilling rig, contracted by a Russian firm to drill closer to shore, was hard at work. Raúl Castro might drop dead, and then what? We invariably agreed to take another look at the situation in a few years.

The New Coalition

On Wednesday evening, March 28, 2012, I sat in the lovely, sprawling, tree-shaded back garden of the Hotel Nacional overlooking the Gulf of Mexico, waiting for ABC's Christiane Amanpour and her producer and cameraman to finish up a final piece for *Nightline* and join me for a farewell drink. It would be her last assignment before moving back to CNN and, as it turned out, Pope Benedict XVI's last overseas trip. It had been a true privilege and learning experience working with Christiane and her team over five days as they covered the papal visit to Cuba. I had joined forces with many television crews over the years, but, as one would expect of people who were at the top of the heap in so competitive a business, the three of them were extraordinarily skilled in their respective jobs.

So what was the pope's visit, most of which had been televised live in Cuba, really all about? I mused as I sipped my beer and watched a few hundred other journalists wrapping up their work while peacocks strolled, strutted, and pecked, seemingly oblivious to the commotion. Raúl Castro's government had gained more international legitimacy and perhaps more sympathy from the Grey Zone. The papal visit was a rebuke to U.S. policy and the more extreme members of the exile establishment and dissident groups who supported that policy. A handful of dissidents had tried to dissuade the pope from coming and then demanded time with him, creating much ado on U.S.-government-run Radio and TV Martí and various U.S.-government-sponsored Internet platforms. The Miami-based Cuban Republican Party had "led" a thirteen-person occupation of a Havana church. They were dislodged by police. Another Miami group had paid eight young Mexicans to come into town, distribute leaflets supposedly written by Cubans, and make as much noise as possible. Four of the eight were arrested, interviewed by state security—a video of which was broadcast on state-run television—and deported.

Benedict's visit signaled the Vatican's full support for the local Catholic Church's decision to embrace Raúl Castro's efforts to mend fences and "modernize" the economy, albeit critically and while pushing for a wider and deeper political opening. But there was something far more important in play. The visit was not just about freedom of religious thought and expression. It signaled the new tolerance of differing beliefs and views in general. Raúl, ever since he took over for his brother, had hammered away at the need for diversity of thought and the legitimacy of expressing one's views and listening to those of others, albeit within certain limits and established channels and never on the street. Some dissidents' mobile and home phones, after all, were cut by the state communications monopoly upon Benedict's arrival and were not restored until he and the journalists had departed. Nevertheless, the papal visit was the latest step in the decompression process. Cuba was like a diver slowly coming up from the deep to avoid the bends and with a big white shark circling overhead. The Cubans were already speaking their minds like never before, even to journalists, and giving their full names with less hesitation. The trip could only embolden them further.

I continued to mull over the week's events as I waited to say goodbye to Amanpour and her team. There had been Benedict's arrival that Monday, March 26, and his first Mass in Santiago de Cuba, after which he paid homage to the Caridad del Cobre. The pope traveled on Tuesday to Havana, where he met with Raúl. That Wednesday morning he presided over a second Mass, followed by a brief encounter with Fidel Castro. Benedict had all but whispered his Havana Mass on a podium placed at the base of the huge statue of national apostle José Martí, front and center in Havana's Revolution Square. Pope John Paul II in 1998 had also presided over Mass in the emblematic plaza, but to the side with the national library as backdrop. The shift of location reflected the political parameters of the new relationship Castro had forged with the Roman Catholic Church and by implication wanted to establish with all Cubans at home and abroad. The Communist Party had always jealously guarded the space at the foot of the Martí statue for "revolutionary events" and claimed only its members and followers were the successors to the nation's independence martyrs. Now Raúl Castro had moved the goal posts (and literally the pope) as he sought support for potentially destabilizing reform and broke fifty-year-old taboos. The message could not have been clearer. He was willing to share those symbols as long as his partners put the nation first. The "patriots" and not "annexationists" still ruled the roost, but it no longer was the exclusive domain of the Communists.

"Benedict will arrive in a country in the process of transformation . . . begun precisely after a change of head of state and evidence of the exhaustion of the real, paternalist socialism . . . that John Paul II knew so well," Cardinal Ortega's top aide and spokesman, Orlando Márquez, had written on the Bishops' Conference's web page in March.

"Relations between the Church and government in Cuba today are at a qualitatively better level than 14 years ago. . . . There is a dialogue between different parties that has as its focus the common good of Cuban society as a whole."[1]

Benedict laced his sermons with references to freedom, reconciliation, and the spiritual needs of human beings and critiques of both the ideological materialism of Communism and the materialistic consumerism of the developed world's capitalism. My grandfather Waldo, a mystic in the end, most certainly would have applauded Benedict. And perhaps Sylvia Cannon, who had scribbled furiously in the margins of his book on Cuba in the 1960s, would have felt somewhat vindicated. But two remarkable events that week, mere sidebars to the larger story, struck me as perhaps the most important for Cuba's future.

That Tuesday the archbishop of Miami, Thomas Wensky, had presided over a Mass in Havana Cathedral, assisted by Father Felipe Estévez of Saint Augustine, Florida, and Father Octavio Cisneros, of Brooklyn, New York. This was yet another first since the Revolution. They had traveled to Cuba along with some 800 Cuban Americans for the papal visit. A similar attempt to be with John Paul II in 1998 was met by protests in Miami and canceled. Archbishop Wensky echoed Benedict's call for a third way into a "future of hope" and a "transition worthy of human beings and Cubans. . . . To emerge from an ideo-logical materialism only to fall into crude materialism would not be worthy of man, either," he said, adding, "Cubans want to be the forgers of their own history." Speaking in the packed cathedral, Wensky said to applause: "At this moment we want Cubans to learn to be brothers, and in this brotherhood have knowledge of diversity, and that this diversity does not have to divide a people which continue to be one people."

A few days later, on Friday, Cuban American businessman Carlos Saladrigas delivered a speech titled "Cuba and the Diaspora" to a packed room of aca-demics, dissidents, clergy and lay people, government supporters, and foreign diplomats at the Church's Felix Varela Cultural Center in downtown Havana. Saladrigas was a self-made millionaire who had arrived as a boy in Miami in the early 1960s. For decades the insurance magnate supported U.S. efforts to topple the Castros. He opposed plans in 1998 for Cuban Americans to be with Pope John Paul II in Cuba. Saladrigas had since broken with the more extreme sector of the exile establishment to advocate engagement as president of a Cu-ban American business organization called the Cuba Study Group. "Cuba's problems are great, but they are our problems, and we have to resolve them between all Cubans. It won't be easy, but we have no other option. . . . We will take down the walls we have built on both sides and construct the bridges that are lacking and set to the task of building a new Cuba," Saladrigas vowed.

The Cuban media blacked out both events, and the Cuban American es-tablishment condemned them. Firebombs soon destroyed the Coral Gables offices of ABC Charters, which had brought the Miami pilgrims to Havana for the papal visit. There was still a long road ahead to the peace and reconciliation Pope Benedict called for and most Cubans, on and off the island, longed for. Yet the two events—and the Cuban Americans flooding into the country and their relatives visiting the United States—signaled that the process had begun.

"Life is a book. We simply turned the page and moved on," a Vietnamese official told a Cuban friend when asked how his country came to terms with the United States and those who had sided with it during the war. "If the Viet-namese could do it after losing millions of lives it shouldn't be all that difficult for us," my friend said.

The head of the Vietnamese Communist Party visited Cuba in late April 2012. The trip was not about strengthening already excellent bilateral relations. He spent his time lecturing to national and local leaders at the Party and gov-ernment cadre schools in Havana and proselytized for market socialism, appar-ently at the behest of Raúl Castro, who was still meeting stiff resistance in the ranks.

"The most difficult has been changing how Vietnamese in general, and individuals, think," Nguyen Phu Trong said in a front-page interview in *Granma*, after reviewing the economic and social success of Vietnam's reforms. He said many people believed when the reform process—known as Doi Moi and begun in the 1980s—got under way that it would lead to the restoration of capitalism, and instead it had resulted in a new socialist model that had lifted the country out of poverty.

"During these days in Cuba, talking with its leaders, it appears to me that you are going through the same process. The change of thinking has to take place at all levels, from top to bottom," Nguyen said.[2] He might have added, and among all Cubans, be they living at home or abroad.

In February 2013 a new slate of 612 National Assembly deputies was voted into office and on the twenty-fourth the new legislature met and approved a new Council of State. The parliament's average age was 48, and 80 percent of the deputies were born after the Revolution. Half its members were women and more than a third black or of mixed race. Of the thirty-one members of the Council of State, 41.9 percent were women and 38.6 percent black or of mixed race. The average age was 57 years, and 61.3 percent were born after the triumph of the Revolution. Raúl Castro, 81, speaking to the country, announced he would step down in 2018, effectively ending the Castro era, and called for a constitutional referendum to establish term and age limits, among other matters. Miguel Díaz-Canel, 52, replaced Machado Ventura as first vice president of the Council of State and Council of Ministers, meaning he would take over if Raúl Castro could not serve his full term. Díaz-Canel, a member of the Politburo, had come up through the Communist Party ranks over many years to become a national cadre, minister of higher education, and vice president of the Council of Ministers. The successor, neither a Castro nor a military man, had finally appeared. Machado took a vice president slot, while Commander of the Revolution Ramiro Valdés, 80, and Gladys Bejerano, 66, the comptroller general, were reelected as vice presidents. Two other newcomers, Mercedes López Acea, 48, first secretary of the Havana Party, and Salvador Valdés Mesa, 64, head of the official labor federation, also earned vice presidential slots. All the top members of the Council of State, with the exception of Bejerano, sat on the Politburo. Esteban Lazo, 69, a vice president and member of the Politburo, left his post upon being named president of the National Assembly, replacing Ricardo Alarcón, 75, who had served in the job for twenty years.[3]

A stooped and now rapidly aging Fidel Castro, who turned 87 in August 2013, would appear to vote in the February general election and chat, with obvious effort and a frail voice, with Cuban reporters for over an hour. He also attended the inaugural session of the National Assembly to signal his endorsement of a gradually changing leadership. Raúl, who turned 82 in June 2013, looked like he would weather a few more years on the planet and in office, especially with Díaz-Canel expected to gradually take over presidential duties as he was groomed for the job.

The Obama administration was unimpressed, State Department spokesman Patrick Ventrell once more implying that only a restoration of democracy and capitalism could move relations forward.

> Question. Do you have a reaction to Raul Castro saying he will not seek reelection in five years' time?
>
> Mr. Ventrell. So, Brad, we are indeed aware of the reports that President Castro, Raul Castro, announced his intention to step down in 2018 after another five-year term. We also saw the announcement that Mr. Miguel Diaz-Canel was named First Vice President.
>
> We remain hopeful for the day that the Cuban people get democracy, when they can have the opportunity to freely pick their own leaders in an open democratic process and enjoy the freedoms of speech and association without fear of reprisal. We're clearly not there yet.
>
> Question. Hold on, hold on, I'm glad you're aware. I guess that confirms that not everybody in the U.S. Government slept through the entire weekend. But do you have an actual reaction? Do you have a position on whether this is a good step, whether this is helpful in that process toward a freer, fairer, Cuba as you stated?
>
> Mr. Ventrell. I think—
>
> Question. Or just that you know that things happened in the world over the last 48 hours?
>
> Mr. Ventrell. Well, no. I mean, I think, Brad, what we're saying is that we've noted that it's happened, but clearly, a change in leadership that, absent the fundamental democratic reforms necessary to give people their free will and their ability to pick their own leaders, won't be a fundamental change for Cuba.
>
> Question. So this is not enough; they still need to do more if they want to, one, improve the state of their country and, two, repair relations with the United States?
>
> Mr. Ventrell. Absolutely.[4]

A week later March brought a cold front, moving west to east along the island, drenching the tropical Cubans and chilling them to the bone. The cold settled in, and the inevitable news that came on the fifth sent new shivers down their spines. Cancer-stricken Hugo Chávez, who had returned to Venezuela in February after his fourth cancer operation in Cuba, was dead.

Three days of mourning were declared, and millions turned out to pay their last respects at memorial services across the country. In Havana the venue was the José Martí Memorial in Revolution Square, where only farewells to revolutionary Comandantes and one foreigner, Che Guevara, had been held in the past. The cannon atop the old Spanish fort overlooking Havana roared with a twenty-one-gun salute on the eighth, as a state funeral got under way in Caracas.

Chávez's resolute political support of Cuba had played a huge role in the country's reintegration within the region, and oil-rich Venezuela's largesse had proved a lifesaver for the embargoed and bankrupt Cuba after the collapse of the Soviet Union.

Many Cubans viewed Chávez as an irreplaceable leader of the region and savior of socialism, portrayed day and night by official media as a champion of regional unity, independence, social justice, and the island.

The Cubans had come to know the Venezuelan leader better than any people did, with the exception of the Venezuelans themselves, Chávez having enjoyed far more media coverage than any other foreign leader since the Revolution, and arguably more than President Raúl Castro.

There were tears for the fifty-eight-year-old Venezuelan and his family, and there was dread that Cuba would once more lose a strategic ally and be plunged back into a grave economic crisis similar to the 1990s after the demise of the Soviet Union.

It was left to Díaz-Canel, standing at a podium with Raúl Castro at his side, to speak for Cuba's leadership as he pronounced his first political discourse since becoming the second most powerful man in the land. The setting was the Sierra Maestra on March 6, and the event was to mark the founding of the Third Front of the revolutionary war fifty-five years earlier. His speech had been designed to demonstrate continuity between the past, the present, and the future, but now it began differently.

"History can always surprise us. We have come here to celebrate our past and she has appeared painfully from the present, as if to warn us that what takes place now cannot be separated from the roots that nurture us and bring us together," Díaz-Canel said. "From this sacred place, let our first words be for the family of Chávez, which is the grand Venezuelan and Latin American family. Let our emotional embrace be for the courageous people who lament the loss of the noblest and most generous of their sons, with pain but also with determination, because no tear has value if it is not accompanied by the commitment to guarantee the survival of the work of the beloved leader. This must be the pledge of all of Our America."[5]

Chávez's impact on contemporary Cuba was so great that barely a word in this book would be the same if not for that folksy follower of Simón Bolívar. Those written in the future will inevitably differ, even if his socialist party continues to govern. Only time will tell how Chávez's passing will affect the new Cuba being born, that *criatura* still in swaddling clothes facing an always promising and always perilous future.

Acknowledgments

My clients and editors at Thomson Reuters, the *Financial Times*, and ABC News all deserve special acknowledgment for their support and improvement of my reporting over the years. Some of the quotations and phrasing in the text first appeared in articles published by all three clients, and I appreciate their authorization to include them. This book would not have been possible without the knowledge and guidance of my wife Marlene and her vast extended family and network of friends inside and outside of Cuba. Nor would I understand much about the always mysterious island if it were not for my dear friend and guide to all things Cuban, Eduardo Machin, my daughter Dhara, my step-daughter Ivet, and all their acquaintances. I owe special thanks to Havana University's Center for the Study of the Cuban Economy for all the fine work they have produced over the years, on which I have always relied for guidance. *Temas* magazine, and its brilliant editor Rafael Hernández, deserve credit for being way out in front of the curve and keeping their readers and the author thinking. Finally, I must mention the myriad Cuban friends and foreign experts, and my sources among Cubans, diplomats, and foreign businessmen, for their insights and encouragement over the years.

Notes

Electronic versions of references are provided where possible, preceded by a comma if a direct link, or by "Online at" if secondary.

Introduction

1. Castro's off-the-cuff remarks were not included in the official transcript.

2. Recorded and transcribed by Reuters in Havana.

3. Wright, *Cuba*, vii–viii.

4. Since 1951 the average temperature has increased 0.9 degrees Celsius (1.62 degrees Fahrenheit), according to the Cuban Meteorological Institute.

5. Johnson, *History of Cuba*, 5: 1.

6. Strode, *Pageant of Cuba*, 320.

7. Hermer and May, *Havana Mañana*, 258–59.

8. Nelson, *Rural Cuba*, 9.

9. Fergusson, *Cuba*, 260–61.

10. "As a man of genius, he of course identifies himself with the substance of his work. But if the identification becomes possessive he will no longer be the good leader. The great question about Fidel Castro is whether he has enough intellectual detachment to recognize in himself the evils of the lusting ego, which he shares with all men and which might distort his vision and stultify his uses" (W. Frank, *Cuba: Prophetic Island*, 141–42).

Chapter 1. Trauma

1. Since the early days of the Revolution, the government had provided a subsidized, World War II–like food ration to the population; after the Soviet Union's demise, the ration was drastically reduced, and today it is gradually being eliminated.

2. Miramar was an upper-class neighborhood spotted with mansions and swimming pools before the Revolution and remains a relatively well-off district, located across the Almandares River, west of the city proper. Further to the west lie the far more posh Siboney and Cubanacán districts.

3. According to UNICEF's 1989 report "On the State of the World's Children," at the close of 1987 Cuba's infant mortality rate stood at 15 per 1,000 live births, as against Mongolia at 46, the USSR 25, Romania 22, Poland 18, Hungary 17, Bulgaria 15, Czechoslovakia 10, and East Germany 9. Cuba's life expectancy had reached 74 years, exceeding

Mongolia at 64, the USSR 70, Romania and Hungary 71, and Bulgaria, Czechoslovakia, and Poland 72, with only East Germany on a par with Cuba at 74.

4. Alexandra Silver, "Mikhail Gorbachev, Pizza Hut," *Time*, August 24, 2010, time.com/time/specials/packages/article/0,28804,2012633_2012652_2012665,00.html.

5. There was an existing immigration agreement that in essence said the United States would accept a minimum of 20,000 Cubans a year. However, in practice the United States granted only a few thousand permanent immigrant visas a year. At the same time, in accordance with a 1960s law called the Cuban Adjustment Act, any Cuban rafter who was picked up at sea or managed to set foot on U.S. soil was given legal status and aid, while those from any other land were considered illegal aliens and deported. In 1994 a new agreement basically said the United States would live up to its commitments and provide 20,000 permanent entry visas per year, while another signed in 1995 committed the United States to returning Cubans intercepted at sea to the island, while those who managed to set foot on U.S. soil could stay, a policy known as wet foot/dry foot.

6. Chávez's failed coup followed the bloody 1989 riots in Caracas and other cities, which left hundreds dead and thousands wounded and in jail. The army was used, artillery and all, to brutally put down protests over International Monetary Fund–imposed austerity measures. This caused deep divisions within the military's ranks, drawn mostly from the 60 percent of Venezuelans who lived in poverty.

7. Vedado is the intellectual district built up around Havana University, and was also the urban home of some of the island's wealthy before the Revolution. To the east of Vedado lies Central Havana, which in turn leads to the old town, the three districts running from the bay westward along the Malecón, Havana's seaside drive, to the Almendares River.

8. Before the revolution, when the Capri hotel and casino were owned by mob boss Santo Trafficante, U.S. tough-guy actor George Raft was the meeter-and-greeter at the Salón Rojo to draw gambling Americans.

9. When terrorists flew hijacked planes into the World Trade Center and the Pentagon on September 11, 2001, and another aircraft crashed in Pennsylvania, more than 3,000 innocent people died, the equivalent of one in every 94,000 inhabitants of the United States. Twenty-five years earlier, in 1976, an exile-organized bombing of a Cuban commercial airliner out of Barbados killed all 73 people aboard—the equivalent of one in every 130,000 of the country's inhabitants at the time. The Cubans were every bit as shocked by that heinous attack as Americans were in 2001. Americans remember, and so do the Cubans.

10. The National Accounting Office was established in 1995 within the Finance Ministry, as was the National Tax Office to administer the Revolution's first income tax, levied on cultural figures and the self-employed. By the summer of 2001 the Accounting Office was replaced by the more powerful Ministry of Auditing and Control, which in turn morphed into the Comptroller General's Office in 2008 as the battle against white-collar crime—called guayabera crime, after the Cuban dress shirt—continued. Havana University boasted a full-fledged accounting school by the turn of the century, and accountants were praised far and wide, by Fidel Castro on down.

11. Omar Everleny Pérez Villanueva, and Pavel Vidal Alejandro, "Cuba's Economy: A Current Evaluation and Several Necessary Proposals," *Socialism and Democracy* 24, no. 1 (2010): 71–93, sdonline.org/52/cubas-economy-a-current-evaluation-and-several-necessary-proposals.

12. Domínguez, Pérez Villanueva, and Barberia, *Cuban Economy*, 209.

13. Unpublished 2009 report by the Working Group to Reduce Inequality, which was comprised of leading sociologists and economists and commissioned by the Central Committee of the Cuban Communist Party.

14. Ibid.

Chapter 2. Castro Falters

1. Ben Macintyre, "Castro's Collapse Shocks Cubans," *London Times*, June 25, 2001. Online at groups.yahoo.com/group/CubaNews/message/3912.

2. This account of my encounter with Fidel Castro first appeared online at ABC News.

3. Marc Frank, "Castro Fractures Knee, Hurts Arm in Fall," Reuters, October 21, 2004. Online at lvracingscene.com/forum/showthread.php?20367-HaHa.

4. Ibid.

5. Elián González went on to lead a relatively normal life as a military cadet and Union of Young Communists member, largely sheltered from the media by the government. Miguel, his father, became a National Assembly deputy through 2012, when he was replaced.

6. The Cuban government issued a 37-DVD set on the Tribunas, which gave the dates and number that were held.

7. Fidel Castro, "Speech Delivered . . . at the Commemoration of the 60th Anniversary of His Admission to University of Havana, in the Aula Magna of the University of Havana, on November 17, 2005," cuba.cu/gobierno/discursos/2005/ing/f171105i.html.

8. "Condi Rice Chairs Anti-Castro Panel," Associated Press, December 20, 2005. Online at archive.newsmax.com/archives/articles/2005/12/20/94757.shtml.

9. The National Assembly usually meets just twice a year, when deputies gather for a few days of closed-door committee meetings and then a day or two of full sessions. Foreign journalists and diplomats were allowed in for the opening moments of the full session, after which deliberations were closed to the public. Since 2008 the entire proceedings have been closed.

10. Francisco Soberón, "Socialism Is Not a Chance Option for Cubans," *Granma International*, December 24, 2005. Online at walterlippmann.com/docs367.html.

11. See Marc Frank, "Cuba Begins to Think about Life after Castro," *Financial Times*, January 2, 2006, ft.com/intl/cms/s/1/235dbc72-7bd5-11da-ab8e-0000779e2340.html#axzz2EP4jzr9g.

12. Castro and Ramonet, *My Life*.

13. Katiuska Blanco Castiñeira, *Fidel Castro Ruz: Guerrillero del Tiempo* (Havana: Abril, 2011–).

14. Vanessa Arrington, "Castro's Brother: Cuba Will Stay Communist," Associated Press, June 15, 2006. Online at alldeaf.com/war-political-news/29812-castros-brother-cuba-will-stay-communist.html.

Chapter 3. The Big Bang

1. For by far the best description in print and drawings of Havana and Cuba in the late 1800s, see Samuel Hazard's truly remarkable and unique *Cuba with Pen and Pencil.*

2. No one does justice to Old Havana like Irene Aloha Wright in the first chapter of her book *Cuba*, where she also explains the street names on pages 15–17.

3. Fidel Castro, "Proclamation by the Commander in Chief to the People of Cuba," July 31, 2006, cuba.cu/gobierno/discursos/2006/ing/f310706i.html.

4. Fidel Castro, "Message Sent by the Commander in Chief to the People of Cuba and Friends from All Over the World," August 1, 2006, cuba.cu/gobierno/discursos/2006/ing/f010806i.html.

5. The ration had gone from eight eggs per month, at 15 centavos each, to ten eggs, five at 15 centavos each and the remainder at 90 centavos each, compared with 2 pesos on the street.

6. "U.S. Sees No Thaw in Ties with Cuba after Transfer," Reuters, August 1, 2006. Online at news.oneindia.in/2006/08/02/us-sees-no-thaw-in-ties-with-cuba-after-transfer-1154464432.html.

7. Anthony Boadle, "Castro Stays Out of Public View," Reuters, August 4, 2006. Online at theage.com.au/news/World/Cuba-shows-support-for-Raul-Castro/2006/08/05/1154198361922.html.

8. Whenever the Bush administration announced that it was increasing TV Martí's signal, or trying a new tactic to get the signal inside Cuba, I would consult my "sugar network" to see if anyone around the country had caught a glimpse. (I covered sugar for Reuters and, over many years, developed a network in most provinces that would let me know how the harvest was proceeding.) The people in my network would call family and friends to tune in to TV Martí, and they invariably reported that no one had picked up the signal.

9. James C. McKinley Jr., "Cuban Officials Say Castro Is Recovering and the Nation Is Stable," *New York Times*, August 8, 2006, nytimes.com/2006/08/08/world/americas/08cuba.html.

10. July 26 is a national holiday marking Fidel Castro's failed 1953 storming of a military fort, Santiago de Cuba's Moncada Garrison, which nevertheless signaled the start of the Cuban Revolution. The president traditionally delivers a state-of-the-nation speech to mark the Day of Rebellion.

11. The "energy revolution" consisted of establishing groups of generators instead of traditional power plants, replacing infrastructure (power lines, transformers, etc.), and substituting lightbulbs and old appliances with new, energy-saving ones from China.

12. This was later confirmed by Fidel Castro's official biographer, Katiuska Blanco Castiñeira, in the introduction to the first volume of *Fidel Castro Ruz: Guerrillero del Tiempo*, where she describes the commotion on his plane upon returning to Havana from Holguín on July 26, 2006, and her first discussion with Castro on August 1, after his operation.

13. Richard Lapper was the *Financial Times*'s Latin American editor at the time.

14. "Spanish Doctor: Fidel Castro Does Not Have Cancer," Associated Press, December 26, 2006. Online at foxnews.com/story/0,2933,238842,00.html.

15. Translated by ABC News.

16. "Spanish Doctor Disputes Castro Health Report," Reuters, January 17, 2007, reuters.com/article/2007/01/17/us-cuba-castro-report-idUSN1735124220070117.

17. Mark Oliver, "Chavez: Recovering Castro 'Almost Jogging,'" *Guardian*, January 25, 2007, guardian.co.uk/world/2007/jan/25/venezuela.cuba.

18. For an abridged transcript of the conversation, see BBC News, "What Castro and Chavez Spoke About," news.bbc.co.uk/2/hi/americas/6403683.stm.

19. "Castro Talks over Phone with Chávez, Preval on Aid to Haiti," *People's Daily* (China), March 14, 2007, english.peopledaily.com.cn/200703/14/eng20070314_357442.html.

20. "Castro Informally Resuming Governing Role: Chavez," Reuters, April 13, 2007, reuters.com/article/2007/04/13/us-chavez-castro-idUSN1322693520070413.

21. Ibid.

22. Fidel Castro, "For the Deaf Who Won't Listen," *Reflections*, May 23, 2007, en.cubadebate.cu/reflections-fidel/2007/05/23/for-deaf-who-wont-listen.

23. Carmen Lira Saade, "Llegué a estar muerto, pero resucité," (I came to be dead, but revived) *La Jornada* (Mexico), August 30, 2010. Online at ziomania.com/articles2010/09/Fidel%20answers%20questions%20from%20the%20editor,%20Carmen%20Lira%20Saade.htm.

24. India's president visited Castro during a Cuban-hosted Nonaligned Movement summit in September 2006. Indian diplomats told me the visit was at the Palace of the Revolution, Communist Party and government headquarters, where there was a secure clinic.

Chapter 4. Raúl Pinch-Hits

1. The Royal Spanish Academy (Real Academia Española) is the official institution responsible for regulating the Spanish language.

2. Luis Sexto, "Burocracia, Distorsión y Rigidez," (Bureaucracy, Distortion, and Rigidity), *Patria y Humanidad*, blog, luisexto.blogia.com/2007/090702-burocracia-distorsion-y-rigidez.php.

3. The best example was the "temporary" food ration, which was established more or less at the same time and is being eliminated only today.

4. Fines levied on farmers should not be confused with the stiff prison sentences—up to fifteen years, though usually less—handed down for cattle rustling and selling black-market beef, a punishment that gives rise to the common saying that you get more years for killing a cow than for manslaughter.

5. See table 9.15, "Bovine Cattle by Sex and Category," in "Agriculture, Livestock, Forestry and Fishing," *Anuario Estadística de Cuba 2011*, Oficina Nacional de Estadísticas (National Statistics Office), www.one.cu/aec2011/esp/20080618_tabla_cuadro.htm. Online, the *Anuario Estadística* (Statistical Yearbook) presents only the most recent year

for which figures are available. For earlier statistics, see the same table in the print edition of earlier *Anuarios*, in particular for 1989.

6. See table 9.17, "Selected Indicators of Cow Milk Production" on the same website as note 5.

7. If you love old cars and happen to be in Havana, I suggest you take a trip to the country's prime farmland to the south. Find yourself one of the better-off family farmers in the area and take a look in the barn. If you're lucky, you may be treated to a vintage vehicle, in near-perfect condition, sheltered within.

8. "Raúl Castro Rips U.S. in First Remarks," *Washington Times*, August 18, 2006, washingtontimes.com/news/2006/aug/18/20060818-113943-6206r/?page=all.

9. Klepak, *Cuba's Military*.

10. Latell, *After Fidel*.

11. "Raúl Castro Tells Union to Fight Corruption," *Morning Star Online*, September 28, 2006, morningstaronline.co.uk/news/content/view/full/35675.

12. Anthony Boadle, "Raúl Castro Tackles Cuba's Shortcomings," Reuters, December 23, 2006. Online at washingtonpost.com/wp-dyn/content/article/2006/12/23/AR2006122300338_pf.html.

13. Anita Snow, "Cuba's Raúl Castro Signals More Openness to Divergent Ideas than Fidel," Associated Press, December 21, 2006. Online at washingtonpost.com/wp-dyn/content/article/2006/12/21/AR2006122100442.html.

14. See note 12.

15. For an excellent and brief summary of the model, see Phil Peters, "State Enterprise Reform in Cuba, an Early Snapshot," Lexington Institute, 2001, lexingtoninstitute.org/library/resources/documents/Cuba/ResearchProducts/state-enterprise-reform.pdf.

16. Susana Lee, "No es perfecto pero ha demostrado su eficiencia" (It isn't Perfect, but has Demonstrated its Efficiency), *Granma*, January 23, 2007.

17. See Raúl Castro's speech delivered July 26, 2007, in Camagüey, available only in Spanish at Cubagob.cu. Online in English at walterlippmann.com/rc-07-26-2007.html.

18. Ibid.

19. See Marc Frank, "Eye Surgeons Bring a Ray of Hope to the Caribbean," *Financial Times*, October 21, 2005, ft.com/intl/cms/s/0/58352e98-41cf-11da-a45d-00000e2511c8.html#axzz2EP4jzr9g.

20. Under PetroCaribe, Venezuela offers beneficiary countries long-term loans at interest rates of 1 to 2 percent to cover as much as 60 percent of their oil purchases, depending on the international price. Some of what is owed can be written off for local social and economic development projects, where Cuba often provides personnel.

21. See table 5.17, "External Balance of Goods and Services," in "National Accounts," *Anuario Estadística de Cuba 2009* (Havana: Oficina Nacional de Estadísticas, 2010), 185.

Chapter 5. Fidel Steps Down

1. Many Cubans practice Afro-Cuban religions in which the Caridad del Cobre represents the orisha (goddess) of love, money, and happiness, called Ochún.

2. Marabú is much like sickle bush, a hardwood bush with thorns; it can grow up to

five meters tall and is very difficult to clear and keep under control because its roots are hard to eradicate and its seeds are spread by cattle and other animals' dung.

3. Camilo Cienfuegos was a Comandante of the Revolution and a much-beloved man who died in 1959 when the small plane he was piloting disappeared at sea.

4. Fidel Castro, "Message from the Commander in Chief," February 18, 2008, cuba.cu/gobierno/discursos/2008/ing/f180208i.html.

5. Fidel Castro, "I Hope I Never Have Reason to Be Ashamed," *Reflections*, February 28, 2008, en.cubadebate.cu/reflections-fidel/2008/02/28/i-hope-i-never-have-reason-be-ashamed.

Chapter 6. From Clinton to Bush

1. See "Trent Lott Resigns from U.S. Senate," Associated Press, December 18, 2007. Online at foxnews.com/story/0,2933,317402,00.html.

2. The e-mails are online in Spanish at desdecuba.com/polemica/index.shtml.

3. "Cuban Poet Hails Banned Writers in Front of Raul, Apparatchiks," Spanish News Agency (EFE), February 13, 2007. Online at business.highbeam.com/436103/article-1G1-159262847/cuban-poet-hails-banned-writers-front-raul-apparatchiks.

4. See, for instance, Sarah Rainsford, "Cuba's Ban on Anti-Castro Musicians Quietly Lifted," BBC News online, August 8, 2012, bbc.co.uk/news/world-latin-america-19174552.

5. "Denuncian negación de visas EE.UU. a intelectuales cubanos" (Denial of U.S. visas to Cuban intellectuals denounced), Prensa Latina, February 7, 2007.

6. Anita Snow, "U.S. Groups Hope Obama to Allow More Travel to Cuba," Associated Press, April 26, 2009. Online at jamaicaobserver.com/news/150239_US-groups-hope-Obama-will-allow-more-travel-to-Cuba.

7. Anita Snow, "Cuba's Roman Catholic Cardinal Charges Rude Treatment by US Immigration Officials," Associated Press, March 3, 2005. Online at highbeam.com/doc/1P1-105960466.html.

8. Marc Frank, "Despite Sanctions Cuba Now 35th U.S. Food Market," Reuters, February 17, 2004. Online at latinamericanstudies.org/us-cuba/market.htm.

9. Wayne Smith and Seema Patel, "Commission for a Free Cuba Sets Restrictions on Americans," *International Policy Report*, June 2004, ciponline.org/research/entry/commission-for-a-free-cuba-sets-restrictions-on-americans.

10. John Solomon, "More Agents Track Castro Than Bin Laden," Associated Press, April 29, 2004. Online at news.google.com/newspapers?nid=1683&dat=20040501&id=hDUqAAAAIBAJ&sjid=dkUEAAAAIBAJ&pg=6574,62901.

11. Cuba said the 138 black flags, each with a lone white star, represented the years since its independence struggle began against Spain in 1868. The black background symbolized the country's mourning for what Havana alleged were the 3,400 Cubans killed by U.S. violence over the years, from the Bay of Pigs invasion to the 1976 bombing of a Cuban commercial plane off Barbados.

12. "U.S. Recommendations for a 'Free Cuba' Spark New Tensions," Spanish News Agency (EFE), July 1, 2006. Online at business.highbeam.com/436103/article-1G1-147707776/us-recommendations-free-cuba-spark-new-tensions.

13. Nancy San Martin, "Raúl Castro Hints at Readiness for Dialogue with Washington," *Miami Herald*, August 19, 2006. Online at groups.yahoo.com/group/CubaNews/message/53920.

14. "U.S. Will Not Reach Out to Castro's Brother," Deutsche Presse-Agentur, August 1, 2006. Online at news.monstersandcritics.com/northamerica/article_1186044.php/US_will_not_reach_out_to_Castros_brother.

15. Oscar Corral and Pablo Bachelet, "Increasing Cuba Broadcasts a Top U.S. Priority," *Miami Herald*, August 3, 2006. Online at cubanet.org/CNews/y06/ago06/04e6.htm. Scroll down to find the article.

16. "Mission Manager for Cuba and Venezuela Announced," *Global Security*, August 18, 2006.

17. Pablo Bachelet, "U.S. Creates Five Groups to Monitor Cuba," *Miami Herald*, September 13, 2006. Online at newsgroups.derkeiler.com/Archive/Soc/soc.culture.cuba/2006-09/msg00602.html.

18. Frances Robles, "New Task Force to Target Cuba Ban Offenders," *Miami Herald*, October 11, 2006. Online at cubanet.org/CNews/y06/oct06/13e4.htm. Scroll down to find the article.

19. George W. Bush, "President Bush Visits Naval War College, Discusses Iraq, War on Terror," June 28, 2006, georgewbush-whitehouse.archives.gov/news/releases/2007/06/20070628-14.html.

20. "Havana: Initial Thoughts on the Way Forward," Wikileaks, August 1, 2008, wikileaks.org/cable/2008/08/08HAVANA614.html.

Chapter 7. Conservative Reformers

1. State-run *Radio Rebelde* newscasts, February 25, 2008.

2. See, for example, Fidel Castro, "I Hope I Never Have a Reason to Be Ashamed," *Reflections*, February 28, 2008, en.cubadebate.cu/reflections-fidel/2008/02/28/i-hope-i-never-have-reason-be-ashamed.

3. Talía González Pérez, "Raúl Castro Speaks on the 50th Anniversary of the Cuban Revolution," *Granma International*, January 11, 2009, 3. Online at links.org.au/node/841.

4. Cubans working abroad on paid missions at the time earned wages in dollar equivalents. The formula gave them a small stipend to live on, another sent to family in Cuba, usually $50 per month, with the remainder of their wages, usually a few hundred dollars per month, placed in a bank account payable on their return to the island. Many also became eligible to buy a used rent-a-car with the money they earned, and some for housing. Many also shipped back goods bought abroad for resale. Salary depended on one's profession and location, as well as the number of years served abroad.

5. "Speech by Eusebio Leal Spengler . . . at the Seventh Congress of UNEAC," *Progresso Weekly*, April 10–16, 2008. Online at groups.yahoo.com/group/CubaNews/message/83034.

6. For the latest U.N. Human development reports, see hdr.undp.org/en/statistics.

7. The Transparency International report is available at cpi.transparency.org/cpi2012, select year.

8. Raúl Castro's inaugural speech is available only in Spanish at Cubagob.cu. An online English version is available at hcvanalysis.wordpress.com/2008/02/24/cuba-pres-raul-castro-speech-at-the-national-assembly-of-peoples-power-havana.

Chapter 8. Computers, Cell Phones, Hotels, and More

1. The National Statistics Office released 2008 telecommunications data showing there were 1.4 million telephones, fixed and mobile, in the country of 11.2 million inhabitants. This gave a total density of 12.6 telephones per 100 inhabitants, the lowest in the region, according to the United Nations International Telecommunications Union.

2. In 2011 ETECSA, the state telephone monopoly, charged the equivalent of $0.45 a minute to make or receive a local in-country call on a mobile phone, and $0.10 between 11 p.m. and 6 a.m. Obtaining a line cost $30.00. Messages cost $0.16. In January 2012 ETECSA eliminated all charges for receiving calls from other cell phones and reduced the message rate to $0.09. In January 2013 the per-minute rate of $0.45 was reduced by $0.10.

3. By 2013 more than 180,000 people had taken advantage of the land lease program, 70 percent farming for the first time.

4. Marc Frank, "Raúl Castro Takes Aim at Cuban Construction Woes," Reuters, July 10, 2008, reuters.com/article/2008/07/10/us-cuba-reform-idUKN1646747820080710.

5. Lourdes Pérez Navarro, "Reordenar es sinónimo de ahorrar" (To reorganize is the same as to save), Granma, February 6, 2010.

6. "Cuban Education at UNESCO Levels," Cubaheadlines.com, November 30, 2007, cubaheadlines.com/2007/11/30/7374/cuban_education_at_uncsco_levels.html.

7. Dalia Acosta, "CULTURE-CUBA: The Times, They Are A-Changin'," Inter Press Service, April 7, 2008, ipsnews.nct/news.asp?idnews=41895.

8. Marc Frank, "Cuba Cuts Education Spending, Shifts Priorities," Reuters, October 3, 2012, reuters.com/article/2012/10/03/us-cuba-education-idUSBRE89217O20121003.

9. Although it was not always the case, it is important to note that by the time my daughters attended the Lenin school, admission was by grade point average and exam scores only, not politics, and the same was true for Havana University and the medical school.

Chapter 9. Disaster, Man-Made and Natural

1. "La economía Cubana, actual y perspectivas" (The Cuban economy: Current situation and prospects), Ministry of Planning and Economy, 2009, unpublished report.

2. "Discurso de Carlos Lage Dávila en la reunión de los presidentes municipales del Poder Popular" (speech by Carlos Lage Dávila in the meeting of municipal presidents of People's Power), Juventud Rebelde, June 8, 2008. Online at cubasource.org/pdf/Chronicle 062008.pdf, then find by date.

3. Esteban Israel, "Raúl Castro Dashes Expectations for New Reforms," Reuters, July 27, 2008, reuters.com/article/2008/07/27/us-cuba-castro-revolution-idUSN 2643611020080727.

4. Jim Loney, "Cuba and Haiti Hard Hit in Hurricane Season," Reuters, November 14, 2008, reuters.com/article/2008/11/14/uk-storm-hurricanes-season-idUKTRE4AD19420081114.

5. "Official information on preliminary data of damages caused by Hurricanes Gustav and Ike," *Granma International*, September 21, 2008, 8. Online at monre.gov.vn/v35/default.aspx?tabid=675&CateID=59&ID=50884&Code=UPWN950884.

6. A year after the storms, the last of 500 home-schools closed, but Raúl Castro on July 26, 2009, said there were 600,000 houses and apartments damaged to one extent or another by these hurricanes and previous ones and that only 43 percent, or 260,000 homes, had been repaired.

Chapter 10. Obamamania

1. "Havana Mercenaries Vote for McCain," *Granma International*, November 16, 2008, 3. Online at groups.yahoo.com/group/CubaNews/message/94670?var=1.

2. Fidel Castro, "The November 4 Elections," *Reflections*, November 3, 2008, en.cubadebate.cu/reflections-fidel/2008/11/03/november-4th-elections.

3. Fidel Castro, "Swimming Up Stream," *Reflections*, December 4, 2008, en.cubadebate.cu/reflections-fidel/2008/12/04/swimming-up-stream.

4. Ibid.

5. Fidel Castro, "The 11th President of the United States," *Reflections*, January 22, 2009, en.cubadebate.cu/reflections-fidel/2009/01/22/11th-president-united-states.

6. Jeremy Pelofsky, "U.S. Congress Sends Last 2009 Spending Bill to Obama," Reuters, March 11, 2009, reuters.com/article/2009/03/11/us-usa-budget-idUSN105441192 0090311.

7. Doug Palmer, "Businesses Urge Obama to Loosen Cuba Embargo," Reuters, December 4, 2008, reuters.com/article/2008/12/04/us-usa-cuba-trade-smb-idUSTRE4B379 120081204.

8. Patrick Markey, "Caribbean Nations Urge U.S. to End Cuba Embargo," Reuters, December 8, 2008, reuters.com/article/2008/12/09/us-cuba-usa-caribbean-idUSTRE4B76AB20081209.

9. "Raúl Castro: The Blockade Has No Future; Cuba Ready for Dialogue among Equals," Prensa Latina, December 18, 2008. Online at forumdesalternatives.org/en/raul-castro-the-blockade-has-no-future-cuba-ready-for-dialogue-among-equals.

10. It is important to note that a number of heads of state, including those of Trinidad and Tobago, Nicaragua, and Haiti, received regular medical treatment in Cuba.

11. Andrew Cawthorne and Brian Ellsworth, "Latin America Rebels Against Obama over Cuba," Reuters, April 15, 2012, reuters.com/article/2012/04/16/us-americas-summit-idUSBRE83D0E220120416.

Chapter 11. Old Foes Get Reacquainted

1. Steve Clemons, "Hillary Clinton on Cuba Questions: I Give Her a 'C+,'" *Huffington Post*, February 16, 2009, huffingtonpost.com/steve-clemons/hillary-clinton-on-cuba-q_b_158497.html.

2. Anne Flaherty, "Sen. Lugar Says US Must Rethink Cuba Embargo," Associated Press, February 22, 2009. Online at foxnews.com/wires/2009Feb22/0,4670,US Cuba,00.html.

3. Karen DeYoung, "Lugar Urges Obama to Open Talks with Cuba," *Washington Post*, April 2, 2009, washingtonpost.com/wp-dyn/content/article/2009/04/01/ AR2009040103777.html.

4. Lesley Clark, "Cuba Trade Proponents Unveil Bill to Lift U.S. Restrictions," *Miami Herald*, March 31, 2009. Online at groups.yahoo.com/group/CubaNews/ message/99423.

5. Martin Kady II, "Martinez Not Keen to Travel to Cuba," *Politico*, April 1, 2009, politico.com/news/stories/0309/20735.html.

6. The delegation, all Democrats, was led by Barbara Lee of California and included Mel Watt (North Carolina), Emanuel Cleaver (Missouri), Marcia Fudge (Ohio), Bobby Rush (Illinois), and Michael Honda and Laura Richardson (California).

7. "Brazil's Presidential Foreign Policy Advisor on Relations with New USG," *Wikileaks*, January 22, 2009, wikileaks.org/cable/2009/01/09BRASILIA95.html.

8. For an excellent overview of U.S. travel and remittance regulations, see Mark P. Sullivan, "Cuba: U.S. Restrictions on Travel and Remittances," *Congressional Research Service*, January 18, 2011, assets.opencrs.com/rpts/RL31139_20110118.pdf.

9. It is a myth that Cubans cannot travel abroad and emigrate, as the long lines that formed every day at the U.S. Interests Section and the Canadian, Mexican, and other diplomatic missions beginning in the 1990s demonstrate. It was true up until 2013 that government permission was required and costly and involved an excessive amount of paperwork, and there were real restrictions placed on the travel of health-care personnel, computer science engineers, dissidents, and young people in general before they put in their required two years of social or military service.

10. Fidel Castro, "Not a Word about the Blocake [*sic*]," *Reflections*, April 13, 2009, en.cubadebate.cu/reflections-fidel/2009/04/13/not-word-about-blocake.

11. Barack Obama, "Choosing a Better Future in the Americas," op-ed, *Miami Herald*, April 16, 2009. Online at whitehouse.gov/the_press_office/Op-ed-by-President-Barack-Obama-Choosing-a-Better-Future-in-the-Americas.

12. "U.S. Urges Cuba to Free Prisoners, Push Changes," Agence France Presse, April 16, 2009. Online at google.com/hostednews/afp/article/ALeqM5hKjb4_0KJMe22 U18OX9AiQ_b0PTQ.

13. Indira A. R. Lakshmanan, "Clinton Says She Expects Cuba Response to Overtures," Bloomberg, April 16, 2009, bloomberg.com/apps/news?pid=newsarchive &sid=acqyFc_vlBiY&refer=us.

14. Ben Feller, "Raúl Castro: I'm Willing to Talk to U.S.," Associated Press, April 17, 2009. Online at guardian.co.uk/world/feedarticle/8459284.

15. "Venezuelan-Led Bloc Fires Shot Across Bow of Americas Summit," *Latin American Herald Tribune*, April 16, 2009, laht.com/article.asp?categoryid=10717&article id=332164.

16. "Background Briefing (Cuba Portions Only)," *Capitol Hill Cubans*, April 18, 2009, www.capitolhillcubans.com/2009_04_12_archive.html.

17. "Remarks by Secretary Clinton at Foreign Affairs Day," May 1, 2009, *IIP Digital, U.S. Department of State*, iipdigital.usembassy.gov/st/english/texttrans/2009/05/2009 0501151637xjsnommis0.3517681.html.

18. Mary Beth Sheridan, "Cuba Agrees to Resume Immigration Talks with U.S.," *Washington Post*, June 1, 2009, washingtonpost.com/wp-dyn/content/article/2009/05/31/AR2009053101078.html.

19. For the U.S. take on Williams's visit, see the U.S. Interests Section cable "GOC Signals 'Readiness to Move Forward,'" *Wikileaks*, September 25, 2009, files.vpro.nl/wikileaks/cable/2009/09/09HAVANA592.html.

20. Jordan Levin, "Some Musings about the Havana Concert," *Cuban Colada*, blog of the *Miami Herald*, September 29, 2009, miamiherald.typepad.com/cuban_colada/2009/09/some-musings-about-the-havana-concert.html.

Chapter 12. Shock and Awe, Raúl Style

1. Rory Carroll, "Raúl Castro Promotes Military Allies to Key Cuban Cabinet Positions," *Guardian*, March 3, 2009, guardian.co.uk/world/2009/mar/03/raul-castro-cuba-fidel-cabinet-shakeup.

2. Raúl Castro's inaugural speech is not available in English on the official government website, Cubagob.cu. Online at hcvanalysis.wordpress.com/2008/02/24/cuba-pres-raul-castro-speech-at-the-national-assembly-of-peoples-power-havana.

3. Phil Peters, *State Enterprise Reform in Cuba: An Early Snapshot,* Lexington Institute, 2001, lexingtoninstitute.org/library/resources/documents/Cuba/ResearchProducts/state-enterprise-reform.pdf.

4. Marc Frank, "Military Man to Head Cuba's Biggest Company," Reuters, September 27, 2010, reuters.com/article/idUSTRE68Q54H20100927.

5. Table 5.17, "External Balance of Goods and Services," in "National Accounts," *Anuario Estadística de Cuba 2011*, Oficina Nacional de Estadísticas (National Statistics Office), www.one.cu/aec2011/esp/20080618_tabla_cuadro.htm.

6. Fidel Castro, "Healthy Changes in the Council of Ministers," *Reflections*, March 3, 2009, en.cubadebate.cu/reflections-fidel/2009/03/03/healthy-changes-council-ministers.

Chapter 13. Blueprint for Survival

1. I later obtained an unpublished report from the Economy and Planning Ministry, "La economía Cubana, actual y perspectivas" (The Cuban economy: Current situation and prospects), which confirmed the source's account.

2. Cuba replaced the U.S. dollar with a local equivalent, the convertible peso, and slapped a 10 percent tax on exchanging the greenback for the local script in November 2004. Fidel Castro said at the time the measure was in response to the Bush administration's pursuit of foreign banks that processed dollars coming into the country from remittances and tourism. Under the embargo it is illegal to do business with Cuba in U.S. currency. Beginning in November 2004, international traders and joint venture partners were paid through deposits in the local currency in state-run banks and could transfer

the money abroad in foreign exchange, as the convertible peso was worthless outside Cuba. Then in November 2008 they were informed Cuba had no real money to back up its currency, and their local accounts were frozen until further notice. The Cubans eventually made good on the accounts, but the credibility of the convertible peso was all but destroyed and most traders insisted they be paid offshore.

3. Table 5.17, "External Balance of Goods and Services," in "National Accounts," *Anuario Estadística de Cuba 2011*, Oficina Nacional de Estadísticas (National Statistics Office), www.one.cu/aec2011/esp/20080618_tabla_cuadro.htm.

4. The Cuban government began estimating the market value of free social services and subsidized goods and services in its calculations of gross domestic product in 2004. Earnings from the export of such items as medical services were also included, though in other countries they are part of the gross national product. This resulted in the statistics office revising upward by 15 percent its GDP series for the previous years. The new formula also masked the ensuing decline of internal manufacturing and agriculture as spectacular increases in economic activity were reported.

5. "La economía Cubana, actual y perspectivas" (see note 1).

6. Ibid.

7. See note 3.

8. Hedelberto López Blanch, "El fortalecimiento de la economía angolana" (The strengthening of the Angolan economy), *Opciones*, November 24, 2011, opciones.cu/internacionales/2011-11-24/cl-fortalecimiento-de-la-economia-angolana.

9. "La economía Cubana, actual y perspectivas" (see note 1).

10. The report said there was a natural population growth of 596 people per day in 1965, of 99 in 2005, and of only 84 in 2007. At the same time, the over-sixty age group steadily increased to 16.6 percent of the population, or 1.8 million in 2007.

11. Marc Frank, "Havana Eyes Easing of Retail Sector Controls," *Financial Times*, September 2, 2009, ft.com/intl/cms/s/0/1d344b52-9758-11de-83c5-00144feabdc0.html#axzz2JfKIUX9W.

12. "Confronting Challenges Serenely and with More Determination than Ever," *Granma International*, August 8, 2009. Online at changesincuba.blogspot.com/2009_07_01_archive.html.

13. Raúl Castro, "Speech at the . . . National Assembly," August 1, 2009, en.cubadebate.cu/opinions/2009/08/01/speech-3rd-regular-session-seventh-legislature-national-assembly-peoples-power.

14. Leticia Martínez Hernández, "Dar, mas que quitar" (Give, more than take), *Granma*, September 25, 2009. Online at decub.de/CubaJournalEs/Articulos/Granma.htm.

15. "He's Paternalistic, You're Paternalistic, I'm Paternalistic," *Granma International*, October 9, 2009. A version of the article is available Online at desdecuba.com/generationy/?p=1157. Scroll down to page ten comment by Julio de la Yncera.

16. The letters are archived in Spanish at the *Granma* website, granma.cubaweb.cu, in the "Cartas a la dirección" (Letters to the Editor) section that appears on Fridays, www.granma.cubaweb.cu/secciones/cartas-direccion/art-001.html.

Chapter 15. Obama versus Raúl

1. Erikson, *Cuba Wars*.

2. Fidel Castro, "The Coup Dies or Constitutions Die," *Reflections*, July 10, 2009, en.cubadebate.cu/reflections-fidel/2009/07/10/coup-dies-or-constitutions-die, and "What Should Be Demanded from the United States," *Reflections*, July 16, 2009, en.cubadebate.cu/reflections-fidel/2009/07/16/what-should-be-demanded-from-united-states.

3. Fidel Castro, "Seven Daggers at the Heart of the Americas," *Reflections*, August 5, 2009, en.cubadebate.cu/reflections-fidel/2009/08/05/seven-daggers-at-heart-americas, and "The Yankee Bases and Latin American Sovereignty," *Reflections*, August 9, 2009, en.cubadebate.cu/reflections-fidel/2009/08/09/yankee-bases-and-latin-american-sovereignty.

4. "Questions from Yoani Sánchez to Potus," *Wikileaks*, U.S. Interests Section cable, August 28, 2009, wikileaks.org/cable/2009/08/09HAVANA527.html.

5. Robert Mackey, "Cuban Blogger Posts Interview with Obama," *New York Times*, November 19, 2009, thelede.blogs.nytimes.com/2009/11/19/cuban-blogger-posts-interview-with-obama.

6. Jeff Franks, "U.S. Contractor Jailed in Cuba Not a Spy: Wife," Reuters, February 18, 2010, reuters.com/article/2010/02/18/us-cuba-usa-contractor-exclusive-idUSTRE-61H2IT20100218.

7. Jeff Franks, "Cuban Document Details Charges Versus Jailed American," Reuters, January 20, 2012, reuters.com/article/2012/01/21/us-cuba-usa-contractor-idUSTRE80K00M20120121.

8. Tracey Eaton, "Secrecy, Politics at Heart of Cuba Project," *Along the Malecon*, January 17, 2013, alongthemalecon.blogspot.com/2013/01/secrecy-politics-at-heart-of-cuba.html.

9. Juanita Darling, "Cuba Complained to U.S. about Flights, Havana Says," *Los Angeles Times*, February 29, 2006, articles.latimes.com/1996-02-29/news/mn-41418_1_flights-havana-cuba.

10. Raúl Castro, "Speech at . . . the National Assembly," December 20, 2009, cuba.cu/gobierno/rauldiscursos/2009/esp/r201209e.html, and excerpts in English at miamiherald.typepad.com/cuban_colada/2009/12/castro-has-some-harsh-words-for-us.html.

11. Jeff Franks, "Cuban Minister: Obama 'Imperial, Arrogant,'" Reuters, December 22, 2009. Online at tvnz.co.nz/world-news/cuban-minister-obama-imperial-arrogant-3316832.

12. The United States Treasury Department reported in April 2012 that it had seized $245 million from Cuba in 2011, 61 percent of all funds frozen from four nations classified as state sponsors of terrorism. The figure was $248.1 million in 2010 and $223.7 million in 2009.

13. "U.S. to Drop Extra Security Against 'Terror Prone' Muslim Air Travelers," *London Times*, April 2, 2010. Online at sanfranciscosentinel.com/?p=67168.

14. "U.S.-Cuba Chill Exaggerated, but Old Ways Threaten Progress," *Wikileaks*, U.S. Interests Section cable, January 6, 2010, wikileaks.org/cable/2010/01/10HAVANA9.html.

15. "US Mission in Cuba Meets with Mercenaries," Prensa Latina, February 20, 2010. Online at www.radioguaimaro.co.cu/english/index.php/news/national-news/1435-us-mission-in-cuba-meets-with-mercenaries.html.

16. Tracy Wilkinson, "U.S.-Cuba Talks Overshadowed by Recriminations," *Los Angeles Times*, February 21, 2010, articles.latimes.com/2010/feb/21/world/la-fg-us-cuba21-2010feb21.

17. "Cuba Investigates Psychiatric Hospital Deaths," BBC News, January 16, 2010, news.bbc.co.uk/2/hi/8462844.stm.

18. "Statement by the President on the Human Rights Situation in Cuba," White House, March 24, 2010, whitehouse.gov/the-press-office/statement-president-human-rights-situation-cuba.

19. Patricia Mazzei, "Gloria Estefan's Obama Fundraiser Angers Some in Miami," *Miami Herald*, April 15, 2010. Online at mcclatchydc.com/2010/04/15/92201/estefans-hosting-obama-dnc-fundraiser.html.

20. Fidel Castro, "The U.S. Healthcare Reform," *Reflections*, March 24, 2010, en.cubadebate.cu/reflections-fidel/2010/03/24/us-healthcare-reform.

21. See note 18.

22. See note 20.

23. "Washington Seized 245 Million Dollars to Cuba in 2011," *Ahora*, April 10, 2012, www.ahora.cu/en/sections/world/2702-washington-seized-245-million-dollars-to-cuba-in-2011.

24. Josh Rogin, "House Panel Votes to Defund the OAS," *InterAmerican Security Watch*, July 20, 2011, interamericansecuritywatch.com/house-panel-votes-to-defund-the-oas

25. Ileana Ros-Lehtinen would rotate from her post in 2013 even as Bob Menendez was scheduled to take over the chair of the Senate Foreign Relations Committee when John Kerry became secretary of state. Connie Mack would lose a bid for the Senate and David Rivera failed to win reelection in 2012.

26. "Kudos to the State Department," *Capital Hill Cubans*, December 17, 2010, www.capitolhillcubans.com/2010/12/kudos-to-state-department.html.

27. Raúl Castro, "Speech at . . . the National Assembly," December 18, 2010, cuba.cu/gobierno/rauldiscursos/2010/ing/r181210i.html.

28. "Statement from the Cuban Ministry of Foreign Affairs," *Granma International*, January 17, 2011, www.granma.cu/ingles/news-i/17january-Statement.html.

Chapter 16. Wired

1. Chapter 17, "Information and Communications Technologies," *Anuario Estadística de Cuba 2011*, Oficina Nacional de Estadísticas (National Statistics Office), www.one.cu/aec2011/esp/20080618_tabla_cuadro.htm.

2. Marc Frank, "Cuban Revolution Meets Digital Revolution," ABC News, February 8, 2011, abcnews.go.com/International/cuban-revolution-meets-digital-revolution/story?id=12867146.

3. Marc Frank, "Venezuela Clicks In for Web-Starved Cubans," *Financial Times*, January 9, 2011, ft.com/intl/cms/s/0/9b442028-2409-11e0-bef0-00144feab49a.html#axzz2EIfXzPJP.

4. See clip, "La ciber policía en Cuba," by Coral Negro, vimeo.com/19402730.

5. The English translation comes from *Translating Cuba*, translatingcuba.com/minint-cyber-lecture-video-english-transcript.

6. The series *Las razones de Cuba* is available on various Cuban websites, including cubadebate.cu.

Chapter 17. Castro, the Cardinal, and the Damas

1. Laura Pollán passed away in 2011.

2. The translation of the cardinal's interview is available at *Progreso Weekly*, May 4, 2010. Online at cuba-l.unm.edu/?nid=78884.

3. Many Cubans prefer the less formal syncretism of Afro-Cuban religions best known as Santería, practiced by thousands of *babalao* priests out of their homes, or various other forms of spiritualism. Most Cubans, including my wife and most of her family, keep some sort of makeshift shrine to La Caridad del Cobre (Our Lady of Charity, the patroness of Cuba) in their homes, and many an assortment of water-filled glasses, representing the spirits of loved ones, and offerings such as a cigar, a glass of wine, fruit, or candy to the gods in hopes they will protect them. There are also Methodists, Baptists, Jews, quite a few Jehovah's Witnesses, Evangelicals, and the list goes on. A walk through Havana neighborhoods on a Sunday brings to one's ear a joyous chorus from the faithful.

4. Marc Frank, "Castro Meeting Signals Wider Role for Church," *Financial Times*, May 23, 2010, ft.com/intl/cms/s/0/4c369170-666b-11df-aeb1-00144feab49a.html#axzz2EIfXzPJP.

5. The cardinal said much the same in a briefing he gave European ambassadors in September 2010.

6. Juan Tamayo, "Spain Unlikely to Take More Political Prisoners from Cuba," *Miami Herald*, April 8, 2011. Online at groups.yahoo.com/group/CubaNews/message/123035.

7. Raúl Castro, "Speech at . . . the National Assembly," August 1, 2010, cuba.cu/gobierno/rauldiscursos/2010/esp/r010810e.html and in English at granma.cu/ingles/cuba-i/2agosto-discursoraul.html.

8. "Number of Cuban Political Prisoners Dips—Rights Group," BBC News, July 5, 2010, bbc.co.uk/news/10517497.

9. Patrick Worship, "Cuba Signs U.N. Rights Pacts that Castro Opposed," Reuters, February 28, 2008, reuters.com/article/2008/02/28/us-un-rights-cuba-idUSN2848640020080228.

10. Marc Frank, "Cuba's Raúl Castro Commutes Most Death Sentences," Reuters, April 28, 2008, reuters.com/article/2008/04/29/idUSN28211608.

11. Jacey Fortin, "Cuba Denies Torture in Prisons; Is Their Incarcerated Figure Accurate?" *International Business Times*, May 24, 2012, ibtimes.com/cuba-denies-torture-prisons-their-incarcerated-figure-accurate-699790.

12. Internally, the two countries refer to each other as the enemy, and the United States does so officially through the Trading with the Enemy Act of 1917, the legal basis for the embargo—which was renewed by President Obama in September 2012.

Chapter 18. Fidel, Born Again

1. Michael Voss, "Fidel Castro's Timely TV Interview," BBC News, July 13, 2010, bbc.co.uk/news/10609575. For a transcript of the interview, see *Granma International*, July 18, 2010, 5.

2. "Cuban Revolution Leader Fidel Visits National Center for Scientific Investigations," Cuban News Agency, July 11, 2010, www.cubanews.ain.cu/2010/0711-cuban-revolution-leader-fidel-castro-visits-national-center-scientific-research.htm.

3. Fidel Castro, "The Source of Wars," *Reflections*, July 12, 2010, en.cubadebate.cu/reflections-fidel/2010/07/12/source-wars.

4. See note 2.

5. Yoani Sánchez, "Fidel Castro, Present and Past," *Washington Post*, August 5, 2010, washingtonpost.com/wp-dyn/content/article/2010/08/04/AR2010080405455.html.

6. "The Message of Fidel and Exchange in the National Assembly," *Granma International,* August 15, 2010, 1. Online at juventudrebelde.co.cu/cuba/2010-08-10/the-message-of-fidel-and-exchange-in-the-national-assembly.

7. Raúl Castro, "Address . . . at the Closing Session of the 9th Congress of the Young Communist League," April 4, 2010, cuba.cu/gobierno/rauldiscursos/2010/ing/r030410i.html.

8. Fidel Castro, "The Ninth Congress of the Cuban Union of Young Communists," *Reflections*, April 8, 2010, en.cubadebate.cu/reflections-fidel/2010/04/08/9th-congress-young-communist-league-cuba.

9. Fidel Castro, "Speech Delivered . . . at the Commemoration of the 60th Anniversary of His Admission to University of Havana, in the Aula Magna of the University of Havana, on November 17, 2005," cuba.cu/gobierno/discursos/2005/ing/f171105i.html.

10. Jeff Franks, "Castro Says Comment on Cuban Economy Misunderstood," Reuters, September 11, 2010, reuters.com/article/2010/09/10/us-cuba-castro-idUSTRE6894UK20100910.

Chapter 19. Pink Slips and Permits

1. "Cuba to Cut One Million Public Sector Jobs," BBC News, September 14, 2010, bbc.co.uk/news/world-latin-america-11291267.

2. Ibid.

3. Table 7.2, "Workers employed in economic activities according to the statistics on employment," *Anuario Estadística de Cuba 2011*, Oficina Nacional de Estadísticas (National Statistics Office), www.one.cu/aec2011/esp/20080618_tabla_cuadro.htm.

4. Raúl Castro, "Speech at . . . the National Assembly," August 1, 2010, *Granma International,* August 2, 2010, granma.cu/ingles/cuba-i/2agosto-discursoraul.html.

5. Unpublished speech delivered by Marino Murillo to professors of the new National Cadre School, September 19, 2011.

6. Marc Frank, "Cuba Cuts State Payroll, Private Sector Jobs Grow 23 pct in 2012," Reuters, December 27, 2012, reuters.com/article/2012/12/27/cuba-economy-reform-idUSL1E8NQ23A20121227.

7. Ledys Camacho Casado, "Una experiencia que adelanta el futuro," (An experiment that brings forward the future), *Opciones*, January 4, 2013, opciones.cu/cuba/2013-01-04/una-experiencia-que-adelanta-el-futuro.

8. Leticia Martínez Hernández, "The Self-Employed Sector, Much More Than an Alternative," *Granma International*, September 27, 2010, granma.cu/ingles/cuba-i/27septiembre-3acpropia-a.html.

9. Marc Frank, "Cuba Unveils New Tax Code for Small Business," Reuters, October 22, 2010, reuters.com/article/2010/10/22/us-cuba-reform-taxes-idUSTRE69L3WY20101022.

10. Marc Frank, "Cuba's Brave New Economic World," ABC News, September 15, 2010, abcnews.go.com/Business/International/cubas-brave-economic-world/story?id=11644606#.UMUWxawQUgQ.

11. Yaima Puig Meneses and Anneris Ivette Leyva, "Socialismo por sendas propias (II)" (Socialism Our Own Way (II)), *Granma*, October 29, 2011. Online at walter lippmann.com/docs3320.html.

Chapter 20. Requiem for the Command Economy

1. For Raúl Castro and Hugo Chávez comments, see *Granma International*, November 14, 2010. Online for Raul's comments at granma.cu/ingles/cuba-i/9noviembre-45R-discurso.html, for Chavez, granma.cu/ingles/cuba-i/8noviembre-45Chav-int.html.

2. A good example was Cuba's more-than-two-decades-long treatment of thousands of child victims of the Chernobyl nuclear accident. Ukrainian president Viktor F. Yanukovich visited Cuba in October 2011 and announced his government would begin reimbursing Cuba for the program.

3. An English translation of the proposals can be found online at walterlippmann.com/pcc-draft-economic-and-social-policy-guidelines-2010.pdf.

4. The figure did not include some $20 billion that Russia claimed Cuba owed the former Soviet Union and that Cuba disputes on the grounds that contracts were broken at the time of the Soviet Union's demise and that the loans were in overvalued convertible rubles.

5. "Key Trading Partners See No Big Economic Reforms in 2010," *Wikileaks*, U.S. Interests Section cable, February 9, 2010, wikileaks.org/cable/2010/02/10HAVANA84.html.

6. Marc Frank, "Cuba Bows to Pressure to Reform Its Economy," *Financial Times*, December 13, 2010, ft.com/intl/cms/s/0/e6fc6374-06d9-11e0-8c29-00144feabdc0.html#axzz2EP4jzr9g.

7. Raúl Castro, "Speech at . . . the National Assembly," December 18, 2010, cuba.cu/gobierno/rauldiscursos/2010/ing/r181210i.html.

Chapter 21. On the Road Again

1. José Alejandro Rodríguez, "Cuba: Economy of Commands or Earnings," *Juventud Rebelde*, December 12, 2010, links.org.au/node/2086.

2. See note 7 to chapter 20.

3. At the time, just 10 percent of the land in the suburban plan nationwide was irrigated, according to Dr. Nelson Companioni Concepción, a member of the national executive committee overseeing suburban farming.

4. The government said in 2012 there were one hundred local projects up and running in the country and it had assigned $1 million in revolving credits to municipalities in western and central Cuba and $2 million to municipalities in eastern Cuba for the local projects.

5. Spain provided citizenship to anyone whose parents or grandparents fled the country under Franco and during the 1936–39 civil war. Cubans took advantage, mainly in search of a passport that would allow them to circumvent Cuban emigration regulations, visa requirements in Europe, and a yearlong wait even to get an appointment for a visa to the United States. Some 80,000 Cubans had obtained their Spanish passports by the time the program ended in 2011, and some 100,000 applications were pending.

6. Fidel Castro, "My Shoes Are Too Tight," *Reflections*, March 22, 2011, en.cubadebate. cu/reflections-fidel/2011/03/22/my-shoes-are-too-tight.

Chapter 22. Forward March

1. See note 7 to chapter 20.

2. An English translation of the economic and social guidelines adopted by the Party Congress can be found at normangirvan.info/wp-content/uploads/2011/12/cuba-guidelines-debate-pdf-english.pdf.

3. Raúl Castro, "Central Report to the Sixth Congress of the Communist Party of Cuba," April 16, 2011, cuba.cu/gobierno/rauldiscursos/2011/ing/r160411i.html.

4. See "Strategic Retreat," Conflict Research Consortium, University of Colorado, colorado.edu/conflict/peace/treatment/retreat.htm.

5. See note 3.

6. See note 4.

7. See note 3.

8. Raúl Castro, "Speech by Army General Raúl Castro Ruz . . . closing the 1st National Conference of the Party . . . January 29, 2012," *Granma International*, January 30, 2012, granma.cu/ingles/cuba-i/30enero-Our%20responsibility.html.

9. Fidel Castro, "My Absence from the Central Committee," *Reflections*, April 19, 2011, en.cubadebate.cu/reflections-fidel/2011/04/19/my-absence-from-central-committee, and "The Congress Debates," *Reflections*, April 18, 2011, en.cubadebate.cu/reflections-fidel/2011/04/18/congress-debates.

10. See note 8.

Chapter 23. Cheers and Jeers

1. Marc Frank, "Steep Hike in Customs Fees Leaves Many Cubans Fuming," Reuters, July 22, 2012, reuters.com/article/2012/07/22/us-cuba-customs-idUSBRE86 L0AC20120722.

2. Raúl Castro, "Speech at . . . the National Assembly," August 1, 2011, *Granma International*, August 7, 2011, 4, granma.cu/ingles/cuba-i/2agosto-The%20greatest.html.

3. Marc Frank, "Cuba Targets Military Firm in Corruption Probe," Reuters, December 13, 2011, reuters.com/article/2011/12/13/us-cuba-corruption-idUSTRE7BC1P220111213.

4. Raúl Castro, "Speech at . . . the National Assembly," December 23, 2011, *Granma International*, January 1, 2012, 6, granma.cu/ingles/cuba-i/26dic-01r-discur.html.

5. Victoria Burnett, "Relenting on Car Sales, Cuba Turns Notorious Clunkers into Gold," *New York Times*, November 5, 2011, nytimes.com/2011/11/06/world/americas/relenting-on-car-sales-cuba-turns-notorious-clunkers-into-gold.html?pagewanted=all&_r=0.

6. Rosa Tania Valdes and Nelson Acosta, "Cubans Line Up to Buy, Sell Homes

under New Reform," Reuters, November 11, 2011, reuters.com/article/2011/11/11/uk-cuba-housing-idUSLNE7AA01P20111111.

7. "Cuba Loosens Internal Migration Law," *Havana Times*, November 22, 2011, havanatimes.org/?p=56244.

8. See note 2.

9. For details of the new immigration regulations, see Sergio Alejandro Gómez, "New Cuban Migration and Travel Policy," *Granma International*, January 18, 2013, granma.cu/ingles/cuba-i/18ener-migration.html.

10. "New Measures Announced to Deepen Relations with the Emigration," *Juventud Rebelde*, October 25, 2012, www.juventudrebelde.co.cu/cuba/2012-10-25/new-measures-announced-to-deepen-relations-with-the-emigration.

11. David Adams and Tom Brown, "Cuban Perks Under Scrutiny in U.S. Immigration Reform," Reuters, February 8, 2013, reuters.com/article/2013/02/08/us-usa-immigration-cuba-idUSBRE9170F920130208.

12. Marc Frank, "Cuba Sweetens Pot for New Private Farmers," Reuters, December 19, 2011, reuters.com/article/2011/12/19/us-cuba-reform-agriculture-idUSTRE7BI1S920111219.

13. Presentation by Marino Murillo, head of the Communist Party reform commission, before the National Assembly, July 24, 2012, broadcast by state-run television on July 25, 2012.

14. For more details, see Sheyla Delgado Guerra and Anneris Ivette Leyva, "New Measures to Improve Functioning of UBPC," Granma International, September 18, 2012, granmai.cubasi.cu/ingles/cuba-i/18sep-Autonomy basic.html.

15. Marc Frank, "Cuban Government to Contract with Private Sector," Reuters, November 28, 2011, reuters.com/article/2011/11/28/us-cuba-reform-private-idUSTRE7AR26420111128.

16. Isaac Risco, "Cuba to Rent Out Workshops to Private Sector," Deutsche Presse-Agentur, December 26, 2011. Online at groups.yahoo.com/group/CubaVerdad/message/69929.

17. Marc Frank, "Cuba Moving Some State-Run Cafes into Private Hands," Reuters, January 13, 2012, reuters.com/article/2012/01/12/us-cuba-reform-services-idUSTRE80B24G20120112.

18. See note 13.

19. "Cuba Eliminates Sugar Ministry, Ending an Era," Agence France Press, September 29, 2011, google.com/hostednews/afp/article/ALeqM5jAm5SLjVcV1hU2JmUMYb_dDOadNw?docId=CNG.11b830e74e89175fd9b015ca71842771.1b1.

20. Ledys Camacho Casado, "Potencialidades de una provincia en desarrollo" (The potential of a developing province), *Opciones*, December 14, 2011, opciones.cu/cuba/2011-12-14/potencialidades-de-una-provincia-en-desarrollo.

21. O. Fonticoba Gener, "New Enterprise Group Established to Manage Biotech and Pharmaceutical Industries," *Granma International*, December 28, 2012, article.wn.com/view/2012/12/28/New_enterprise_group_established_to_manage_biotech_and_pharm/#/related_news.

22. See note 13.

23. O. Fonticoba Gener, "Non-Agricultural Cooperatives," *Granma International*, December 20, 2012. Online at wendyholm.com/granma.cu.Non-ag.coops.pdf.

24. Ivette Fernández Sosa, "New Tax Law Decisive in the Updating of Cuba's Economic Model," *Granma*, November 27, 2012, www.granma.cu/ingles/cuba-i/27novi-Decisive%20in.html.

Conclusion

1. Marc Frank, "Pope Benedict XVI Goes to Cuba; Thousands Wait," ABC News, March 25, 2012, abcnews.go.com/International/cuba-awaits-pope-benedict-xvi/story?id=15987673.

2. "Renovation Has Not Been an Easy Task," *Granma International*, April 22, 2012, 4, granmai.cubasi.cu/ingles/cuba-i/16abril-fidel-Phu-Trong.html.

3. Raúl Castro, "Speech at . . . the National Assembly," February 24, 2013, *Granma International*, February 26, 2013. Online at http://july26coalition.org/wordpress/raul-castro-speech-at-the-national-assembly-2013.

4. Daily Press Briefing, Department of State, February 25, 2012, state.gov/r/pa/prs/dpb/2013/02/205179.htm#CUBA.

5. Miguel Díaz-Canel, "Aquí venimos a reverenciar, no solo al Comandante legendario, sino a un pueblo y a un ejército nacido de ese pueblo" (We have come here to venerate not only the legendary Comandante but a people and an army born of that people), *Granma*, March 6, 2013, www.granma.cubaweb.cu/2013/03/07/nacional/artic01.html.

Selected English-Language Bibliography

Bangs, John Kendrick. *Uncle Sam, Trustee*. New York: Riggs, 1902.

Bardach, Ann Louise. *Cuba Confidential: Love and Vengeance in Miami and Havana*. New York: Random House, 2002.

Beals, Carleton. *The Crime of Cuba*. Philadelphia: J. B. Lippincott, 1933.

Bourne, Peter G. *Fidel: A Biography of Fidel Castro*. New York: Dodd, Mead, 1986. Published in England as *Castro: A Biography of Fidel Castro*. London: Macmillan, 1987.

Brenner, Philip, William M. LeoGrande, Donna Rich, and Daniel Siegel, eds. *The Cuba Reader: The Making of a Revolutionary Society*. New York: Grove, 1989.

Castañeda, Jorge G. *Compañero: The Life and Death of Che Guevara*. Translated by Marina Castañeda. New York: Alfred A. Knopf, 1997.

Castro, Fidel, and Ignacio Ramonet. *My Life: A Spoken Autobiography*. Translated by Andrew Hurley. New York: Scribner, 2008.

Chapman, Charles E. *A History of the Cuban Republic: A Study in Hispanic American Politics*. New York: Macmillan, 1927.

Domínguez, Jorge I., Omar Everleny Pérez Villanueva, and Lorena Barberia, eds. *The Cuban Economy at the Start of the Twenty-First Century*. Cambridge, Mass.: Harvard University Press, 2004.

Dubois, Jules. *Fidel Castro: Rebel—Liberator or Dictator?* Indianapolis: Bobbs-Merrill, 1959.

English, T. J. *Havana Nocturne: How the Mob Owned Cuba . . . and Then Lost It to the Revolution*. New York: William Morrow, 2008.

Erikson, Daniel P. *The Cuba Wars: Fidel Castro, the United States, and the Next Revolution*. New York: Bloomsbury, 2008.

Fergusson, Erna. *Cuba*. New York: Alfred A. Knopf, 1946.

Frank, Waldo. *Cuba: Prophetic Island*. New York: Marzani & Munsell, 1961.

Franklin, Jane. *The Cuban Revolution and the United States: A Chronological History*. Melbourne: Ocean Press, 1992.

Gallenga, A. *The Pearl of the Antilles*. London: Chapman and Hall, 1873.

Green, Nathan C. *The Story of Spain and Cuba*. Baltimore: International News and Book, 1896.

Guerra y Sánchez, Ramiro, José M. Pérez Cabrera, Juan J. Remos, and Emeterio S. Santovenia, eds. *A History of the Cuban Nation.* Translated by Emilio Chomat. Havana: Editorial Historia de la Nación Cubana, 1958.

Hazard, Samuel. *Cuba with Pen and Pencil.* 1871. Whitefish, Mont.: Kessinger, 2010.

Hermer, Consuelo, and Marjorie May. *Havana Mañana: A Guide to Cuba and the Cubans.* New York: Random House, 1941.

Johnson, Willis Fletcher. *The History of Cuba.* 5 vols. New York: B. F. Buck, 1920.

Klepak, Hal. *Cuba's Military 1990–2005: Revolutionary Soldiers during Counter-Revolutionary Times.* New York: Palgrave Macmillan, 2005.

Latell, Brian. *After Fidel: The Inside Story of Castro's Regime and Cuba's Next Leader.* New York: Palgrave Macmillan, 2005.

Matthews, Herbert L. *Castro: A Political Biography.* London: Penguin, 1969.

Miller, Tom. *Trading with the Enemy: A Yankee Travels Through Castro's Cuba.* New York: Atheneum, 1992.

Nelson, Lowry. *Rural Cuba.* Minneapolis: University of Minnesota Press, 1950.

Pérez, Louis A., Jr. *On Becoming Cuban: Identity, Nationality, and Culture.* Chapel Hill: University of North Carolina Press, 1999.

Phillips, R. Hart. *Cuba, Island of Paradox.* New York: McDowell, Obolensky, 1959.

———. *Cuban Sideshow.* Havana: Cuban Press, 1935.

Quirk, Robert E. *Fidel Castro.* New York: Norton, 1993.

Rathbone, John Paul. *The Sugar King of Havana: The Rise and Fall of Julio Lobo, Cuba's Last Tycoon.* New York: Penguin, 2010.

Roberts, W. Adolphe. *Havana, the Portrait of a City.* New York: Coward-McCann, 1953.

Spadoni, Paolo. *Failed Sanctions: Why the U.S. Embargo against Cuba Could Never Work.* Gainesville: University Press of Florida, 2010.

Strode, Hudson. *The Pageant of Cuba.* New York: Harrison Smith and Robert Haas, 1934.

Sweig, Julia E. *Cuba: What Everyone Needs to Know.* London: Oxford University Press, 2009.

Thomas, Hugh. *Cuba, or, The Pursuit of Freedom.* Rev. ed. Cambridge, Mass.: Da Capo, 1998.

Verrill, A. Hyatt. *Cuba Past and Present.* New York: Dodd, Mead, 1914.

Woon, Basil. *When It's Cocktail Time in Cuba.* New York: Horace Liveright, 1928.

Wright, Irene Aloha. *Cuba.* New York: Macmillan, 1910.

Index

Page numbers in italics refer to illustrations.

Journalist Marc Frank is currently based in Cuba, where he writes and consults for the Thomson Reuters News Agency, the *Financial Times*, and ABC News. Mr. Frank, who has covered the Caribbean island since 1984, is considered by many Cuba watchers around the world—in government, business, and academia—to be the most informed English-language foreign correspondent working in Cuba today. Mr. Frank has won various Thomson Reuters awards, including Latin American and global best for general and political news and best scoop for Latin America in 2008 for his coverage as the island moved toward a more market-oriented economy. He has lived in and reported on Cuba during the best days of the Revolution, the fall of the Soviet bloc, the great depression of the 1990s, the stepping aside of Fidel Castro, and the reforms orchestrated by Raúl Castro. Mr. Frank was born in Chicago in 1951, grew up in Cambridge, Massachusetts, and is a graduate of Rutgers University. His first book, *Cuba Looks to the Year 2000*, was published in 1993. Mr. Frank has written and consulted for numerous media and publications over the years, and his articles have appeared around the world in both English and Spanish.

Contemporary Cuba

EDITED BY JOHN M. KIRK

Afro-Cuban Voices: On Race and Identity in Contemporary Cuba, by Pedro Pérez-Sarduy
and Jean Stubbs (2000)

Cuba, the United States, and the Helms-Burton Doctrine: International Reactions, by
Joaquín Roy (2000)

Cuba Today and Tomorrow: Reinventing Socialism, by Max Azicri (2000)

Cuba's Foreign Relations in a Post-Soviet World, by H. Michael Erisman (2000)

Cuba's Sugar Industry, by José Alvarez and Lázaro Peña Castellanos (2001)

Culture and the Cuban Revolution: Conversations in Havana, by John M. Kirk and
Leonardo Padura Fuentes (2001)

Looking at Cuba: Essays on Culture and Civil Society, by Rafael Hernández, translated
by Dick Cluster (2003)

*Santería Healing: A Journey into the Afro-Cuban World of Divinities, Spirits, and
Sorcery*, by Johan Wedel (2004)

Cuba's Agricultural Sector, by José Alvarez (2004)

Cuban Socialism in a New Century: Adversity, Survival, and Renewal, edited by Max
Azicri and Elsie Deal (2004)

*Cuba, the United States, and the Post-Cold War World: The International Dimensions of
the Washington-Havana Relationship*, edited by Morris Morley and Chris McGillion
(2005)

Redefining Cuban Foreign Policy: The Impact of the "Special Period," edited by H.
Michael Erisman and John M. Kirk (2006)

Gender and Democracy in Cuba, by Ilja A. Luciak (2007)

Ritual, Discourse, and Community in Cuban Santería: Speaking a Sacred World, by
Kristina Wirtz (2007)

The "New Man" in Cuba: Culture and Identity in the Revolution, by Ana Serra (2007)

U.S.-Cuban Cooperation Past, Present, and Future, by Melanie M. Ziegler (2007)

Protestants, Revolution, and the Cuba-U.S. Bond, by Theron Corse (2007)

The Changing Dynamic of Cuban Civil Society, edited by Alexander I. Gray and Antoni
Kapcia (2008)

Cuba in the Shadow of Change: Daily Life in the Twilight of the Revolution, by Amelia
Rosenberg Weinreb (2009)

Failed Sanctions: Why the U.S. Embargo against Cuba Could Never Work, by Paolo
Spadoni (2010)

Sustainable Urban Agriculture in Cuba, by Sinan Koont (2011)

Fifty Years of Revolution: Perspectives on Cuba, the United States, and the World, edited
by Soraya M. Castro Mariño and Ronald W. Pruessen (2012)

Cuban Economists on the Cuban Economy, edited by Al Campbell (2013)

Cuban Revelations: Behind the Scenes in Havana, by Marc Frank (2013)

*Cuba in a Global Context: International Relations, Internationalism, and
Transnationalism*, edited by Catherine Krull (2014)